THE CREATIVE DESTRUCTION
OF NEW YORK CITY

THE
CREATIVE
DESTRUCTION
OF
NEW YORK
CITY

ENGINEERING THE CITY
FOR THE ELITE

ALESSANDRO BUSÀ

OXFORD
UNIVERSITY PRESS

OXFORD
UNIVERSITY PRESS

Oxford University Press is a department of the University of Oxford. It furthers
the University's objective of excellence in research, scholarship, and education
by publishing worldwide. Oxford is a registered trade mark of Oxford University
Press in the UK and certain other countries.

Published in the United States of America by Oxford University Press
198 Madison Avenue, New York, NY 10016, United States of America.

Library of Congress Cataloging-in-Publication Data
Names: Busà, Alessandro, 1977- author.
Title: The creative destruction of New York City : engineering the city
for the elite / Alessandro Busà.
Description: New York, NY : Oxford University Press, [2017] |
Includes bibliographical references and index.
Identifiers: LCCN 2017005675 | ISBN 9780190610098 (cloth)
Subjects: LCSH: City planning—New York (State)—New York. |
Urban renewal—New York (State)—New York. |
Gentrification—New York (State)—New York.
Classification: LCC HT168.N5 B87 2017 | DDC 307.1/216097471—dc23
LC record available at https://lccn.loc.gov/2017005675

1 3 5 7 9 8 6 4 2
Printed by Edwards Brothers Malloy, United States of America

To New York City, the only city where
I ever really felt at home

Contents

Foreword

We're masochists. We doll ourselves up every night for a city that's just going to end up giving us a black eye anyway.[1]

I landed in New York City in 2006, with a J-1 visa in my hand, an over-packed suitcase, an all-too-tight grant from my university in Berlin, and the prospect of an unpaid research position in one of the most expensive cities in the planet. I must have been crazy.

My first pad in New York was a one-bedroom roach-infested short-term rental near Hudson Street in the West Village, with a shower in the kitchen, which I rented for $700 a month. It took a while to clean it up, but that shabby dump, which belonged to an elderly actor who in the 1970s used to perform in the gritty theaters of the Village, really had some charm to it, and after a few weeks I felt home. I was a young visiting scholar at Columbia University, and I really didn't mind commuting uptown every day, as long as I could enjoy some taste of the life downtown. I loved it there, but it didn't last long. After a few months the lease was over and I had to move, this time to an $800-per-month, 90-square-foot room in a five-story walk-up in Chinatown. The room was no larger than a prison cell, and the stench from the Chinese deli downstairs invaded the apartment. But I was in heaven: I loved to sit on the rusty fire escape and smoke my early-morning cigarette while watching the bustling streets below. It was a dilapidated apartment I shared with two roommates whose jobs I never understood, who had moved to the city from somewhere in the Midwest. The place looked like it was straight out of one of those Chelsea Hotel gritty photographs of the 1970s—half artist atelier and half the perfect spot for a heroin addict to be found dead. Our landlord was Chinese, as were all the other tenants in the house—extremely populous families crowding in tiny apartments—so we were technically the only "white pioneers" in this working-class tenement. But we soon realized we were not the gentrifiers of the desired kind: after a few months, our landlord almost doubled our rent, forcing all of us to move almost literally overnight. In the meantime, most of my friends and colleagues—students, artists, musicians, photographers, models, actors, writers, bartenders—who once had stayed in Manhattan had already moved to Brooklyn, most of them to the now very trendy areas of Williamsburg, Greenpoint, and Fort Greene.

By 2007, rentals in Manhattan had become so tight for my pockets that I had no other choice but to follow the fleeing wave. Thanks to a friend who was shooting a short film about the Chelsea Hotel's shady past, I got a chance to meet legendary hotel manager Stanley Bard, and spent two weeks inside the Chelsea's infamous walls—it was my romantic way of saying goodbye to Manhattan. I then reluctantly moved out of the island, to what everyone considered one of the least appealing neighborhoods of Brooklyn—Bedford-Stuyvesant. But the flat I rented together with my African American roommate, a chef in a trendy fusion restaurant in Manhattan, was really the most decent I had seen in a long time. The neighborhood was mostly black, and most people there were poor. It had a liquor store with thick metal grates, a few bodegas, some 99-cent stores, and a huge Super Clean Laundromat by the Kosciuszko Street J train station. Two teenage boys were killed down the street in a drive-by shooting just a few weeks after I moved in. May their souls rest in peace. But on Sundays, dressed-up children and families crowded the church of Pastor Taylor down the street and sang gospel songs. Sometimes at night I used to go to the roof and watch the towers of Manhattan shine from a distance. I felt very isolated. I hated the enervating, hour-long commute I had to make each day to get Uptown and back. But others in the neighborhood had it way harder. Almost every early morning I used to meet this lady at the Kosciuszko Street station. She lived in the homeless shelter near our block and took the J train every morning to work as a janitor in a Manhattan hotel.

These were the times where single rooms in the more trendy areas of Brooklyn were already priced at over $1,200. By comparison, the rent for our whole two-bedroom apartment in Bed-Stuy was $1,400. But even this accommodation was short-lived. Our landlord announced he would increase the rent 80% to $2,400. Even Bed-Stuy was getting its share of gentrification, and the landlord assumed he could make more money by planting a tree on the sidewalk and finding better tenants. We had a few weeks to move out. During subsequent craigslist housing hunts, I saw it all: a couch space in the kitchen of an Upper East Side studio for $1,000, a 10×10-square-foot room in the Lower East Side for $1,500, a basement with no windows in Harlem for $900. I've seen elderly people in their 60s subletting portions of their living rooms to students or even to grown-up professionals to make ends meet, and a family of six in the housing projects of the Lower East Side subletting their kids' rooms to NYU students. Finally, in 2008, I was able to move back to Manhattan. I first moved briefly to 125th Street in Harlem, then returned to my beloved Chinatown, where I found a room in a tiny apartment I shared with the noisiest Mexican roommate for a thick $1,400.

After my research period came to an end, I left the United States, and returned to New York only in the spring of 2010. This time I was lucky enough to stay in one of the few remaining flophouses near the Bowery—a gritty pension populated by artists, actors, and other New York City outcasts, where I finally found a tiny room for myself, the tiniest I've ever seen: 8×6 square feet, with shared toilets down the hall, for around $250 a week. No joke, but this turned out to be one of the best deals I've ever found in my troubled New York years: it was great being back in Manhattan, having my early-morning cup of coffee in the streets of the East Village, sitting on the stoops with perfect strangers at night, enjoying my regular El Paso burger at Paul's Da Burger Joint, and feeling again part of the energy of the city. The last time I returned to New York, the building had been boarded up. Nearby, a swish 72-room boutique hotel would rise, according to the banners at the construction site.

In my New York years I experienced first-hand how hard it is to survive in the city when your budget nears the poverty line, and it was not a pretty picture. I also witnessed what the inexorable rise in rental prices did to the networks of friends and colleagues I had in the city. Based in the island at the beginning, all of us were forced to move out of Manhattan, first to Williamsburg, Greenpoint, Long Island City, Astoria, or Jackson Heights, and then farther out, to the eastern ends of Brooklyn (Bushwick, Bedford-Stuyvesant) or to Harlem. The increasing distances between us and the exhausting workdays made it very hard to keep our network alive. It also made many of us feel pretty disempowered, as we started to fear that as much as we went on in our careers, the quality of our lives (location, connection, networks) was not improving.

Don't get me wrong: living in New York is absolutely fantastic. That thrilling spectacle of life is the closest to heaven I have ever experienced.

Also, I was young. New York's loud, restless streets gave me an adrenaline rush that made me immune to all bad things and transformed my adventures and even my hardships into some wonderful movie script. But now that I'm slightly older, I must tell the truth: New York is really fantastic as long as you have the money. If you don't, you can bet on a restless existence made of constant moving, constant threats, and a continuous process of starting all over again. I wrote this book as a testimony to the strains I endured to survive here, and those of all the people who each day wake up dreaming of making a life in this magnificent city but are finding that dream to be more and more out of reach.

Global Troubles

It wasn't only my personal experience of living in New York City, both as a precarious visiting researcher and an irredeemable big city lover, that persuaded me to write this book. It was also the realization that what I endured wasn't that scary when compared with some of the horror stories I heard in the streets of New York: a single mother of four from the Rockaways who commutes over two hours each day to work as a clerk at a Gap downtown, a young guy living with his elderly family in a dark basement in Astoria, or the kind African American lady that was stuck in the homeless shelter in Bed-Stuy. It was also the realization that this tough life is becoming the daily reality for innumerable friends and acquaintances of mine, who are striving to keep themselves afloat in big cities around the world, from London to San Francisco, from Paris to Milan, from Singapore to Dublin. Ironically enough, most of them could be called members of the fabled "creative class" celebrated by urban theorist and new-economy guru Richard Florida, yet very few of them seem to enjoy the fabulous lives of some of Florida's "creatives" who earn their living in the world of finance, banking, or real estate. They are the broke adjunct professors on short-term contracts at CUNY, the hipster writers at VICE magazine, the penniless students living on a pack of future loans, the freelance software designers, the fashion photographers, the eternal trainees at architecture studios, the apprentice editors, and the self-employed journalists and graphic designers. Many of them are trapped in low-paying jobs with no benefits or security, some have dropped health insurance altogether, and many need a second or even a third job to carry on. And this is happening in cities where the

housing market has become scandalously unaffordable, and where finding
a decent rental—not to mention buying a home—has become a pipe dream
for most. The biggest irony of it all is that, from New York to London, from
Sidney to Amsterdam, local politicians keep repeating that they are working hard on solutions to fix these problems: they all seem to have some
plan up their sleeve that will provide affordable housing for those on low
incomes, yet what we witness are more luxury condos piercing the skyline,
and a housing market that keeps getting tighter and tighter. As naive as our
elected officials may think we are, we have all become disenchanted enough
to discern, as a *Metropolis Magazine* reporter puts it, that "solving a housing
crisis by building penthouses would be like trying to solve an automobile
shortage by manufacturing Bentleys."[2]

We live in citadels of unimaginable wealth, surrounded by crumbling out-
skirts where a growing class of under-laborers (the minimum-wage clerks,
runners, janitors—the so-called service economy that makes the other half of
the city function) endures its daily struggle just to hang on. Meanwhile, once-
working-class districts are revolutionized by studio galleries and vegan bistros,
coffee shops and music clubs, farmers' markets and gluten-free beer gardens,
bike lanes and river walks—safe environments for a brand-new class of consumers, without the pesky vestiges of actual working-class people, who in the
meantime have long been kicked to the curb. And this is a global phenomenon.

Take Berlin, for instance. The city has been branding itself to the world
as the European capital of creativity and "coolness," in an age where EU
austerity measures have obliterated much of the economic vitality of spectacular cities like Madrid, Paris, and Milan. Berlin's "poor but sexy" appeal
has sold well for years, as the German capital managed to attract young
professionals and broke bohemians in record numbers, while innumerable
international headlines and TV reports kept celebrating it as the "European
Capital of Cool."[3] But behind the hype, there is a less jubilant reality of
rampant unemployment (the highest rate in Germany, with 30% of social
scientists and 40% of artists being out of work in 2012[4]) and welfare dependency. And if Berlin is poor, that doesn't make it necessarily cheap, courtesy
of an unprecedented influx of foreign buyers who, attracted by the sirens
of real estate bargains, have been buying massive chunks of property all
across the city, inflating a speculative housing bubble in a city where holiday rentals in certain areas have been outpacing legitimate leases.[5] Finding
a home in Berlin today has become a hopeless task for the hundreds of
thousands of young self-employed and freelance workers who can't show

any evidence of a steady income, let alone a decent salary. At a typical open-house viewing you can find lines of potential renters coming from all over Europe, queuing all the way out the door till the end of the block. And it's not uncommon to meet people in their 40s and 50s who are still living in shared flats.

Yet Berlin is a relative bargain compared to Paris. In the City of Love, common listings for rooms and apartments include barely legal (and definitely stretched) definitions of "habitable space," so that if your budget is tight, you may go for a 60-square-foot "studio" whose toilet is in a cupboard that can be pulled out from under the kitchen sink. If you don't mind sharing toilets with your neighbors, for around 500 euros you will find a *chambre de bonne*, a single room in the former maid's quarter in the garret of some apartment building. Or, if you are lucky, you may find yourself a more charming 180-square-foot "loft" studio with a bunk bed for 900 euros plus utilities. In Paris, where rich Middle Eastern and Chinese buyers are now ousting the French from the housing market, even the upper middle classes are being priced out.

And don't get me started on London. In the city where a 188-square-foot apartment (not much larger than a prison cell) can sell for £275,000, a car box in Highgate for £250,000, and a Knightsbridge apartment for £65 million, real estate insanity has become the norm. Even once-unfashionable outer neighborhoods have become unaffordable to the point that "families and young workers...looking to buy their first home, are leaving the capital in their droves to get on to the property ladder, forced out by high house prices."[6] The rental market here is so tight that apartment seekers are aware that any open-house viewing will turn into a bloody bidding war between applicants. In London, the urban legend of the man living in a broom cupboard is no urban legend at all. I found an actual such listing, in the Paddington area, for just £40 a week, the ad calling it a "loft conversion," but noting that "you cannot stand upright in the room....Ideally it would suit someone less than 5'4 tall and with no history of claustrophobia."[7]

Not to mention San Francisco, the new US capital of insane housing prices, and home to the highest concentration of the global super-rich (those making over $30 million) of any city in the United States.[8] Here, venture capitalists, Silicon Valley entrepreneurs, and tech-sector employees have been buying up the most desirable areas in a bidding frenzy for years, driving average rents near $3,500 a month for a one-bedroom apartment, and creating a housing market where most new construction consists of super-upscale condos, and where the *median* home price today is above $1.2 million.[9] The deranged San Francisco housing market has unleashed viral BuzzFeed stories like "9 Private Islands That Cost Less Than an Apartment in San Francisco"[10] or "5 Castles That Are Cheaper Than an Apartment in San Francisco"—if you are smart, you'll sell that dull $985,000 one-bedroom condo in Nob Hill and buy yourself a 13-bedroom 20th-century palace with a pool in Spain for the same price.[11] But if you are not a billionaire and really can't stay away from the City by the Bay, you may be lucky enough to find a "contractor special" decrepit shack in the Outer Mission District selling for just $350,000.[12] And if San Francisco prices are crazy, then prices in cities like Tokyo or Melbourne have long been in the asylum. And the list could go on.

Space is getting tight, courtesy of a new global population of super-rich consumers "whose real estate spending power has changed the game entirely,"[13] and of local governments that are all too eager to oblige.

This is what urban life is becoming for many of us, in a world where big cities are slowly becoming citadels of overpriced offshore properties where the absurdly rich love to park their cash, leaving very little space at hand for anyone else. And in this book I will show how this is not some unexplainable god-given plague like a heat wave or a locust invasion to punish us for our sins, but a man-made disaster—the result of very concrete urban policies that for years have been favoring the influx of a new, extra-national, super-wealthy class of citizens, for which governments and developers have devised brand-new glittering cities that are pushing the lower-, middle-, and even upper-middle-income classes out. "If we can find a bunch of billionaires around the world to move here, that would be a godsend," argued former New York City mayor Michael Bloomberg in an interview with *New York Magazine*.[14] He sure isn't the only one who thinks this way: the rapid, ruthless, corporate-style creative destruction I will describe in New York is happening in similar ways in all major cities around the globe, from London to Tokyo, from Hong Kong to Melbourne. The end game of this era of rampant hypergentrification is a segregated, dysfunctional city that bears very little resemblance to the cities of opportunities to which our fathers and grandfathers migrated. Is the elite city to become the final destination of booming cities around the world? And are our neighborhoods destined to be trampled by multimillion-dollar safe-deposit boxes in the sky for the wealthiest global players?

Introduction

Over the last 15 years, New York City has changed in ways that are at the same time shocking and merciless. For the billionaire CEOs, CFOs, and Wall Street managers, and the elite of super-wealthy investment bankers, hedge fund managers, and traders employed in the financial sector, whose earnings can reach highs unheard of in the rest of the country, New York is more than ever the global capital of multimillion-dollar deals and record fortunes. In the gilded towers of New York City, Wall Street moguls, Eastern European oligarchs, and Hollywood celebrities have created their own fanta-sylands of outrageous luxury, with apartments providing perks beyond one's wildest dreams: private spas, sculpture gardens, outdoor pools, art galleries, meditation rooms, recording studios, wine cellars, and private elevators. For this privileged group of billionaires, New York satisfies all kinds of frivolous consumption fantasies, such as a $100-million duplex on Billionaire's Row or a world-record-smashing $250-million four-floor apartment in a Robert A. M. Stern–designed tower at 220 Central Park South.[1]

For those other few with the means to enjoy it, New York is, more than any other global city, a glamorous haven of work, leisure, luxury shopping, and world-class entertainment. These are the new urban classes made up of employees in the finance, insurance, and real estate (FIRE) industries, highly mobile professionals, and urban residents with higher-than-average incomes and strong purchasing power. Together, they compose a new affluent urban class whose presence is revolutionizing the social landscape of global cities such as London, Tokyo, Singapore, New York, Hong Kong, and Paris. In New York, they may be found drinking coffee in the cafes of the Village, snooping around at gallery openings in NoHo, or boutique shopping in trendy areas like the Meatpacking District.

For ordinary people, however, living in the city has become more and more of a challenge, and for those at the lower end of the social and eco-nomic ladder, surviving in today's New York can be a living hell. These are the broke college students in Astoria and the starving artists in Bushwick, the teachers and the firefighters, the small business owners, the shoemakers and the dry cleaners, the minimum-wage clerks at the Duane Reade and Starbucks, the Mexican runners and janitors in the trendy restaurants of the Village. But even those able to make a middle-class income—salespeople, nurses, managers, executive assistants, graphic designers, copywriters, and other professionals—are being priced out of the city. During the years of Bloomberg, New Yorkers on middle incomes have struggled to survive in the least affordable American city because of the constant pressure of exorbitant rents in their neighborhoods. Before Bloomberg took office, the percentage of apartments that were unaffordable to median-income households was at around 20%. By 2010, almost 40% of all rental units had become unaffordable to average New Yorkers. While the city was being relentlessly remodeled for the wealthy, middle- and low-income residents became accustomed to never-ending cycles of instability and housing insecurity.

This is the result of the most aggressive urban development agenda ever adopted in the history of New York City. Even more aggressive than that of Robert Moses, the infamous "Power Broker" of post–World War II New York, Bloomberg's agenda has rezoned immense swaths of the city's working-class, manufacturing, and waterfront areas into a wonderland for lavish real estate. The speculative fever prompted by the presence of super-wealthy consumers, and encouraged by a political agenda all too prone to subsidize luxury development, has resulted in the widespread multiplication of over-priced, exclusive condominium buildings that are unaffordable but to the wealthiest. This is what "gentrification" has come to be in today's New York: whereas in the past the reach of gentrification strategies was to rehabilitate working-class neighborhoods to middle-class standards, today's super-gentrification is "upgrading" the city to standards that are unaffordable but to the very wealthy, pushing out even those who had been accused of gentrification in the past: New York's middle class.

Welcome to the shadow side of Bloomberg's "luxury city": a segregated New York with the elites employed in the high-end sectors of the economy residing in the opulent enclaves of Manhattan and the Brooklyn/Queens waterfronts, and the low-wage and middle-income earners pushed farther and farther away from the city center—a dysfunctional city in which the low-wage service workers from Jamaica, Astoria, and Bed-Stuy suffer the most exhausting commute times in the country to get to their workplace, often as runners, dishwashers, and cleaners in the gleaming hotels, condos, restaurants, and cafes in Manhattan.

Enter de Blasio. New York City's public advocate until 2013, Bill de Blasio was a fervent social activist in the 1980s and 1990s. His "tale of two cities" mayoral campaign, which placed the issue of inequality at the center of the political agenda, galvanized progressive urban activists, trade union leaders, and middle-class New Yorkers. Some media even depicted him as a dangerous socialist who would make a radical U-turn not only from the "luxury city" agenda of his billionaire predecessor, but also from the capitalist consensus on a neoliberal, free-market approach to city building. A parade of prominent liberal New Yorkers and Hollywood stars gave de Blasio their public endorsement. This buzz was reminiscent of the halo the media created around the figure of Barack Obama during the 2008 presidential elections. But the city's real estate lobbies knew better, and lined up in support of the new mayor. And just as with Obama, radical change has yet to be seen.

The Bloomberg legacy was a city plagued with the most severe dearth of affordable housing for its middle- and low-income citizens seen in recent times. Yet de Blasio's approach to solving this crisis didn't differ much from that of Michael Bloomberg. Just like Bloomberg did before him, de Blasio hired a Goldman Sachs executive to be his deputy mayor for housing and economic development, the top position in New York's urban development machine. One year later, he appointed the vice president of development for Forest City Ratner, one of the largest realtors in the city and fundraiser of his mayoral campaign, to join the Rent Guidelines Board—the panel responsible for annual rent adjustments for the over one million apartments that are under the city's rent stabilization program. And his housing strategy, which he called "the largest, fastest affordable housing plan ever attempted at a local level," seems to rely almost exclusively on the same strategies that made big real estate so fond of Bloomberg: giving out subsidies and tax exemptions to luxury developers with the condition that they include a percentage of affordable units in the upscale developments that continue to pop up in gentrifying neighborhoods across the city. But will they ever be enough, in a city where affordable housing is consistently lost at a much faster rate than it's produced? In 2014, almost 60,000 people filed applications for 105 affordable units in Greenpoint. One year later, over 80,000 people found themselves applying for 38 newly built affordable units in Brooklyn.[2]

City officials' talks of fostering "social inclusion" through these initiatives may have to be taken with a grain of salt: seven months into de Blasio's term, the city approved a 33-story luxury tower at Riverside Drive in which the required-affordable-housing tenants must enter through a "poor door" located in the tower's back alley. As the developer of a similar project in Williamsburg candidly admitted, it's unfair to expect that the elite buying million-dollar apartments would wish to share their entrance with the likes of the lower or middle class. Such rich-door/poor-door developments, a legacy of Bloomberg's housing strategy, have become yet another test for de Blasio, who had won based on his promise to bring an end to the "tale of two cities." Despite the promises of the new mayor, and to the disappointment of many, little is changing in the day-to-day struggles of ordinary New Yorkers. More luxury development is about to come, and with it more rent increases and displacement are on their way.

The truth is that mayors, although powerful, can't change the rules of a game that was started way before they came to power. And Bloomberg and de Blasio are only the latest chief executive officers of a powerful "urban regime" that was in place before their administrations, and that will continue to reign over the city after they are gone. In this book, I not only tell the story of 15 years of dramatic urban changes in New York, but also identify the powerful, yet unelected regime of city producers and city consumers that covertly rules the city. I describe a governing coalition that includes elected officials, local and extra-local property owners, real estate developers, the business and corporate industry, and the other power players who hold all the cards in the city building game. These city producers existed before Bloomberg and de Blasio, and will outlive their administration. For years, they have been on the front lines of a new kind of corporate-style urban development, one that has actively redesigned, rebranded, and repackaged the city, as if New York were a product targeting the elite or luxury market. Their main goal is to ensure the city is custom-tailored to a global, mobile, and exceptionally affluent population of city consumers. These are the new urban classes of professionals in the higher-paid echelons of the knowledge-based and creative sectors, local and international corporations, property investors and developers, urban tourists and resident-consumers, and an ever-growing elite of super-wealthy individuals. Their presence in the city is strongly encouraged by the regime of city producers, because, so the logic goes, it is through their consumption patterns that they keep the city's elite markets and high-value industries alive.

In this book, I explain how since the early 1970s, New York's city producers have worked to reinvent the city as an entertainment and consumption-based playground for this favorite target group of consumers. I tell the story of the once vastly industrial landscapes along the Brooklyn–Queens shoreline, which have been transformed into South Beach–like enclaves of gleaming condos on the waterfront. I talk about the once-shady neighborhoods of Hell's Kitchen and downtown Brooklyn, and how they are being transfigured into spectacular islands of luxury towers for the well-off.

But I also tell the story of loss—the loss of legendary, iconic neighborhoods that have made New York what it is in the history of popular culture. I chronicle the developments that have radically changed the face of Harlem's "Main Street," where today, franchises like Gap, H&M, and Starbucks, coupled with gourmet Italian restaurants or cafes charging $5 for a cup of coffee, dominate a landscape that was once made of cheap bodegas, bookstores, liquor stores, and hair salons. And I describe the limbo of Coney Island, whose turn-of-the-century ballrooms and gritty arcade game parlors have been sacrificed to make room for a new wave of corporate retail. From Hell's Kitchen to downtown Brooklyn, from Williamsburg to the Meatpacking District, I tell the story of the merciless years that have obliterated innumerable traces of old New York: of the thousands of historical buildings that have disappeared from the city map; of the innumerable diners, drugstores, bookstores, hardware stores, and laundromats that have shut their doors over the last decade; and of the shimmering condos, boutiques, cafes, and chain stores that are taking their place.

My journey starts in Harlem, the legendary African American neighborhood that has been caught in the midst of a development storm over the last two decades. In chapter 1, "The New Face of Harlem's Main Street," I visit 125th Street. I tell the story of Harlem's most iconic boulevard, from its beginnings as a popular commercial thoroughfare in the 1910s and 1920s, through the decay of the neighborhood during the Great Depression and in the post–World War II years, to its real estate renaissance in the late 1990s and 2000s. This chronicle is accompanied by an investigation of the changing media representations of the area through the years, from frightening accounts of a crime-ridden ghetto plagued by poverty and drugs during the late 1960s and 1970s to the image of a vibrant and fashionable community by the late 2000s. In my account, I expose the pivotal role of city producers in the retelling of the story of Harlem's Main Street to the world and to its own residents. I then examine the rezoning plan for 125th Street, which was approved by the city during the Bloomberg years. I identify the city producers who backed the plan and describe the contentious decision-making process that led to its approval. I investigate its impact on the physical, social, and symbolic space of the neighborhood. Finally, I focus on Harlem's new consumers, a population of affluent black and white urbanites that are the main drivers of the so-called New Harlem Renaissance, the much-celebrated multicultural and economic transformation of what once was considered nothing but a barren urban ghetto. But beneath this shining surface, I illustrate the crafty dynamics behind the residential and commercial gentrification of 125th Street and its surroundings.

In chapter 2, "How Capital Shapes Our Cities," I introduce some necessary background that will help readers understand why neighborhoods like Harlem, and cities like New York more generally, are doomed to never-ending cycles of creative destruction. I explain how the physical, social, and symbolic space of our cities is dominated by the imperatives of capital, in its relentless struggle to conquer every corner of our cities and to extract profit from it. I demystify the concept of "urbanization" and explain how urban land creates wealth for developers and land owners, and how this accumulation of wealth is favored by the daily works of elected officials. I offer a brief, compelling history of the evolutions in New York City's urban policies that, particularly since the 1970s, have contributed to the urbanization we see today, and explain how, through the years, the relentless obliteration of traces of old New York has paved the way for the creation of a brand-new, more profitable city. In this chapter I explain how cities not only are crucial nodes and stages of consumption but also have become commodities in their own right. I argue that the physical fabric of our cities, their social environment, and even their representations in the popular media are manufactured and consumed. I theorize the existence of powerful elites of city producers, coalitions of interest groups that are actively engaged in manufacturing and branding the city. I investigate their activities and explain how they contribute to the production of a specific physical, social, and symbolic space: a repackaged wonderland for affluent city consumers. In turn, city consumers' demand for specific urban experiences, strongly influenced by the media, leads to the production of a city that is more and more tailored to their demands and desires. I describe a new kind of cost-prohibitive, super-gentrified space as the product of the interlocking practices of city producers and city consumers.

In chapter 3, "The Producers and Consumers of New York City," I identify several categories of producers that are active in New York City. These include the local government, the local and extra-local real estate industries, the business world, the media and city branding and marketing industry, and a corollary of nongovernmental organizations that operate within the local community and are active in the making of urban policy. Naming names, I investigate their activities and how they contribute to the production of a specific physical, social, and symbolic space that is custom-tailored for the new hordes of city consumers. I then identify these new consumers—individuals and groups who play a crucial role in dictating the guidelines of New York City's urban agenda. These include geographically mobile urban residents, local and international corporations and businesses, local and extra-local property investors and developers, urban tourists, resident-consumers, and the new elites of super-wealthy players. I investigate their consumption patterns and clarify how their consumerist demands play a strategic role in the production of a repackaged, overdesigned, and super-commodified urban space.

In chapter 4, "Rezoning New York City," I explain the strategies that city producers have adopted since the 1970s to physically transform New York into a consumption- and entertainment-based playground for new consumers. I start by introducing a brief history of zoning in New York City through the years, from the 1811 Commissioner's Plan through the 1961 zoning resolution, which is still in vigor today, although it has been subjected to innumerable amendments since its adoption. I then investigate the rezoning agenda implemented by the Department of City Planning since the mayoralty of Michael Bloomberg. I demonstrate how, compared to comprehensive master plans, site-specific rezonings have proven more flexible and accommodating to the erratic demands of a fluid and globalized real estate industry. I describe in detail the plans for New York City's 2012 Olympic bid, the operations of the Department of City Planning under rezoning "czar" Amanda Burden, and PlaNYC 2030, Bloomberg's plan for a postindustrial, ecologically friendly city unveiled in 2007. I examine two among the largest and most contested rezoning plans adopted by the city during Bloomberg's first two terms in office, the Atlantic Yards and the Hudson Yards development plans, respectively in Brooklyn and Manhattan's Far West Side. Both plans, I argue, epitomize a top-down approach to planning that has eschewed formal public review procedures, using state and city government powers to push development forward in spite of local opposition, often against the interests of the local communities. I criticize the key arguments that form the discursive framework of the Department of City Planning's rezoning agenda for New York City, and I challenge official discourses of comprehensiveness, citizen participation, affordable housing, mixed-use development, and contextual development. In so doing, I highlight the many contradictions of the key discourses that have shaped Bloomberg's, and are shaping de Blasio's, urban agenda. Whether under Bloomberg or de Blasio, I argue, rezoning has been used as a tool for the physical upgrading of neighborhoods as much as a device for the social re-engineering of existing communities: with its insistence on the production of exclusive housing, high-end retail, and new infrastructures in disadvantaged neighborhoods, rezoning has institutionalized the gentrification of marginalized districts as a government-sponsored development program. This agenda also operates within already-gentrified districts, acting as a form of regentrification or, as urban scholar Loretta Lees calls it, "super-gentrification," in which new generations of super-wealthy individuals from the corporate and financial industries are revolutionizing middle-class areas whose residents had in turn been responsible for the displacement of former working-class residents years ago.

In chapter 5, "The Rezoning That Almost Killed Coney Island," I hit the streets once again to explore another iconic working-class neighborhood that has undergone tremendous change over the last 15 years. I tell a brief history of Coney Island's heyday in the 19th and early 20th centuries and of its long decline after World War II, and I chronicle the popular representations of the neighborhood in the movies and the media from the 1970s to today. I investigate the rezoning plan for Coney Island approved in 2009 and illustrate its troubling impact on Coney's legendary businesses and on the local amusement industry. I chronicle the property speculations that occurred prior to and immediately after the plan's approval, and their impact on the neighborhood's historic buildings, small businesses, and old amusement operators. The city's ambitious visions of turning Coney Island from one of the city's poorest residential areas into a luxury year-round seaside destination is still far from reality, but in the meantime, many small businesses, amusement parlors, and historical buildings have been wiped out to make room for a tide of retail chains that would have been unthinkable only a few years ago.

In chapter 6, "The Power Branders of New York City," I demonstrate how, since the aftermath of New York's fiscal crisis in the mid-1970s, city producers have consistently worked on remodeling the image of New York City through concerted marketing and branding efforts. But in recent years, the scope and scale of city branding has reached unprecedented highs. From Bloomberg to de Blasio, a corporate-style, vertically managed branding machine has contributed to the production of a new, hegemonic representation of the city as a commodity, and has dictated the guidelines of a growth-prone, luxury-oriented development agenda. By expanding the scope of branding initiatives across all five neighborhoods, and by incorporating elements of underground and off-culture into the compass of the tourist market, the branding of New York City has hastened a process of commodification of the urban experience that is unprecedented in its pervasiveness, and that is likely to become a prototype for the branding of big cities worldwide in the coming years.

In chapter 7, "A Different Brand of Mayor," I tell the story of Mayor de Blasio and of his rise to power at a time when New Yorkers were afflicted by skyrocketing housing prices and low- and middle-income households, along with small independent businesses, were being priced out of the city in droves. A crusade against inequality became the central theme of de Blasio's mayoral campaign, which was widely viewed as a repudiation of Bloomberg's time in office. But the radical stances of pre-election de Blasio have loosened up quickly once in office. His substantial continuation of Bloomberg's rezoning and housing agenda and his half-hearted commitment to the cause of small business owners have baffled those New Yorkers who believed in a radical cut with past policies. In opposition to the anti-Bloomberg rhetoric of his campaign, they suggest a choice of continuity with past policies, announcing that more of the same is on its way. Drawing mostly on de Blasio's rezoning and housing plans, I explain how the new mayor has tried to broker a deal between his electoral promises and the imperatives of the "urban regime" of city producers that rules New York City. The de Blasio experience is showing that a new mayor won't reverse the course of urban policy: undeterred by changes in leadership, New York's city producers will strive to ensure that their achievements will be sustained in the years ahead. One thing is sure: in New York City, more years of creative destruction are on their way.

THE CREATIVE DESTRUCTION
OF NEW YORK CITY

I

The New Face
of Harlem's Main Street

And yet, this new army of developers, speculators, and investors marches
through Harlem behind the wrecking ball of global capital, banking on the
neighborhood's rich history as the center of black culture and art.[1]

In the spring of 2013, the Real Estate Board of New York launched its
first "Harlem Open House Expo." It was an exclusive event in partnership with Chase Manhattan, geared at "potential buyers looking to get a
peek at the hot Harlem real estate":[2] brokers from all major real estate
firms operating in Harlem hosted viewings of pricey co-ops, condos, and
townhouses for sale. The listings included a brownstone at West 126th Street
selling for $2.5 million and a two-bedroom apartment at East 126th Street
for $805,000. A few years before, "Harlem Is Booming" was the title of an
eight-page advertising supplement that appeared in the *New York Times*:[3] it
depicted Harlem as a new hip and sophisticated destination for the well-off
newcomers, listing the dozens of luxury development projects taking place
in the neighborhood. These included the 2280 FDB at 123th Street, a 12-
story luxury condominium building with prices ranging from $509,000
to $1.889 million; the Livmor Condominium at 115th Street, whose pent-
houses sold for almost $2 million, and which includes amenities such as a
state-of-the-art fitness center and a media lounge; and the Apex, a luxury
condo at 124th Street and Frederick Douglass Boulevard on top of the
boutique Aloft Hotel, with a panoramic rooftop terrace, bar, and fitness
center. Sponsored by the largest realtors with ventures in the district, the
New York Times supplement celebrated the new wave of luxury development in Harlem, asking the readers, "Are we witnessing a second Harlem

Renaissance?" The answer was of course a sound yes, although the supplement gave the rather clear impression that what drove this renaissance was a wave of luxury real estate, rather than a cultural and political awakening.

From the 1960s through much of the 1980s, Harlem had made headlines as one of the most infamous urban ghettos in America, plagued by poverty, gang violence, and drugs. But during the Bloomberg and de Blasio years, the neighborhood that had frightened middle-class Americans for decades has emerged as one of the city's luxury real estate hotspots. Nowhere are these changes more remarkable than around 125th Street, once the bustling focal point of the "Harlem Renaissance," the street where the history of black America was made in the 1920s and 1930s, and which entered a phase of steep decline in the late 1960s. Over the last 15 years, the swift pace of development has radically changed the face of the strip: today, Old Navy, H&M, CVS, Starbucks, Subway, Applebee's, and Gap have made it almost undistinguishable from major commercial crossroads downtown, like 14th, 23rd, or 34th Street. A few blocks down, new lavish condos are popping up everywhere, bringing with them an army of new, hip, and moneyed city consumers. But it's not hard to see what's behind that gleaming surface. In today's Harlem, pricey brownstones and luxury condominium buildings stand next to public housing projects that are still home to a poor and segregated community. While *Sunday Times* real estate sections routinely list Harlem properties to affluent professionals from downtown, along with anecdotes of black and white yuppies snapping up wonderful mansions for bargain prices, the old Harlemites lament the loss of their community. Over the past 10 years, I've spoken with both long-time residents and newcomers to the area, and I've witnessed first-hand the simmering conflicts over class that gentrification has brought about in the neighborhood. Heather is a young white woman I met while she was walking her dog at Marcus Garvey Park. She moved to Harlem in 2010 and is quite knowledgeable about the changes that are happening in the neighborhood:

> All these new cafes and Whole Foods and the cupcake shops, these places are not catering to the people that were originally here. They are catering to those like us. New people who just moved in the neighborhood. Black or white doesn't matter, but it's still the newcomers they are building all this new stuff for.

That seems to be the case with new stylish restaurants like Red Rooster, opened in 2010 by world-class chef, TV star, and new Harlem transplant Marcus Samuelsson, whose patrons are majority white and nonlocal.

Located between 125th and 126th, just nearby the historical soul food diner Sylvia's, it was called a "game changer" in Harlem, as reported by a *Guardian* journalist:

> Business owners speak about "before Red Rooster" and "after Red Rooster," referring not just to its power in terms of drawing outsider crowds, but also in defining a specific kind of Harlem chic.[4]

But if a new trendy Harlem is being made for newcomers, what about those who lived here before? I talked to Gale, a black woman in her 50s whom I met in front of the therapy center for HIV patients at 125th Street and Malcolm X Boulevard. Although she still works here every day, she was recently forced to leave Harlem:

> I don't live in Harlem anymore. I stayed here 28 years, I had to leave in 2012, they took the apartment back, the landlord wanted all the apartments back so they could give them over to the new rich people.... This happened everywhere. They did no longer need us. I had to move in the Bronx by the new Yankee Stadium, and then I had to move from there again, 'cause my rent there was doubled too.

Gale is outraged by the changes in the neighborhood. To her, the new businesses along 125th Street are catering not to people like her, but to a brand-new population of consumers who don't have any real bond with the community she knows:

> These new people, they do not spend any money in the moms and pops. They spend their money only at Starbucks. They do not buy stuff from here. They go downtown. All these companies they come with their own people over here, they don't bring new jobs, they promise they'll hire people from the area, that's the hoop-la to get all the paperwork to get approval from the city. We don't benefit at all.

Although the commercial and residential gentrification of the areas surrounding 125th Street had been set in motion in the years of Rudolph Giuliani, the pace of these transformations has accelerated tremendously under the administrations of Bloomberg and de Blasio. According to Gale, it was the city's rezoning of 125th Street, approved in 2009, that put the final nail in the coffin of what was once a predominantly black, working-class neighborhood:

> That's what they do all the time. They need to push those zoning changes. They need to change the blocks, they need to change an area that has been

existing way before you even thought about coming here. This has been a growing neighborhood for years now. This ain't no abandoned area. These rezonings are not for the average person. They spent $6 million for the park [Marcus Garvey Park], they made it for those white people living in those luxury condos over there. But we, the average people, we are stuck in a box. We see our shops close. They buy them out. We are not supposed to live here any longer.

The rezoning for 125th Street came at a very sensitive time for Harlem residents, who were already under pressure from escalating housing prices, massive development schemes by neighboring Columbia University, and extensive waves of foreclosures and bankruptcies of small businesses in the recessive economy of the late 2000s. And 125th Street, Harlem's largest and most famous thoroughfare, has become the latest battleground between the ambitions of New York's city producers, the demands of new city consumers, and the fears and outrage of many long-time residents.

History of "Harlem's Main Street"

Laid out in the 1811 Commissioner's Plan for Manhattan (the "grid plan"), 125th Street is a broad cross-town street that runs from the Hudson to the East River, crossing West, Central, and East Harlem. Around the end of the 19th century, Harlem was a prestigious residential suburb lined with streets of beautiful row houses and freestanding mansions, but also of five- and six-story tenements for middle-class families. The beginning of construction work for the IRT subway in 1900 was the catalyst for a wave of rampant property development and the construction of new tenements in the area, and after the completion of a subway stop at the corner with Broadway in 1904, 125th Street established itself as Harlem's central commercial thoroughfare. But the opening of the subway did not have the desired effect on property values: the improvement of mass transit to the outer boroughs instead drove many of Harlem's middle-class residents away. As landlords were unable to find white tenants for their dwellings, they started renting to a growing African American community: during and after World War I, large numbers of African and Caribbean migrants from British, Dutch, and French colonies in the West Indies migrated to Harlem. By 1914, Harlem's African American population was estimated at about 50,000.[5]

In the 1920s and 1930s, Harlem experienced a period of cultural and political ferment that was unique in the history of African American culture. Black intellectuals and artists were attracted to a neighborhood they saw as a promised land of opportunities for emancipation. This Harlem Renaissance was a moment of glorious artistic and literary achievements that for the first time in American history exposed black artists, activists, and intellectuals to an audience far beyond the traditional confines of the African American community. The works of writers like W. E. B. DuBois and Langston Hughes and artists such as Jacob Lawrence and Romare Bearden were applauded well beyond the boundaries of Harlem. In these years, 125th Street became the beating heart of Harlem's nightlife, with its innumerable theaters, dance halls, lounges, speakeasies, cafes, and bars. Legendary jazz clubs, like the Cotton Club, the Lenox Lounge, and the Savoy, opened, along with numerous theaters. Harlem became the "Black Capital of the World," and 125th Street became the bustling focal point of this extraordinary blossoming of culture (Figure 1.1). In 1917, the Loew's Victoria Theater opened

Figure 1.1 View of the Apollo Theater marquee, New York, between 1946 and 1948.

on 125th Street as a luxury vaudeville and motion picture theater; in 1934, the world-famous Apollo Theater opened in a former burlesque house on 125th Street. It was here that the careers of prominent black entertainers like Billie Holiday and Ella Fitzgerald were launched.

But the cultural ferment of the Harlem Renaissance did not extirpate a long history of racial and social injustice. Most of the 125th Street bars, nightclubs, and stores were in fact owned by white landlords, and most were "white only" establishments that did not accept blacks as customers or even as clerks. Even housing opportunities were limited for black people, and home ownership was thwarted by the infamous redlining practices of banks, which denied loans to residents of black inner-city neighborhoods. In 1920, one-room apartments in central Harlem rented for about $40 to whites, but the price was up to three times more for black tenants.[6] These and other forms of racial segregation, which persisted through the mid-1970s, encouraged the formation of political groups fighting for the emancipation and the self-determination of black Americans, and rampant political and social activism in defense of the rights of black people became a hallmark of Harlem in the early decades of the 20th century.

In the 1910s and 1920s, political leader Marcus Garvey galvanized the community with his struggles for the rights of African Americans. Many in Harlem joined the Black Nationalism and Pan-Africanism movements, which advocated for racial pride and the self-determination and independence of American blacks. But the Great Depression of 1929 ended this moment of cultural and political ferment for the Harlem community. In the early 1930s, employment among black New Yorkers dropped dramatically, and activist groups started boycotting white-owned stores under the slogan "Don't buy where you can't work." Protests escalated with the 1934 public demonstration at 125th Street in front of Blumstein's Department Store for the right of African Americans to work in white-owned establishments.[7] Rampant unemployment and persisting social conflict, which culminated in the Harlem Riot of 1935 at 125th Street,[8] convinced those wealthier whites who had supported Harlem's entertainment and retail businesses to leave.

Circumstances worsened after World War II, when 125th Street and the surrounding areas entered a phase of precipitous decline as middle-class blacks started moving away, leaving only the very poor and the unemployed in the neighborhood. With the passage of the Federal Housing Act in 1949, urban renewal and "slum" redevelopment processes changed

Figure 1.2 The Riverside Park Community apartment complex at 3333 Broadway between West 133rd and 135th Streets, in Harlem.

the face of many areas of Harlem (Figure 1.2). While the impact on 125th Street was limited and focused only on its east and west ends, other public housing schemes in Harlem were responsible for the large-scale obliteration of entire portions of the historic fabric and the extensive displacement of long-time residents. Traditional tenements were replaced with monolithic high-rise, low-income housing complexes, surrounded by vast gardens and parking lots, which severely exacerbated the geographic segregation of the poor in Harlem. At the west end of 125th Street, the General Ulysses S. Grant Houses were completed in 1956 between Broadway and Morningside Avenue, from 123rd Street to 125th Street. The complex, the tallest housing project in New York City at the time it was built, hosted 1,940 apartment units in eight buildings at twenty-one stories, and was managed by the New York City Housing Authority (NYCHA), established as the first public housing authority in the country by Fiorello La Guardia in 1934. At the east end of 125th Street, the Senator Robert F. Wagner Sr. Houses were completed in 1958 between Second Avenue and FDR Drive, between East 120th and East 124th Streets. The complex consisted of 22 towers with 2,154 apartments for around 5,290 residents.

The 1960s were the beginning of a three-decade-long age of decline for Harlem. When landlords could not afford property taxes or repairs, buildings were abandoned and boarded up, or even burned down to collect insurance money. More and more tax-delinquent buildings in Harlem (called "in-rem") were foreclosed and taken over by the city, which by the 1960s came to own almost 40% of the area's housing stock. As the building stock deteriorated, private landlords converted their buildings into privately run flophouses and homeless shelters. Meanwhile, in the 1950s and 1960s, the heroin epidemic hit Harlem like a storm. Drug-related crime, such as robbery, burglary, and murder, was six times higher in the neighborhood than the city average. The critical housing conditions in the neighborhood contributed to more social unrest.

In the summer of 1964, Harlem became the scene of a new riot unleashed by the fatal shooting of an unarmed black teenager by a white police officer. Other riots followed the shocking assassination in 1968 of Martin Luther King Jr., leader of the African American civil rights movement.[9] During the late 1960s and 1970s, Harlem, like the South Bronx and the most deprived parts of Brooklyn, continued to experience widespread abandonment and arson. In the 1970s, the process of abandonment escalated to the point that Harlem reached a lower population density than the rest of Manhattan for the first time since before World War I. Also 125th Street's fortune as a premiere commercial street declined dramatically. The famous Apollo Theater shut down in 1976. Few bars and clubs remained open on the street. Most storefronts were boarded up or left vacant. This is how a *New York Times* reporter described the street in 1978:

> Empty, boarded-up stores along the once bustling 125th Street shopping corridor; burned-out abandoned buildings demeaning almost every block … ; hundreds of idle men clustered at corners, drowning empty days in wine and whisky; youths barely into their teens selling drugs as openly as other boys hawk newspapers.[10]

The lack of access to credit and the unaffordable insurance fees (due to Harlem's vertiginous crime rates, among the highest in the nation) discouraged black storeowners from holding on to their businesses. Nonblack business owners, on the other hand, were threatened by the frequent "buy black" boycott initiatives launched by local groups. As a result, commerce gradually shifted to the sidewalks of 125th Street, where peddlers and street vendors started selling soul food and bootleg goods. A large illegal market emerged on the sidewalks of the street and on a vacant lot between 125th and 126th Streets. Dreams of a revitalization of Harlem and of its Main Street in the late 1970s and early 1980s were short-lived. The vision of a Harlem International Trade Center at 125th Street and Lenox Avenue never materialized. There also had been plans to create a major shopping mall and a center for the arts, but shrinking federal subsidies, coupled with the uneasiness of private investors to invest in a risky territory like Harlem, shattered the hopes of those who dreamt of a new Harlem revival.

There were some exceptions, however. In 1982, the Studio Museum, first opened in 1968 as a small loft exhibiting African American artists' work at 5th Avenue and 125th Street, reopened in a new location on 125th Street between Lenox and Adam Clayton Powell Jr. Boulevard. In 1983, the Apollo Theater was eventually purchased by City Broadcasting, a firm owned by former Manhattan borough president Percy E. Sutton.[11] The theater obtained federal, state, and city landmark status, and fully reopened in 1985. But despite these few encouraging signs, the prospects for the neighborhood remained bleak.

In 1982, Mayor Ed Koch commissioned a "Redevelopment Strategy for Central Harlem," prepared by a special "Harlem Task Force." The report called for public–private investments in selected anchor areas around Harlem, especially at 125th Street. In the early 1980s, the Koch administration also began auctioning the city's in-rem properties back to private investors and to nonprofit organizations, in an attempt to foster private investment in the neighborhood. However, the results of the first auction in 1982 were discouraging, as most of the purchased properties were not rehabilitated, but flipped over to other investors for a profit. As a consequence, a second auction in 1985 remained open only to households with a substantially higher income than the Harlem average,[12] mainly middle-income residents from other neighborhoods. Already around the mid-1980s, urban geographers Richard Schaffer and Neil Smith noted that activities in the housing markets of certain areas of Harlem were pronounced enough to signal the onset of the first forms of gentrification.[13] In the early 1990s, a few national chains also opened their first branches on 125th Street. The first was a Body Shop at the corner of Fifth Avenue, followed by a Ben & Jerry's ice cream franchise right across the street. But despite these signs of commercial upgrading, the long recession of the early 1990s once again frustrated city officials' ambitions of a revitalized Harlem.[14]

125th Street from Giuliani to Bloomberg

On October 17, 1994, Harlem was again in turmoil, as hundreds of police officers swooped in to displace the many street vendors and peddlers populating the sidewalks of 125th Street. One *New York Times* reporter described the scene as follows:

> In place of the vendors yesterday were police officers standing along the street in clusters of three, with metal barricades on the sidewalks, giving 125th Street an air of an area under siege.... Police officials declined to say how many officers were assigned to the area yesterday, but some officers estimated their numbers at more than 500. And while many Harlem residents found the scene disquieting, some praised how the Giuliani administration was dealing with what many had considered a perennial severe problem whose solution had eluded previous mayors.[15]

The illegal vendors were moved to a temporary market site at Lenox Avenue and 116th Street. The aggressive raid against them signaled the advent of that "law and order" platform that would become the hallmark of the Rudolph Giuliani administration in the following years, and would change the face of 125th Street for good.

The end of Harlem's "crack wars" in the mid-1990s and the staggering drop in crime complaints in Harlem coincided with a new era of aggressive police enforcement in the neighborhood. Although crime in New York City as a whole had been declining since the Dinkins years, it was during the period 1993–2001 that the three Harlem police precincts (28, 30, and 32) reported the most remarkable drops in crime in the whole city—especially drug-related crimes such as burglaries and murders.[16] The mid-1990s were also a time of rapid real estate appreciation citywide, but certain areas of Harlem hit record sales. During the 1996–2006 period, East and Central Harlem were among the neighborhoods with the largest increases in sale prices, with 499.6% and 270.2%, respectively,[17] signaling a strong reactivation of the real estate market in a neighborhood that for decades had been off limits for developers. Harlem was becoming safer for investors. In 1993, the creation of a 125th Street Business Improvement District (BID) to promote shopping along the strip paved the way for the long sought-after revitalization of Harlem's Main Street. In its early years, the BID installed security lighting to make the street safer at night, improved sanitation, created promotional maps and brochures, and organized summer concert series, sport and fashion galas, jazz programs, and business conferences. The closing months of 1999 witnessed the appearance of the first Starbucks on West 125th Street and Lenox Avenue—a very reliable indicator that something on the street was definitely changing.

In 2001, as former US president Clinton's staff moved its offices to 55 West 125th Street, reporters described the event as a psychological boost to the Harlem community, despite ambivalent local reactions, as some residents started fearing that gentrification was about to make its way into the neighborhood.[18] In fact, one of the main catalysts for a new wave of commercial development on 125th Street was the Upper Manhattan Empowerment Zone (UMEZ) legislation backed by Clinton and introduced in 1994 in Congress by Harlem Representative Charles Rangel. It was one of nine empowerment zones established by the Clinton administration in distressed areas across the country with the goal to stimulate economic growth by granting tax breaks and low-interest loans to private investors. The UMEZ's initial 10-year program was based on a federal grant of $100 million, alongside funds from the governor of New York State and the mayor, creating an investment pool of $250 million available for development in Harlem.[19] However, the UMEZ's funding to small businesses represented only about 10% of the total money allocated;[20] most of the funds went to attract giant corporate retailers in the neighborhood. In true Darwinian fashion, while many locally owned establishments closed shop, global chains started opening their first branches on 125th Street, with the promise of hiring local residents. Most of the new jobs created, however, turned out to be mainly entry-level positions as cashiers or clerks, with minimum-wage salaries and few benefits.[21] According to a Harlem businessman, "the Empowerment Zone is not empowering people, it is permitting them to be clerks."[22]

A pilot project that received a major share of the UMEZ's public financing was Harlem USA, a 285,000-square-foot, six-level retail and entertainment complex that opened at 125th Street in 2000. Anchored by large chain retailers including Old Navy, New York Sports Club, JP Morgan Chase Bank, and the "Magic Johnson Theaters" multiplex, it was a pioneering venture on 125th Street, and the trailblazer for such kinds of developments on the strip. In 2002, a large retail and office complex called Harlem Center followed suit at the corner of Lenox and 125th: its mall at the ground floor hosted Marshall's, Washington Mutual, Payless Shoesource, Duane Reade, and an H&M outlet in a side pavilion close to the Adam Clayton Powell Jr. Federal Office Building. In both developments, ground-floor rents were way beyond the reach of most local businesses, so that only corporate retailers could afford a space there.[23] By 2002, the west end of 125th Street, which only a decade before was still dotted with abandoned buildings, started to look undistinguishable from the major cross-town retail strips downtown.

Meanwhile, the commercial makeover of the east end of 125th Street, between Lexington and 3rd Avenue, was carried out in the form of large, suburban-like superstores. A Pathmark supermarket, with a parking lot occupying the entire block between Lexington and 3rd Avenue, was completed in 2002. The three-story, 90,000-square-foot Gotham Plaza retail center opened the same year right across the street, filling an entire lot of East 125th between Lexington and 3rd. The huge enclosed shopping mall hosts the offices of Commerce Bank and AT&T and chain brands such as Sleepys and Radioshack. The Gateway Building, which opened in 2002 diagonally across from the Pathmark center, is a smaller, three-story, 39,000-square-foot commercial complex hosting franchises such as Duane Reade and Seaman's Furniture (Figure 1.3).

Commercial development coincided with a new wave of extensive residential construction and rehabilitation of decrepit single- and multifamily buildings. The rehabilitation of old houses and the development of new units were spearheaded by the action of several community development

Figure 1.3 The Gateway Building at 125th Street and Lexington Avenue.

corporations active in Harlem since the late 1980s, including the Abyssinian Development Corporation, whose efforts by the late 1990s shifted from providing housing to moderate- and low-income Harlem residents to the development of middle- to upper-income condominium apartments, and of massive commercial complexes along 125th Street, including the Pathmark supermarket and Harlem Center in partnership with the UMEZ. The Harlem Community Development Corporation (HCDC), created as a subsidiary of the Empire State Development Corporation in 1995, was also crucial in the redevelopment of the neighborhood. By the late 1990s, tenement-style dwellings and row houses around 125th Street and in Central and West Harlem gradually started attracting increasing numbers of affluent in-movers, mostly black and white professionals from other parts of Manhattan, who could profit from the relative bargains and the excellent transportation options of the area.

Representations of 125th Street from the 1970s to the Bloomberg Years

Throughout the 1960s, the 1970s, and much of the 1980s, journalistic, literary, and cinematographic accounts of Harlem routinely portrayed the neighborhood as the underbelly of a city in chaos, a slum plagued by poverty and gang violence. Blaxploitation and action movies such as *Cotton Comes to Harlem* (1970), *Shaft* (1971), and *Black Caesar* (1973) told the US public stories of crime and mobsters in the most dangerous American urban ghetto (Figures 1.4 and 1.5). Sensationalistic articles in magazines and newspapers

Figure 1.4 Movie still from the movie *Black Caesar* (1973).

Figure 1.5 Movie still from the movie *Shaft* (1971).

were adding fuel to the fire, portraying Harlem like a nightmarish urban jungle to a frightened American audience.

But in the late 1980s and early 1990s, the mass perception of danger that had long been associated with Harlem started to dissipate. Sociologist Sharon Zukin notes that it was in these years that mainstream media gradually began portraying the virtues of Harlem as a conveniently located Manhattan neighborhood just waiting to be discovered by brave urban pioneers:

> Beginning in the 1980s mainstream media such as the *New York Times* and *New York Magazine* published occasional stories of gentrifiers, more black than white, who bought brownstone houses cheap because of the neighborhood's decline and then confronted drug addicts, gangs and rubble-strewn lots. Through the 1990s, when the empowerment zone set up shop, the stories about new residents grew more optimistic, and after 2001 they focused on more whites than blacks.[24]

The rediscovered media interest for Harlem was also the result of two-decade-long efforts of local business alliances and city agencies to encourage tourism in the neighborhood. The Uptown Chamber of Commerce (UCC) had been launching timid initiatives to persuade visiting out-of-towners to add Harlem to their Manhattan itineraries since the early 1970s. Their aim was to promote a tourist-friendly image of a neighborhood that had long been associated with crime and poverty. In 1974, the UCC's launch of "Harlem Day" (a one-day summer event celebrating the neighborhood and its culture, arts, religion, entertainment, and sports) proved successful, and the event was soon expanded into a week-long festival showcasing the best that Harlem had to offer.[25] More initiatives to market Harlem as a viable tourist destination followed suit. In 1979, the UCC launched a "Do It Up in Harlem" campaign that was officially linked to the state's glob-ally successful "I ♥ New York" initiative. In the mid-1980s, the Harlem Visitors and Convention Association (HVCA) was created to promote tourism in the neighborhood. In 1985, the "I ♥ New York" campaign had Harlem as its centerpiece and an "I ♥ New York Harlem Travel Guide" was produced to highlight shopping and entertainment in the neighborhood. The Apollo Theater at 125th Street, which had finally reopened after many years of neglect, started featuring a tourist-friendly entertainment program with jazz nights, gospel Sundays, and the famous Wednesday amateur night shows. Since 1993, the activities of the 125th Street BID were also cru-cial to reinforce the image of Harlem's Main Street as a vibrant shopping thoroughfare. The BID produced promotional maps, worked on streetscape improvements, and launched a series of initiatives to attract visitors to the area, including the "Holiday Lighting Program" during Christmas (1994), the "Harlem Summer Concert Series" (1996), and walking tours of the neighborhood's landmarks. Also, the UMEZ dedicated part of its resources (through a $25 million Cultural Investment Fund) to promote tourism to some of the iconic attractions of Harlem, most of which were located on 125th Street or in its immediate surroundings. These included the Apollo Theater, the Boy's Choir of Harlem, the Dance Theater of Harlem, the Studio Museum, and the Museum for African Art.[26]

By the late 1990s, the mainstream press was keener than ever to highlight the pleasures of visiting Harlem, and dazzling reviews of its best restaurants, bars, and jazz parlors filled the lifestyle and food sections of the *New York Times* and *New York Magazine*. By the early 2000s, tourism in the area was on the rise. In 2000, about 800,000 tourists visited Harlem's attractions.[27] But it wasn't until the election of Michael R. Bloomberg that Harlem experienced its most staggering increase in tourist numbers. With Bloomberg in office, massive efforts were invested in the production of a new brand for Harlem and for its Main Street. Marketing initiatives by the UMEZ, the Uptown Chamber of Commerce, the 125th Street BID, and other local stakeholders were reinforced and coordinated by NYC & Company, Bloomberg's newly created branding machine. In 2003, the UMEZ partnered with NYC & Company to open a visitor information center at the New York State Office Building Plaza on 125th Street. The BID, meanwhile, continued its initia-tives to create a "friendly business atmosphere" on 125th Street and started partnering with larger companies:[28] in 2000, it launched the "American

Express Holiday Stroll Program" and a series of "Thursday Is Business Day" events, sponsored by Chase, the UMEZ, and Citibank. In 2009, a new visitor information center was opened in the Studio Museum, also on 125th Street. One year later, the opening of the Aloft Hotel, a 124-room Starwood franchise just one block south of 125th Street, was cherished by the press for being the first hotel to open in Harlem in decades.[29] In 2012, NYC & Company launched "Destination Harlem," a one-month-long campaign to highlight cultural events at renowned Harlem institutions, including the famous amateur nights at the Apollo, gospel concerts at the Dwyer Cultural Center, readings at the Schomburg Center for Research in Black Culture, cabaret shows at the Harlem Stage, and poetry readings at El Museo del Barrio. The campaign also promoted some of the few traditional local businesses that had managed to survive and thrive in the midst of the gentrifying neighborhood, like Sylvia's Soul Food Restaurant, Amy Ruth's, or the famed Lenox Lounge.[30] The message conveyed to visitors and New Yorkers was that Harlem was no more a no-go area: instead, it had become just another welcoming, vibrant, and trendy Manhattan destination—with some black flavor. Only passing references to African American culture, and no mentions of the historical struggles for self-determination of Harlem's blacks, were included in these new representations:

> While it's too soon to call it a full-fledged neo-Renaissance, Harlem is unquestionably happening. Buoyed by an influx of former downtowners and emboldened by a tradition of culture and creativity, the neighborhood is chockablock with new high-end shops, restaurants, music halls, lounges and even a luxury hotel.... Harlem may still be beloved for its hundreds of churches, elegant row houses, unexpected parks and tiny home-cooking joints, but there's another side of the neighborhood in the making these days: sleek, chic and sophisticated. It's Manhattan at its colorful best.[31]

By the mid-2000s, city newspapers and magazines celebrated Harlem's "Second Renaissance": its vibrant atmosphere, its lively culture, but most of all its charming residential properties made headlines. Meanwhile, new trendy media were launched to show New Yorkers the coolness of living uptown. In 2004, *Uptown Magazine* was created by two young black entrepreneurs who set office at East 125th Street. The glossy lifestyle magazine speaks directly to the growing population of affluent black professionals living in Harlem. Articles featured in *Uptown* are about successful black businesspeople, CEOs, hedge fund managers, doctors—the new Harlem elites:

From ultra-elite Madison Avenue events and black tie galas to Fashion Week at Lincoln Center, New York City is the epicenter of style and status. UPTOWN gives you a firsthand look at the life and times of the city's affluent African-Americans.[32]

The magazine's readership includes "180,000 socialites, business executives, financial gurus, celebrities, power players, and style mavens with annual incomes exceeding $132,000 ... a new audience of noteworthy influencers who inspire trends across the country."[33] The launch of the *Uptown Flavor* online magazine in 2006, presented as "the premiere online lifestyle destination in Harlem" and featuring pieces such as "The Ultimate Guide to Yoga in Harlem" and the "Holiday Wine Guide," was also indicative of the emergence of a brand-new population of wealthy city consumers in a rapidly gentrifying Harlem. This same affluent and trendy population was the focus of a TV show produced in 2009 by BET Networks called "Harlem Heights." The show celebrated the glamorous lives of the young black elite in gentrifying Harlem. In the show, gentrification, far from being a dirty word, had become an indication of status.[34] Although the show lasted one season, the launch of this production was a clear indication that, by the late 2000s, representations of Harlem in the mainstream media were indeed undergoing a radical makeover.

Enter Bloomberg: Rezoning Harlem's Main Street

> This Rezoning will reinforce the 125th Street Corridor as an important regional business district and bolster its historic role as an arts, entertainment and retail corridor.[35]

In 2003, the Department of City Planning (DCP), in partnership with the New York City Economic Development Corporation (NYCEDC), the Department of Housing Preservation and Development (HPD), the Department of Cultural Affairs, the Department of Transportation (DOT), and the Department of Small Business Services, crafted a development framework for a sweeping rezoning of 125th Street. An advisory committee of local actors, composed of local businesses, civic groups, cultural institutions, and community boards 9, 10, and 11, was included in the planning process, but a key role was played by business-oriented Harlem organizations like the 125th Street BID. The proposal came at a time when many projects in Harlem were already under way or in their first planning stages. These included Columbia University's 17-acre campus expansion in Manhattanville at the western end of 125th Street and an oversized mixed-use project for the East Harlem Media Entertainment and Cultural Center on its eastern end. The so-called river-to-river proposal envisioned the rezoning of all blocks between 124th Street and 126th Street, from Second Avenue to Broadway. By increasing residential densities and encouraging mixed-use development, the plan called for approximately 2,600 new apartments and over 600,000 square feet of new office and retail space. Eighty percent of the new housing units would be market rate, and 20% would be set aside as "affordable" according to the city's inclusionary zoning program, which offers developers floor area bonuses in exchange for including a percentage of non-market-rate housing in new developments. The proposal also introduced a height restriction of 290 feet for all new construction to discourage out-of-scale development in the area. The proposal was described by the DCP as a way to "sustain the ongoing revitalization of 125th Street as a unique Manhattan Main Street, enhance its regional business district character and reinforce the street's premier arts, culture, and entertainment destination identity."[36] According to the DCP, the rezoning plan was the result of a substantial participatory process, made of over 150 meetings held from 2003 to 2007 with "stakeholders, property owners, residents and elected officials to discuss and refine the plan."[37] But many claim that these meetings repeatedly avoided discussing topics that were vital to local residents—particularly their fears that the rezoning would displace low-income households and small businesses, and concerns that the new housing units would be unaffordable to Harlem locals.[38] In 2007, the DCP stated that the foreseen displacement of 71 small businesses and their 975 employees resulting from the rezoning would "not constitute a significant adverse economic impact." Likewise, the indirect displacement of 500 residents and the threat of demolition of some of the street's century-old buildings were not considered worthy of particular consideration.[39] On December 5, 2007, community boards 9 and 11 (East and West Harlem) voted for conditional approval of the rezoning (i.e., they approved the plan, provided certain modifications were made), while community board 10 (Central Harlem) objected that at least 2,077 units, with an estimated 5,400 residents, would be under threat of displacement under the new zoning and disapproved of the DCP's assessment that the displacement of 71 businesses would not constitute a significant adverse economic impact; the board also expressed concern about the impacts of an overproduction of market-rate housing units (80% versus 20% reserved as "affordable") in a very low-income area like Harlem. All three community boards agreed that the plan did not guarantee a sufficient amount of housing affordable to local residents, nor any provision to protect existing tenants from eviction. They also called for the establishment of provisions to retain local businesses in the area. On January 30, 2008, the City Planning Commission held a public hearing at the City College of New York at West 135th Street. Over 100 residents, business owners, and local community organizers attended to voice their opposition to the rezoning.[40]

Before final approval was due on April 30, 2008, Councilwoman Inez Dickens, who represented the portion of 125th Street where the largest upzoning was proposed (CD 10), was holding the balance of power. Dickens, the daughter of real estate millionaire and three-term assemblyman Lloyd E. Dickens, is a woman strongly tied to the Greater Harlem Chamber of Commerce and to its development arm, the Greater Harlem Housing Development Corporation, and active in the Harlem real estate business with her own firm.[41] Although the community board she represents was the one voting for conditional disapproval of the plan, the board had traditionally been siding with large development plans for Harlem.[42] Dickens had promised to not approve the plan until she could extract some benefits for the local community. But after negotiations with the board of the DCP, Dickens came to an undisclosed agreement, and a modified version of the plan was presented to city council for approval. According to the modified plan, 1,785 of 3,858 of the apartments planned for Harlem (46%) would be indeed "affordable," with 900 set aside for those earning $46,000 or less a year for a family of four, and 200 set aside for families earning a maximum of $30,750 a year.[43] Other revisions included height restrictions capping buildings at 190 feet, a $750,000 forgivable loan program for businesses adversely affected by the plan, the creation of a local arts advisory board, and a $5.8 million fund for capital improvements at Marcus Garvey Park.[44] On April 30, 2008, Council gathered to decide whether to approve or reject the plan. Harlem Congressman Charles Rangel (among whose donors were real estate firms with development plans for 125th Street)[45] and Governor David Paterson backed the plan. Dickens voted yes, along with other council members Robert Jackson and Melissa Mark-Viverito (today's city council speaker in the de Blasio administration).[46] The modified version of the rezoning plan was eventually approved by an overwhelming majority of council members (47 to 2) in what became a tensed and emotionally charged session. The public, mostly composed of black Harlem residents opposing the plan, shouted at and booed Dickens from the chamber balcony. As the session ended, Dickens had to be escorted out of City Hall through a rear door.[47] Council members Tony Avella and Charles Barron, the only two who voted against the rezoning, called it "top down" and "a sellout." Barron protested: "Ten to 12 years from now, they will see that the housing will not be affordable. This will be the wholesale sellout of Harlem from river to river."[48] The same day, gleeful press accounts listed the generous concessions that Dickens had managed to extract from the DCP and boasted the large amount of affordable housing that the rezoning would create. The *New York Post* wrote of an "unprecedented 46 percent" of new housing units that would be reserved for low- and moderate-income families.[49] Dickens said of the affordable housing agreement: "It's an inclusionary program never before done in the history of this great city." She added: "I'm fighting to support and protect my community.... With this rezoning, Harlem's historically indigenous cultural institutions will be protected."[50]

The Plan in Detail

The rezoning established a new contextual "special district" for 24 blocks between 124th and 126th Streets, from Broadway to Second Avenue, crossing through West, Central, and East Harlem. It allows for denser and taller buildings and introduces mixed-use developments in lots that were once zoned for commercial activity (Figures 1.6 and 1.7). To create new commercial space that is more suitable to large-scale retail, the rezoning increases the allowable commercial and residential densities. In all, the plan allows for approximately 3,900 new apartments and around 600,000 square feet of new office and retail space, which is expected to fill in the vacant lots and replace the one-story retail shops that line 125th Street. In an effort to create a pleasant pedestrian experience, the rezoning aims to enhance "ground-floor retail continuity" and regulates uses located on the ground floor in all new developments with street fronts on 125th Street. "Dead" uses (including bank and hotel lobbies, offices, and residential uses) are prevented from fully occupying the ground floor of new developments: they are allowed

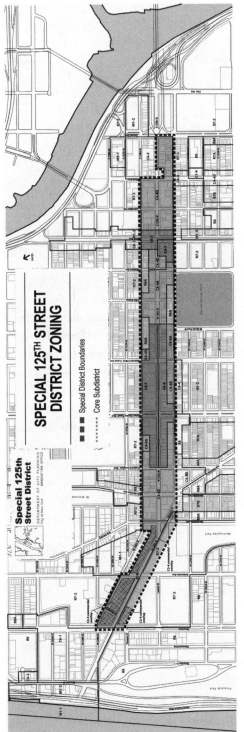

Figure 1.6 Special 125th Street District Zoning Map.

SPECIAL 125TH STREET DISTRICT ZONING - As adopted on November 19th, 2008

Use:	Allowed Density within Special District (FAR):							Building Form:		
	RESIDENTIAL			COMMERCIAL			COMMUNITY FACILITY	Special District bulk controls		
Underlying Zoning District	Base FAR	Inclusionary Housing or Arts Bonus	Max. FAR	Base FAR	Arts Bonus	Max. FAR	Max. FAR	Building base (streetwall): min. max.		Building height: max.
R6A	-	-	3.0	-	-	-	3.0	40'	60'	70'
R7-2	-	-	3.44	-	-	-	6.5	not required		none
C2-4 overlay	-	-	-	-	-	2.0	-	-		-
R7A	-	-	4.0	-	-	-	4.0	40'	65'	80'
C2-4 overlay	-	-	-	-	-	2.0	-	-		-
C4-4A	-	-	4.0	-	-	4.0	4.0	40'	65'	80'
C4-4D	5.4	1.8	7.2	4.0	1.4	5.4	6.0	60'	85'	120'
C6-3 within core*	5.4	1.8	7.2	6.0	2.0	8.0	6.0	60'	85'	160'
C6-3 outside core	6.0	2.0	8.0							
C4-7 within core	5.4	1.8	7.2	7.2	1.45	8.65	7.2	60'	85'	195' within core
C4-7 outside core	9.0	3.0	12.0	10.0	2.0	12.0	10.0			330' outside core

* core subdistrict

Figure 1.7 Special 125th Street District Zoning Chart.

only on the upper floors, and can have only limited space for entrances and lobbies on the ground floors. The same goes for offices and hotels. The plan also outlined a "special arts and entertainment district" between Frederick Douglas Boulevard (8th Avenue) and Malcolm X Boulevard (Lenox Avenue), the area where major landmarks such as the Apollo and Victoria Theaters, the Blumstein Department Store, and the Hotel Theresa are located. To maintain a vibrant street environment, new developments in this area are required to dedicate 5% of their total floor area to arts- and entertainment-related uses such as museums, performance venues, and restaurants. The proposal also includes regulations to enhance the streetscape by preventing shop owners from coating storefronts with roll-down metal grates—probably too reminiscent of the old ghetto days—and promoting instead "distinctive signage," for example, allowing theaters to build marquee signs reminiscent of the old times of the Harlem Renaissance. An "arts bonus," usually in the form of additional floor area, is available to developers in exchange for the provision of nonprofit visual or performing arts spaces in their developments.

Voices Against the Plan

The 125th Street rezoning received a chorus of criticism from local residents, community advocacy groups, tenant organizations, and even urban planning think-tanks. Although objections have targeted almost every aspect of the plan, most concerns addressed its lack of affordable housing provisions, the threats of displacement of existing residents and businesses, and its impact on the physical character of the neighborhood.

Impact on Housing

> I don't think the average person can like the rezoning, 'cause it works against them. As far as apartments, if they are kicked out, and they are, they won't ever find another apartment in the area.[51]

The strongest opposition from residents and civic groups addressed the lack of guarantees that new housing developments would be within the reach of local residents. They were right.

Talks of a 46% share of affordable housing, considered by the popular press the biggest win for Councilwoman Dickens, were just smoke and mirrors. The plan approved has no mandate to produce even a single affordable unit. It only offers developers the option to take advantage of incentives if they decide to reserve a percentage of the newly developed units as "affordable." These units can be placed on-site (within the rezoned area) or off-site, in the immediate surroundings. But in boom times and in heated property markets, the majority of developers have generally chosen to opt out of these subsidies, in search of higher returns from market-rate developments. Furthermore, the few units that may be produced won't be affordable to the local residents of Harlem. The average median income for the zip codes included in the plan was approximately $22,000 in 2008. Since the affordability standard is measured with respect to the area median income (AMI) of New York City as a whole (around $71,000 in 2008), by these measures only 5.18%, or 200 units, out of a proposed 3,858, would be available to households whose annual incomes are $30,750 dollars or less (the average Harlem resident)—if they ever get built.

In addition to worries about housing affordability, concerns have addressed the threat of displacement of long-time residents. According to Community Board 10, at least 2,077 units will be directly impacted by the rezoning, in addition to the indirect impacts caused by development, including pressures to tenants in rent-stabilized buildings. Massive displacement would happen because, even if the developers took advantage of the inclusionary zoning incentives, most of the new residential developments will be market rate, versus a much lower percentage set as "affordable." Nellie Hester Bailey, human rights activist and cofounder of the Harlem Tenants Council, a tenant rights advocacy organization that is active in fighting the displacement of residents and businesses in the neighborhood, pointed to the increasing number of residents' complaints about landlords illegally raising rents, harassing tenants, and evicting people to make way for new affluent in-movers,[52] and to reports on family homelessness in New York City showing that Central Harlem ranked among the top 10 neighborhoods in the city with the highest displacement rate.[53] She described the proposal as "a plan that seeks to replace a working class community of color with an affluent white community."[54] Other locals voiced their concerns that the rezoning would force African Americans out of the area. Sharifa Rhodes-Pitts, a Harlem resident and author, claimed: "Their plan basically says that working-class people don't have the right to live here.... The soul of the city is being drained out of veins."[55] According to Craig Schley, the head of Vote—Voices of the Everyday People, a group engaged in a campaign (eventually unsuccessful) to stop the 125th Street rezoning plan, "People talk about gentrification, but this would be Katrina-fication done by a swipe of a pen rather than a hurricane."[56]

Impact on Local Businesses

> They are closing all these stores. Lenox Lounge just closed. They asked him $10,000 a month, like three times what he was paying before. That's not Roseland [Ballroom]. You don't have the kind of space to make that kind of money. So they had to shut down.[57]

Local mom-and-pop store owners bemoaned that the rezoning would force their businesses to close due to rising competition from large retail chains or escalating rental prices. Again, they were right.

In 2008, Community Board 11 (East Harlem) made several recommendations aimed at preserving small businesses in the neighborhood. The board suggested the introduction of provisions that would require developers to reserve a space to host existing local businesses in their developments and recommended incentives to developers in exchange for the commitment of new establishments to hire locals. The plan didn't include any provisions to protect existing small businesses other than the establishment of a $750,000 no-interest, forgivable loan program for businesses that were forced to close shop or relocate. But this meant only a paltry $10,000 per business—a ridiculous amount to offset the costs of displacement and relocation. Meanwhile, a staggering $5.8 million was allocated for improvements to Marcus Garvey Park, an initiative that no local group had ever requested or supported, but that sure pleased the developers of several new luxury residential condominium buildings facing the park—most of which were on the drawing board by the time the rezoning was adopted (among these, the 28-story condominium tower, 5th on the Park, completed in 2009). A great many small, locally owned businesses have left their locations along 125th Street since then. According to the Greater Harlem Chamber of Commerce, approximately one-third of businesses in Harlem closed only between July 1, 2008, and June 30, 2009. This was not a merit of the national recession alone. As will be demonstrated in the following pages, dozens of small businesses along 125th Street were directly evicted by their landlords so that they could take full advantage of the increased density coming with the rezoning and make room for more lucrative developments. Needless to say, this happened at the same time that big chains were tirelessly expanding their presence along the strip—even in the midst of a global economic slump.[58]

Impact on Neighborhood Character

> I was just driving west on 125th street last week.... I truly couldn't believe how quickly that long stretch of street has literally become a long large mall. Anything with any sort of personality and history to it is being wiped out at a really rapid pace.[59]

The plan was presented by the press as one of the most meticulously crafted initiatives to come out of the DCP under the chairmanship of "rezoning czar"[60] Amanda Burden. Burden herself claimed she had spent more time working on the 125th Street proposal than she had on any other prior rezoning plan.[61] The rezoning promised to promote the development of "building forms that are compatible with existing neighborhood character,"[62] but has missed opportunities to incorporate measures to preserve historical landmarks in the area. Aside from two public libraries, both landmarked in 2009, no other historically significant building was given landmark status during the planning process. The city admitted that the rezoning "could result in significant adverse impacts due to potential demolition of four Register-eligible resources on potential development sites, including: the former Harlem Savings Bank, the Marion Building, the Bishop Building and the Amsterdam News Building," none of which was calendared for designation as a city landmark.[63] The list of iconic buildings on 125th Street that are not protected by landmark laws, however, is much longer, and should also include Blumstein's Department Store (completed in 1923), which was the site of Adam Clayton Powell's "Buy Where You Can Work" campaign, and the glorious Victoria Theater, which was hailed at the time of its opening in 1917 as one of the most beautiful theaters in the city.[64] At several public meetings in preparation of the rezoning plan, Michael Henry Adams, Harlem historian and author, pointed to the difficulties he encountered when struggling for preservation against Bloomberg's development-prone administration: "Harlem has the same cultural and architectural significance as New Orleans, Charleston and Savannah.... Our local law is flawed. It's old and timid. Mayor Bloomberg essentially dictates what gets designated or not."[65]

The modified plan also sets height restrictions of 190 feet, or about 17 stories, on the north side of 125th Street and of 160 feet, or about 14 stories, on the south side. City officials said that this was necessary, as the 1961 zoning did not incorporate any height limits. However, it was the old zoning that kept too-tall buildings from being built in practice, as it incorporated narrower limits to the allowable building density. This is why most buildings along the corridor have remained predominantly low scale for decades. Because of the increased allowable densities, instead, the new zoning actively encourages the demolition of low-scale structures to build taller and more profitable ones.[66]

Harlem's New Consumers

Yesterday's demilitarized zone is today's luxury condo haven. Double-wide strollers wheel down sidewalks where yuppies once feared to tread. This has been the pattern everywhere from the East Village to Hell's Kitchen—and don't even start with Brooklyn—but nowhere has the resurgence of development and renewed real estate interest been quite as clear as it has been in Harlem.[67]

I bow down to the Gods of real estate every night the rezoning passed! I'm moving to Harlem soon, and I'm already dreaming how it will soon be like Hell's Kitchen. I lived there for years and welcomed the change. I will be so happy in my condo, and very happy when 125th street is nice! So long, Ghetto![68]

The same neighborhood that middle-class New Yorkers were fleeing for decades has finally morphed into one of the city's real estate hotspots. Today, rehabilitated townhouses and new luxury condominium apartments keep drawing a brand-new population of black and white newcomers in the area.

In the midst of this Harlem boom, the website of 5th on the Park, the luxury residential condominium tower completed just a few blocks from 125th Street at 5th Avenue and 120th Street (Figure 1.8), where two-bedroom units were listed for over $2 million, talked of a "New Harlem" and celebrated its brand-new population of affluent "urban pioneers":

> Located in upscale New Harlem in the heart of Manhattan, 5th on the Park Luxury Condos are the ultimate in fine living. New Harlem is now welcoming thousands of upwardly mobile new home owners of various backgrounds. These are sophisticated urban pioneers, who will settle for nothing less than the finest apartments.[69]

On the website of Douglas Elliman, one of the largest residential brokerage firms in New York, Harlem is described as a neighborhood in transition, revived by an injection of new residents:

> Harlem's newest population is refreshingly diverse, made up of residents who enjoy the neighborhood's history, the gorgeous homes and unrenovated gems, oozing with potential.[70]

So, who are these "sophisticated urban pioneers"? Who makes up "Harlem's newest population"?

Figure 1.8 Construction at 5th on the Park, a luxury condominium building in Harlem built in 2007.

Today, a large share of Harlem's new residents is made up of middle-
or upper-middle-class families, Columbia University students, and young
professionals squeezed by the impossible costs of living in Manhattan and
attracted by the area's quick connections to midtown and downtown.

While the number of white in-movers has grown in recent years, a large
share of Harlem's new residents is made up of black professionals. Recent
studies have emphasized the importance of the "black gentry" as an active
agent—just as much as its white counterpart—of sweeping social change in
the neighborhood. Columbia University Professor Lance Freeman points
to the almost doubling of black Harlem residents holding a college degree
between 1980 and 2000 as an indicator that a solid black middle class has
been settling in Harlem, resulting in "a critical mass of potential black gentrifiers."[71] In his investigation of the "new urban renewal" in Chicago's
Bronzeville and New York's Harlem, urban affairs scholar Derek S. Hyra
also contended that it is mostly middle-class blacks that are transforming the
social fabric of both neighborhoods.[72]

But the popular press has been generally keener to emphasize the influx
of white residents into what had once been an African American enclave.
To be sure, the influx of whites in Harlem has escalated in the last two
decades—they made up 2% of the total population in 2000, while now
they account for nearly 10%. Still, these numbers are modest in compar-
ison to a still-overwhelming black and Hispanic majority. Freeman notes
that "although the black middle class or gentry was perhaps a more potent
force than whites behind gentrification...their presence did not attract
the attention that the statistically smaller white populace did. Nonetheless
it was whites who figured prominently in narratives of gentrification."[73]
Particularly in Central Harlem, long a bastion of black America, black residents still make up the large majority (63%) of the population. The most
dramatic ethnic shift in Harlem in the latest years has been instead the
major increase in the Hispanic population: Hispanics accounted for 4.3%
of Harlem residents in 1980, but their number reached 18.6% in 2006.[74]
Other changes in the social fabric of the neighborhood indicate that a
new population of city consumers is settling in Harlem. The number of
college-degree holders has doubled during the 2000–2010 time span to
28%, while the young population has also risen and now accounts for
about 19.6% of Harlem.[75] This is also a reflection of the increasing number
of Columbia University students who have been steadily streaming uptown
in recent years, renting apartments especially in the area of Morningside

Avenue between 110th and 125th Streets. Median income levels have also increased across the whole neighborhood, indicating a growing influx of wealthier residents. By 2010, one of the most gentrified census tracts in Harlem—between Morningside Avenue and Frederick Douglass and 122nd and 126th Streets—registered an average annual income of $33,500, a 124% increase over the previous decade.[76] Harlem is, indeed, in transition.

Conflict

> Then comes the motherfuckin' Christopher Columbus Syndrome. You can't discover this! We been here.... You can't just come in when people have a culture that's been laid down for generations and you come in and now shit gotta change because you're here? Get the fuck outta here. Can't do that![77]

The community that a *New York Times* reporter has enthusiastically renamed the "21st-century laboratory for integration"[78] is still far from being a conflict-free zone, however. The integration of a brand-new population of city consumers into a neighborhood that for decades has been geographically and racially segregated is not going to be a smooth ride.[79]

Questions related to who are the main beneficiaries of the neighborhood's transformations spark controversy among Harlem locals: a common perception among many long-time residents is that "the improvements taking place are ... targeted to others," that is, the new gentrifiers.[80] Most people I talked to during my interviews feel like they didn't have any say in the major decisions affecting their neighborhood. In the words of one of my interviewees:

> They are opening a new bank every other month on 125th Street to finance the loans for all these new people to buy these houses.... We do not have anybody representing us here in Harlem. When they have a conversation on television, they never talk about people like us. It's like we don't even exist. People that make, say, $10,000 a year. We don't exist. We don't benefit at all.[81]

The presence of new businesses such as upscale wine stores, gourmet restaurants, or cafes charging $5 for a cup of coffee is seen as catering not to long-time residents but to a brand-new population of more affluent, mostly white city consumers.

The issue of race has taken center stage during the process for the rezoning of 125th Street. Many have bemoaned that Harlem's black cultural identity would be erased to make the neighborhood suitable for a population of affluent whites. Historian Michael Henry Adams said of the rezoning: "If the only black presence in Harlem is a memory in the form of museums and place names, to hell with that."[82] The increased presence of police officers patrolling newly opened stores has also inspired resentment, as locals do not feel that police were protecting them in the bleak days of Harlem's decay. If Giuliani's war on crime managed to dismantle whole patterns of community life in Harlem, with crackdowns on street vending, public drinking, loitering, and block parties, the Bloomberg years were no better for black residents in Harlem, with a skyrocketing increase in stop-and-frisk searches, mostly targeting young black males. And more police enforcement has come under de Blasio, with the NYPD announcing in 2015 the creation of a 38-officer unit to be stationed at 125th Street to deal with the homeless roaming the street.[83]

Many long-time Harlem residents also complain that the demands of the new residents, whether black or white, have disrupted their daily habits.[84] The case of the African and Caribbean drummers of Marcus Garvey Park is emblematic. The drummers have played in the park every summer Saturday since 1969. But across the street from the park is now 5th on the Park, where a three-bedroom apartment can sell for over $3 million. In 2008, some of its residents, mostly young professionals, complained about the noise and had the Parks Department remove the drummers more than once. The situation got tense as a racist email against the drummers was sent by a white co-op tenant to the other residents, and the controversy "bubbled over into a dispute about class, race and culture and has become a flash point in the debate over gentrification."[85] In 2012, when plans were unveiled to build an eight-story building for low-income families on a parking lot on 123rd Street between Adam Clayton Powell Jr. and Frederick Douglass Boulevards, both black and white middle-class residents of the brownstones that line the street voiced their opposition to the plan. The building, to be built by the Abyssinian Development Corporation to relocate residents from "the projects"—the adjacent and decrepit public housing complex called Ennis Frances Houses—was contested for being "out of character." But what residents really feared was people from the "projects" moving in front of their middle-class homes. They deplored the drug sales and violent crimes that had long been associated with the dwellers of the ill-famed Ennis Frances Houses.[86] This resentment was representative of the simmering conflicts over class that gentrification has brought about in the neighborhood, where pricey brownstones and luxury condominium buildings, symbols of a new Harlem of affluence and success, today stand next to public housing projects that are still home to a poor and segregated community.[87]

The Gentrification of Harlem
from Bloomberg to de Blasio

Since the early 2000s, the influx of a new population and the rising average incomes have consistently driven up prices in Harlem. Increases in the average price of housing in the neighborhood have been steady and remarkable in the last two decades: from $190,000 in 1995, they rose to $412,000 in 2001.[88] Average prices registered a decline after 9/11 but soared again as the economy rebounded. In 2007, Harlem's average sale prices had already peaked to $713,000,[89] and the staggering costs of living in the neighborhood were making headlines. The 2008–2010 recession brought a drop in real estate values, with foreclosures and bank takeovers that hit Harlem very hard, and left 125th Street blighted by stalled developments and fenced-off construction sites. However, the slump was short-lived, and sale prices rose again swiftly in 2010–2011. By 2011, the most luxurious condominium developments in Harlem commanded prices of over $715 per square foot.[90] Among these were developments like 5th on the Park, the Langston, the Lenox, the Lenox Grand, and the Dwyer—the kinds of condos that provide luxury amenities like 24-hour concierges, gyms, and landscaped roof gardens. By 2012, in the highly gentrified tract around 110th Street, home values had jumped 39% compared to 2007 levels—the highest increase in all of Manhattan. In 2012, a luxury penthouse located in the One Museum Mile building on 110th Street and 5th Avenue sold for $3.1 million. One year later, an East Harlem townhouse was purchased by actor Neil Patrick Harris for just under $4 million.[91] In 2016, another neighborhood record was set, with a townhouse in Hamilton Heights selling for close to $5 million, after having been purchased for $1.7 million back in 2007.[92]

Residential Gentrification
and Displacement in Harlem

I was born here, lived in Harlem all of my life. I lost my apartment in 2011. My landlord kicked me out 'cause I was renting a room in the apartment. I did it to pay the rent.... Everything had become too expensive. Now I'm here living in the shelter, and let me tell you, it is horrible to be here. I'm tired to be searched every time I go to bed. But what are you gonna do? What happened to people like me, and, you know, many others, is, we are left here to die. What happens to us? We just live under a garbage can or in a homeless shelter for 20 to 30 years, and then we die. Where is the afford-able housing? I haven't seen any of that.[93]

Change is good; we are doing something good for this neighborhood. More services, more housing for all. We are making the neighborhood diverse.[94]

I met Carlos, a Puerto Rican man in his 60s, by the entrance of the Pathmark supermarket, at the east end of 125th Street. He is one of the many home-less folks populating this stretch of the strip, the hub for many that come by bus from the shelters at Randall's and Ward's Islands. Some are here for treatment in the methadone clinics nearby; others are waiting for the Relief Bus to provide food and clothing. Some are junkies waiting for their push-ers, or just killing time before returning to the shelters. Many stand by the bottle deposit machines of the Pathmark at the corner. Some sleep on the sidewalks on flattened cardboard boxes; others push shopping carts piled with all their belongings. Carlos is one of those who have been tossed to the curb while landlords and speculators were making a killing in Harlem.

For years, advocacy groups like the Harlem Tenant's Council, the Coalition to Preserve Community, and Buyers and Renters United to Save Harlem have worked to help struggling tenants by providing access to legal counseling and training and educating the local community about their rights. By the time the rezoning was passing, these associations reported complaints by hundreds of Harlem tenants being threatened with eviction or being displaced because of escalating rental prices, aggressive landlord harassment, or expiring rent regu-lations.[95] City Planning chairwoman Amanda Burden rebuffed criticism and referred to the "over 90%" of existing rent-protected housing units in the neigh-borhood to reassure residents that their fears of displacement were unfounded. It is true that subsidized housing still makes up a large share of the housing stock in Harlem. In 2006, the districts of East, West, and Central Harlem had a total of 51,216 units for people of moderate and low incomes. Another 24,207 units were in the public housing projects.[96] However, with rent regulations phasing out throughout the city, the question is how many of these residents will man-age to stay in their community in the coming years.[97] In 2005 alone, New York City lost a record 5,518 rent-protected apartments whose landlords opted out of subsidy programs: nearly 80% of the units lost were in the South Bronx and especially in Harlem, where the landlords of three large housing complexes (Riverside Park Community, Schomburg Towers, and Metro North Houses) decided to opt out of the Mitchell-Lama program, a program established by New York State in 1955 that offers developers tax abatements and low-interest mortgages for the development of middle-income housing.[98]

In too many cases, the weakening of rent regulation laws, combined with the overheated Harlem property market, has encouraged the proliferation of "predatory equity" schemes. Predatory equity is a form of real estate speculation whereby private equity firms purchase apartment buildings with rent-regulated units in gentrifying neighborhoods and promise their investors very high returns that can only be achieved by aggressively driving out existing rent-controlled tenants. After a tenant leaves, the landlord can sell or rent the vacant units at market price. This can mean, for instance, managing to earn $5,200 a month for a Manhattan two-bedroom apartment that was renting for $1,700 with the old tenant.[99] This happens all the time in New York City, where about 266,000 apartments have been deregulated since 1994.[100] In just the time span between 2004 and 2008, private equity firms have acquired almost 75,000 rent-regulated apartments in the city.[101] To speed the turnover, many employ illegal tactics to kick rent-regulated tenants out. Often, they neglect maintenance works, cut gas or electricity service, or intimidate tenants with bogus legal proceedings: there have been innumerable cases of tenants being baselessly sued by their landlords for alleged illegal sublets or unpaid rents.

In March 2008, Bloomberg signed legislation that allows tenants to take their landlords to court if they file repeated and groundless proceedings to force them out of their homes. A day late and a dollar short: only few low-income tenants have the legal skills to file a lawsuit against their landlords, and many drop it altogether, fearing their landlord may retaliate and eventually win in court. It goes without saying that complaints of tenant harassment have nearly doubled in the following years, particularly since 2011.[102] A few years later, in 2015, de Blasio signed new laws to protect tenants from harassment and authorized funds for offering counseling to troubled tenants in hot development areas. But these initiatives will not even start to offset the impact of the speculative craze that the new administration's rezonings have unleashed.

Another threat to subsidized housing is caused by landlord mismanagement or neglect. In cases of extremely bad maintenance, the federal government can cut off subsidies or even sell the properties through foreclosure if they are deemed uninhabitable. Between 1991 and 2006, the Department of Housing foreclosed on 17 low-income housing complexes in New York City, with 2,264 housing units. More than half of these units were located in Bedford-Stuyvesant and Harlem.[103] Horror stories of tenants displaced because of abusive landlords' tactics increased as the Harlem real estate market boomed in the mid-2000s. In 2005, as the massive public housing complex at 3333 Broadway (135th Street) opted out of the Mitchell-Lama program, rental units were deregulated. The residents filed a class action lawsuit claiming that the new firm that purchased the building used illegal tactics to kick them out.[104] The same has been happening over and over again at Lenox Terrace, a middle-income housing complex at 135th Street and Lenox Avenue, whose landlord has been planning since 2003 to turn the complex into a more upscale complex with six brand-new towers and new commercial space[105]—a dream that is finally approaching reality under de Blasio.[106] There are innumerable cases of landlords' violations, including violations for not providing heat, hot water, maintenance, and repairs to tenants. Sometimes landlords can keep their apartments in such bad conditions that tenants are forced out by city authorities because of structural damages or health hazards. In 2007, 27 families were evacuated from a Harlem building at 305 West 150th Street that had a long history of violations.[107] In 2012, dozens of families living in two buildings at East 120th Street were forced out of their homes after the Department of Buildings deemed the buildings unsafe due to fire code violations and structural damage.[108] The same year, dozens of other tenants were evacuated from their apartments at 3750 Broadway after the FDNY deemed the structure unstable.[109] In many such cases, displaced tenants have never been allowed back into their homes.

Obviously, homeownership can be an effective antidote against displacement. In fact, in gentrifying neighborhoods, it is homeowners who generally stand to benefit from the unabated increase in home values. This is not the case for the majority of Harlem residents, however. According to the 2010 census, 87.5% of Central Harlem residents were renters. In West Harlem and East Harlem, 12.6% and 7.9% of residents were homeowners, respectively.[110] Such a small share of homeownership in Harlem is also the result of a long history of redlining, which for decades has made it impossible for residents of black neighborhoods to receive loans and mortgages by private banks.[111]

The truth is, housing for low- and middle-income residents is dropping out of sight. And the construction of the much-trumpeted new "affordable" housing in Harlem so far hasn't even remotely made up for the amount of affordable units lost because of recent development pressures.

At 121 West 125th Street, plans were approved in 2013 for a city- and state-backed 400,000-square-foot complex that will house the national headquarters for the National Urban League and a civil rights museum. The complex should also include 114 "affordable" housing units. A new $415 million luxury development made of two 32-story towers at Park Avenue and 125th Street, called 1800 Park Avenue, may soon rise on the site where Harlem Park, a project abandoned after the recession, was once supposed to be built. It will become the tallest building in Harlem and should have a total of 650 residential units. In 2014, East Harlem residents demanded more than the 70 affordable units set aside in the original plan.[112] As of today, it is not known how many affordable units will eventually be included in the project.[113] Three lots across the street were recently purchased for $37 million by Waterbridge Capital, which plans to build a mixed-use residential and retail tower.

At the eastern end of 125th Street, the NYCEDC is moving forward with the development of E125, a mixed-use development on a massive site spanning from 125th to 127th Streets along Second and Third Avenues that was seized by the city through eminent domain in 2008. When completed, it will provide for 950 housing units. Of these, 295 should be reserved for households earning less than 60% of the AMI.[114]

Commercial Gentrification of 125th Street

> Old Navy, Blockbuster Video, ColdStone Creamery, RadioShack, FHM, Citarella, Pathmark, Verizon, Dr. Jays, CVS, Marshalls, White Castle, Starbucks. All of these chain and more are already on 125th Street. I just don't understand the call to protect the mom and pop shops from the rezoning, when they clearly lost that battle years ago.[115]

Over the last decade, the swift pace of development has changed the face of Harlem, and particularly that of its Main Street, where innumerable locally owned stores (bookstores, clothing stores, fried-chicken joints, bodegas, hair salons) have been substituted by large corporate retailers. Where this still hasn't occurred, banners on the dozens of empty storefronts are there to inform us that brokers are on the hunt for new A-list tenants. This process of commercial gentrification, which was boosted by the new developments brought about by the UMEZ funds in the late 1990s, has been steady since then, and has only intensified in the Bloomberg and de Blasio years.

In the early 2000s, as the rezoning of 125th Street was in the making, cases were reported of commercial rents in the area soaring almost 300% in the time of only one year. By the spring of 2005, rents along the corridor had become comparable to those of the rest of Manhattan—the average asking rent for retail space at 125th Street amounted to $90 per square foot, compared $103 per square foot for an average rent in Manhattan.[116] After rents peaked in 2007, an abrupt drop marked the onset of the national recession, which hit Harlem and other low-income neighborhoods in the city particularly hard. In 2008 and 2009, Harlem's independent businesses experienced record bankruptcies and foreclosures, which by 2009 resulted in a 37% store vacancy rate in some of Harlem's main shopping corridors[117] and in a 16% vacancy rate along certain sections of 125th Street.[118] After the frenzy of development of the previous years, Harlem's Main Street entered a limbo: the large superstores and newly built shopping malls stood next to empty lots and boarded-up buildings vacated in expectation of the rezoning. In 2009, the largest urban void was at 125th Street and Park Avenue, where plans for Harlem Park, the $435 million office tower that at one point was to include TV studios for the Major League Baseball Network, were scrapped in December 2008. A *New York Post* reporter describes Harlem's Main Street in 2009 as follows:

> Dreams of a Harlem renaissance have been deferred.... Instead of planned office and retail towers, a pro-sports television station, high-rise hotels and a culinary-arts school, there are vacant storefronts and trash-strewn lots. Dozens of often bitter mom-and-pop businesses ... were booted for high-rises that never rose.[119]

Most of the boarded-up storefronts belonged to small businesses that had been in the neighborhood for decades. Many of these were forced to leave because of unaffordable rents; others, unable to compete with large corporate retailers or confronted with a changing customer base in the gentrifying neighborhood, had no other choice but to close. Most were directly evicted by landlords who took advantage of zoning changes and rushed to vacate lots to build taller, denser, and more profitable buildings. The casualties of the 125th Street rezoning include a number of stores that had become cultural fixtures and that for decades had served the Harlem community. In 2007, Sigfeld Group and Kimco Realty Corporation purchased a $50-million, 110-year-old building on the northwest corner of 125th Street and Frederick Douglass Boulevard with the intent of clearing the land and building a new mixed-use retail and office building. The 16 tenants forced to move included the legendary soul food restaurant Manna's and the Bobby's Happy House music store (among the first African American–owned businesses in Harlem). Some of the businesses were offered a paltry $5,000 for relocation costs.[120] Several store owners left immediately, while Manna's and five remaining neighbors united into the Save Harlem Association and filed a lawsuit against the developers. The lawsuit was successful, and the businesses managed to eventually settle for a restitution of over $1 million[121] before leaving the building by September 2008. Today, a 100,000-square-foot box-shaped four-story retail building is on the site, anchored by a 30,000-square-foot Designer Shoe Warehouse, a Joe's Crab Shack, a Blink Fitness, and the offices of Capital One Bank occupying almost all of the ground floor. So much for the "distinctive signage" and "ground-floor entertainment uses" envisioned in the rezoning plan!

On the east end of the strip, plans for a $700 million East Harlem media, entertainment, and cultural center also collided with the interests of existing long-time small businesses. The area, located between 3rd and 2nd Avenues, had been designated as a blighted urban renewal area since 1968 because of soil contamination and the many abandoned lots. In 2008, the city approved the project of developers General Growth Properties, Archstone, Richman Group, and Monadnock Construction for a huge mixed-use development that would include 385,000 square feet of retail space, 250,000 square feet of class A office space, a 98,000-square-foot hotel, 600 housing units, community and cultural space, and a public plaza. The city moved to the court to condemn six acres of properties and leave them empty in preparation for the project.[122] But in 2009, half a dozen remaining businesses joined in the East Harlem Alliance of Responsible Merchants and filed a class lawsuit against the DCP's determination to make use of eminent domain for the benefit of private developers. Their lawsuit was dismissed on October 12, 2010. In 2011, however, the ruling was making headlines once again after an appellate judge lambasted the city for falsely claiming "blight" in the neighborhood as a means to transfer private properties to a private developer.[123]

Other casualties of rezoning-led development are to be seen all along 125th Street (Figures 1.9 and 1.10). The Boro Hotel, at 125th and 5th, has been boarded up and slated for demolition in April 2008. Its first floor once hosted a small restaurant and jazz club called La Famille, opened in 1958 by two sisters who were among the first African American women to work on 125th Street.[124] Also, the legendary M&G Diner at West 125th Street between Morningside Avenue and St. Nicholas Avenue, known in the neighborhood for its extravagant marquee sign and its cheap southern food, was sold in 2008 and now sits vacant. The world-famous Lenox Lounge

Figure 1.9 Vacated building with "for sale" banner at 69 East 125th Street, in 2008. The building was demolished to make way for a 12-story mixed-use building.

at 125th and Lenox, a legendary bar with a striking art deco interior and signage, hosted performances by the greatest names of jazz, including Billie Holiday, Miles Davis, and John Coltrane. After 73 years in Harlem, it closed its doors on December 31, 2012, its rent having been literally doubled.[125]

If in just a few years a large number of small businesses on 125th Street went out of business for good, the crisis was a golden opportunity for corporate retail chains. During the national recession, while independent stores were dropping like flies, large retailers heavily increased their presence along the strip.[126] These included Starbucks, which in 2008 inaugurated its second 125th Street branch, and Applebee's, which in 2009 opened a new store along the strip. As the recession ended, commercial rents along the 125th Street corridor climbed again. By the fall of 2011, they soared to about $129 per square foot.[127] To put these numbers into perspective, average asking rents in midtown Manhattan were at $130 per square foot, while the Manhattan average was at $112 per square foot. Such asking prices are enabling only corporate retailers to settle in on 125th Street. In

Figure 1.10 The vacated M&G Diner at West 125th Street.

2012, there was an 11.2% rise in corporate chain retail in Harlem compared to 2011—the biggest growth in new chain retail openings recorded in New York City in that year—bringing the total number of chain stores in Harlem to 338.[128] The same year, more stores that had been around for decades, like the Harlem Lanes bowling arcade, the black-owned Hue-man Bookstore, and the delicious MoBay Restaurant, were all forced to shut down. In 2013, a new Gap store opened on 125th Street next to Mart 125, replacing a locally owned kids clothing store. Just across the street, next to the Apollo Theater, a $14-million, three-story retail building anchored by a Red Lobster and Banana Republic was built on a long-vacant site by the developers of Harlem USA, Grid Properties, and the Gotham Organization.

At the eastern end of 125th Street, the Pathmark supermarket shut its doors in 2014, leaving behind a shady boarded-up storefront that occupies an entire block at the corner with Lexington Avenue. The closure has left 236 workers jobless and is making this part of Harlem virtually a food desert, as East Harlem residents are forced to travel further downtown to find any well-supplied supermarket.[129] The land, once property of the East Harlem Abyssinian Triangle Limited Partnership, backed by the Abyssinian

Development Corporation, was sold for $39 million to Extell Development Company, which according to rumors has planned to build luxury condos on the 69,000-square-foot site. No plans have yet been filed, however.[130]

As Pathmark has left 125th Street, a much more glamorous grocery store—and with it a much fancier clientele—is on its way to the strip. Whole Foods, the high-end grocery chain that is rightfully considered the pièce de résistance of gentrification, and a solid indicator of neighborhood affluence, will be the anchor of a five-story glassy retail development at 125th Street and Lenox Avenue.

Not far, near the intersection with 5th Avenue, Bed Bath & Beyond and WeWork will be the anchors of a new 130,000-square-foot building at 5-15 West 125th, which should be topped by 30 residential rental units.

From "Main Street of Black America" to Just Another Main Street of American Franchise?

In the 1980s, when Harlem was to the American public nothing more than one of the most infamous ghettos in the country, urban scholars Richard Schaffer and Neil Smith called it "a supreme test for the gentrification process."[131] After 40 years of relentless creative destruction, it's fair to say that gentrification has passed the test, especially in the blocks around 125th Street, a neighborhood that has changed at lightning speed. Today, the homologating force of corporate retail is compromising the community's uniqueness and, according to some observers, even jeopardizing its potential as a tourist destination. In 2012, the executive director of the Harlem Business Alliance told the *New York Daily News*: "The risk of a homogenized, cookie-cutter landscape filled with chains is that we become less interesting: We're not there yet, but we're near the tipping point."[132] Today, the tipping point has clearly been reached. Subway, Applebee's, McDonald's, Dunkin Donuts, Old Navy, H&M, CVS, and Starbucks dominate a completely revolutionized physical, social, and symbolic space, and the "Main Street of Black America" is morphing before our very eyes into just another main street of American franchise. Assisted by rezoning and branding, the steadfast forces of corporate capital have managed to penetrate almost every corner of the famed thoroughfare in their relentless struggle to conquer Harlem and to extract profit from it.

2

How Capital Shapes Our Cities

A far cry from the "Main Street of Black America" of times past, by 2015, 125th Street counted 77 chain retailers and 15 commercial banks.[1] But the shocking tide of urban change is by no means unique to Harlem. Walking through the streets of New York City, from Manhattan to the Rockaways, from the Bronx to downtown Brooklyn, block after block, each empty retail window and each "premium residences" banner at construction sites remind us that the forces of capital are constantly at work. They are behind the lavish towers along the Williamsburg waterfront and behind the boarded-up storefronts along 5th Avenue, behind the new megamalls in the Bronx and the ravaged empty lots of Coney Island. Across the globe, wherever we turn, whether in Shanghai or in London, in Berlin or in Los Angeles, we see capital at work, in its relentless struggle to conquer every corner of our cities and to extract profit from them. Welcome to the urban space under capitalism: it is a space that, as French philosopher Henri Lefebvre argued, has been entirely occupied and commodified by the forces of capital. It is a space whose "urban fabric, with its multiple networks of communication and exchange, is part of the means of production."[2] It is a space where everything, from the busy office districts to the quiet housing wards, from the seedy industrial areas to the new up-and-coming neighborhoods, is part and parcel of capital. The shape of our cities is the physical materialization of these forces at work, and the very process of city building is nothing but a reflection of capital's compulsory need to ensure its survival. This is what neo-Marxist scholars like David Harvey call the "urbanization of capital":[3] capitalism can survive only by subjugating more and more of the urban experience under its rules.

We live in the era of the most rapid urbanization in human history, an era in which our cities are playing an ever more strategic role in facilitating the accumulation, consumption, and reproduction of capital.[4] After all, what else is the city if not "a giant machine for making money"?[5] Anyone who pays a rent or collects a rent from a property he or she owns knows all too well what I am talking about. And in times where cities are gradually substituting nations as global economic engines, city building has become a very profitable venture. This is why private players and local governments are eager to invest monumental resources in the production and promotion of this ever more sophisticated, ever more seductive money-making machine. And the space created by capital is a very seductive space indeed—provided you have the money. Yes, because the driving motor of the process of capitalist urbanization is the quest for profit. And the transformation of the city into a pricey commodity for sale is one of the most profitable ventures in this phase of capitalism. Despite what we may have heard in the campaign speeches of this or that elected official, one of the fundamental duties once they are in office will be to create the conditions where urban land can be turned into profit. This is the key to a deeper understanding of the functioning of our cities. This explains why, despite their political color or campaign promises, elected officials in successful global cities from London to New York, from San Francisco to Beijing, routinely adopt strikingly similar, ubiquitous policies, whose bottom line, apart from a few tweaks here and there, is always one and the same: the redevelopment of underperforming property markets (i.e., working-class or ex-manufacturing districts) into high-revenue urban land that can accommodate the most profitable uses (swanky residential enclaves, high-end retail rows) and attract the most profitable consumers (international companies and their employees, wealthy newcomers, tourists). In more technical terms: to create an environment that is capable of accommodating new cycles of capital investment and profit, a spatial arrangement that is suitable for the production, consumption, and reproduction of capital.

In New York City, we know all too well how this works on the ground: low-income neighborhoods and former industrial areas are relentlessly being transformed into more upscale residential enclaves with amenable parks and high-end retail, driving up the overall cost of land and pushing low- and middle-income long-time residents out of their communities. But this process is global. From Beijing's *hutong* settlements to London's Docklands, from Berlin's Soviet-era *Plattenbauten* to Chicago's public housing projects, in capitalist cities, demolition, displacement, and reconstruction are the order of the day. This is why the process of urban development is a highly contested political process, as demonstrated by the fierce protests of grassroots activists fighting for their communities from the global North to the global South. These groups, often representing low-income and working-class communities living at the margins of the political arena, are engaged in constant crusades against government plans, sometimes to preserve the existence of affordable homes, at other times to oppose the demolition of beloved historical buildings or to prevent the placement of hazardous facilities in their neighborhoods. Capital's tendency to make space a commodity in the marketplace is the harbinger of severe social conflicts, and the history of capitalist urbanization is nothing but a centuries-old war between powerful groups seeking to extract profit from the urban land and ordinary citizens who value their space simply as a basis for living and creating communities, and who are engaged in a perpetual fight to keep it that way.[6]

A Brief History of Capitalist Urbanization from Post–World War II America to Today

From the suburbanization of the United States in the 1950s, through the entrepreneurial urban regimes established after the global financial crisis of the early 1970s, to the "back to the city" movement starting in the 1980s, capital has ensured its survival through a constant writing and rewriting of the form of urban America.[7]

In the booming post–World War II era, which in the United States was marked by a Fordist economy based on mass production and mass consumption, the demands of capital contributed to the most radical restructuring of space in the history of the country, and suburbanization became the key allowing for the absorption of immense capital surpluses. A system of high wages and welfare provisions contributed to the creation of a rather affluent, consumerist middle class, which escaped the city in search of the comforts of the suburbs, while the state, in concert with the oil and automobile industries, was responsible for the production of an automobile-centric sprawling geography of highway networks, suburban villages, and shopping centers surrounded by vast parking lots to sustain an unprecedented consumption of oil and cars.

In major US cities, this was also the era of urban renewal, an era of unprecedented public works that have changed the shape of urban America for good. With the passing of the Housing Act in 1949, the federal state initiated programs of "slum clearance" that obliterated hundreds of working-class neighborhoods across the country. It also massively subsidized the construction of new housing for the poor and the working class, often in the form of segregated "towers in the park" public housing estates—the infamous "projects" that have been so loathed from Chicago to New Orleans, and that urban activist and author Jane Jacobs defined as "worse centers of delinquency, vandalism, and general social hopelessness than the slums they were supposed to replace."[8] Urban renewal has left an enduring legacy in the space of major American urban areas: the annihilation of once-bustling inner-city neighborhoods has left permanent scars in the urban fabric, while most public housing complexes have resulted in islands of decay surgically segregated from the rest of the city.

The temporary balance of post–World War II economic growth did not last long, however. The Arab oil embargo and the global property market crash of 1973, followed by the collapse of the very banking institutions that had powered the post–World War II property bubble, precipitated the system into a major global crisis. And "to the degree that urbanization had become part of the problem, so it had to be part of the solution. The result was a fundamental transformation of the urban process after 1973."[9] The dismantling of the welfarist regime of post–World War II America and the dissolution of federal commitments to city building brought about yet more transformations in the shape of urban America. This shift was epitomized by the handling of New York City's near default in 1975, which culminated with the notorious "Ford to City: Drop Dead" front page of the *Daily News*, in which President Ford likened the city's spending for health care, education, and other forms of public service to an "insidious disease."[10] The handling of this crisis signaled the onset of a process of aggressive neo-liberalization of urban governance in the United States: shrinking federal subsidies left municipal governments no other choice but to rely on their own strengths (their local fiscal capacity) to sustain their economies, and this made them increasingly dependent on the private initiative for the financing of public works. In these years, private actors became increasingly involved in the making of urban policy, while the local authorities embraced the role of facilitators of private investment through the creation of public–private partnerships and generous business-oriented fiscal policies.[11] While cities started engaging in bidding wars with each other for investment capital from the private sector, business and property developers learned to rely on the public government for sweetheart deals and publicly funded financial incentives and tax benefits. In light of these phenomena, David Harvey speaks of a new "entrepreneurial" form of governance that emerged in these crucial years.[12] In this entrepreneurial era, the aim of local governments shifted from the provision of welfare to sustain consumption to the pursuit of "growth," especially in the form of local tax returns from real estate development.[13]

A series of events in the 1970s marked this shift in planning paradigms in the United States. In 1974, Congress terminated the Urban Renewal Program that had been launched in 1949, while a moratorium was imposed on federal housing subsidies, putting an end to the public housing programs. These programs were substituted by federal grants whose target shifted from large-scale housing plans to site-specific, privately led development projects. Such policy shifts brought about remarkable changes to urban planning strategies in American cities, and New York was definitely no exception.

The Shape of New York City After 1975

In New York City, the flight of the middle class to the suburbs in the 1960s and the shrinking of industrial jobs across the metropolitan area had led to the progressive erosion of the municipal tax base—one of the very foundations upon which the strong local welfare state had ensured its survival. A radical shift in public policy occurred in the aftermath of the city's near bankruptcy in 1975, when the City Planning Commission (CPC) lost its control over the city's capital budget, and its resources were severely curtailed. Privately led development efforts were strongly encouraged and touted as the antidote to the failure of government bureaucracies. Cuts in social services were paralleled by generous tax incentives to large corporate and financial institutions, while urban policy started focusing on creating "business-friendly" environments to attract large corporations and their employees, and on promoting large-scale development plans as catalysts for consuming visitors and a new urban middle class.

This resulted in a new course for land use and planning regulations, which became more accommodating both to private investment and more generally to the demands of the market. It also led to a burgeoning of new city agencies committed to subsidizing private investment throughout the city.

The Public Development Corporation (PDC), a quasi-independent local development corporation created in 1966 (it was renamed the Economic Development Corporation, or EDC, in 1991), was aimed at encouraging development with the sale of city-owned properties to private investors. From 1966 to 1991, it became the powerful force behind the most spectacular

development projects in Manhattan, including the revamping of Times Square
and the rehabilitation of the South Street Seaport. As reconstituted in 1991,
the EDC's primary functions included the development, marketing, selling,
and managing of city-owned land; the financing of private development
plans; the establishment of incentives for business retention and attraction; and
the provision of financial assistance for developers. While the EDC acted as a
catalyst for private development, the Department of City Planning, the government department responsible for preparing land use plans, became more
and more dependent on the dictates of the EDC's agenda. The PDC/EDC
worked closely with the Urban Development Corporation (UDC), another
public authority created in 1968 by the New York State Urban Development
Corporation Act. In 1975, the Urban Development Corporation was reorganized and its mission shifted from developing housing to facilitating mixed-
use developments that included retail and office uses.

Under the administration of Abraham Beame (1974–1977), the channeling of financial incentives into large private development plans in downtown
Manhattan went hand in hand with Housing Commissioner Roger Starr's
controversial policies of "planned shrinkage" in the South Bronx and in other
disadvantaged neighborhoods, a strategy which consisted of the deliberate
withdrawal of city services and investments from blighted neighborhoods to
encourage the exodus of the poor. By the 1980s, 26% of rental apartments,
especially in Harlem, the South Bronx, Bedford-Stuyvesant, and the Lower East
Side, were in arrears, and many were abandoned or torched by their landlords, as
they deemed that the buildings were worth more for the insurance money than
as sources of income. By the mid-1970s, the Bronx had 120,000 fires per year,
for an average of 30 fires every two hours. Forty percent of the housing in the
area was destroyed. The net loss of housing from 1970 through 1984 amounted
to 360,000 units.[14] By 1979, the city had taken ownership of over 100,000 housing units that had been foreclosed or abandoned, making the Department of
Housing Preservation and Development (HPD) the second-largest landlord in
the city. In the years of Ed Koch (1978–1989), the city handed out massive tax
breaks and incentives to large corporations, subsidizing one of the most remarkable office building development booms ever recorded in Manhattan. In these
years, private developers could take advantage of a broad range of tax incentives
for new construction. The Industrial and Commercial Incentives Board (ICIB),
although initially intended to serve as a tool to revive the manufacturing industry, was soon employed as a catalyst for a wave of speculative construction of
office buildings in midtown and downtown Manhattan.[15] In the words of labor

writer Kim Moody, the influx of the first affluent white professionals in once off-limits areas of Manhattan like the Lower East Side in the early 1980s constituted "the safety valve for the vast army of well-paid professionals who populate the city's central districts."[16] This influx was a direct result of these shifts in policy, and in particular of a reorganization of the city's tax incentive programs, notably with the creation in 1971 of the 421-a tax abatements for new residential construction[17] and the extension of the J-51 tax exemption for the conversion of low-income housing to upscale condominium buildings and co-ops.[18]

Years of incentives to luxury development resulted in a growing dearth of affordable housing in Manhattan, which became particularly severe in the late 1980s. During Koch's first term, 81,000 units of affordable housing had disappeared as a result of demolition, conversion, or gentrification.[19] Paralleling the growth in the luxury market in Manhattan was the decline of districts like Harlem, the Bronx, and parts of Brooklyn and Queens. Staggering criminality, housing abandonment, and poverty in these areas contributed to make New York City a national symbol of urban decay.[20] As a response to the housing crisis, in 1986 Koch announced a 10-year, $5.1-billion city-financed program to support the privately led production or rehabilitation of 252,000 low- and moderate-income housing units. Koch's housing plan eventually managed to rehabilitate or build a staggering 150,000 homes, contributing to the economic recovery of vast swaths of city land that had fallen into disrepair over the years.[21] Starting in the early 1980s, the real estate market started to rebound on the back of a strengthening national economy, and Koch presided over an array of remarkable development projects, mostly located in Manhattan, to accommodate the extraordinary growth of employees in the city's finance, insurance, and real estate (FIRE) industries. Through the EDC/PDC and the UDC, federal subsidies for economic development were used to subsidize major image-enhancing projects such as the South Street Seaport, Battery Park City, the Javits Convention Center, and hotel construction in Times Square to catalyze tourism in the city. But the development boom ended abruptly with the stock market crash of 1987: the city was left with empty office buildings and vacant flats, rising unemployment in the financial and business sectors, a steep collapse in real estate values, and a recession that lasted until 1991.

David Dinkins (1990–1993), who took office as the recession unfolded, launched a 1990 National Urban Summit—a plea for more federal aid to cities, which brought together 35 mayors from cities across the United States. The effort proved fruitless, as federal money to municipalities continued to drop throughout the 1980s and 1990s, following a trend that had been in motion since the 1970s.

As former US attorney Rudolph Giuliani (1993–2001) took office, he ignited a new wave of fiscal austerity with cuts across the board on municipal services, which included curtailing the programs for affordable housing construction initiated by Koch. Giuliani stopped city hall from purchasing tax-foreclosed properties and introduced the "Building Blocks!" program in 1994, which was designed to return city-owned property to private entrepreneurs or community-based not-for-profit groups. During the Giuliani years, the number of affordable housing units in the city dropped precipitously: in only 2 years, from 1996 to 1998, over 1.3 million affordable units were lost, according to Moody.[22] Almost 50,000 market-rate new units were built between 1994 and 1999, but none of them were really affordable to middle-income families.[23] Meanwhile, hundreds of millions of dollars were spent to retain large companies and banking and financial institutions in the city, while corporate tax rates were aggressively curtailed to encourage development in midtown and Lower Manhattan.

Giuliani was followed by Michael Bloomberg, who served from 2002 to 2013 and performed as another distinctly "pro-growth" mayor: with the most aggressive urban development agenda since the times of Robert Moses, the Department of City Planning under his control has rezoned over one-third of the whole New York metropolitan area, re-engineering immense swaths of New York City's working-class, manufacturing, and waterfront areas into brand-new, mixed-use developments. But this is a story I will tell in chapter 4. And the new mayor in office, Bill de Blasio, hasn't detached himself from the grand ambitions of his predecessors, making rezoning across the board the centerpiece of his planning agenda, as we will see in chapter 7.

The Creative Destruction of New York

Manhattan is the primary locus of global capitalism, the most voracious force for change in history. Best to pick a different place to try to render fixed and solid that which inexorably melts into air.[24]

No phrasing can describe decades of whirlwind urban transformations in New York City better than "creative destruction." Across different phases of capitalism, from the Keynesian era of post–World War II economic expansion to the postindustrial era of rampant neo-liberalism starting in the 1970s, the relentless destruction of traces of old New York has constantly paved the way to a brand-new, more profitable city. Be it through the obliteration of working-class districts to make room for towering housing projects in the times of urban renewal or through the construction of slender high-rise condos and green promenades along waterfronts that were once home to bustling port activities in the times of Bloomberg, the city has constantly endeavored to find new ways to create profit for land owners and developers through a relentless process of destruction and rebuilding.

But this history of constant change is by no means a New York prerogative. The oxymoron "creative destruction,"[25] popularized by Schumpeter in 1942, captures the functioning of capitalism in its centuries-long evolution: the process of relentless transformation and innovation that is implicit in capitalism "incessantly revolutionizes the economic structure from within, incessantly destroying the old one, incessantly creating a new one."[26] This also applies to the process of capitalist urbanization, which, as Lefebvre argued, is driven by the dictates of capital profitability under conditions of shifting social, economic, and cultural circumstances.[27] The production of space under capitalism is characterized by a relentless tendency toward the destruction of obsolete (i.e., unprofitable or underperforming) space and the constant engineering of a brand-new space allowing for a profitable "excavation of value."[28] Our cities are arenas of relentless processes of creative destruction, "insofar as their constitutive socio-spatial forms—from buildings and the built environment to land-use systems, networks of production and exchange, and metropolitan-wide infrastructural arrangements—are sculpted and continually reorganized in order to enhance the profit-making capacities of capital."[29] The incessant restructuring of the built environment is a reflection of capital's ability to constantly find new avenues to reproduce itself.

According to urban scholar Rachel Weber, "capital circulates through the built environment in a dynamic and erratic fashion. At various points in its circulation, the built environment is junked, abandoned, destroyed, and selectively reconstructed."[30] Whenever space is destroyed, rearranged, or recreated from scratch, capital is extending its reach to incorporate more and more of the urban land under its grip.

The consequence of capital's push for constant innovations, however, is not only the obliteration of specific property markets and built legacies, but also a relentless disruption of existing communities, social ties, and cultural identities. In the recent history of New York City, this happened during the era of urban renewal, with the aforementioned passing of the Housing Act in 1949 and the adoption of a new zoning resolution in 1961, both responsible for the wholesale demolition of old working-class districts and their substitution with modernist public housing estates, and with the creation of a whole new sprawling infrastructural system during the era of suburbanization. It happened again during the "back to the city" era of urban upgrading and rampant gentrification of inner-city districts since the 1980s, when cities experienced an out-migration of industry workers and an in-migration of middle-class "pioneers" who embraced the diversity, freedom, and "authenticity" of the postindustrial inner city.[31]

In the following chapters, I will show how the creative destruction of New York City has been advanced in recent years, and specifically under the administrations of Michael Bloomberg and Bill de Blasio. This time, it was done through a systematic use of amendments of old zoning regulations, which has managed to unlock development potential in what were once unprofitable or underperforming property markets across the city, leading to one of the most remarkable building booms in the history of New York. While in the times of Robert Moses creative destruction went under the name of urban renewal, in the times of Bloomberg and de Blasio it goes under the name of rezoning.

The Production and Consumption of the City

Behind the building and rebuilding of New York City, we see capital at work in its relentless effort to subjugate more and more of the urban space under its rules. But the ravenous appetite of capital is not limited to the physical space of our cities alone. The forces of capital are striving to conquer all other possible dimensions of our urban experience: they not only shape the material form of the built environment around us—streets, squares, and buildings—they also condition our social routines and daily habits, and even influence our very personal perceptions of what living in the city is, or ought to be. In other words, the imperatives of capital accumulation dominate the physical, social, and symbolic space of our cities. If, as Lefebvre said, "space is a social product,"[32] then under capitalism the production of a distinctive material infrastructure (physical space), as well as the manufacturing of specific narratives and representations of space (symbolic space) and the development of specific policy instruments and regulations (social space), is dominated by the logic of capital profitability. In sum: we inhabit a space that has been designed by capital and that is fundamental to its survival.[33]

As such, the space of our cities becomes a commodity in its own right. And cities, just like any other commodity, are produced, marketed, and consumed. We are all, to some extent, caught in this never-ending cycle of production and consumption of the urban space. But under capitalism, certain powerful groups play a particularly crucial role in it. As I will explain in the following paragraphs, the production and consumption of our cities have a tendency to be commanded by powerful social groups of producers and consumers. They are the ones who hold all the cards of the urban development game.

City Producers

"All animals are equal, but some animals are more equal than others," wrote George Orwell in his 1945 dystopian novel *Animal Farm*. A retired lady in *El Barrio* may well have the same constitutional rights as her landlord, but does she have the same legal staff and financial means when it comes to fighting in court against a two-week eviction notice? And when it comes to planning for the future of their community, be it in Harlem or in Brooklyn, are the voices of local grassroots activists being heard just as loud and clear as those of well-connected multinational developing firms?

Every day we witness the striking transformations occurring in our cities. We observe shiny towers rise to the sky while the grocery store and the shoemaker next door shut down. We see our rents soar while our salaries dwindle. And we realize that someone else is calling the shots. Yes, because the production of the space in our cities is commanded by a very selected elite of landlords, developers and financiers, always in search of strategies to boost the market value of urban land. And this—like it or not—is one of the most powerful rationales for the process we call "urban development."

Theirs is not necessarily a totalitarian, Soviet-style endeavor: the transformations we see around us are the result of clashes, compromises, or cooperations of a number of different interest groups, from the powerful developer to the local councilperson, from the state government to the local community association. Many times a developer may come with a plan that is strongly endorsed by an administration but finds no backing once a new mayor is in office; other times, a developer may find total support from local politicians but fierce resistance from enraged local communities; still other times, developers must downgrade the size of their development ambitions or negotiate concessions to the community for their visions to move ahead. But, especially in booming economic times and in thriving cities, certain interests always tend to prevail, and certain visions of the city have it easy, while others really don't stand a chance. Resident groups may fight for decades to preserve a beloved community garden from being replaced by luxury condos, but it can take no more than two years for a million-square-foot megaproject like New York University's 2031 expansion in the heart of Greenwich Village to be almost unanimously approved by city council.[34] The truth is, cities are increasingly being built for the rich to invest in rather than for regular people to live in. This dynamic is accelerating, and doing so globally.

In the 1970s, American sociologists Harvey Molotch and John Logan described the city as a "growth machine"—a machine that is captained toward land growth by powerful coalitions of interests:

> A city and, more generally, any locality, is conceived as the areal expression of the interests of some land-based elite. Such an elite is seen to profit through the increasing intensification of the land use of the area in which its members hold a common interest.... Governmental authority, at the local and nonlocal levels, is utilized to assist in achieving this growth at the expense of competing localities.[35]

According to this view, local interest groups in any given city join forces in a political machine to promote growth by boosting the market value of urban land.[36] Harvey also associates the rise of urban-based class alliances of "landlords and property owners, developers and financiers, and urban governments desperate to enhance their tax base"[37] with the launching of large development ventures that were initiated since the mid-1970s as a response to the threats of deindustrialization and the rise of interurban competition. The "growth machine" thesis claims that the goal of growth, in the form of profit extracted from urban land, is capable of uniting otherwise conflicting social groups into coherent local governing coalitions. These alliances are composed of actors that are more or less directly associated with the property market[38] and include developers, investors, landlords, speculators, and financing and banking institutions, but also corporate businesses, cultural institutions, local policymakers, and even the local media. Among such elite groups, there is a general consensus about growth, and this consensus is so powerful that it invalidates "any alternative vision of the purpose of local government or the meaning of the community."[39] These coalitions strive to influence political decisions related to city building and to orientate the public opinion in support of their ambitious development ventures by emphasizing the value of growth as a collective good that is supposedly beneficial to all citizens.

A classic example of how growth machines have formed and functioned in the crucial post-1973 crisis years can be found in the aforementioned case of New York's 1975 near default, when the business elites managed to seize an unprecedented degree of influence in city politics and to dictate their own agenda for the years to come. In the summer of 1975, a "crisis regime" governed by members of these elites was put in place in New York City. The state authorized the creation of the Municipal Assistance Corporation (MAC) headed by leaders of the banking industry, which was in charge of selling bonds issued by the city to enable cash flow to return to the city's government, and enacted the New York State Financial Emergency Act in an attempt to bring city finances under control. The State Emergency Financial Control Board (EFCB) was created, which wielded powers of oversight over city government and public authorities.[40] The EFCB, which included key members of the business elites, was given full authority on all financial and fiscal decisions, including the power to approve or disapprove of labor contracts.[41] A *Village Voice* journalist and a political consultant, Jack Newfield and Paul Du Brul, in 1977 dubbed this network of unelected power brokers New York's "permanent government."[42] The reforms enacted by the "crisis regime" led to a balanced budget by 1978, but only at the cost of escalating social wreckage: massive layoffs resulted from the cutbacks adopted in almost every sector of public expenditures, from education to affordable housing, from health care to infrastructure maintenance. By the early 1980s, a massively downsized public service system was the enduring legacy of these reforms, which for Harvey represented "a coup by the financial institutions against the democratically elected government of New York City."[43]

The growth machine theory was not alone in its analysis of the functioning of urban-based class alliances. Since the late 1980s, urban regime theory has studied how local governments and private actors have coalesced into governing coalitions through formal institutions and informal networks.[44] Urban regimes emerge from the cooperation of representatives of local governments and members of the business world: while government enjoys political legitimacy and authority, business possesses the capital needed to spur development and generate jobs and revenues. A very important aspect of urban regimes is their relative stability: regimes embody orientations and coalitions that are capable of outliving different governing administrations.[45] In this book, I talk of city producers.[46] City producers are a network of local or extra-local individuals and social groups who have a say in the production of the urban space in a given locality because of their social, economic, and political leverage. Their scope of action is not limited to property development alone, but extends to interventions affecting the social and symbolic restructuring of the space of the city (legislation, policymaking, place marketing). They include local and extra-local authorities, the real estate and corporate industries, the media, marketing and branding agencies, and, although in different measure, the myriad neighborhood groups, civil rights organizations, nonprofits, and more or less institutionalized community-based alliances that operate within the community. City producers enjoy a position of overpowering influence in decisions affecting the production of the city. As opposed to ordinary citizens, whose access to the institutional decision-making mechanisms of urban development are prevented by their low level of political, social, and economic influence, city producers are deeply ingrained in the inner workings of the city because of their access to the corridors of power. Through lobbying, campaign contributions, promises of tax returns or job creation, and other levels of pressure, they are capable of massively influencing and affecting political decisions to their own benefit. City producers are on the front lines of urban development and are proactively engaged in "producing the city" at different levels, contributing to reshaping its social, economic, and physical fabric, as well as to manipulating its image in the media and news outlets. The power wielded by city producers in fueling the development of a brand-new urban experience is nigh on unstoppable: city producers, and the formal institutions and informal networks they consolidate, are the main engines of production of the physical, symbolic, and social space of our cities.[47]

In the next chapters, I will investigate the two major tools in use by New York's city producers to re-engineer the physical, social, and symbolic space of New York City. In New York, a systematic rewriting of obsolete zoning codes (rezoning) has been used to unlock development potential in once-unprofitable working-class and ex-manufacturing districts across the five boroughs (see chapter 4). This sweeping rezoning of the city has been paralleled by the production of seductive representations of a consumerist

New York experience through city branding, that have reframed the city as an attractive postindustrial, tourist-friendly destination for more affluent residents and consumers (see chapter 6). While branding strategies have contributed to produce new glittering representations of a commodified urbanity, rezoning plans have produced the physical framework where the spatial practices of a new population of city consumers occur.

The Consumption of the City

In capitalist societies, increasingly more aspects of our social experience have become subject to the laws of the market. As I mentioned above, space is one of them. Capital has subjugated the space of our cities, turning it into just yet another marketable commodity.[48] This commodification[49] of space is quintessential to the survival of capitalism, because the profits amassed from the exploitation of land are fundamental to the process of capital accumulation: the commodification of the urban space represents a political strategy to open up new channels for capital accumulation by expanding the scope of the private market for housing, retail, infrastructure, and services.[50] The privatization of municipal housing stocks, the transfer of public land ownership and management to private landlords and developers, the devolution of municipal services to private providers, the privatization of public spaces, and the establishment of public–private partnerships to support development ventures are all remarkable examples of how the local state and private actors are directly involved in creating market conditions to facilitate the exploitation of space for profit.

But, as Marx argued, "production is thus at the same time consumption, and consumption is at the same time production":[51] the consumption of space is also "productive," as consumption has the power to constantly stimulate new cycles of investment and development. In their hunt to attract new consumers and stimulate consumption, our cities have reinvented themselves as entertainment- and consumption-based wonderlands for residents and visitors alike: the multiplication of spectacular shopping malls, entertainment zones, and even themed ethnic neighborhoods is part of an agenda that seeks to emphasize consumption as the economic engine of a city that has forsaken its industrial past.[52] From New York City to Shanghai, from Tokyo to Berlin, city users are increasingly becoming consumers of a space that has been produced for them by policymakers, technocrats, urban planners, and the forces of the market.[53]

City Consumers

> The Miracle of our modern age is that we do have a choice. For the first
> time ever, a huge number of us have the freedom and economic means to
> choose our place. That means we have an incredible opportunity to find
> the place that fits us best.... As the most mobile people in human history,
> we are fortunate to have an incredibly diverse menu of places—in our own
> country and around the world—from which to choose.[54]

City consumers are those high-profile individuals and social groups whose
consumption patterns have the power of deeply influencing the urban development agenda. They include the "new urban classes" composed of highly
mobile professionals in the knowledge-based sector of so-called creative
workers,[55] and, more generally, geographically mobile urban residents with
higher-than-average incomes and with a strong discretionary purchasing
power; local and international corporations and businesses who are enticed
by city governments to locate in the city; local and extra-local property investors and developers; urban tourists; resident-consumers; and the elites of
super-wealthy consumers. What these groups have in common is their social
and political leverage, and the growing attention that entrepreneurial public
policy pays to indulge their preferences and consumption demands. Their
presence in the city is strongly encouraged by city producers, because it is
through their consumption patterns that they keep the processes of capital
accumulation alive. Their lifestyle concerns are increasingly determinant in
the process of city building, in an era in which "quality of life is not a mere
byproduct of production; it defines and drives the new processes of production."[56] Their demand for space plays a strategic role in the production of a
brand-new urban space, which is constantly revolutionized by their evolving
consumption practices. Thus, far from being mere passive beneficiaries of the
produced space, city consumers are active producers of it. In fact, the consumption of the city fuels urban development efforts (production of adequate
housing, retail, and infrastructure), legitimates policy guidelines (development
blueprints and regulations intended to foster an attractive built environment),
and engenders new narratives and representations of space (new sophisticated
urban brands are manufactured to cater to new populations of consumers).[57]

Of course, there would be no city producers without city consumers: while the first strive to constantly create demand for consumption (by
educating consumers through marketing and branding campaigns and by
anticipating and guiding their consumption preferences), the latter's demands
for specific urban forms in turn lead to the creation of a city that is more and

more tailor-suited to their expectations and desires.[58] In capitalist societies, the patterns of consumption offered to consumers do not necessarily coincide with what is best for the individual, but align themselves with the goals of market expansion and capital accumulation.[59] The consumerist habits of city users can hence be conditioned in order to satisfy city consumers' insatiable demand for profit. The construction of city consumers can be powered by narratives and images propagated by the media, official branding and marketing agencies, and the private real estate industry. These industries manufacture enticing images of "business-friendly," "green," "vibrant," "diverse" urban idylls that are meant to stimulate endless demand for consumption (of specific housing, services, and amenities). In this framework, architecture and urban design, together with branding and marketing efforts, are employed to sell the city as an attractive place in which to live, work, and invest.

But the symbolic and material consumption of the city constitutes the experience not only of those who have access to economic capital and are capable of influencing the urban agenda, but also of those who are disenfranchised from consumer culture. In fact, not all citizens are invited to the big party of urban consumption: those unable to participate due to their economic marginality are excluded from the "produced" city. Unequal access to consumption between "strong" and "weak" consumers results in different degrees of political empowerment and different abilities to actively influence the dominant agenda of consumption-based development. As a result, unequal access to consumption comes to determine new forms of social inclusion or exclusion in the city.[60]

While the consumption patterns of powerful consumers are increasingly dictating the agenda of urban development, other city users are all too often merely abiding by the arrangements of an urban agenda that is not speaking in their name. This is why the rise in political leverage and consuming power of city consumers challenges common notions of citizenship, in an urban society where the inability to consume comes to define new forms of social disenfranchisement and new geographies of segregation.

City Producers Reshape the City for City Consumers: The Gentrification of the City

Gentrification has become quite the buzzword of our urban age. We all know stories of infamous urban ghettos that were once plagued with crime and poverty and that suddenly have morphed into fashionable hot spots for artists and hipsters, or stories of a beloved neighborhood that was once bustling with life and color and was gradually converted into a dull, off-limits enclave for the wealthy alone.

According to urban scholar Neil Smith, by the 1990s gentrification evolved into a global development strategy, sponsored by local governments from the global North to the global South:[61] today, "gentrification blueprints," under the guise of municipal strategies for "livability" or "sustainability," are advanced more or less explicitly by all local authorities willing to compete in the global marketplace.[62] The advocates of such strategies routinely emphasize the benefits of their pro-gentrification policies, like increased tax revenues to support municipal services, increased average incomes to sustain commerce and keep the economy vibrant, increased home equity benefiting homeowners, and increased order, cleanliness, and safety in neighborhoods that were once underserved and in disrepair. But they routinely dismiss or overlook their downsides, like the displacement of long-time residents and businesses.

The role of the public sector as the "enabler" of gentrification is that of easing the regulatory boundaries that may prevent it, for example, by loosening strict zoning regulations (rezoning), by creating special development districts or enterprise zones, or by granting direct subsidies to encourage private ventures in underperforming areas. Gentrification is also promoted by government-led strategies of urban branding, which under the various banners of "urban renaissance," "urban revival," and the like, call attention to assets and perks of gentrifying districts.

This is why I define gentrification quite succinctly as "the process through which city producers produce a space to be consumed by city consumers." In this context, gentrified space is produced both in response to the demands of specific consumers and as an active producer of such demands. This physical space includes not only fashionable housing for the newcomers but also a fully redesigned urban landscape that is rich in entertainment and consumption opportunities for the new consumers.

Neil Smith saw gentrification as a restructuring process that allows global capital not only to penetrate the urban cores of our cities but also to infiltrate any remaining urban frontier, including peripheral, off-limits neighborhoods, in its perpetual search for profit.[63] This is the case of New York City under the administrations of Bloomberg and de Blasio, where gentrification, far from being a localized phenomenon occurring in specific central areas, has become a vast, generalized, and geographically pervasive urban restructuring operation. As I will explain in chapter 4, these administrations have implicitly promoted the wholesale gentrification of New York City as an engine of economic growth. Much of their development policies have been based on the re-engineering of peripheral and underperforming property markets to encourage high-end investment and the influx of new, more affluent city consumers. By promoting gentrification across the board, the city has enabled capital to penetrate in residual and disadvantaged communities across the five boroughs, leading to their physical, social, and symbolic makeover.

3

The Producers and Consumers of New York City

The Producers of New York City

Sometimes it doesn't take much hassle to turn a New York City nursing home into luxury condos, provided you are on the right side of the track. This is exactly what happened in 2016 with the Rivington House, a health care facility on the Lower East Side that was operated as a hospice center for AIDS patients, and that was locked by a deed restriction that prevented any use other than nonprofit residential health care. It took only about a $16 million fee for the new buyer to have a city agency lift the deed restriction that prevented a conversion, enabling him to flip the property one year later to a condo developer for a thick $116 million.[1] The buyer ended up with a $72 million profit, while the community has remained with one less health care facility and yet one more luxury development down the road.

In matters of urban development, we, regular people, rarely have a say. City producers are the ones in charge. From the local government to the real estate industry, from large corporations to banking giants, they are the main players in the game we call "production of the city." They are reshaping its neighborhoods and streets, reframing its social policies and regulations, and manipulating its images and representations in the popular culture. And we are becoming nothing but consumers of an urban experience that has been entirely designed and packaged by these powerful players. City producers are reshaping the city as a commodity for sale to the highest bidder.

The Real Estate Industry

The real estate industry is the single most powerful engine of urban development, and its activities are relentlessly revolutionizing the shape of our cities.

In New York, this industry employs legions of developers, planners, consultants, market researchers, financial analysts, engineers, architects, designers and landscapers, appraisers, property managers, construction workers, inspectors, attorneys, and so forth. In 2012 alone, New York City's private real estate industry accounted for about $106 billion in total economic output, or 13% of the gross city product, and employed around 519,000 people. Such a huge industry generates a multiplier effect in direct, indirect, and induced economic activity, which translates into an enormous fiscal impact for the city budget: in 2012, the real estate industry generated $15.4 billion, or 38% of the city's overall tax revenues.[2] For better or for worse, New York City would not be the spectacular metropolis it is today if it were not for the grand visions, the over-the-top ambitions and the insatiable quest for profit of those in the real estate business.

Real estate firms invest in properties from which they can extract the most profitable returns. In New York, some companies deal with large-scale development schemes in former manufacturing areas where mixed-use rezonings have increased commercial and residential development potential; others set their sights on purchasing low-priced rental units in subsidized housing complexes in overheated markets, evicting lower-income tenants and charging higher rents to more affluent residents; yet others choose to rehabilitate vacant structures that have fallen in disrepair, or to invest in the development of brand-new mixed-use projects in prime central areas. Some firms may choose to purchase and rehabilitate commercial properties and keep them vacant for years if necessary (a phenomenon called "warehousing"), in expectation of upscale retail (and with it, exorbitant rental profits) settling in. Others prefer to buy huge chunks of property in low-priced areas, only to flip them to the next investor when the market heats up.

In New York City, the real estate industry includes a bundle of established real estate dynasties (think of the Dursts, the LeFraks, the Rudins, the Milsteins, the Fishers, and the Trumps), powerful landlords (including the city, universities, and the largest banking conglomerates), local and international developers, and thousands of small and medium-sized real estate firms. All of these entities are represented in the Real Estate Board of New York (REBNY), the industry's leading trade association, which lobbies the city and state governments for development opportunities and fiscal incentives, and whose heavy support to the local political elites (through lobbying and political campaign contributions) has been traditionally paid off through legislations and directives aimed at encouraging development and absorbing the risks of real estate operations through public subsidies. In 2015, the REBNY member firms gave $21.7 million in campaign contributions to state-level elections.[3] The board's ranks consist of around 12,000 owners, builders, brokers, managers, banks, insurance companies, pension funds, real estate investment trusts (REITs), attorneys, architects, marketing professionals, and many other individuals and institutions involved in the New York real estate machine. The board monitors all legislation of interest to the industry before the city, state, and federal legislatures, preventing the passage of bills that could obstruct development or hurt profit margins, like commercial rent increase caps or rent control expansions, and has consistently pressured the state's and city's lawmakers to enact measures to benefit real estate expansion, including incentives to rezone industrial and waterfront sites as mixed-use developments. In 2016, the REBNY has pushed for the extension of the controversial 421-a multiyear tax abatement program,[4] which for years has been used to subsidize luxury developments at a cost to the city of hundreds of millions in foregone tax revenues.[5] The 421-a program has been one of the major allies of the real estate industry in New York City, but not the only one. Over the last 40 years, the state and the city have strived, and succeeded, to entice real estate development by leveraging tax breaks, credits, free infrastructure costs, and various other rewards in the hopes of fostering investment and thus capturing tax revenues that would otherwise go to other cities. The policies enacted since the aftermath of the 1975 fiscal crisis have made New York City's real estate particularly attractive to foreign investment, and the city's real estate market has been traditionally propelled by massive injections of foreign capital. In the 1980s, the Japanese takeover of the city was epitomized by the purchase of a majority stake in the Rockefeller Center by the Mitsubishi Estate Company.[6] In the late 1990s, investors from Hong Kong sank capital into New York real estate after the colony became part of China in 1997, fearful that the new regime would devalue their local investments. The early 2000s marked a new boom of foreign investment in New York City's real estate: in a phase characterized by a weak dollar and a booming property market bred by Bloomberg's growth agenda, investors from Europe, China, Dubai, Canada, and Australia started pouring money into New York City's residential and commercial real estate. In 2007, before the global financial crisis, international buyers in New York accounted for over 30 percent of all condo sales in the city.[7] As the country slowly recovered from the 2008 financial bust, more and more foreign investors have been buying high-end properties in the constantly growing New York City market, elevating the city as the global "capital of

foreign real estate investments" in 2015 and 2016.[8] Recently, Chinese investors have entered the game in droves, investing heavily in commercial and
residential projects throughout the city: Chinese companies have cofinanced the
stalled Atlantic Yards development in Brooklyn and signed major leases at the
Empire State Building and at the One World Trade Center site. They have also
increasingly made their way into the booming hotel business, which has developed at an unprecedented scale over the last decade: Chinese insurance company
Anbang purchased the Waldorf Astoria in 2015 and a $6.5 billion portfolio of
high-end hotel properties from Blackstone in 2016.[9]

Among the largest players in New York City's real estate business today
are globally traded REITs, such as SL Green Realty Corporation, AvalonBay
Communities, Boston Properties, Vornado Realty Trust, and Kimco Realty
Corporation, and private equity real estate investing firms (PEREs), such
as the Blackstone Group (currently the world's largest private equity real
estate investor), Tishman Speyer, the Carlyle Group, and Brookfield Asset
Management. REITs and PEREs are corporations or trusts that pool the
capital of many investors around the globe to purchase real estate or mortgage loans, mostly in prime areas in the city center. In particular, shares
in a REIT are publicly traded on stock exchanges and as such present
opportunities for global investors to hold property assets around the world.
Some REITs operating in New York invest specifically in one area of real
estate—shopping malls, for example (this is the case of Kimco Realty
Corporation)—or have a diversified portfolio in one specific region (this is
the case of Vornado Realty Trust, which owns and manages over 22 million
square feet in over 50 properties in Manhattan only, including Class A office
buildings, luxury residences, stores, and showrooms). REITs haven't yet displaced the traditional family-owned companies that continue to own and
develop large amounts of property in New York City, but since they have
access to low-cost public capital, they are capable of fast expansion through
acquisition of more and more parcels and properties. The growing market
share of these new entities represents a challenge for the economy of cities,
as their budget and fiscal policies are destined to be more and more tied to
the ebbs and flows of the global financial markets.[10]

But national real estate companies whose portfolios are distributed across
major American urban areas remain among the largest players in New York City.
A few names we will encounter in this book are the Related Companies (owner
of the Time Warner Center and developer along with Oxford Properties of
the Hudson Yards mixed-use mega-development project in Manhattan), Forest

City Ratner (developers of the Atlantic Yards site in downtown Brooklyn), Thor Equities (whose portfolio includes retail properties on Fifth Avenue, SoHo, the Meatpacking District, and Brooklyn, including at Coney Island), and Extell (developer of One57, among the most expensive residential towers ever built in the city, and which has recently purchased the former Pathmark property at 125th Street in Harlem).

The Corporate Industry

A company's choice of locating or opening branches in a city is strongly determined by the city's so-called business climate. This can be forged by producing a specific physical, social, and symbolic space: business-friendly locations not only deliver state-of-the-art office space, fashionable residences for their managers and employees, hotels, conference halls, and other perks (cultural venues, a vibrant nightlife, and a safe and clean street environment) but also offer a range of tax incentives and other subsidies for companies willing to relocate or expand; finally, business-friendly cities heavily invest in branding and marketing campaigns to portray themselves as safe and enjoyable places to conduct business.

Making New York City a business-friendly location has been the goal of policymakers since the mayoralty of Ed Koch in the late 1970s, and the out-spoken objective of every administration since then. For decades, New York State and New York City have employed all possible economic subsidies to help companies locate or expand their operations in the region. New York State spends billions per year to subsidize companies with property tax abatements, corporate income tax credits, cash grants, low-interest loans or loan guarantees, rebates and reductions, sales tax refunds, free land and land write-downs, infrastructure aid, or development grants.[11] More sub-sidy agreements are made by the city-controlled New York City Economic Development Corporation (NYCEDC) and the Industrial Development Agency (IDA) to finance the expansion of top companies in New York City. The NYCEDC officially oversees the programs of the IDA, while the IDA's board decides which companies and projects may receive discretion-ary subsidies. Despite being presented to the public as essential to promote or retain jobs in the city, subsidies granted by the NYCEDC and the IDA are not required to incorporate job quality mandates (such as living wage requirements).[12] As a result, incentives have often been granted to facilitate development projects that produced few quality jobs or no jobs at all: in some cases, subsidy recipients have been large companies that, after cashing the deal, have actually reduced their workforce.[13] In other cases, large subsidies have been employed to retain large corporations that had no intention of leaving the city in the first place—something that had become customary during the Giuliani years, for instance when he signed a controversial subsidy package with the New York Stock Exchange (NYSE) in 1998, which included a staggering $1.4 billion in enticements and tax abatements to retain the NYSE in Manhattan after its officials had threatened, quite unrealistically, to move to New Jersey.[14] The claim of "job creation" has traditionally enabled large corporations to extract massive public subsidies in exchange for quality jobs, even when they failed to deliver them. This is a system that penalizes taxpayers, as well as smaller businesses that do not possess the legal expertise required to apply for such grants.

Thanks to decades of policies favorable to large companies and to its reputation as a global business capital, New York City today hosts the headquarters of an outstanding number of major international corporations, including the highest number of Fortune 500 companies of any metropolitan area in the nation. Until 2012, when the torch was passed to London, New York was constantly ranked as the most attractive city in the globe for business, ahead of Singapore, Paris, and Tokyo, according to Japan's Mori Memorial Foundation's Global Power City Index.

Most of the city's major corporate, entrepreneurial, and investment giants today are represented in the Partnership for New York City, which was formed in 2002 out of the merger of the New York Chamber of Commerce and Industry and the New York City Partnership. It is a nonprofit membership organization composed of an elite group of around 300 CEOs from the city's top corporate and investment firms and real estate giants, committed to lobby the government, labor, and nonprofit sector for legislation favorable to business expansion. The partnership has enormous sway at city hall and in Albany, where it advocates for fiscal abatements, infrastructure development, and support to emerging industries. Through its affiliate, the New York City Investment Fund, the partnership also directly invests in economic development projects in the five boroughs.

New York City also has among the highest numbers of global retailers of any city in the world. Particularly over the last 20 years, corporate retailers have multiplied their ventures even in neighborhoods that only a few years ago were severely underserved. While Manhattan hosts the highest concentration of national retailers in the United States, with a staggering 2,804 chain stores, the outer boroughs are also experiencing a record increase in their number. As of 2016, New York City had 596 Dunkin Donuts, 433 Subways, 317 Starbucks, 303 Duane Reade, and 217 McDonald's locations.[15] Particularly during the Bloomberg and de Blasio years, this "attack of the chains"[16] was paralleled by a steep decline in independent mom-and-pop stores. The rezonings of large swaths of land across the city have put no restrictions on sizes or rental prices for commercial space, leaving it to the free market to ensure the survival of the fittest. Skyrocketing rental prices, which haven't declined significantly even during the 2009 recession, coupled with the fierce competition from national and international chains, have made it harder and harder for thousands of independent retailers to keep operating. Add to that the fact that small businesses in New York face some of the highest tax rates in the United States: according to the Small Business Tax Index, which ranks the friendliest policy environments for small entrepreneurship, New York State has consistently ranked among the least friendly tax environments for small businesses in the country.[17]

As the city has strived to produce a business climate favorable to large corporations, it has neglected its small local merchants: in fact, most of the city's "business-friendly" policies have directly or indirectly threatened their survival, leaving the smaller ones more vulnerable to shocking rent hikes or outright evictions.[18]

The Local Government

The Mayor

The mayor has enormous power in steering New York City's development machine. The mayor is elected by popular vote to a four-year term and is responsible for the administration of all functions of city government. His office oversees the largest municipal budget in the United States, which in 2016 amounted to $82 billion, larger than some US states. In his or her executive functions, the mayor is advised by the public advocate, the city comptroller, and the five borough presidents.[19] The mayor is the chief executive officer of the city, and as such is responsible for all city services, including police and fire protection, education and sanitation, the enforcement of all city and state laws within the city, and the management of municipal property. The mayor also appoints the chairs of about 50 city departments without any need for approval by any legislative body and, through his or her direct appointments at the Department of City Planning (DCP), the Department of Housing

Preservation and Development (HPD), the City Planning Commission (CPC), and other public–private agencies like the NYCEDC, holds decisive power in all decisions that matter in urban development.

The Deputy Mayor for Economic Development and Rebuilding
(Now Deputy Mayor for Housing and Economic Development)
The mayor appoints several deputy mayors to head critical offices with specific executive competences. In particular, the deputy mayor for economic development and rebuilding has a massive influence over the scope and pace of urban development in the city, as he or she oversees and coordinates the operations of a massive number of city agencies and departments related to economic development and land use.[20] Since the years of Michael Bloomberg, only high-profile individuals from the world of finance and banking have been chosen for this position. First was Daniel L. Doctoroff, former investment banker at Lehman Brothers and managing partner of private equity investment firm Oak Hill Capital Partners. Doctoroff had strong ties to the development community and had been an active promoter of a New York City bid for the Olympic Games since the mid-1990s. As deputy mayor, Doctoroff administered the rebuilding of Lower Manhattan after 9/11, launched the city's bid for the 2012 Olympics, worked on the rezoning of the Far West Side of Manhattan, and was the mastermind of the mayor's "green" plan, PlaNYC 2030, which was released in 2007. Doctoroff stepped down from the Bloomberg administration in 2007, only to become president of the mayor's firm Bloomberg LP in January 2008. The next to pass through the revolving door between corporate boardrooms and government jobs was Robert C. Lieber, former managing director at Lehman Brothers, who served until 2010, during the national recession. Lieber focused on more large-scale plans, including the redevelopment of Coney Island, the redevelopment of panoramic parklands at Governors Island, and the rezoning of Willets Point in Queens, only to return to the world of banking in 2010, when he became executive managing director for Island Capital Group. He was followed by Robert Steel, another former banking executive who had been vice chair of Goldman Sachs and CEO of Wachovia/Wells Fargo until 2010, and had served as under-secretary for domestic finance in George W. Bush's Treasury Department during the financial crisis of 2007 and 2008. He spearheaded new massive-scale developments including Hunters Point South and Flushing Meadows-Corona Park in Queens, the South Bronx, and the Stapleton waterfront development on

Staten Island's North Shore. He became CEO of global financial services firm Perella Weinberg Partners in 2014.

Appointing former banking executives to this crucial position has also become the norm under de Blasio. After his election, the title, which was changed to "deputy mayor for housing and economic development" to strengthen its central role on housing policy, was passed to Alicia Glen, who had previously served 12 years as head of the Urban Investment Group at Goldman Sachs, a fund that has invested over $2 billion in over 100 projects across the city. In 2016, the group invested $200 million in the first phase of the Essex Crossing megaproject in the Lower East Side, which will transform one of the largest stretches of empty land in Manhattan into a mixed-use development with 1,000 housing units and 850,000 square feet of commercial space.[21]

The Department of City Planning

The Department of City Planning is responsible for land use matters, including the acquisition or sale of city-owned land, the manufacturing of plans, the rezoning of districts, and the advising of the mayor, the borough presidents, the council, the 59 community boards, and other local government bodies on all issues related to the physical development of the city. The mayor appoints the director of the DCP, who also serves as the chair of the City Planning Commission (CPC), and 6 of the 12 DCP members who serve terms in office for five years.[22] Over the last decade, the DCP has focused on delivering an efficient and attractive built environment for residents and investors, fostering the development of brand-new mixed-use districts, iconic architectures, and a state-of-the-art street environment. This has been achieved mostly through a meticulous process of amending zoning regulations on a case-by-case basis: rezoning has been used to loosen the strict segregation of uses across the five boroughs, to direct development along transit corridors, and to convert manufacturing districts and waterfront areas into upscale residential enclaves (see chapter 4).

Under Bloomberg, the director of the DCP was "rezoning czar" Amanda Burden, heir of the Standard Oil fortune and a respected urban planner, who had served as vice president for planning and design of the Battery Park City Authority in the 1980s. Today, she is a principal at Bloomberg Associates, the high-powered international consulting service founded by Bloomberg in 2013 to spread the gospel of innovative city planning around the globe. Under de Blasio, the torch has passed to Carl Weisbrod, a veteran insider who was formerly founding president of the NYCEDC, head of the Lower Manhattan Development Corporation (LMDC), and founding president of the Alliance for Downtown New York, which oversees the Lower Manhattan Business Improvement District, New York City's largest business improvement district. After Weisbrod's resignation in early 2017, de Blasio appointed Marisa Lago, former president of the Empire State Development Corporation and a former Citigroup executive, whose long resume has included key roles in City, State and Federal government.

The City Planning Commission

All DCP decisions have to be approved by the City Planning Commission, which currently operates under the terms of the revised 1989 City Charter, with 7 of its 13 members, including its chair, being directly appointed by the mayor. The commission adopts or vetoes the land-use plans or recommendations of the DCP. Since they are considered legislative acts, amendments to the text or maps of the zoning resolution must ultimately be voted into law by the city council.

The New York City Council

The city council is the legislative body of New York City and is represented by 51 members from the different council districts throughout the city. The council has sole approval authority over the city's budget and spending and has the power to approve or reject zoning changes, city plans, and community development plans. This power makes the council the most significant decision-making body in issues related to city building after the mayor.[23]

The speaker of the council, selected by the 51 council members, is the second most powerful political post in New York City's government. The council speaker under Bloomberg was Christine Quinn, a Democrat who backed Bloomberg all along, including the controversial 2008 bill that overturned term limits, allowing Bloomberg to run for a third term in 2009. In March 2013, Quinn announced her candidacy to succeed Michael Bloomberg in the 2013 mayoral election, but she came in third in the Democratic primary after former city comptroller Bill Thompson and then–public advocate Bill de Blasio. The current speaker of the city council is Puerto Rican–born and de Blasio ally Melissa Mark-Viverito, heir to the fortunes of her millionaire father,[24] and yet representative of one of the poorest districts in the city, which includes the South Bronx and East Harlem. Under the new administration, both areas have been earmarked for massive rezonings.

The Department of Housing Preservation and Development

The Department of Housing Preservation and Development, headed by a commissioner who is appointed directly by the mayor, is responsible for the preservation and development of housing. In the last decades, HPD has made a decisive shift away from public ownership of properties and has promoted private investment and public–private partnerships to stimulate the production of new housing. The first commissioner of the HPD under Bloomberg was Shaun Donovan, who oversaw the city's multi-billion-dollar "New Housing Marketplace" agenda to finance the creation and preservation of 165,000 units of "affordable" housing, and who later served as the US secretary of Housing and Urban Development (HUD) in the cabinet of former president Barack Obama until 2014. After the financial crisis hit, Bloomberg appointed Rafael E. Cestero for the position. Cestero later became president and CEO of the Community Preservation Corporation, a nonprofit organization specializing in affordable housing that was founded in 1974 by David Rockefeller, the world's oldest billionaire and only living grandchild of Standard Oil founder John D. Rockefeller. At the peak of the real estate boom in 2007 and 2008, the Community Preservation Corporation's for-profit arm, C.P.C. Resources, invested millions of dollars in condo developments and megaprojects across the city, and defaulted on a $125 million loan on the 11-acre Domino Sugar Factory site in Williamsburg, which was then sold to developer Two Trees Management.[25] In April 2015, one year after a massive $1.5 billion redevelopment plan for the site was approved by the city, Two Trees donated $100,000 to de Blasio's now-defunct nonprofit Campaign for One New York, whose fundraising operations came under federal investigation in 2016.[26] In 2015, de Blasio appointed former professor at New York University and director of the Furman Center for Real Estate and Urban Policy Vicky Been as HPD Commissioner. Been worked for two years on the implementation of de Blasio's ambitious 10-year housing plan, before resigning in 2017.

The New York City Economic Development Corporation

One of the most influential agents of urban development in New York City is the NYCEDC. It was born in 1991 out of a merger of previous development corporations that promoted business expansion in the city, including the Public Development Corporation and the Financial Services Corporation. It is a nonprofit local development corporation that is set up to work more like a private corporation than a city agency. Even though its board is almost entirely under the mayor's control, its activities are not subject to review or oversight by the Department of City Planning or the City Council. According to urban scholar and community planning activist Tom Angotti, "EDC probably has more to do with planning the city— where, how and when new development happens—than all the city agencies that are entrusted with doing so. Despite that, the agency receives little scrutiny or even attention."[27] Through its annual contracts with the city, the NYCEDC has played a leading role in almost all major development schemes launched over the last 15 years. The NYCEDC has negotiated, backed, and sponsored some of the largest development projects across the five boroughs, including the World Trade Center, the Hudson Yards in the Far West Side of Manhattan, and the Atlantic Yards in downtown Brooklyn, just to name a few.

During Bloomberg's mayoralty, all of the NYCEDC's executive directors came from the world of banking. The first was Andrew Alper: prior to his appointment in 2002, he had spent 21 years in the Investment Banking Division of Goldman, Sachs & Co. Next was Seth Pinsky, appointed in 2008, who had been an associate at the law firm of Cleary Gottlieb, where he worked as an investment analyst and lawyer, and a financial analyst at James D. Wolfensohn Incorporated. As Pinsky left the NYCEDC in 2013 for a private-sector appointment in a real estate firm, the *Observer* commented:

> In his role as NYCEDC president, Mr. Pinsky was, in many senses, Mayor Bloomberg's right-hand man when it came to locking down the complicated development projects most likely to secure the mayor's legacy: Atlantic Yards, Hudson Yards, the Cornell tech campus on Roosevelt Island, Willets Point, the Kingsbridge Armory. Under Bloomberg, the not-for-profit arm of the mayor's office tasked with promoting economic development across the five boroughs shifted from an organization that largely paired tenants with office space to a policy-setting, city-altering powerhouse.[28]

Pinsky was followed by Kyle Kimball, former vice president at Goldman, Sachs & Co. and at J.P. Morgan. He later became vice president of government relations for Con Edison. In 2015, de Blasio temporarily overturned Bloomberg's legacy of banking executives–only appointments for this position and hired Maria Torres-Springer, who had previously served as commissioner of the New York City Department of Small Business Services (SBS). After two years, Torres Springer was sent to replace Vicky Been as Commissioner of Housing Preservation and Development, and James Patchett became the new head of the NYCEDC. Patchett had served as vice president of the Urban Investment Group at Goldman Sachs before becoming Deputy Mayor Alicia Glen's chief of staff. In this position, he had negotiated tax breaks in exchange for affordable housing at Stuyvesant Town/Peter Cooper Village on Manhattan's East Side, and at the Riverton Housing Complex in Harlem.

City Marketing Agencies

Today, all city branding and marketing initiatives are crafted by NYC & Company, a not-for-profit whose chair is directly appointed and overseen by the mayor's office. The tireless activities and tremendous influence of this massive branding powerhouse will be investigated in chapter 6.

The Landmarks Preservation Commission

The Landmarks Preservation Commission holds a strategic role in affecting decisions around development, as its stated role is to prevent unwanted forms of development from taking place in areas whose buildings have a particular historic value. In the global capital of creative destruction, the commission is in a very delicate position, as it strives to "strike a balance between protecting architecture and accepting economic realities, between a responsibility to history and a knowledge that the city must evolve."[29] Landmarking can be an effective tool to preserve the historic fabric of neighborhoods in times of development fury, and the Landmarks Preservation Commission each year designates neighborhoods or individual buildings that deserve to be spared from the wrecking ball: for instance, in 2015, the commission designated six individual landmarks and protected over 2,000 buildings through the creation of four "historic districts" across the city. But the Landmarks Preservation Commission, whose chair is directly appointed by the mayor, has also been criticized for "backing off too readily when important developers' interests are at stake," for instance by denying landmark designation to historically significant buildings that stood in the way of development.[30] This has also happened in the districts I have visited in my journey, and particularly at Coney Island, where, in the aftermath of the city's rezoning frenzy, only a few buildings that made the history of the neighborhood have managed to survive the wrecking ball.

The Community Boards

Today, the city is divided in 59 administrative districts, each served by a community board (CB). Community boards serve as advocates for the voices of local residents and communities. Each board has up to 50 voting members, with one-half of the membership appointed each year for two-year terms; there are no term limits. But community board members have only an advisory role in land-use decisions such as zoning changes and urban renewal plans. The final decisions on all these matters belong to the CPC and the city council.

Community-Based Groups

There are hundreds of community-based coalitions in New York City. Besides groups specifically committed to issues related to housing and land use, such as the Association for Neighborhood and Housing Development (ANHD), Real Affordability for All, Housing Here and Now!, Citizens Housing and Planning Council, New York City Environmental Justice Alliance, and so forth, other coalitions, like the New York City Small Business Congress and the Coalition to Save New York City Small Businesses, advocate to protect the rights of small business owners, an endangered species in today's highly competitive New York habitat. Hundreds of other community-based organizations in New York City are fighting for the provision of community service, health, educational, personal growth and improvement, social welfare, and self-help for the disadvantaged, including the homeless and the LGBT community.

Many more or less institutionalized grassroots groups have formed in response to specific rezoning plans in their community and struggle to have a say in the planning process or to craft their own alternative plans. These include groups such as Develop Don't Destroy Brooklyn, Save Coney Island, the Harlem Tenants Council, Good Old Lower East Side, the Chinese Staff and Workers Association, the Chinatown Working Group, the Bowery Residents Committee, the Movement for Justice in El Barrio, the Red Hook Tenant Association, and other groups whose fights I will describe in the following chapters.

The Consumers of New York City

Here, I identify influential groups of city consumers whose consumption patterns play a crucial role in dictating the agenda of urban development in New York City today, and clarify how their demands for specific urban experiences play a strategic role in the production of a brand-new, fully repackaged, hyper-commodified city.

The New Urban Classes

In recent times, economists, think tanks, and policymakers have been preaching the virtues of a somehow nebulous social group of urbanites, comprising professionals in the knowledge-based sector, and so-called creative workers,[31] whose presence, so they say, has the thaumaturgic ability to ensure economic growth and prosperity to almost any city. Research involving the preferences and values of this socioeconomic group shows that these new urban classes tend to base their location patterns on the "amenities" of a place, rather than on more traditional factors like the headquarters location of established employing firms.[32] According to the creative class theory,[33] this educated and mobile workforce is made up of professionals in the fields of science, law, technology, design, the arts and architecture, entertainment and media, education, and health care. They are attracted to places that host diversified labor markets and offer a range of quality-of-life advantages such as fashionable housing, a hip cultural life, and a wealth of trendy lifestyle options. They value urban density over sprawling suburbs and bike lanes over private car use; they look for an urban environment that facilitates easy networking and that promises upward mobility and career development. Most of these qualities are specifically urban, and these new urban classes, although often made up of former out-of-towners or suburban individuals, take pride in images and symbols of urban living. Their appetite for all that is "urban," in turn, is fueled by a brand-new global industry of urban trends and lifestyles, in an era in which lifestyle marketing has become an industry of its own. Thus, this rediscovered infatuation with urban living can be seen as the product of evolving cultural preferences as much as the result of recent shifts in the politics of marketing and branding of cities.

Often, the new urban classes include educated people whose careers or lifestyle choices require them to relocate. These are the flexible employees in the finance, insurance, real estate (FIRE), and in other sectors of the service economy—but also temporary residents such as college students,[34] visiting researchers and professionals, "permanent tourists,"[35] or "global nomads,"[36] and, more generally, geographically mobile urban residents with higher-than-average incomes and with strong purchasing power. Contrary to most traditional workers, the new urban classes enjoy a cosmopolitan lifestyle that empowers them to select the location they deem better tailored to suit their personality or their career ambitions. They possess "the means, resources and inclination to seek out and move to locations where they can leverage their talents."[37]

According to the creative class theory, cities that are successful in attracting these skilled workers will ensure their economic success through increased tax revenues and an overall diversification of their economic base. In the context of interurban competition, in which cities strive to gain a competitive edge to attract outside investment, the presence of this class of consumers is seen by policymakers as quintessential to success: according to urban theorist and creative class guru Richard Florida, a city that isn't capable of attracting these urbanites is doomed to lose in the global arena—which may lead to a spiral of capital disinvestment, economic decline, and out-migration.[38] In advanced capitalist cities, the presence of these new urban classes is thus almost universally encouraged by city producers, much of whose agenda revolves around meeting their wishes and satisfying their consumption demands.

Even though a large scholarship has exposed the weaknesses of the creative class doctrine,[39] these theories can't seem to lessen their appeal to entrepreneurial local governments. The assumption that attracting this class of consumers will bring prosperity to cities remains unchallenged among policymakers, and, according to urban geographer Jamie Peck, "a large number of cities have been ready, willing and able to join the new market for hipsterization strategies,"[40] since these can be easily ingrained into the framework of a market-driven, consumption-oriented "business as usual."[41] In the last decades, small and large cities around the globe have devised "creative agendas" to attract these groups of hip professionals in the hopes of fostering economic growth. Whereas a number of smaller US cities such as Portland or Houston have only recently turned to creative strategies to attract this new population of consumers, New York City historically has always been a catalyst for creative types. During the last decades and particularly in the Giuliani and Bloomberg years, the city has become "a leading player in the postindustrial global creative economy, an economy that relies on the innovation, ideas, and creativity of human capital."[42] Traditional creative industries like publishing, advertising, entertainment (art, theater, cinema, music), fashion and design have joined emerging and high-tech industries (biotechnology, pharmaceutics, software development, game design, green technologies) as drivers of New York City's "creative economy."

By 2015, 18% of the 3.7 million private jobs located in the city were in the professional services and information sector, which includes the tech industries, architecture and engineering, legal services, media and film, publishing, and research—a sector that has grown steadily over the past five years. Another sector in strong surge, particularly after the 2008 recession, is the FIRE industry, which accounted for 12% of private-sector jobs in 2015. Another 24% was represented by the health care, educational, and social assistance services, while 12% of private-sector jobs were in the recreation and hospitality industry, including restoration and entertainment.[43] A substantial portion of these urbanites are not married, and many have relocated from other parts of the country in search of new career opportunities: according to Eric Klinenberg, author of *Going Solo*, nearly 50% of all households in Manhattan today consist of just one person, "a number that seems impossibly high until you discover that the rate is similar in London and Paris, and even higher—a staggering 60%—in Stockholm."[44] Such a massive presence of young single professionals opens up innumerable possibilities for consumption-related development. To satisfy the consumerist appetite of this new powerful group of consumers, the city is reinvented as an "entertainment machine,"[45] a consumption-based playground that continually strives to emphasize and reinvent its cultural, recreational, and commercial offerings.

The entrepreneurial policy toolkit aimed at attracting the new urban classes is usually based on the rehabilitation of historical neighborhoods; the construction of brand-new housing; the refurbishing of parks and public spaces; the beautification of facades, parks, and streetscape improvements; the introduction of bike lanes; and so forth. Such interventions generally amount to nothing less than carefully designed forms of government-sponsored gentrification[46] in districts with "potential." This is exactly what we have seen happening in New York City under the administrations of Bloomberg and de Blasio, courtesy of an unprecedented wave of rezonings of former working-class and manufacturing districts across the five boroughs. From Fort Green to Williamsburg, from Long Island City to Bushwick, from Bedford-Stuyvesant to the East Village, city producers have hammered away to enhance housing, amenities, and retail options to make them into hot, revamped destinations for these hordes of new consumers.

Resident-Consumers

Regardless of their social background, the residents of an urban area inhabit the city's housing supply, employ its services and infrastructures, populate its public and private spaces, and enjoy its amusements, nightlife, and cultural attractions. They shop in the city's stores, visit its museums and galleries, and crowd its nightlife venues. And housing, goods, groceries, entertainment, shopping, culture, services, education, medical care, and even natural resources like water and gas to run their homes are all commodities that come with a price.

Like it or not, the everyday lives of city residents are structured around the lines of their consumption patterns, which vary depending on their age, gender, income, occupation, and education.[47] While the consumer behavior of some is characterized by a strictly utilitarian rationale (to satisfy functional or economic needs), the consumption patterns of other groups are inspired by more hedonistic reasons (shopping as a leisure activity or consumption of certain goods as a statement of social status). Compared to their suburban counterparts, today's city consumers spend on average much more of their disposable income on shopping for goods and services: cities today are filled with enthusiastic alpha and beta shoppers with strong hedonistic shopping motivations[48] who, in the talks of consumer behavior experts, "hold high expectations for products, customer service, store prestige, brand recognition, and value."[49] In marketing reports, the talk is of "citysumers," which *Trendwatching* in 2011 described as "the experienced and sophisticated urbanites (with disposable income), from San Francisco to Shanghai to São Paulo, who are ever more demanding and more open-minded, but also more proud, more connected, more spontaneous and more try-out-prone, eagerly snapping up a whole host of new urban goods, services, experiences, campaigns and conversations."[50] Retailers in recent years have fine-tuned their approach to cater to this new pool of urban consumers: big-box companies have been overhauling their marketing strategies and inventing new, smaller formats to adapt to the density of urban centers, while major brands have been seeking to tailor their products and marketing campaigns to an exquisitely urban audience by delivering urban-specific products and services and by promoting more daring and "edgy" marketing campaigns.

The close association of city residents with a pool of consumers has been the rule of market consulting firms for years. In recent times, however, this association has departed from the secretiveness of marketing reports of private companies to become the outspoken agenda of policymakers and elected officials. In the entrepreneurial era, both businesses and city governments strive to provide an urban environment that will stimulate high levels of consumption. Increasingly larger portions of urban land are being devoted to shopping and entertainment activities: historic streets turn into showcases for global brands, sidewalk cafes, food courts, and entertainment complexes, while new spectacular malls are incorporated into development blueprints because of the revenues they are expected to generate. The spread of development zones, festival marketplaces, entertainment centers, and ubiquitous chain retail stores in gentrifying districts are all manifestations of an entrepreneurial urban agenda that actively promotes consumption as an engine of urban and social change.[51]

In the United States, in the early years of the "back to the city" movement in the 1980s and 1990s, big swaths of the inner city were still in disrepair and remained out of the reach of large-scale retail. For big national retailers, the "return to the city movement" of the middle and upper middle classes opened up a long-awaited opportunity for expansion: capturing the buying power of inner-city shoppers became the target of their marketing efforts since the 1980s. In the reports of private business consulting firms, the inner city had become "the next retailing frontier":

> The moneymaking potential of inner-city retailing may be one of the industry's best-kept secrets. Inner-city markets are attractive because they are large and densely populated. Despite lower household incomes, inner-city areas concentrate more buying power into a square mile than many affluent suburbs do. But they are badly underserved, often lacking the types of stores that inundate suburban areas—supermarkets, department stores, apparel retailers, pharmacies and so forth....Thus, many inner-city residents must travel outside their neighborhoods for the kind of world-class shopping suburbanites take for granted.[52]

We know the rest of the story: large companies started lobbying governments for an injection of pro-big-business economic development strategies. These would be based on reducing regulatory obstacles and improving urban infrastructure to pave the way for retail development of the kind that prospered in the suburbs. In the years following, the vision of a corporate retail-friendly city was eventually fulfilled, and most city centers in the United States have been reshaped as safe and attractive havens for forms of shopping that were once exquisitely suburban.

Making the inner city safe and accommodating to national retailers has been a priority of urban policies in New York since the late 1970s. But especially in the last decade, rezoning plans have given the ultimate boost to the proliferation of generic, large-scale retail stores across the five boroughs, and massive shopping and entertainment complexes have often been designated as the centerpiece of large development schemes, like at

Hudson Yards, where a spectacular, seven-story 750,000-square-foot concourse, when completed in 2018, will include 20 restaurants and over 100 luxury shops, including Dior and Chanel, and the habitual array of Banana Republic, H&M and Zara.

Elsewhere across the five boroughs, the presence of chain retail is quietly revolutionizing the landscape of the city's main commercial corridors, from the Fulton Mall in downtown Brooklyn to 125th Street in Harlem, from Jamaica Avenue in Queens to Surf Avenue in Coney Island. Today, the "suburbanization of New York"[53] is a done deal. And while the city is reinvented as a mecca for national retail, shopping as a frantic leisure activity is gradually becoming the everyday practice of choice for a larger and larger number of us.

Urban Tourists

The multiplication of spectacular revitalization plans in postindustrial cities over the last decades has gone hand in hand with the exponential growth of urban tourism.[54] In the entrepreneurial era, city producers have increasingly integrated tourist-related development blueprints into their planning agendas, and an ever-increasing number of urban areas have been made accessible to more or less mainstream forms of urban tourism. In New York, tourist-related developments have become a crucial element of urban policy since the times of Rudolph Giuliani, and were given a tremendous boost under Michael Bloomberg, the mayor who touted the tourism industry as the employment future for hundreds of thousands of New Yorkers: tourism, he noted, "is our answer to the old-time industries' declining."[55] Through his mandate, fostering tourism has been presented as the unavoidable solution to deindustrialization, becoming the alibi for innumerable revitalization efforts across the city while giving a tremendous boost to the city economy. Thanks to Bloomberg's rampant efforts to attract tourism, the city has broken all-time records in tourist numbers, becoming the undisputed number-one tourist destination in the United States year after year. Today, the whole of New York City is being reshaped with what sociologist John Urry called the "tourist gaze"[56] in mind: the city is actively encouraging tourists to venture into districts that only a few years ago would have been considered off-limits, unsafe, or simply too dull. In these areas, the city capitalizes on bits and pieces of local flavor to satisfy the tourists' appetite for authenticity: as we have seen in the previous chapter, the rezoning plan for 125th Street in Harlem set rules to bring distinctive signage reminiscent of the grit and buzz of the old Harlem Renaissance days. Likewise, the rezoning plan for Coney Island is trying to bank on the amusement area's legendary past, although purified of its grit, to cater to a more mainstream tourist target.

Meanwhile, "starchitectures" have spread all over the metropolitan area, and buildings like the Time Warner Center at Columbus Circle, the new Apple Store on 5th Avenue, 100 Eleventh Avenue, New York by Frank Gehry, 432 Park Avenue, and Calatrava's World Trade Center transit terminal, among many others, have made the city an open-air catalog of the contemporary architectural stardom franchise. While private developers know that more buyers will be willing to pay premium rates for apartments and facilities designed by star architects, city officials realize that iconic architectural brands will help sell their development projects as major tourist attractions too. This has definitely been the case for the Highline, the chic elevated park designed by international architects James Corner Field Operations and Diller Scofidio & Renfro on the once-derelict freight railway line that runs near the Hudson River from Gansevoort Street to West 34th Street. Particularly since the opening of its phase II in 2011, the park has become such a "tourist-clogged catwalk"[57] that it has inspired resentment from New Yorkers complaining that every spot the Highline touches has turned into a jam-packed version of Disneyland's Main Street. The seedy streets that were once homes to meatpacking businesses, small manufacturers, and car workshops have turned into a spectacular "architects' row" of gleaming, ultramodern architectures by the likes of Jean Nouvel and Frank Gehry, while property values nearby have been driven literally to the sky by the presence of the new park.[58]

The pedestrianization of parts of major crossroads and streets in Manhattan and in the outer boroughs, which was initiated under the guide of Department of Transportation commissioner Janette Sadik-Khan in the mid-2000s, has turned into a powerful tourist magnet as well. In the summer of 2009, portions of Times Square were closed to car transit and turned into a pedestrian mall with chairs, benches, and café tables with umbrellas. This experiment was the trailblazer for a huge number of similar interventions across the city, and today such plazas are to be found everywhere around New York City, from 37th Road Plaza in Queens to Albee Square in Brooklyn.

Besides such acupunctural interventions, the city has kept investing massively in the most internationally renowned tourist sites. After a slow start, reconstruction at the World Trade Center site is now almost completed.

The National 9/11 Memorial was unveiled on September 11, 2011, in a special ceremony for the victims' families and opened to the public the day after. The memorial features two enormous artificial waterfalls and reflecting pools, each nearly an acre in size, sitting within the footprints where the Twin Towers once stood. One World Trade Center, once known as the Freedom Tower, was completed in 2013. The 105-story tower by David Childs is currently the tallest skyscraper in the Western Hemisphere, with an antenna reaching a symbolic 1,776 feet (541 meters) in reference to the year of the United States Declaration of Independence. The long-delayed World Trade Center transit terminal by Santiago Calatrava opened in March 2016, over 10 years after work began, and with a staggering cost of nearly $4 billion (the Burj Khalifa in Dubai, the tallest skyscraper on the planet, was built for less than half the cost), making it the most expensive train station ever built, and bringing another piece of international architectural stardom to the World Trade Center site. The entire area is expected to become one of the most visited tourist destinations in the entire world.

Especially in recent years, new frontiers are being opened to the tourist market, allowing visitors to move beyond traditional destinations and to explore less established urban areas that were once off-limits to tourism (ethnic neighborhoods, ex-industrial areas, artists' districts), as much as new, deliberately configured redevelopment zones (brand-new waterfront promenades, festival marketplaces, entertainment and shopping clusters).[59] While new tourist development zones are created from scratch, ex-manufacturing areas can be turned into hip artists' districts with exhibition rooms and loft galleries, and former working-class neighborhoods gradually morph into "urban entertainment destinations"[60] filled with specialty stores, fashionable restaurants and cafes, galleries, and lounge bars. These are the favored spots for a new type of urban tourists whose demand for nonstandardized, "authentic" urban experiences sets them apart from the likes of mass tourism. These are generally younger, more affluent and more sophisticated tourists who look for that certain "authentic" *je ne sais quoi*. In their urban wanderings, they search for the "buzz" or the atmosphere of a particular place. In New York City, they'll look for a cute, well-rated Airbnb in the next up-and-coming neighborhood rather than book a hotel through a travel agency. They'll steer clear of traditional tourist bubbles like Times Square or the Statue of Liberty, stay away from the long lines to get to the top of the Empire State Building, and refuse to pile up souvenirs in gadget stores. Instead, they'll be found drinking coffee in the cafes of the Lower East Side, snooping around at gallery openings in Williamsburg, or boutique shopping in more specialized areas like the Meatpacking District or Nolita. What they look for is that "authentic" New York lifestyle experience: artsy boutiques and galleries and, most of all, bars and restaurants. But as tourism crawls in, small businesses close, restaurants open, hotels multiply and homes morph into bed-and-breakfasts, one has to wonder: Is this the authenticity they were looking for?

The Super-Wealthy

It is no mystery that global and national policy reforms adopted since the 1970s to deregulate financial markets and privatize public resources have massively contributed to boosting the profits of the upper ranks in the financial, banking, and real estate sectors, while depressing wages for middle- and low-income US workers. Over the past four decades, as a result of the global and nationwide enforcement of aggressive neoliberal economic policies, those at the very top of the income pyramid have increasingly accrued a disproportionate share of economic gains, especially when compared to the standards of post–World War II America.

In New York City, this trend has been aggravated by the city's position as one of the major global financial capitals, where immense wealth in the upper crust of the corporate and financial industries collides with growing poverty in the lower sectors of the economy. New York is home to Wall Street, the world's largest investment banks, and the highest number of corporate headquarters in the United States. Such a concentration of capital has traditionally reflected in a vertiginous income inequality that, although paralleling that of other major American cities, has reached in New York, and particularly in Manhattan, its highest historical peaks.[61] Over the 1980–2007 time span, the incomes of the richest 1% in New York has increased 10 times as fast as those of the middle class, skyrocketing from about $447,000 in 1980 to $2.731 million in 2007, while the income of poor New Yorkers has actually decreased to levels lower than those of 1980 when adjusted to inflation.[62] New York State has the highest polarization of incomes in the United States, and New York City has always ranked among the most unequal cities in the nation.[63] According to the Fiscal Policy Institute, "if New York City were a nation, it would rank 15th worst among 134 countries with respect to income concentration, in between Chile and Honduras. Wall Street, with its stratospheric profits and bonuses, sits within 15 miles of the Bronx—the nation's poorest county."[64]

The concentration of so much money in so few hands has created a brand-new elite of "super-wealthy" individuals residing, doing business, or just depositing foreign cash in the city's most exclusive properties. Due to the global role of New York City as a capital of financial transactions, this class includes a core of billionaire CEOs, CFOs, and Wall Street managers, followed by an elite of super-wealthy investment bankers, analysts, and traders, whose personal earnings in the form of salaries, direct compensation, and bonuses often amount to a large slice of the total revenues of their employing firms;[65] and hordes of foreign buyers looking for safe deposit boxes in the booming New York City luxury condo market. Not only do common definitions of extraordinary wealth not apply to New York City, where individual wealth reaches highs unheard of in the rest of the country, but also the definition of extraordinary wealth in the city has changed altogether over the last few years, reaching unprecedented, outrageous highs. According to a *New York Magazine* reporter, "having $1 million in assets as of 2001 placed you in the top 7 percent of families nationwide, according to the Federal Reserve. In New York, it means you own an average co-op in Manhattan outright."[66] The city has never had such a concentration of super-wealthy individuals: in 2011, there were about 90,000 people in the top 1% of the income scale.[67] Their average annual earnings of $3.7 million translate into a daily income of over $10,000. Ten thousand dollars *a day*. To put these numbers into perspective, they make in a day more than what those New Yorkers living in deep poverty make in an entire year. Yes, because despite its reputation as a city for the wealthy, half of New York City households have annual incomes below $30,000—"an amount that the top 1 percent receives over the course of a holiday weekend."[68]

The incredible concentration of wealth in the hands of this privileged elite is constantly revolutionizing the cityscape of New York, a city that has traditionally known how to meet the extravagant demands of billionaires. Many of the rezoning schemes implemented by the City have targeted this and other groups of wealthy city consumers by incentivizing the production of spectacular luxury towers across the city, from the Lower East Side to midtown, from Lower Manhattan to Long Island City. This is among the factors that have contributed to propel the super-gentrification of Manhattan and the outer boroughs over the last 15 years, creating a system where "the thousands of highly-compensated employees on Wall Street and related businesses can afford to bid up the price of brownstones, cooperative apartments and condominiums,"[69] literally ousting average and even upper-income New Yorkers from the housing market.

In the mid-2000s, the speculative fever prompted by the presence of the super-wealthy, and encouraged by a political agenda all too prone to subsidizing luxury development, has resulted in the widespread multiplication of overpriced, exclusive condominium buildings for the elite of global billionaires. The fiscal recession of 2009, triggered by the bursting of the housing bubble caused by the very speculative financial instruments that Wall Street managers and bankers had devised, painted at first a less rosy picture. Postcrisis New York was a city filled with incomplete or largely empty luxury condos, both in Manhattan and in the outer boroughs.[70] But while it took years for the national economy to recover, the luxury end of the residential market bounced back in no time. By 2011, headlines were dominated by stories of foreign buyers snapping up apartments in Manhattan for prices none had ever heard of before. For example, Russian billionaire Dmitry Rybolovlev paid a record-breaking $88 million for a 10-bedroom apartment on Central Park West for his 22-year-old daughter Ekaterina Rybolovleva, who "plans to stay in the apartment when visiting New York."[71] At $13,000 per square foot, it was the most expensive apartment ever sold in New York City, and the trailblazer for a series of record purchases for "safety-box apartments" for ultra-rich individuals parking their cash in the city.[72] In 2012, as the national housing market continued to falter, three New York City penthouses designed by Frank Gehry were rented at a price of $40,000 to $60,000 per month.[73] Only five years later, a five-bedroom apartment at the Time Warner Center would reach an outlandish $110,000 monthly price tag, becoming the most expensive non-hotel rental ever recorded in New York City.[74] In 2013, a stunning $95 million penthouse with six bedrooms was sold at 432 Park Avenue, the tallest residential building in the Western Hemisphere and the second-tallest building in the city.[75] But it was 2015 that broke an all-time New York record, with the sale of a $100.47 million penthouse on top of One57,[76] Extell's 90-story blue glass condominium tower, also known in the city as "the Billionaire Building." Note that most record purchases in the top Manhattan condos have benefited from million-dollar tax breaks[77]—sweetheart deals of a generosity that no small investor will ever enjoy, let alone other acts of largesse, like legal immigration status granted to foreign millionaires in exchange for big-money investments through the controversial EB-5 federal visa program.[78]

So who are these buyers? A big part of the sky-high end of the condo market is dominated by individuals looking to store money whose source may be dubious. Nobody seems to know their names, protected as they are by layers and layers of opacity. As a *New York Magazine* reporter writes:

> Behind a New York City deed, there may be a Delaware LLC, which may be managed by a shell company in the British Virgin Islands, which may be owned by a trust in the Isle of Man, which may have a bank account in Liechtenstein managed by the private banker in Geneva. The true owner behind the structure might be known only to the banker.[79]

In many cases, such deposit boxes for foreign cash are rarely used, if not as *pied-à-terre.* The number of properties that stay vacant at least 10 months a year has reached 30% in the blocks between Fifth and Park Avenues between 49th to 70th Streets: "And so New Yorkers with garden-variety affluence— the kind of buyers who require mortgages—are facing disheartening price wars as they compete for scarce inventory with investors who may seldom even turn on a light switch."[80]

The money of Wall Street's top executives, Middle Eastern tycoons, and exiled Russian oligarchs is also fueling a new super-luxury market for posh services and pricey gadgets no regular New Yorker could ever dream (or maybe care?) to afford. A $222,000 diamond-encrusted Hermès Birkin handbag?[81] Check. A $4 million pair of sneakers covered in "hundreds of carats of tailor-made white diamond pieces and blue sapphires set in 18k gold"?[82] Check. A $25,000 ice cream sundae gilded in edible 24-carat gold and fresh whipped cream?[83] And what about a $295 burger? Or a "69-dollar haute dog made with truffle oil, foie gras and heirloom ketchup"?[84] In today's New York, even the chic 212 area code has become a luxury brand—a status symbol that is almost as sought after as an Upper West Side apartment, and that can be bought online from brokerage firms for prices ranging from a few hundred to a few thousand dollars.[85]

For years, New Yorkers have been told that the presence of the filthy rich in the city is more than good: it's a gift from heaven. It's the old trickle-down adage that promises that their exorbitant wealth will ultimately spread from the top to the bottom. It is something that Michael Bloomberg, a member himself of these elites, has repeated with pride and conviction throughout his mandate, crowning Wall Street executives as the city's most important job creators and revenue generators:

> The city depends on Wall Street. Let's not forget, those taxes pay our teachers, pay our police officers, pay our firefighters. Those taxes we get from the profits companies and the incomes, they go to pay for this library.[86]

It is undeniable that many of the ultra-rich pay huge amounts of taxes, and that many are indeed great job creators. But such tributes make no mention of the tremendous speculative pressure that the buying power of these elites has unleashed on New York's real estate market, nor of the inflationary effects of their extravagant consumption demands on the costs of living in the city. Their ability to outbid any other buyer when it comes to real estate, as well as their demands for outrageously priced housing, services, and amenities, which are met by developers eager to extract all the profit they can from this luxury craze, is one of the crucial engines of the massive gentrification waves that today have made Manhattan, and even parts of Brooklyn and Queens, an off-limits territory even to upper-middle-class New Yorkers.

But the luxurification of New York wouldn't have happened without a municipal government way too pleased to oblige. In the next chapter, I will describe the policy toolkit that the city has devised over the years to re-engineer itself as a luxury wonderland for the new favored class of city consumers.

4

Rezoning New York City

Rezone It Till It Bleeds

Harlem is not the only area of New York that has radically changed during the last decade. Many blocks down, in the Far West Side of Manhattan, between West 30th and West 39th Streets, a brand-new district of flagship high-rise towers is on the making. This part of Hell's Kitchen, which was once home to a mix of warehouses, small-scale businesses, and turn-of-the-century walkups, is now undergoing a shocking wave of luxury development, spurred by Bloomberg's rezoning of the area in 2005. Today, the neighborhood is unrecognizable. The railway tracks that gave the area the name of Hudson Yards are being swiftly covered by a massive platform that by 2018 will host 16 high-rise towers, a retail complex, a six-acre public square, and cultural facilities, courtesy of developers Related Companies and Oxford Properties. Downtown, the final leg of the High Line, once a derelict elevated freight railway, opened to the public in September 2014, creating an uninterrupted park from Gansevoort to 34th Street that attracts five million visitors a year. New constructions in the surrounding area include the Abington House, a residential tower whose rental prices start at $3,675 for a studio apartment and that features glamorous lounge bars, an Equinox-inspired gym, a 1,000-square-foot dog-sitting and grooming facility, and a sun rooftop terrace. Across the East River, in Brooklyn, another large chunk of the city has been radically transformed. The business district that had been intended for downtown Brooklyn since the opening of the Williamsburg Savings Bank in 1929 and was halted for decades after the Great Depression is finally on the rise, thanks to the rezoning of the area of the old Vanderbilt Yards in Prospect Heights in 2004. Forest City Ratner, one of the largest real estate firms in the country, has built a brand-new sport arena called Barclays Center, surrounded by a colossal construction site of 17 high-rise buildings, which will become a mixed-use commercial and residential development called Pacific Park. Formerly named Atlantic Yards, the developer has rebranded the project in 2014, probably due to its troubled history and the many controversies it created for its use of eminent domain and for the displacement of long-time residents and businesses in the area.

Rezoning: as of late, it has become a buzzword loaded with rather negative connotations in New York City. While for some residents it's nothing more than some technocratic yawn-inducing mumbo-jumbo, for others this loathed word means a call to arms. For now over a decade, concerned New Yorkers have seen elected officials come to their communities with promises that the magic wand of rezoning would bring "unprecedented" affordable housing and services to their neighborhoods. What they have witnessed time and time again, however, is rezoning serving as a Trojan horse for unaffordable developments, gentrification, and displacement.

Technically speaking, zoning refers to the classification of urban land into zones that regulate the activities, form, and density accepted in new developments. New York City's current zoning resolution dates back to 1961, and today it is considered obsolete by all possible standards: it was adopted at the height of the Urban Renewal era, which in New York was embodied by the figure of Robert Moses, the infamous "power broker" who presided over the building of innumerable housing complexes on condemned city land, often replacing dense, lively communities with isolated, monolithic "towers in the park" public housing projects, and who was responsible for the displacement of thousands of low-income and minority New Yorkers.[1] But in the years after 1961, the decline in the manufacturing industry, accompanied by the rise of a new postindustrial economy and the "back to the city" movement of white middle-class professionals, resulted in a radical shift in planning approaches in New York. Rather than engaging in a comprehensive work of reassessment of the 1961 zoning code, in the following decades city officials have chosen to focus instead on an area-by-area reclassification through zoning amendments (rezoning) to ensure ad hoc new regulations that were more attuned to the specific neighborhoods and to new planning concerns and market demands. City officials recognized that any attempt at a comprehensive overhaul of the 1961 zoning ordinances would be fought hard by the city's major real estate players. They also understood that any form of static plan for the city would become obsolete before its launch, and would prevent a flexible and discretionary management of land uses—a mandatory requirement in an increasingly fast-paced and globalized real estate market upon which the economy of the city depends. As city consumers constantly redefine their demands for housing and consumption spaces, developers seek more flexibility to address these new demands than a rigid zoning ordinance would allow. Likewise, regulators need flexibility to adapt to the city's evolving demography and changing needs, and to facilitate private injections of capital into the urban environment. Because of their flexibility and their detachment from any rigid blueprint, rezoning plans have proven to be the device of choice for policymakers eager to facilitate development in areas where opportunities for profit arise.

The rezoning of city land allowing for new infill developments, mixed-use conversions of manufacturing districts, and development of brand-new waterfront residential enclaves where port facilities once stood, is capital's way of opening profitable outlets in areas that were once unexploited or underperforming. In other words, rezoning can provide capital with a much needed "spatial fix,"[2] a sort of safety valve that allows for new waves of capital investments in territories that were once out of its reach.

Starting during the Giuliani years, and more massively under the administrations of Michael Bloomberg and Bill de Blasio, rezoning has managed to unlock development potential in once-unprofitable or disadvantaged property markets across the city, leading to a radical transformation of the city's physical, symbolic, and socioeconomic environment. In the Bloomberg years, rezoning has expanded the geographical scope of property investment and development to unprecedented extents, remodeling well over one-third of city land in little more than 10 years, and paving the way for one of the biggest building booms in the history of New York. And many more large-scale rezoning plans are now under way, from East New York in Brooklyn to Jerome Avenue in the Bronx, courtesy of Mayor Bill de Blasio.

How Rezoning Works

New York's 1961 zoning resolution is still on the books today and divides the city into three basic zoning districts: residential, commercial, and manufacturing. These basic districts are further categorized into a variety of lower-, medium-, and higher-density residential, commercial, and manufacturing districts. Each zoning district regulates the use, the density (measured through a floor-to-area ratio called FAR), the amount of parking space required, and more nuanced prescriptions on the allowable bulk and height of buildings. Any of these districts can be overlaid by "special purpose" zoning districts that are tailored to the specific characteristics of certain neighborhoods (e.g., the Theater District in midtown Manhattan). Most developments in New York City occur "as of right": if the Department of Buildings ratifies that a proposed development meets the requirements of the zoning resolution and the building code, a building permit is issued. Sometimes, however, certain developments are not allowed under the current zoning regulations, and a zoning text or zoning map amendment is required (e.g., because the proposed use is not permitted on a specific location, or because the height and bulk of the proposed structure exceed zoning limits for the area). Such an amendment is called rezoning. Rezoning is a reclassification of a specific plot of land to enable different uses and development forms. Rezoning plans may reclassify areas by either downzoning or upzoning them. Downzoning is a reclassification to a lower building density, while upzoning allows for a more intensive use. Rezoning plans can be proposed by the Department of City Planning or other public entities to guide development along specific planning guidelines (for instance, transit-oriented development). But rezonings can also be initiated by private actors to carry out specific development proposals, as well as by community boards, borough boards, borough presidents, the Land Use Committee of the city council, the City Planning Commission, or the mayor. They must be assessed for their potential environmental impacts and are subject to a lengthy public review process, known as the Uniform Land Use Review Procedure (ULURP), whose function is to allow the different stakeholders and the local communities to be involved in the planning process. To be enforceable, a rezoning plan must be approved by the City Planning Commission and ultimately adopted by city council.

A Brief History of Zoning in New York City

The first form of land regulation for the island of Manhattan was enacted with the so-called Commissioner's Plan adopted in 1811, which established the use of a grid of avenues and streets between 14th Street and Washington Heights in uptown Manhattan. The plan imposed a regular grid of avenues and streets, without regard to the particular topography of the island, to promote an orderly development and facilitate the sale and exchange of property lots, but didn't provide for large public squares and parks, except for a few tracts where the grid was interrupted. Central Park, created in 1853, wasn't part of the plan, but was created at a later stage on 700 acres of land that had limited development potential because of drainage problems.

In the early 1900s, the introduction of steel beam construction and improved elevators gave rise to higher and higher skyscrapers. Slender towers seemed to mushroom uncontrollably, giving the Manhattan skyline its spectacular, chaotic, quartz-like form. Furthermore, as New York was rising to become a world capital of industry and commerce, it became customary for residential neighborhoods to stand next to noxious factories. To regulate its chaotic urban growth, in 1916, New York City adopted the first zoning resolution of the nation. The 1916 Zoning Law precluded particularly tall or bulky buildings from preventing light and air from reaching the streets below them. It didn't impose height limits, but restricted skyscrapers through series of setbacks to a percentage of their lot size. These regulations resulted in the distinctive pyramidal, ziggurat-like shape of many Manhattan buildings (Figure 4.1).

The spectacular multitiered skyscrapers of the 1920s through the 1940s were a direct result of this resolution, which set an iconic design standard that is still widely implemented today across the globe.

Figure 4.1 Empire State Building, New York City. [View from], to Chrysler Bldg. and Queensboro Bridge, low viewpoint.

While other US cities started adopting the New York model, however, the model itself was the object of constant amendments to become more responsive to major shifts in population and building technologies. By mid-century, the prescriptions of the grid plan and of the 1916 zoning code proved obsolete and inadaptable to the changing times. Both plans were focused on the island of Manhattan, leaving areas in the outer boroughs "unrestricted" and thus subject to the vagaries of the market. Moreover, the 1916 zoning had been designed to potentially accommodate a population of 55 million residents, which never materialized, yet it didn't forecast the future expansion of automobile use, which would become a major concern of urban planning programs after the economic expansion of the post–World War II era. The "wedding cake" skyscraper form that resulted from the zoning regulation was also criticized, as developers claimed that, by requiring larger lots, it made buildings uneconomic and inefficient.

By the end of World War II, the city was badly in need of new instruments to guide its surging growth. Post–World War II planning policy at the federal level unleashed an era of massive public works that would have a tremendous influence on the urban form of large cities like New York. Title I of the Housing Act of 1949 introduced an "urban renewal" program that would forever reshape American urban areas: it established heavy federal subsidies to help cities acquire so-called blighted areas and clear them for public housing construction led by private developers and local authorities. Urban renewal plans made broad use of eminent domain to condemn private property for development purposes and often dictated the demolition of buildings and the forced relocation of residents in low-income and minority neighborhoods.[3] In those years, a new planning philosophy inspired by the theories of Swiss architect Le Corbusier was emerging, which promised to address the problems connected with the demographic explosion—acknowledging, and at the same time encouraging, the emergence of a new, automobile-oriented, utopian city. In New York, such "modernist" planning ideas were blatantly espoused by then park commissioner and "master builder" Robert Moses (1888–1981), who initiated an era of unprecedented public works (Figure 4.2). Throughout his 44-year-long career, from 1924 to 1968, spanning the administrations of five mayors and six governors, Moses headed 12 governmental entities and wielded more influence than anyone else in New York State. He was the force behind nearly every major city planning initiative in the city. He was responsible for the construction of the bridges, expressways, parkways, and highways that

Figure 4.2 Sponsor of Battery Bridge/*World Telegram & Sun* photo by
C. M. Spieglitz, 1939.

linked the five boroughs together; for the many public parks and for innumerable housing projects; and for a number of monumental architectural
complexes like the Lincoln Center, the UN headquarters, Shea Stadium,
the NY Coliseum, and the 1964–1965 World's Fair facilities.[4]

In the early 1960s, half a century after the enactment of the first zoning law,
a new zoning code was adopted. The zoning resolution approved in 1961 was
a response to a demographic increase from 5 million in 1916 to almost 8 million residents in the late 1950s, and acknowledged the growth of automobile
use and the demand for new mass transit routes, the spread of suburbanization, and the introduction of massive government housing programs. It was
designed to accommodate about 12 million residents (a more realistic down-
sizing compared with the projections of the 1916 code) and embodied a radical vision for a sprawling, automobile-oriented city. The resolution set limits
on use and bulk of buildings, mandated lower densities, and established parking requirements for all new residential developments outside of Manhattan.
It strictly divided New York City into residential, commercial, and manufacturing areas[5] and regulated building density through the introduction of

a floor-to-area ratio (FAR), a maximum ratio of permitted floor area based on the area of a zoning lot. The new regulations also eliminated the set-back, wedding-cake skyscraper to accommodate a new type of monolithic high-rise office building with large floors surrounded by public plazas: Le Corbusier's "towers in the park" visual aesthetics began to take hold even in the dense, chaotic island of Manhattan.[6] Across the city, vibrant communities were lost to towering public housing estates or nonresidential public works.

Gradually, Moses's reputation began to fade. In 1961, the publication of Jane Jacobs's seminal work *The Death and Life of Great American Cities* unleashed a heated urban planning debate that drew attention to the virtues of lively urban fabrics and respect for the human scale. Jacobs, a resident of a West Village that was moving away from its industrial past, led a vocal civic struggle against the principles of modernist orthodoxy and their failure to produce a healthy and vibrant urban environment (Figure 4.3). The opposition gained momentum over the demolition of one of the city's architectural jewels, Penn Station, completed in 1910. Its demolition was the catalyst for the enact-ment of the city's first architectural preservation laws in 1965[7] and prompted the opposition of a rising number of local activists against Moses's plans to

Figure 4.3 Mrs. Jane Jacobs, chairman of the Comm. to save the West Village holds up documentary evidence at press conference at Lions Head Restaurant at Hudson & Charles Sts/*World Telegram & Sun* photo by Phil Stanziola, 1961.

build an expressway across Jacob's Greenwich Village and the area today called SoHo. The city government eventually rejected the proposed expressway in 1962, signaling an epochal turn that would change urban planning approaches in New York City in the years to come. Public opinion was radically turning against the massive development schemes embodied in Robert Moses's agenda, and so had the interests of developers and government.

Revisions in the Late 1960s and 1970s

Combined with the growing concerns for preservation, the planning debate in the late 1960s and early 1970s started to focus on environmental issues that had been fully neglected by the 1961 resolution. In 1976, the state required all governmental agencies to assess the environmental impact of zoning changes before approval. In New York City, the City Planning Commission established a complex and lengthy procedure for the review of land use plans, known as the ULURP. Environmental review provisions required that proposals include a detailed study of their potential impacts, including effects on air or water quality, traffic, historic resources, socioeconomic makeup, and character of a neighborhood. Another important trend of the late 1960s was a growing engagement of local communities in issues affecting their neighborhoods, and their increasing involvement in local politics through participatory decision-making vehicles such as the city's community boards.[8] As discussed earlier, in 1975 the city was divided into 59 community districts, each represented by a board with up to 50 unsalaried members appointed by the borough president, with half nominated by city council members. Community boards were given an advising role in planning and on matters such as the city budget, city services, and facilities to be located in their community. Through public hearings where plans are discussed, the system brought ordinary citizens for the first time into the urban development arena. Community boards were given the opportunity to make recommendations before any city council vote, although, as already anticipated, these recommendations are nonbinding.[9] Some progress in community participation was introduced in 1989 during the Koch administration, when another charter revision legitimized, through section 197-a, community-based plans. This enabled community boards to prepare their own plans and submit them to the City Planning Commission and city council for approval. This at first seemed like a departure from top-down city planning, providing the opportunity for residents to have a voice in planning and land use decisions affecting their communities. But the City Planning Commission undermined any effectiveness of these plans, determining that their existence should not prevent city agencies from crafting their own plans for the same area—even if these include developments that are incompatible with the visions expressed in the community plan.[10] These rules, adopted in 1991, rendered community plans de facto powerless. As a result, it took 12 years before the first community-sponsored plan was submitted to the city. As of today, only a few community plans have been crafted, and they were either ignored or encountered numerous hurdles along the way.[11] According to a *City Limits* reporter:

> Again and again communities have invested years in putting together a 197-a plan only to see its acceptance by DCP essentially serve as a death certificate. In the nearly 20 years since the charter was changed, only 10 such plans have won the city's approval.... The city has at best ignored the results of the 197-a process, and at worst implemented zoning changes explicitly contravening their recommendations.[12]

Another reason for the ineffectiveness of 197-a plans lies in the fact that community boards have never been granted anywhere near the budget or resources necessary to craft plans. There are also great disparities in budget between community boards that serve wealthy neighborhoods and those serving low-income communities: as hiring lawyers and planning firms to initiate a 197-a plan can be very costly, affluent communities are more likely to develop such plans than poor communities. To make matters worse, community boards are not politically independent. As their members are appointed by the borough president, there have been numerous cases in which "Community Board members who voted against projects that were priorities for borough presidents found themselves removed from the board when the next round of appointments came."[13] Such was the case for members of a Bronx board who voted against the Yankee Stadium project, which was strongly supported by Mayor Bloomberg and borough president Adolfo Carrión, who were then disinvited from the board. Similar was the fate of five members of Community Board 6 in Brooklyn who had expressed reservations about the scale of the Atlantic Yards redevelopment plan: none of them were reappointed.[14]

First Amendments to the 1961 Zoning Resolution

Over the years the city's zoning resolution has incorporated several incentives, whereby certain height or setback restrictions could be waived if the developer agreed to provide or pay for public improvements, such as public plazas, parks, transit improvements, or affordable housing. The adoption of rezonings with provisions for affordable housing (also called "inclusionary zoning" programs) epitomized a major shift from the government-sponsored housing developments of the post–World War II era to a market-driven approach that has become dominant since the late 1970s. Inclusionary housing programs were formally introduced in the United States in 1975, but it was not until 1987 that such a zoning program was adopted in New York. Here, a specific program was applied to high-density housing areas (R 10 zones) and granted developers a floor area bonus in exchange for providing, or preserving, housing affordable to households earning up to 80% of the area median income (AMI). The affordable housing could be on-site or off-site (within the same community district or within a half mile of the subsidized development). Starting in the 1970s, "mixed-use zoning" areas, which integrated industrial and residential uses, were introduced in specific parts of Brooklyn, allowing for the expansion of manufacturing uses in districts that were once off-limits to the industry— the opposite of what is happening today, when former industrial areas across the city are being rezoned for residential uses. The first residential-industrial mixed-use zoning district was officially established in 1970 in the north side of Williamsburg, in Brooklyn. In Manhattan, on the other hand, in the late 1970s, contextual conversions from manufacturing to residential use allowed a generation of artists, squatters, and urban pioneers to legally live in the ex-industrial lofts of SoHo. In addition, in the 1970s, the city established a number of "special zoning" districts with their own unique regulations and prescriptions on land use. One such special zoning was adopted in 1967 to protect the Theater District in the area surrounding Times Square, where new office buildings were in strong demand at a time when theater culture was declining. The Theater District stretched from 57th Street to 40th Street, an area that once had bustled with legendary theaters, night clubs, and cabarets. It offered developers incentives in the form of floor area bonuses in exchange for the promise to build a theater as part of the project: it was not meant to prevent office expansion in the area, but to facilitate it while preserving the cultural charm of the district. By 1991, five theaters were built under this program,[15] indicating that, with a smart use of zoning amendments, efforts at maximizing the value of property could coexist with concerns for heritage preservation. The number of special zoning districts multiplied over the years. By 1991, New York City had 40 special purpose zoning districts to ensure up-to-date regulations for specific sites, including the Lower Manhattan Mixed Use District, the Garment Center District, the Broadway/Lincoln Center District, and Greenwich Street in downtown Manhattan. The enactment of so many special regulations resulted in a zoning ordinance that was becoming increasingly complex. By the 1990s, the continuous amendments had made the 1961 zoning resolution "a collage of ad hoc, jerry-built and thoughtful inspirations, grafted onto a long-disowned armature."[16]

From the Fiscal Crisis to the Giuliani Years: Toward Developer-Driven Planning

On the heels of New York's near bankruptcy in 1975, an aggressive private market was increasingly mobilized to guide the city's economic recovery. As private requests for development were increasingly guiding the pace of the urban agenda, governmental agencies narrowed their scope to that of technical facilitators of the private initiative.[17] Privately led development efforts, touted as the antidote to the failure of public government bureaucracies, were strongly encouraged and generously subsidized by government. With the creation of the Emergency Finance Control Board in September 1975, the City Planning Commission lost its control over the city's capital budget, and its resources and influence were severely diminished.[18] Meanwhile, new city agencies like the already mentioned Public Development Corporation (which in 1991 merged with the Financial Services Corporation to form today's New York Economic Development Corporation, or NYCEDC) were launched to increase revenues by spurring private development and selling city-owned properties to private developers. In the late 1980s, the city's very governmental structure was largely revised, as a 1989 charter revision gave the mayor and city council more power in land use decisions.[19]

In the Giuliani years, the use of amendments of the 1961 zoning code became unstoppable. The City Planning Commission under Chairman Joseph B. Rose adopted a staggering number of rezoning proposals across the city's five boroughs, covering more territory than all five previous mayoral administrations combined. One of the most remarkable was the rezoning of Times Square, which helped transform the legendary crossroad from a seedy center for erotic shops, game parlors, and peep shows to a district where media outlets and studios, theaters, financial companies, megastores, and restaurants were paramount. To cleanse the whole area, new strict zoning rules were introduced that banned erotic parlors and any other sex establishments in commercial and residential areas. In 1995, Giuliani also pushed for zoning amendments that would have made it easier for warehouse-style megastores such as Walmart to enter the city. Under the proposed plan, any store up to 200,000 square feet would have been able to open in manufacturing areas without a zoning exception. Although the plan was defeated in 1996, megastores have since then managed to find their way into the lucrative New York market, and by 1999, super-stores like Kmart, Home Depot, and Target had found their locations even in the dense island of Manhattan, for example in midtown, Chelsea, and even Harlem and the East Village. Another large rezoning plan approved during the administration of Giuliani was the 2001 rezoning of Long Island City, which allowed for towering high-rises on the waterfront in an area that had been traditionally devoted to manufacturing.[20]

In an effort to disentangle the growing hodgepodge of conflicting and overlying zoning regulations, in 1999, the Department of City Planning (DCP) under Chairman Joseph Rose proposed a "Unified Bulk Program" to "establish reasonable parameters for new development that give communities, developers and regulators a clear sense of what is and is not allowed in a given district, while allowing appropriate flexibility in the design of individual buildings."[21] The plan would have removed the "plaza bonus," a legacy of the 1961 zoning code that had resulted in many misused and unattractive public spaces, and would have set height limits in most areas of the outer boroughs. Most important, it would have made regulations more easily understandable to small developers who couldn't count on the services of major law firms to decipher New York City's maze of zoning ordinances. However, as they feared height limits would be an obstacle to development, the city's largest landlords and developers, united in the Real Estate Board of New York (REBNY), lobbied heavily against the proposal, which was never adopted.[22]

The Bloomberg Years:
The New "Power Broker"

Michael R. Bloomberg had begun his career as a partner at Wall Street investment bank Salomon Brothers in 1973. After being laid off from the firm in 1981, he used a $10 million liquidation package to create his own company, named Innovative Market Systems, which developed state-of-the-art terminals for business information for Wall Street executives. The company was renamed Bloomberg LP in 1987, and through the years it successfully expanded into a global financial data and media company. When Bloomberg decided to run for mayor of New York City in 2001, he used his own fortune (a staggering $73 million of his own money) to finance his campaign, which gave him a massive spending advantage over Democratic nominee Mark J. Green.[23] But despite outspending his opponent five to one, he was elected mayor of New York City with a narrow victory of 50% over Green's 48%.[24] Bloomberg was re-elected in November 2005 by a margin of 20%, the widest margin in history for a Republican mayor of New York. In 2008, in the midst of the Wall Street financial crisis, Bloomberg announced that he would seek to overturn the city's term limit law[25] to run for a third term in 2009, arguing that only his proven business leadership could help the city recover from the economic recession. The majority of the council voted to extend the limit to a third term, after defeating a proposed amendment to submit the decision to a public referendum. In 2009, despite having spent $90 million of his own fortune for its campaign, and outspending Working Families Party nominee and New York City comptroller Bill Thompson by 14 to 1, Bloomberg was re-elected for a third term in office only by a slight 5% margin.[26] Notably, the mayor didn't accept any financial contributions from third parties; he paid for his record-expensive political campaigns himself. However, Bloomberg managed to keep the nonprofit sector close to his side thanks to hundreds of millions of dollars in charitable donations to thousands of institutions,[27] and to curry favor even with those parties that could have opposed his agenda most aggressively:[28] when running for a third mayoral term in 2009, he notably asked some of the beneficiaries of his charity to support his bid for a third term.[29]

When Bloomberg took office in 2002, his net worth was $4.8 billion.[30] In just the 2007–2009 time span, he moved from 142nd to 17th on the list of the world's billionaires.[31] By 2016, with a net worth of $44.8 billion, he was the sixth-wealthiest person in the United States and the eighth wealthiest in the world.[32]

Reshaping the City for City Consumers

The dismissal of Rose's Unified Bulk Program proposal in 1999 had taught city officials that any attempt at a comprehensive overhaul of the 1961 zoning ordinances would be fought hard by the city's major real estate players. City officials had also understood that, in a fast-evolving city with a globalized property market, any form of static, comprehensive plan would become obsolete before its launch. Thus, with Bloomberg as mayor, the city decided once again to eschew a comprehensive overhaul of the 1961 code and focused instead on a meticulous process of amendments of zoning regulations on a case-by-case basis to keep up with the demands of new markets and consumers.

As Bloomberg took office in January 2002, he inherited the devastation of the 9/11 terrorist attacks, and the resulting loss of over 159,000 jobs and over 13 million square feet of office space in downtown Manhattan, the onset of a national recession, and a $4.8 billion budget deficit.[33] The new state of emergency resulting from 9/11 and the ensuing fiscal crisis led city officials and key business groups to invoke measures to retain firms and businesses that were leaving the city in throngs. Right upon taking office, the first concern of the mayor was to close the budget deficit caused by depressed tax revenues by curtailing spending on services while increasing property taxes. Soon after, Bloomberg engaged in a series of marketing campaigns to announce that New York was again "open for business after 9/11"[34] and channeled federal aid for reconstruction to initiate a new era of development across the five boroughs.

To New York's city producers, the launch of an aggressive urban development agenda was imperative if the city wanted to overcome its image crisis and start reattracting businesses.[35] To Bloomberg and his advisers, a successful development strategy had to be based on providing qualified companies with appropriate space and infrastructure, and providing their employees with attractive living environments, rather than focusing only on financial incentives to lure or retain big business in the city.[36] In his 2003 State of the City address, Bloomberg announced:

> We'll continue to transform New York physically—giving it room to grow for the next century—to make it even more attractive to the world's most talented people.... New York is the city where the world's best and brightest want to live and work. That gives us an unmatched competitive edge—one we'll sharpen with investments in neighborhoods, parks and housing.[37]

The production of a brand-new urban space would provide the appropriate environment for the favored class of city consumers: "This involved comprehensive planning for upscale residential projects, the creation of new and enhanced office districts, and improved parks (especially on the waterfront) and cultural resources that would appeal to the city's postindustrial denizens."[38]

Bloomberg gathered around him experienced executives, several of whom had worked for his firm Bloomberg LP, and restructured the city government according to a hierarchical model in which all agencies responsible for land use and economic development would be overseen by a single officer of his choice, the deputy mayor for economic development and rebuilding. In so doing, the mayor created a strong leadership model capable of coordinating and directing the efforts of multiple agencies toward specific development goals, expediting the process of adoption and implementation of an ambitious development agenda. For this crucial position, Bloomberg appointed Daniel Doctoroff, a millionaire investor whose background was in private equity investment. Doctoroff had been an active promoter of a New York City bid for the 2012 Olympic Games since the mid-1990s. Bloomberg appointed Amanda Burden, who had served on the CPC since 1990, as head of the DCP and chair of the City Planning Commission (CPC). From 1983 until 1990, Burden was vice president for planning and design of the Battery Park City Authority.

The mayor chose Andrew Alper as new president of the NYCEDC. Alper was a high-profile manager at Goldman Sachs and new to the world of public administration but, according to the mayor, an able negotiator with the business community: "exactly the right kind of guy to bring in companies to the city and to keep companies here."[39] The NYCEDC was internally restructured, and its operations expanded with the launch in 2002 of the Five Borough Economic Opportunity Plan, a visionary list of redevelopment priorities that set specific economic goals to bring the city through the downturn of the early 2000s. With all land use city agencies vertically reorganized under his direction, Bloomberg went on to lay out his grand visions for a brand-new city.

In the first years after 9/11, the population in the immediate area of the World Trade Center had strongly declined. As the 16 acres called Ground Zero belonged to the Port Authority, development on the World Trade Center site was controlled by the state, the newly created Lower Manhattan Development Corporation (a subsidiary of the Empire State Development Corporation), and Governor George Pataki. The Bloomberg administration thus refrained from playing a significant role in the development of Lower Manhattan and set its sights on other targets. While some former

Lower Manhattan residents had left the city altogether, many looked for new apartments in the outer boroughs or in uptown Manhattan. By the second quarter of 2003, Wall Street profits were rebounding, creating enough momentum to push development to other parts of the island and to the outer boroughs.

Bloomberg's Rezoning Machine in Action (Part I): "How NYC Won the Olympics"[40]

Daniel Doctoroff's proposed bid for the 2012 Olympics became the main catalyst for Bloomberg's massive rezoning agenda across the city. The Olympic bid was managed by NYC2012, a private nonprofit organization Doctoroff had founded in 1994, seven years before joining the Bloomberg administration. Doctoroff commissioned Alex Garvin, director of planning for NYC2012 since 1996 and former city planning commissioner, to develop a comprehensive plan for the whole metropolitan area that used the Olympics as the engine for moving along massive development projects across the city (Figures 4.4 and 4.5). Garvin's plan focused on seven areas

Figure 4.4 Midtown West, aerial, Hudson Yards.

Figure 4.5 The Olympic Village.

of the city that had long been targeted by the city as potential locations for new development.[41] These included the Far West Side of Manhattan, Brooklyn's East River Waterfront, Long Island City in Queens, the Flushing section of Queens, Harlem, the South Bronx, and downtown Brooklyn.

The focal point of the development plans would be a new stadium to be built on the Far West Side of Manhattan, an area that in the vision of Doctoroff and the mayor would be transformed into an extension of the Midtown Central Business District. The Olympic stadium would be built on a platform over the Long Island Rail Road yards (Hudson Yards) and would be the catalyst for the transformation of the Far West Side—a relatively undeveloped portion of Manhattan, once home to bustling manufacturing and garment industries—into a spectacular, high-density, mixed-use development. After the Games, the stadium would be used by the New York Jets and would serve also as a major expansion of the Jacob K. Javits Convention Center, located immediately to the north. In addition, there would be one new major rail line and an extension of the #7 subway line from Times Square west to 11th Avenue and to the Javits Center and the new stadium. After the Games, the subway extension would provide a steady connection to a brand-new part of midtown. Along the East River waterfront, in the largely vacant industrial area in the Hunters Point section of Queens, the plan forecasted a massive residential rezoning allowing for an Olympic Village with 4,400 apartments for athletes, trainers, and team officials, including recreational facilities and a long stretch of parkland along the waterfront.

After the Games, the Olympic Village would be transformed into a residential community with high-end apartment buildings on the waterfront. The Olympic plan also included a new park with an indoor volleyball arena in downtown Brooklyn; a rowing course in Flushing Meadows-Corona Park and a new aquatics center in Astoria, both in Queens; a new waterfront park for beach volleyball in Williamsburg, Brooklyn; a velodrome in the South Bronx; a marina along the coast of the Atlantic Ocean; an equestrian center on Staten Island; and the refurbishment of the historic 369th Regiment Armory in Harlem for boxing and rhythmic gymnastics.

The Olympic bid provided New York's city producers with a golden opportunity to articulate a bundle of different development visions into a comprehensive plan, as Garvin's plan included areas that had long been considered potential locations for new development: the redevelopment of the Far West Side, the expansion of the Javits Convention Center, and the extension of the #7 subway service line had been discussed since the times of Ed Koch. Other areas that had long been considered for development were the industrial waterfronts of Brooklyn and Queens. Furthermore, the strict timetable of the bidding process provided a much-needed "forcing mechanism"[42] to hard-push development that was long sought after, while overcoming potential community opposition and bureaucratic hurdles.

But despite the Bloomberg administration's and NYC2012's attempts to mobilize civic pride and public enthusiasm for the Olympic Games in favor of their development agenda, public opposition from residents in the areas earmarked for development mounted.[43] Fierce criticism was raised especially against the Far West Side plan for resembling the top-down, old-school urban renewal schemes of the infamous Moses era.[44] Critics argued that the construction of a publicly subsidized stadium and other facilities was less than desirable in a predominantly low- to medium-income community like Hell's Kitchen, and that it would heavily advance the gentrification of the neighborhood, displacing residents and businesses, and obliterating the little remaining affordable housing. By the early 2000s, gentrification was already well under way in the area, whose mix of warehouses, small-scale businesses, and housing units was slowly succumbing to a wave of luxury residential development. Since 1998, residents and businesses united in the Hell's Kitchen Neighborhood Association held community meetings to draft an alternative plan for the area,[45] which was submitted to the DCP and the local community board in 2004, but to no avail.

In 2005, when London was eventually chosen over New York as the site for the Games, the plan for the Olympic stadium fell apart. But the rezoning of the Hudson Yards area went on. In January 2005, the city rezoned the 32-block area from 28th to 42nd Street between 8th and 12th Avenues, including the eastern part of the rail yards, from industrial to residential and commercial use. On paper, the rezoning was a mixed-use rezoning allowing for both residential and manufacturing uses. In reality, however, its net impact was to displace manufacturing uses, as a conversion to residential uses granted much higher profits in such valuable properties in the immediate proximity of the Midtown Business District.[46] In 2009, the city also managed to rezone the western portion of the rail yards, totaling 60 blocks of rezoned area. The rezoning allowed for a cluster of condominium and office towers on the rail yards, the expansion of the Jacob K. Javits Convention Center, a waterfront park, plazas, and open spaces, creating 24 million square feet of office space and 13,000 residential units. In 2010, Related Companies signed a 99-year lease with the Metropolitan Transit Authority (MTA) for the 26-acre rail yard site for $1 billion. The massive plan, which is now carried on by Related and Oxford Properties, includes 16 spectacular towers with over 12,000 million square feet of office, residential, and retail space, 14 acres of public space, a public school, an art center, and a massive, high-end shopping concourse. The #7 line extension opened in 2015, and the first 52-story office tower at West 30th Street and 10th Avenue was completed in 2016. Construction also broke ground at the 750,000-square-foot retail complex, and at 30 Hudson Yards, which by 2019 will be the tallest tower to rise in the development.

Another massive rezoning plan that was pushed along by the city and later integrated into the Olympic bid was on the Vanderbilt Yards in Prospect Heights, adjacent to downtown Brooklyn and Fort Greene (Atlantic Yards). In the early 2000s, the area had seen a remarkable explosion of property values and had been rapidly gentrifying. In 2003, Forest City Ratner (FCR), one of the largest real estate development companies in the country, proposed a basketball arena as the centerpiece of a high-density redevelopment plan for the 22-acre area adjacent to the Atlantic Metro Terminal, which by 2003 was a mixture of low-scale walkups, small businesses, and vacant lots. Ratner proposed to build over a million square feet of office space, 8,500 housing units, and an arena above the rail yards. In FCR's initial plan, the arena would be used by the Nets, a Brooklyn team that FCR had purchased the same year. By 2004, however, Bloomberg announced a change to the

Olympic plan that included the yet-to-be-approved Brooklyn arena as the new venue for indoor games for the Olympics, allowing FCR to "wrap his venue in the Olympic flag" and granting government support to its development plans.[47] Using the Olympics to leverage state support, FCR managed to evade the local land use public review process by getting the Empire State Development Corporation (ESDC) to sponsor its project.[48] With the involvement of the ESDC, the plan could also count on government power to condemn private property that stood in the way of development.[49] The justification for eminent domain was "blight," but opponents of the plan charged that the site had been a victim of "developer's blight," as FCR had been purchasing several buildings and leaving them vacant or in a state of disrepair in expectation of a city rezoning.[50]

The loss of the Olympic bid in 2005 and the mounting local opposition didn't stop the plan, which was pushed forward nonetheless. Objections had focused mostly on the loss of almost 1,000 existing housing and businesses, and on the density of the project, which was deemed too high even by Manhattan standards. Most important, the use of eminent domain to condemn existing properties was contested as a violation of the New York State Constitution. Several lawsuits were filed by local groups, such as Develop Don't Destroy Brooklyn, charging FCR with abusing eminent domain for private benefit.[51] In spite of a strenuous opposition from local residents, the plan was approved in 2006. In March 2010, city officials broke ground on the $4.9 billion project. The arena, called Barclays Center, opened two years later. In 2012, FCR broke ground on the first tower, a 32-story residential tower at Flatbush Avenue and Dean Street. In June of 2014, FCR and Greenland, USA closed on a joint venture agreement to develop all future phases of the project, which will include around 6,430 housing units (both affordable and market-rate), 250,000 square feet of retail and 8 acres of public space. By 2016, six towers were on the rise in a completely redesigned neighborhood, now rebranded "Pacific Park" in an effort to purge the stories of past lawsuits and community opposition from the city's memory, while appealing to a hip population of moneyed newcomers.

In sum, by the time New York City lost its bid for the 2012 Olympics, a massive development machine had already been set in motion, which was destined to change the face of the city for good. For years, Bloomberg and Doctoroff had mobilized all city agencies to expedite project approvals on the Olympic timetable, regardless of whether New York would win the

bid or not. Although New York City ultimately lost to London, major rezoning plans had been adopted or were on their way to completion in almost
all of the areas included in the Olympic plan, allowing for "a comprehensive
rezoning of New York City in record time."[52] These included, besides the
Hudson Yards and Atlantic Yards areas, the massive rezoning of 43 blocks
at Hunters Point in Queens (approved in 2004), and of 184 blocks along
the Greenpoint/Williamsburg waterfront (approved in 2006), for high-
density residential uses. The South Bronx's proposed development of
Olympic facilities didn't come to light, but the Olympic plan provided
the pressure to push forward the redevelopment of the old Bronx Terminal
Market, which was substituted with the Bronx Gateway Center mall. Despite
fierce opposition from local merchants, the Gateway project was approved
in 2006 and the old market building was demolished shortly thereafter.
The Bronx Gateway Center opened in 2009 and was recently re-renamed
the Bronx Terminal Market.

Bloomberg's Rezoning Machine in Action (Part II): Undoing the Moses Legacy and the Rezoning "Czar"

It was the zealous activity of DCP Commissioner Amanda Burden, the
"rezoning czar," that helped transform Doctoroff's grand visions into concrete plans through a meticulous process of rezoning across the board, creating brand-new opportunities for high-end development where property
markets had long been dormant. It was under her direction that the DCP
initiated the major rezonings of the East River Waterfront (Williamsburg/
Greenpoint), downtown Brooklyn (Atlantic Yards), Long Island City in
Queens, and Hudson Yards on Manhattan's Far West Side. She has also been
responsible for the major rezoning plans in once-neglected neighborhoods
such as 125th Street in Harlem, Coney Island in Brooklyn, Port Morris in
the Bronx, and Jamaica in Queens.

It is common knowledge that the rezoning plans overseen by Amanda
Bloomberg have represented a radical backlash against the modernist
orthodoxy of the Robert Moses era.[53] According to the New Yorker, the
approach of the DCP under Amanda Burden has been based on "undoing
the Moses legacy"[54]: while Moses had planned for a future expansion of
the manufacturing sector, which eventually failed to materialize, Burden
has rezoned large swaths of declining manufacturing areas for residential

and commercial uses; while the "master builder's" approach to planning had neglected any effort at human-scale development, the DCP under Burden has prided itself for its fine-grained approach to urban design and its attention to the local character of neighborhoods. Burden's planning approach has expanded the territory of zoning regulations to include new tools: arts bonuses for builders who preserve or integrate cultural institutions in their developments, provisions to encourage bike lanes, incentives to neighborhood grocery stores providing fresh produce, and inclusionary zoning regulations to incentivize affordable housing production.

Burden, a talented planner and recipient of several planning and design awards (including the American Planning Association Award in 2006), has championed herself as an heir to Jane Jacobs's philosophy that favored the human scale of lively pedestrian environments over large-scale buildings isolated from the fabric of the city: "I like to say that our ambitions are as broad and far-reaching as those of Robert Moses, but we judge ourselves by Jane Jacobs's standards."[55] She has always been a vocal promoter of a vision of urbanity made of active streetscapes, diverse street fronts, and design elements that foster a vibrant street environment. Burden's vision of the city is a consumer-oriented one, in which urban planning and design can be mobilized to enhance "quality of life" assets such as amenable public spaces and vibrant pedestrian environments. It is a vision guided by a faith that a well-designed urban landscape can attract affluent city consumers and become a catalyst of economic growth: "Good design is good economic development," she said. "What I have tried to do, and think I have done, is to create value for these developers, every single day of my term."[56] Enough said. Along these guidelines, Burden has overseen and facilitated projects that have become successful catalysts for tourism, like the pedestrianization of portions of major New York City crossroads, starting with Times Square, parts of which have been turned into a pedestrian mall with chairs, benches, and café tables with umbrellas, or the refurbishment of the once-derelict High Line in Manhattan into a spectacular elevated park. Such radical transformation of Manhattan's streetscapes has been advanced through the operations of the Department of Transportation (DOT) under Commissioner Janette Sadik-Khan, who was appointed in 2007. The DOT's 2008 Sustainable Streets strategic plan for the city has promoted new rapid transit service routes in the Bronx, Manhattan, and Staten Island; added over 285 miles of on-street bike lanes; created new public spaces in key city locations; and launched the Public Plaza program, which by 2013 had resulted in the opening of 23 public plazas in busy intersections across the five boroughs.

Rezoning Across the Board

Amanda Burden has facilitated the re-engineering of the city as a postindustrial wonderland for the favored class of city consumers. Her rezonings have increased residential density, fostered mixed-use and transit-oriented development, created new attractive parks and open spaces, and led to a wholesale upgrading, and sometimes even over-designing, of the city's built environment across the five boroughs (Figure 4.6).

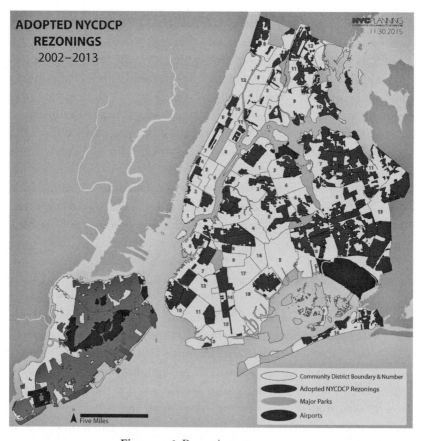

Figure 4.6 Rezonings: 2002–2013.

Under Burden, the DCP has implemented three different categories of rezoning plans: conversions of manufacturing areas (especially along the waterfronts) into mixed-use residential communities that also include office space and retail; upzonings in central business districts and along transit corridors, allowing for higher density of commercial and residential uses; and downzonings that limit development opportunities to preserve neighborhood character, mostly in lower-density neighborhoods outside of Manhattan.

Overall, city-led rezonings have increased residential capacity to accommodate the influx of more residents.[57] Upzoning plans to increase residential density have been mostly implemented in areas with significantly lower incomes compared to the city average, while downzoning plans were mostly launched in more affluent areas.[58] Generally, the DCP's strategy has been to balance upzoning to allow for greater density along major transit thoroughfares and downzoning to preserve the existing character of quiet residential side streets. This is the case of the Lower East Side/East Village rezoning plan in Manhattan and of the 125th Street plan in Harlem. In many cases, upzoning plans have brought about increased traffic, an overall decline in affordable housing options, and phenomena of displacement of long-time residents and businesses. In some cases, downzoning plans have been the result of political pressure from well-off, predominantly homeowner communities. Downzonings in affluent white communities like Riverdale have strongly limited development potential, thus contributing to preserve the character of the neighborhood, while upzoning plans, mostly adopted in working-class communities such as Greenpoint and Williamsburg, have been a boon to developers, and often a burden to long-time residents.[59]

Bloomberg's Rezoning Machine in Action (Part III): Rezoning with a Green Twist and PlaNYC 2030

During Bloomberg's first term in office, the city embarked on an aggressive development agenda based on rezoning plans scattered across the metropolitan area—with little, if any, regard for a comprehensive land use strategic vision for the city as a whole:[60] the Olympic plan, nothing more than an infrastructural program to accommodate the Games, was far from representing a strategic long-term vision to guide the future shape of the city. As public opposition against Bloomberg's visions showed no signs of abating, city officials acknowledged that the formulation of a long-term, comprehensive blueprint to articulate and guide development was necessary to win citizen support for their and the business community's growth agenda.

Consequently, in 2007, Bloomberg announced a "comprehensive" plan that would make New York "the first environmentally sustainable 21st-century city."[61] The plan, called "PlaNYC 2030: A Greener, Greater New York," was crafted by a department created ad hoc by the mayor and named the Office of Long-Term Planning and Sustainability (OLTPS), which was put in charge of coordinating the operations of major city agencies and departments to ensure its smooth implementation.

Most of PlaNYC was based on the guidelines that had been developed in the report prepared by Alex Garvin & Associates for New York City's Olympic bid, but "in a green dress."[62] Based on an expected population growth of one million residents by 2030, the plan outlined specific proposals on energy, land use, water supply, and housing. It suggested strategies for "smart" urban growth—including, among others, the retrofitting of city buildings to improve their energy efficiency; the remediation of Brownfield sites; the development of new land by building platforms over transportation infrastructure, such as rail yards, rail lines, and highways; the provision of energy efficiency tax rebates to building owners; the development of underused or vacant land along the city's 578-mile waterfront; and the conversion of unused schools, hospitals, and other municipal sites for new housing, parks, and public space. The plan also called for the reforestation of 2,000 acres of parkland by planting one million new trees, and aimed to improve streets and sidewalks by adding new pedestrian plazas in every neighborhood.

The proposal was commended for the broad range of innovative initiatives to reduce pollution, increase energy efficiency, and improve the quality of streets and parks. Among the supporters were environmentalists, business leaders, and private sector firms.[63] A report by the International Council for Local Environmental Initiatives applauded PlaNYC "as the gold standard for big-city sustainability plans." The report went on to praise the "methodical, transparent, and inclusive planning process" behind PlaNYC.[64] But, was it so? Although PlaNYC was in all effects a land use plan, it was crafted with no formal participation by the Department of City Planning or the City Planning Commission. Remarkably, it never went through a proper public review process; it was never presented to the city's 59 community boards, nor to the borough presidents or city council; and, most of all, there was no formal approval.[65] Noting that the plan was already being developed when the public outreach process began in the fall of 2006, activist and policy analyst Brian Paul argues that

> public participation in PlaNYC 2030 was an afterthought that was initiated only when the Mayor's office realized it was a necessary component of selling the plan to the public.... And the outreach efforts fell well short of best practices in public participation, involving only meetings with hand-picked non-profit organizations and policy experts and 11 public town hall presentations where the Mayor's slideshow was presented, followed by limited questions from the audience.[66]

Because of the lack of official approval, PlaNYC 2030 doesn't have the formal prerequisites to constitute a legally binding plan for the city. This notwithstanding, within one year of its release, over 97% of the plan's 127 initiatives were launched, initiating a wealth of legislation in a range of different sectors, from land use to water supply, from transportation to housing, from health to waste management.

Between Growth and Sustainability

PlaNYC was the result of environmental concerns as much as a tool to spur a new massive wave of property development and create new markets and services in a rising local and global green economy. Its growth-centered approach to sustainability has expanded opportunities for economic expansion, while providing the city administration with an alibi for development that is virtually unassailable, as new waves of profit-driven development efforts can be mobilized in the name of a collectively shared goal. After all, who wouldn't want a "greener New York"?

But some greenwashing can't conceal the reality of "business as usual" growth policies. These days, "sustainable development" blueprints can be easily incorporated into growth-prone entrepreneurial urban agendas, imbued as they are with market-centered notions of competitiveness, uneven development, and perpetual growth.[67] And PlaNYC is no exception: unsurprisingly, left out from Bloomberg's sustainability agenda is a tangible concern for the social impacts of growth.[68] It is not an accidental omission, however. The exclusionary, technocratic nature of the decision-making process behind PlaNYC 2030 has led to the formulation of a set of policies whose social costs and benefits are unequally shared. One of the explicit goals of PlaNYC 2030 is to make New York City competitive in the global market on the basis of "livability," a concept that the plan measures mostly in terms of "quality of life" assets for a new class of postindustrial consumers and green-tech hipsters. Unsurprisingly, one of the common lines of critique of the plan is that "even the most environmentally sensitive aspects of the plan, from park rehabilitation to bike lanes to tree planting, are in fact merely de facto pro-gentrification tactics that are increasingly remaking the city as a more active site of increasingly affluent consumption."[69]

PlaNYC's underlying assumption that green is good, as long as it doesn't prevent growth, brings about many contradictions, so that discussions of the negative impacts of the growth policies embedded in Bloomberg's green agenda (overdevelopment, housing price inflation, gentrification) are missing in the official debate around sustainability: the words "gentrification" and "displacement" are notably nowhere to be found in PlaNYC 2030.

PlaNYC 2030 and the Affordable Housing Crisis

The severe dearth of affordable housing is the most dramatic issue impacting the lives of middle- and low-income New Yorkers these days. In 2003, before embarking upon his aggressive development agenda, Bloomberg had launched an ambitious five-year plan to develop and preserve apartments for low- to middle-income residents, called the New Housing Marketplace Plan (NHMP). Initially, the plan forecasted the building or preservation of 65,000 units affordable to low- and medium-income families by 2008. In 2006, at the peak of the national housing bubble, the plan's goal grew to create or preserve 165,000 affordable homes by 2013, with the city aiming to build 92,000 units and preserve another 73,000. With the city's slide into a recession and the weakening of the local housing market in 2008, however, the plan was again modified: the deadline was extended to 2014, and a greater emphasis was put on preserving the affordability of 105,600 existing subsidized units, while the plan's building program was reduced to 54,500 units.

The NHMP was the city's largest investment in housing production since the Koch housing plan in the mid-1980s, and has been a powerful internal marketing tool to energize low-income New Yorkers and to persuade them that their mayor cared about their daily struggles. As for providing affordable housing for those households who needed it the most, however, the plan hasn't even come close to starting to solve the issue.[70] Between 2000 and 2007, New York City lost 569,700 units of affordable housing due to rent destabilization and rent increases.[71]

A 2009 study by the Center for an Urban Future showed that in the third quarter of 2008, only 10.6% of housing in the New York City region had remained affordable to people earning the median income for the area—the lowest share of any US city. According to the report, the lack of affordable housing forced thousands of New Yorkers to flee the city in search of less expensive urban areas during the booming years from 2002 to 2006.[72] In the midst of such a disastrous situation, the release of PlaNYC in 2007 gave housing advocates some ground for hope, as the plan promised to give a decisive boost to Bloomberg's NHMP by "making housing more affordable and more sustainable"[73] and by massively expanding opportunities for residential construction across the five boroughs. This would be achieved mostly by rezoning underperforming urban land to increase its residential capacity, and using inclusionary zoning to incentivize private development of affordable units in new market-rate residential developments. From 2007 to 2013, rezoning plans with affordable housing provisions have been approved for the East Village/Lower East Side, the Hudson Yards, West Clinton and various sections of Harlem in Manhattan; for Jamaica, Sunnyside-Woodside, Dutch Kills and Hunter's Point South in Queens; for Coney Island, Bedford-Stuyvesant, Boerum Hill and Fort Greene/Clinton Hill in Brooklyn; for Williamsbridge/Baychester, Hunts Point and the Lower Concourse in the Bronx; for St. George in Staten Island.

Looking back at the five years since the launch of PlaNYC, no one can deny the monumental proportions of the efforts made by the Bloomberg administration in terms of land use changes to maximize residential development. Since 2007, the city has created over 92,000 housing units and adopted 55 neighborhood rezonings. Overall, since Bloomberg's first term in office (2002), the city has completed 119 rezonings, covering over 11,000 blocks and 36% of the city's total built area.[74]

However, these endeavors haven't even come close to alleviating the dramatic shortage of affordable housing in New York City.[75] According to some commentators, these policies have instead exacerbated the dearth of housing options for low- and middle-income New Yorkers, contributing to reinforcing segregation along racial and social lines.[76]

From Bedford-Stuyvesant to Coney Island, from 125th Street in Harlem to the Lower East Side, the city's rezoning plans have increased residential density, fostered mixed-use and transit-oriented developments, created new parks and open spaces, and led to an overall upgrading of the city's physical

environment. But the re-engineering of the city as a postindustrial destination, and the resultant influx of new consumers, businesses, and spending
visitors, has triggered a tremendous increase in land values and rental prices,
sparking a speculative market that has resulted in a net loss of affordable
housing options for the city's middle- and low-income households. Yet city
officials never seemed concerned that their very housing agenda may have
been contributing to aggravate an already prohibitive housing market, making the shortage of affordable housing more severe and intensifying, rather
than alleviating, patterns of gentrification and displacement in the city.[77]

In fact, the Bloomberg administration has shown a rather cynical and
politically savvy approach to the question of affordable housing: while the
rezoning agenda incorporated in PlaNYC 2030 mobilized waves of luxury
construction across the metropolitan area for a new urban class of affluent
city consumers, the New Housing Marketplace Plan was the administration's
half-hearted attempt to alleviate the plight of middle-class New Yorkers
struggling with the consequences of the city's very growth policies.

Unsustainable Housing

Unaffordable housing means unsustainable housing, as there are far-reaching human and social costs associated with housing insecurity or poor
housing conditions.[78] We all know that the lack of affordable and decent
housing options and the resulting life instability can affect family relation-
ships, personal safety, access to employment and economic opportunities,
and even mental and physical health.[79] In 2016, Matthew Desmond's best-
selling book *Evicted* made us aware of the heartbreaking stories of families
on the edge of survival in the American Midwest, and of their struggles in
the face of housing insecurity and the threat of evictions.

Even though Bloomberg's plan included specific provisions to increase
affordability for middle- and moderate-income residents, the plan's solution
to the city's housing crisis was mostly based on the doctrine that increasing
the numerical supply of residential units would automatically drive down
housing prices[80]—the plan notably stated: "Without action our city's housing stock won't be as affordable or sustainable as it should be. That's why
we will expand our supply potential by 300,000 to 500,000 units to drive
down the price of land."[81] However, if "driving down the price of land" was
the aim, something must have gone very wrong. Land values and property
prices have only kept escalating, unsurprisingly. The truth is, the new market-rate residential developments have boosted property values in many

low-income areas that were once actually affordable. And simply increasing the numerical supply does not make a difference when the majority of new housing remains out of reach for local residents. In 2010, in the midst of a contracting economy, the PlaNYC 2010 Progress Report acknowledged the "mismatch between the housing that many New Yorkers, particularly low, moderate, and middle-income New Yorkers, need and can afford and the housing being constructed by the private market."[82] One year later, the 2011 Progress Report eventually admitted: "Making housing more accessible and affordable to New Yorkers requires more than increasing the overall housing supply. New market-rate housing generally serves higher income levels. While new inventory generally relieves pressures on costs in the long run, housing currently is too expensive for many New Yorkers."[83] Although thousands of housing units have been built, a less-than-minimal fraction of them are really affordable to those who need them the most. What's more, in the booming luxury market in the years before 2008 and right after 2009, very few developers took advantage of inclusionary zoning bonuses, while most found it more profitable to focus on the development of exclusively market-rate housing. As a result, by the end of 2011, only about 3,100 inclusionary housing units were started as part of the NHMP.[84] Furthermore, the prices of income-targeted housing in new developments are measured from the AMI of New York City as a whole. In many working-class neighborhoods where rezoning plans were implemented, however, the AMI was much lower, so that a large part of the newly produced "affordable" units remained far out of the financial reach of local residents.

Finally, all too often the rezoning plans spearheaded by PlaNYC have acted as a displacement tool in low-income neighborhoods where rehabilitations, conversions, and new constructions have threatened the livelihood of long-time residents, businesses, and industries. In many cases, the adoption of rezoning plans has brought about overnight surges in property values, pushing landlords to increase rents, evict their tenants, or demolish buildings to make room for more profitable developments. In many rezoned areas, extensive phenomena of "predatory equity" have been occurring, in which building owners and investors have illegally evicted hundreds of tenants to extract higher profits from their properties.

The New York City comptroller report showed that the percentage of New York City households that paid more than 30% of their income on rent has increased significantly in the last three decades: it rose from 39% in 1980 to 41% in 2000. But the steepest increase occurred during the first 8 years of the Bloomberg administration (2002–2010), when the number of households living in nonaffordable housing reached 49% of the population. In 2010, almost 30% of all New York City households spent over 50% of their income on rent. In addition, nearly 20% of all households in the city spent more than 75%—almost all of their income—on rent.[85] This decrease in affordability reflected the steady increase in rental prices during the Bloomberg years. From 1980 to 2000, the percentage of apartments that were unaffordable to households earning the median income was at around 20%. But by 2010, almost 40% of all rental units had become unaffordable to families earning the median income.[86]

Bloomberg's "luxury city" has been expanding unrelentingly out of Manhattan into the outer boroughs, despite the financial crisis of 2007–2008 and the following recession. After a brief halt in 2008, high-end real estate development was back on its feet in no time by 2009–2010 and focused mostly in the outer boroughs, especially along the waterfront areas of Queens and Brooklyn. The boom in the luxury housing market has been paralleled by the loss of thousands of units of housing affordable to middle- and lower-income New Yorkers due to conversion of low-income housing units into priced condos, expiring rent stabilization programs, and inadequate tenant protection laws. Since Bloomberg took office in 2002, any effort at bringing in new affordable units has been far outweighed by the loss of hundreds of thousands of affordable apartments due to gentrification and rent deregulation, as innumerable units that received some form of federal assistance were taken out of subsidy programs and converted into market-rate apartments in expectation of higher returns. Low-income residents who are unable to afford escalating housing costs are oftentimes left with no other choice than to end up in the city's homeless shelter system. Under Bloomberg, homelessness in New York City constantly escalated, reaching the highest levels ever recorded since the Great Depression of the 1930s, with over 50,000 homeless people sleeping each night in the New York City municipal shelter system by March 2013[87]—a tragic record that only the de Blasio administration has been able to surpass.

The continuing upward trend in rents (in a city where 68% of the population rents homes, compared to 33% nationwide) and the difficulty of finding available housing options is a dilemma that Bloomberg's approach was structurally unable to solve. The city has been steadily losing more affordable units than it gained under the NHMP and PlaNYC combined: by the end of his tenure, the mayor's plans didn't even come near to closing the gap between demand and supply for affordable housing in the city.[88]

"Gold Standard of Sustainability" or "Business as Usual" in Green Clothing?

On October 29, 2012, Hurricane Sandy wreaked havoc across the East Coast, devastating homes and infrastructures along the New York and New Jersey shores, and flooding large sections of Lower Manhattan, including Battery Park and the Ground Zero construction site, Queens, and Brooklyn, with particularly severe disruption at Coney Island and the Rockaways. The East River overflowed its banks, flooding subway tunnels and causing the worst damage in the history of the New York City subway system.[89] On November 26, Governor Cuomo estimated costs to New York State at $42 billion, claiming that Sandy had had an even greater economic impact than Hurricane Katrina because of the denser population in the New York City area.[90] In the aftermath of these tragic events, criticism was voiced when Mayor Bloomberg promptly announced that the disaster would not deter the city from pushing for further development along the city's shoreline: "People like to live in low-lying areas on the beach, it's attractive. People pay more, generally, to be closer to the water even though you could argue they should pay less because it's more dangerous. But people are willing to run the risk."[91] Although he acknowledged the necessity to limit future damage by strengthening building code standards for flood protection in these areas, the mayor played down the necessity of undertaking major infrastructural investments to mitigate storm surges, so that future investments in the city's exclusive waterfront properties would not be inhibited.

Many of the development areas incorporated into PlaNYC through the Vision 2020: NYC Comprehensive Waterfront Plan, the 10-year plan for the city's 520 miles of shoreline released in 2011, are located in high-risk areas for flooding—the so-called Zone A evacuation areas.[92] Despite repeated warning reports of rising sea levels and potential storm surges on the city's coastline going back at least a decade,[93] the city never questioned the validity of developing along the waterfronts, one of the main cornerstones of PlaNYC. In the aftermath of Sandy, critics questioned once more whether further development along the city's waterfront was still a desirable choice for the city.[94] But the mayor's "business as usual" response to the tragic events raised the question of whether the city's sustainability vision only goes as far as its quest for growth allows. The mayor's sustainability plan is, after all, an agenda for growth. The tension between growth and sustainability, however, is a highly controversial conundrum in the debate around sustainability. In 1993, Herman Daly and Kenneth Townsend argued that growth is inherently unsustainable and that the notion of "sustainable growth" is simply an "impossible theorem."[95] According to their view, development can be sustainable only as long as it doesn't imply growth. On the opposite side, in its 2011 report "Towards a Green Economy: Pathways to Sustainable Development and Poverty Eradication," the United Nations Environment Program (UNEP) declared that economic progress and environmental sustainability are not mutually exclusive, and that "the greening of economies need not be a drag on growth."[96]

Striking a balance between economic growth and environmental sustainability may prove challenging, however. Bloomberg's agenda, which seeks to balance urban growth with concerns for environmental preservation, has been well received among the business community because of its very unthreatening stance toward development. Sustainability, according to Bloomberg's agenda, can thrive in a competitive, growth-oriented framework of governance where design, technological innovation, and "smart" planning, coupled with incentives to "green" businesses, will do the job of preserving the environment. New York City's "green" agenda has also been a response to the demands of new markets and consumers: by physically transforming the city, it has acknowledged as much as it has facilitated the rise of a postindustrial, eco-friendly and consumer-oriented city. The priority given to high-end housing production has encouraged the development of new glitzy residences in once-disadvantaged neighborhoods, in some cases carving brand-new residential enclaves out of existing communities and remodeling large swaths of New York City's low-income districts as fashionable playgrounds for the new hordes of green-savvy consumers, but hasn't been able to relieve the lack of affordable housing that plagues the city's low and middle classes. Unsurprisingly, the mayor's sustainability approach has been criticized for being "merely another wolf in green clothing, or what environmental expert Susan Owens calls 'rhetoric plus business as usual.'"[97] Although its many environmental efforts are commendable, it does not ensure that new growth will generate equal opportunities for all New Yorkers. PlaNYC is an agenda that, while striving to find market solutions to balance economic growth and concerns for environmental preservation, fails to address issues that are of major concern among the city's most vulnerable residents, like the need for decent and affordable housing. The costly upzonings on flood-prone land and the rise of luxury residential projects in once-bustling manufacturing and working-class districts, raise the issue of whether a "green" New York can be at all sustainable and affordable to most New Yorkers.

Rezoning NYC: Slogans Versus Hard Facts

Citizen Participation

First off, we start by listening to communities, spending time with them, and walking neighborhoods, to understand what makes them special, what challenges they face and what opportunities exist. Then, as planners, we develop detailed neighborhood plans. We strive to make these plans understandable with three-dimensional drawings illustrating exactly how proposed rules would work, so communities can understand and fully participate in the planning process.[98]

The official narrative about the making of rezoning plans in the Bloomberg years was filled with stories of community involvement in the planning process. Amanda Burden stated on several occasions that the city's approach to zoning was based on listening to the needs of communities and neighborhoods. But was it? In too many cases, the concerns of community boards have been downplayed, and their recommendations haven't been incorporated into the final plans. All too often residents, grassroots organizations, and advocacy groups have claimed that their demands fell on deaf ears. This was particularly the case throughout the Hudson Yards and Atlantic Yards decision-making processes, as we saw earlier. In the case of the Coney Island rezoning, the local community board, together with numerous advocacy groups, urged the DCP to correct its plans for luxury high-rise developments in the heart of the amusement district, but all of their requests remained unanswered, as we will see in chapter 5. Similar was the fate of community recommendations during the making of the rezoning plan for 125th Street in Harlem. Here, Community Board 10 requested height limits on the main strip at 160 feet and the guarantee that a substantive amount of really affordable housing for low-income households would be included. Despite negotiations between the City Planning Commission and city council, buildings were allowed to rise to 190 feet. Moreover, since the city incorporated a voluntary incentive for inclusionary zoning, no guarantee has been given to the community that affordable housing units would eventually be produced.

Affordable Housing

> We are working to create a more inclusive city, with economic opportunities for everyone, more affordable housing, a healthy environment to sustain us, and an improved quality of life in revitalized neighborhoods throughout the five boroughs.[99]

The official narrative around development through rezoning was centered on the promise that rezoning plans would provide much-needed affordable housing. During the years of Bloomberg, the city expanded the inclusionary housing program for areas being rezoned to medium- and high-density residential uses and included an inclusionary zoning tool in the rezoning plans for Williamsburg and Greenpoint. Since then, inclusionary zoning was incorporated into many of the rezoning plans adopted by the city, where developers were usually granted a bonus of 20% additional floor area if they agreed to make 20% of the homes "affordable." Amanda Burden declared that "ensuring and encouraging affordable housing for all New Yorkers and maintaining New York's economic diversity is one of the most important planning challenges facing New York City" and presented the inclusionary zoning tool as "a way of mitigating some of the displacement of New Yorkers who might otherwise be forced out by rising land prices and an ever-increasing pool of wealthier tenants and buyers."[100] But the inclusionary tool has proven ineffective in creating a barely adequate amount of housing affordable to residents. First of all, the voluntary nature of the program meant that affordable units could be built or not, at the sole discretion of the developer. Second, most of the units that have been actually produced under this program were never meant to be affordable to those who most needed them in the first place. Each year, the US Department of Housing and Urban Development (HUD) establishes affordability standards that are based on the median family income of entire metropolitan areas, and this number is used to determine eligibility for affordable housing programs. But the New York City region includes some of the wealthiest counties in the nation, so that the AMI has very little to do with the actual wealth of New York City's residents, and particularly of those living in working-class neighborhoods undergoing rezoning like parts of Harlem, Brooklyn, and Queens. Today, New York City's AMI is $90,600 for a family of four. To be considered low income, a family of four has to earn up to 60% of AMI, or $54,360—a figure that would be considered comfortably middle class in most cities across the US. In the New York City region, families making $149,490 a year, which is 165% of AMI, are considered middle income, and as such are eligible for middle-income housing programs.[101]

It is no wonder, then, that of the several thousand housing units built during the Bloomberg years, just a tiny fraction was really affordable to residents struggling to make ends meet, particularly in poor areas of Harlem and Brooklyn where the average income is slightly over $20,000. According to the Independent Budget Office's report on the mayor's housing plan, of the 124,400 housing units that were built by 2012, only 15% percent have been reserved for low- and middle-income groups: this corresponds to about 18,600 units of affordable housing to date, against 75% of units set aside for upper-income households.[102]

Despite these hard facts, the promise of affordable housing through the inclusionary zoning tool has been sold by the city for years as an alibi to justify more development, while making it more palatable to the communities involved.

Mixed Use?

> Housing alone isn't enough to maintain New York's economic diversity and vibrancy. Mixed use development is essential, as is ensuring the health of the city's neighborhoods and commercial, cultural and manufacturing districts.[103]

The narrative of "mixed use" development through rezoning was centered on compensating the "mono-functionality" of industrial districts through the addition of a residential component. In too many cases, however, the net impact of such mixed-use rezonings has been to encourage the near obliteration of former manufacturing areas to make room for a new mono-functionality, only this time made of outright luxury residences. This was remarkably the case of large portions of the Williamsburg, Greenpoint, and Redhook waterfront areas. As Angotti argues:

> The problem is, the new mixed-use zones allow for both residential and industrial uses to compete with one another. But in a hot market, like the one in Greenpoint and Williamsburg, no developers in their right mind would build for industrial tenants when they can sell or rent residential property for 10 times the price. In effect, the mixed-use zoning was a back-door residential rezoning.[104]

In these areas, where factories and houses had stood side by side for decades, land use changes to mixed use have opened the door for large residential projects that have displaced hundreds of manufacturing firms for good.[105]

Preservation

> We have introduced "Contextual Zoning" districts to ensure that growth won't mean the out-of-scale over-development of some of New York truly unique neighborhoods like the Lower East Side, Coney Island, Park Slope, or Greenpoint-Williamsburg, to name a few.[106]

Along the city's shores (particularly in Williamsburg and Greenpoint), upzoning plans have facilitated the construction of gargantuan 30- and 40-story residential towers with pricey waterfront views that have limited access along the water's edge and created a wall between the shoreline and the blocks of 3- or 4-story walkups that lay behind the towers.[107]

In other districts traditionally dominated by low- to midrise buildings, rezoning plans have incorporated height caps meant to protect the human scale of the neighborhoods. But all too often these restrictions have been of little use, as the increased allowable density has encouraged property owners to demolish smaller buildings and replace them with taller ones, even under the new height limits. This is what happened with the rezoning of 125th Street in Harlem: even without explicit height limits, most commercial buildings along the thoroughfare were predominantly low-scale. This was because, despite the lack of specific height caps, the 1961 zoning had implicit restrictions on floor areas that in practice prevented the proliferation of super-tall structures in this area.[108] After the 125th Street rezoning passed in 2009, many of these low-scale buildings were demolished in preparation for taller buildings.

Unlocking Real Estate Through Rezoning

As is now clear, zoning is not just some gibberish for urban planners and government technocrats. It is a powerful tool that directly affects our daily lives.

Zoning can establish restrictions on urban development and capital investment as much as it can endorse and activate them. In areas that are not performing for capital as they should, rezoning is "a device that unlocks value,"[109] a value that was dormant with old zoning regulations and that can be reawakened by changing the rules. For instance, the rezoning of a declining industrial area into a high-density residential community loosens the regulatory barrier that prevented lucrative development of land whose value was "locked" because of the old manufacturing-only zoning rule.

As such, rezoning has a crucial role in translating the dictates of capital in the urban environment, as it allows capital to conquer more and more of the urban space we inhabit. Neil Smith called "rent gap" the hiatus between the ground rent in a disinvested area and the potential ground rent that could be accumulated by maximum exploitation of the land with the most profitable uses.[110] The devaluation of land in neglected neighborhoods allows investors and developers to purchase property for relatively low prices and to evict tenants or demolish old buildings in expectation of future development. Once the government jumps in with a rezoning to more profitable uses, the developer can proceed to ignite development in the hopes of extracting the maximum profit from the land he or she acquired. In other words, rezoning can create the material conditions (providing the legal and administrative framework) under which the "excavation of value" by land owners and developers becomes feasible and profitable.[111] Quite ironically, the systematic rezoning of city land has been at times contested by the real estate lobbies and their advocates as antidevelopment because of its insistence on height limits or other strict design requirements. In reality, rezoning has been a tremendous ally to New York City's development industry. By targeting unproductive areas and re-engineering them to cater to new city consumers, the DCP's rezoning agenda has opened innumerable new avenues for profitable investment in communities that were once off-limits to investment. Even though only some of the rezoning plans implemented by the DCP have taken the form of upzoning, these have been concentrated in disadvantaged neighborhoods whose initial land values were relatively low, and where the expectations of returns from development were therefore particularly high. In so doing, rezoning has expanded the geographical scopes of property investment and development to unprecedented extents, facilitating the "mobilization of urban real-estate markets as vehicles of capital accumulation,"[112] and paving the way for one of the biggest building booms in the history of the city. While rezoning policies have been a boon to the development community, however, they have directly or indirectly harmed the most vulnerable New Yorkers. These are mostly low- to middle-income households and small independent businesses and manufacturing firms that have been priced out of their neighborhoods in the aftermath of rezoning actions, or whose survival in areas undergoing rezoning is under threat.

The "G" Word: Rezoning as a Blueprint for the Gentrification of New York City

Condominium high-rises sprout like weeds along the East River waterfront in Williamsburg. Longtime Harlem residents watch newcomers—often young, affluent and white—sink into the overstuffed couches of the new cafes and coffee shops along 125th Street, the main street of Black America. Owners of small businesses on the dirt and pothole-ridden streets of Willets Point worry they will lose their location, their customers and their livelihood.[113]

Although the term "gentrification" is rarely, if at all, mentioned in policy documents or official statements, the DCP's rezoning agenda has been in fact a blueprint for the gentrification of New York City. By encouraging "mixed communities," "green developments," and "improved public space," it has advanced processes of physical upgrading of once-disadvantaged neighborhoods to make them more attractive to wealthier groups of city consumers.[114]

During Bloomberg's 2002–2013 rezoning wave, gentrification phenomena have been observed in almost every area rezoned by the DCP. In a vicious circle, gentrifiers have become at the same time displacers and displacees: while skyrocketing rental and property prices forced less competitive Manhattanites to look farther away for affordable solutions, they contributed to the displacement of more vulnerable residents in the outer boroughs. Farther afield from Manhattan to Williamsburg, from Williamsburg to Bushwick, from Bushwick to Bedford-Stuyvesant, rezoning has triggered a worrying spiral of displacement of weaker households and businesses that has severely jeopardized the social stability of neighborhoods.[115] And new waves of displacement will soon be occurring in more of the outer boroughs, where a new storm of rezoning plans announced by Mayor de Blasio have already unleashed a speculative craze that will hit residents hard in working-class neighborhoods from East Brooklyn to the South Bronx.

The Social and Economic Costs of Displacement

Improvement of neighborhoods—some people call it gentrification—provides more jobs, provides housing, much of it affordable, and private investment, which is tax revenue for the city.[116]

"Displacement is vital to an understanding of gentrification," writes critical geographer Tom Slater,[117] especially at a time when policymakers try to de-emphasize the class dimension of urban development, and when "stealth forms of gentrification have worked their way into planning manifestos, regeneration proposals, and private market initiatives to maximize profits from residential turnover."[118] Yet, despite the evidence of a causal relationship between the adoption of rezoning plans and the hardships of vulnerable residents, the class nature of the city's rezoning strategies is notably hidden in the public discourse around development. Imbued as they are with positive and morally persuasive notions of "sustainability," "diversity," "affordability," "social mixing," and so on, these official slogans for growth try hard to conceal the social inequalities that development brings about. Gentrification gradually leads to a wholesale social re-engineering of neighborhoods, as more affluent social groups displace less affluent ones who are forced out because they can no longer afford to live in the area.[119] The exorbitant increase in housing values threatens renters on a fixed income, as soaring rents push housing in the neighborhood out of their reach. And for those with low incomes who manage to stay, life isn't rosy: for low-income homeowners who do not wish to sell, survival in a gentrifying neighborhood can imply facing the cost burdens of escalating property taxes they cannot afford; to tenants, it may mean resisting harassment and threats from landlords who will do anything to empty their units in expectations of higher returns from more affluent occupants. The most vulnerable leave the city altogether or end up in the city's shelter system or in the streets.[120] For others, survival in the neighborhood sometimes means developing adaptive strategies like doubling up in a single housing unit with friends or relatives, accepting a substandard quality of living, or illegally subletting rooms to strangers to afford escalating rents.[121] Formal or informal community networks of mutual support also dissolve in the wake of displacement. Services and businesses that long-time residents relied on can become unaffordable to them or disappear altogether, making life harder for those who remain. In an increasingly unaffordable housing environment, illegal settlements and phenomena of overcrowding in tiny apartments have provided the essential minimum to house a growing force of low-wage laborers who work in the city. In the Bloomberg and de Blasio years, cases of low-income New Yorkers who commute even two to three hours a day from their neighborhoods in Queens or East Brooklyn to work as secretaries, cashiers, cooks, cab drivers, nannies, and cleaning ladies in Manhattan have become the norm.

Rezoning and Residential Displacement

The rezoning has been a nightmare here in Riverdale. My neighborhood … has been scarred by ugly, too-tall, garish and unaffordable (to me or any of my neighbors) condos and co-op buildings.… I don't think South Riverdale needs more wrong, inappropriate development along these lines. We need practical, affordable housing for teachers, nurses, city workers, office folks and artists etc.[122]

My neighborhood of the Bowery experienced open season for high rise condo and hotel construction.There was a building near mine (we've lived here 30 years) that was torn down to create a "green" hotel.The construction destabilized a small building that housed two small businesses and now both sites are abandoned.… I don't think Bloomberg actually understands something basic about what a neighborhood is both as a reliable economic engine and as a center for human gathering.[123]

The main forces of displacement of the most vulnerable residents in rezoned areas have been the rising housing values and the staggering number of landlords opting out of publicly subsidized rent protection programs in expectation of higher profits. In downtown Brooklyn and in Hell's Kitchen, for instance, the net effect of rezoning has been a sharp increase in land values, which has become a major engine of displacement of old tenants, as increased allowable densities and heights have encouraged landlords to demolish swaths of old walkups to make room for high-rise condominium towers.

As already mentioned, in too many cases "inclusionary zoning" incentives, supposed to make the construction of affordable housing more palatable to developers, have produced very meager results in terms of housing affordable to those who really need it. Plus, since the standards of affordability of new housing are calculated based on the AMI, even when "affordable" housing was created, it acted as a proper displacement tool in areas whose residents didn't make an income that qualified them to receive the newly produced "affordable" housing. In Williamsburg, the 2005 rezoning pushed land values to the sky: land prices went up 500% from 2002 to 2005, in anticipation of the rezoning.[124] Here, most developers produced a range of exclusive units for upper-income single or couple households, mainly geared to affluent Manhattan transplants— "a far cry from the needs of many of the neighborhood's existing residents."[125]

Rezoning and the Displacement of Manufacturing

New York City's shift from a manufacturing center to a postindustrial global capital in the post–World War II era has brought about a sharp decline in blue-collar employment. In the late 1960s, New York City was still a major hub of apparel manufacturers, while other leading employers were printing and publishing companies. Between 1969 and 1999, however, due to delocalization of production and disinvestment inland, manufacturing employment in New York City fell 68%.[126] The 1961 zoning resolution didn't anticipate such a remarkable decline, and by the early 1990s, vast amounts of city land (particularly along the city's waterfronts) were still zoned for manufacturing and port-related activities, although they were becoming less and less relevant for the city economy.

In 1993, the City Planning Commission conducted an extensive review of industrial areas in New York City and recommended that future land use policy encourage the growth of the finance, insurance, and real estate (FIRE) sectors at the expense of manufacturing areas in these areas.[127] In the Bloomberg years, with Garvin's Olympic plan and later with the release of PlaNYC 2030, government policy became even more explicit in furthering and accelerating the transition from an industrial to a postindustrial urban landscape, targeting manufacturing areas across the five boroughs for mixed-use development to provide prime office space for service-related companies and hip housing environments for their employees.

Although not as central to the city's economy as it once was, manufacturing is still an active sector that provides a large pool of employment opportunities for working-class New Yorkers. In 2011, it accounted for over 16.3% of citywide employment, and 25% of employment outside of Manhattan.[128]

But the survival of a strong industrial sector never was among the main concerns of city government, and particularly of the Bloomberg administration, which instead used rezoning as a weapon against manufacturing and encouraged the quick transition of former industrial areas to brand-new postindustrial residential environments. Between 2008 and 2012, the manufacturing sector in New York lost 74,000 middle-wage jobs, compensated by a gain of 194,000 jobs in low-wage service industries.[129] By 2015, with around 78,000 jobs, employment in the manufacturing industries had sunk to just 2% of the city's economy, down from almost 33% in 1950.[130]

But there is a difference between processes of deindustrialization that result from unavoidable global economic shifts and local industrial displacement that results directly from specific land use policies.[131] In New York City, both elements have been at work. In addition to global economic shifts (globalization and the outsourcing of cheap labor to third-world countries), rezoning actions have directly contributed to the wholesale displacement of manufacturing businesses, especially in the outer boroughs.

Today, the Brooklyn–Queens waterfront is undergoing one of the most spectacular transformations in the city's history (Figure 4.7). What was once a vastly industrial landscape is being transformed into a high-density, luxury residential environment complete with waterfront parkland and promenades. In her investigation of industrial displacement in Williamsburg, scholar Winifred Curran reports of small manufacturers in the neighborhood being actively displaced "through buyouts, lease refusals, zoning changes and increasing rents."[132] As land values escalate together with property taxes and rental costs, many businesses decide to shut down or downsize because of soaring costs, and many are bought out by landlords anxious to empty their buildings, while those who own the buildings in which they are located often become developers themselves and convert their establishments into residential uses. Some other businesses are harmed even when they are not directly threatened with physical displacement—for instance, when other businesses to which they are related for their production network, or their very customers, are forced to leave.[133] The in-moving of new hordes of city consumers in once industry-dominated areas is also a major factor of industrial displacement, as industrial warehouses turn into hip loft apartments or are simply demolished for new residential construction. Before the

Figure 4.7 The Williamsburg waterfront in 2014.

Williamsburg/Greenpoint rezoning, as the neighborhood was experiencing a first wave of residential gentrification, it was common for landlords to vacate manufacturing establishments to extract higher returns through residential conversions. But, with new regulations enabling much higher densities of residential development, the adoption of the 2005 rezoning has only exacerbated this trend.

Rezoning and the Displacement of Independent Businesses

As I watch the luxury high rise buildings sprout in this neighborhood, and the Walgreens and CVSs, Chain Designer stores replace the small drugstores, galleries and individually owned shops that made the East Village so vibrant and desirable, I find myself grieving over the loss of community and culture here.... The same has been happening in Williamsburg, in Harlem, all over the city. It glitters now, more than ever, but the communities are dying.[134]

I live in North Chelsea, or what I call Noche because it's become so dark with all the 33 story hard-front luxury rentals that have gone up in the last 10 years. One a year—the construction hasn't stopped since I moved in 10 years ago. The buildings have a massive and bland character, and invite multinational—not local—shops.[135]

The last 15 years have been a nightmare for small businesses in New York. According to the federal Small Business Administration (SBA), during the second Bloomberg term the number of small-business loans in New York City plummeted 500%, from 4,012 in the 2006–2007 fiscal year to 669 in 2009. In the same time span, the number of commercial eviction warrants amounted to nearly 29,000, indicating the difficulties business owners had keeping their stores alive in the city (Figure 4.8).[136] The recession sparked by the outbreak of the 2007–2008 financial crisis was not the only reason for the plight of small businesses in the city. Remarkably, the greatest turnover was to be found in gentrifying areas where commercial rents escalated while changing demographics brought a brand-new population of consumers.[137]

A rapidly gentrifying area, the Lower East Side of Manhattan was rezoned by the DCP in 2008. That year, a report by Good Old Lower East Side found that almost half of small local businesses surveyed in the area were facing increasing rents (Figures 4.9 and 4.10). Nearly one-third identified rising commercial property rents as the "greatest challenge" to their survival.[138]

At Coney Island, the adoption of a rezoning plan in 2009 has opened the way to a destructive wave of demolitions that has displaced dozens of

Figure 4.8 Shut-down storefronts in Bedford-Stuyvesant, 2007.

Figure 4.9 "Out of Business" sign at a store on Delancey Street, in the Lower East Side, 2008.

Figure 4.10 New luxury high-rise residential developments in the Lower East Side, at East Huston between Orchard, Ludlow, and Essex Streets, in 2014.

long-existing businesses. While the legendary Astroland amusement park was shut down and its land sold, dozens of other active and beloved independent businesses, some of which were in place for over 40 years, have been evicted, their premises vacated, and their buildings demolished or replaced by new corporate establishments. Similar was the fate for 125th Street in Harlem, where many businesses that had been around for years were displaced right before or right after the rezoning plan was adopted. In post-rezoning Williamsburg, there was a tremendous increase in lifestyle businesses catering to the new hipsters (vegan restaurants, studio galleries, apparel stores, beer gardens, and yoga studios), paralleled by a steep decline in hardware stores and small grocery stores that were once patronized by the old residents. The main force behind the displacement of less upscale businesses in the area has been the remarkable increase in property values, which has pushed rents through the roof: between 2003 and 2007, commercial property values in the trendiest area of Williamsburg, the Bedford Avenue corridor, increased by 224%.[139] Further south, downtown Brooklyn has been completely revolutionized by the 2004 rezoning. Here, new regulations have sharply raised land values by allowing skyscrapers to replace the area's mostly low-rise buildings. The city estimated that the rezoning would directly displace 100 businesses and 1,700 jobs, although a report by the Pratt Center deemed these calculations a gross understatement of the rezoning's real impact.[140] By 2008, another report found that 57% of the small businesses surveyed in the area were about to close or were being forced to leave as a result of the rezoning and of growing competition from large corporate retailers:

> More and more buildings are redeveloped for corporate tenants in order to qualify for city and state job-retention subsidies, incentives, and tax credits. The Downtown Brooklyn Partnership's aggressive courting of large chains and national retailers is also driving up rents by recruiting firms to the area which can easily outbid mom-and-pop retailers for coveted commercial-space.[141]

Similar was the fate for the Hudson Yards area. By the early 2000s, gentrification was well under way in the district. But the rezoning has heavily advanced the spectacular luxurification of what was once a predominantly low- to medium-income community. Its net impact was to obliterate manufacturing uses and make room for a dazzling new luxury citadel in the immediate proximity of the Midtown Business District.[142] The sharp increase in land values has become a major engine of displacement, particularly of independent businesses and small manufacturers. Conservative estimates of the impact on existing businesses mentioned a displacement potential "of up to 225 private businesses and up to an estimated 4,269 private employees."[143]

But downtown Brooklyn and the Hudson Yards are by no means an exceptional case. Development under Bloomberg and de Blasio has often favored larger retailers over small stores. In recent years, the growth of corporate retail has consistently outpaced that of smaller businesses, and the process of "malling" New York City has been particularly remarkable in areas where rezoning plans were adopted.

In Brooklyn alone, between 2002 and 2007, the number of large businesses with 500 to 999 employees jumped 50%, compared with a 20% increase for smaller businesses over the same period.[144] In Red Hook, the 2008 rezoning of a plot once restricted to heavy manufacturing opened the doors for an Ikea megastore, replacing the 19th-century dry dock that was still in use by the time the rezoning was adopted. The rezoning of the Hunts Point section of the Bronx, which allowed the development of a new shopping mall and caused the eviction of hundreds of mostly minority wholesalers in the old Bronx Terminal Market, is another of many examples. And more displacement is expected in the South Bronx, along the Jerome Avenue corridor, where a new mixed-use rezoning, approved by the city in 2016, will likely wipe out the old auto repair shops that have been in the area for over 30 years.[145]

The Center for an Urban Future releases a yearly report documenting the growth of chain stores in the city, and its 2010 report found that the recession years were a moment of major expansion for most national chains in New York City: the largest corporate retailers profited mightily from the national downturn, as small businesses were forced to close and chain stores quickly took their spots.[146]

In Manhattan, meanwhile, the process of suburbanization is near completion.[147] As large chain retailers transform the city into a homogenized, cookie-cutter urban landscape, they are displacing small, independent businesses in droves. The loss is also an economic one. According to a *City Limits* reporter, "national studies show that for every $100 spent in a locally owned business, $85 is reinvested in the community—whether in paychecks for employees or goods and services purchased from other local businesses— compared with the $15 that stays local when that $100 is spent at a national chain."[148] Also, contrary to chain stores, which notably offer minimum wages and part-time, temporary positions, small businesses tend to hire full-time workers and to offer more stability for their employees.

Elected officials of all colors love to say that small businesses are the backbone of the city's economy, yet their policies have long forgotten them. Nowhere is this more obvious than along Surf Avenue in Coney Island, where it took a city-initiated rezoning plan to wipe out the old amusement arcades and food joints of times past, clearing the ground for yet another invasion of Manhattan-like corporate chains, as we will see in the next chapter.

5

The Rezoning That
Almost Killed Coney Island

Not that I would ever go there now or after a "revitalization," but being from Brooklyn, modern day Coney Island is a complete ghetto embarrassment to all of New York. Bring on the malls, condos, rides, whatever. Maybe clear the blight first with a fuel bomb or something. Anything.[1]

Wow: 'a ghetto embarrassment'?! People like you do not deserve to be living in New York City. Get thee to the suburbs, bitches![2]

If you are a nostalgic soul longing for the old-fashioned funk of old Coney Island and are planning a visit soon, chances are you may be bewildered by what you'll see. You'll be surprised to jump off the train at the Coney Island Stillwell Station only to be welcomed by a "Thor Equities and Brooklyn Welcome you to Coney Island" banner on top of an IT'Sugar franchise. Across the street from Nathan's Famous hot dogs, you'll see visitors crowding a Nets Shop by Adidas in search of its signature black-and-white apparel and swimwear. Along Surf Avenue, between an empty lot and a "retail space available" placard, you'll spot a Popeyes, an Applebee's, and a Tuscan-styled Subway Cafe franchise—for those unable to find more original food options around the area. And while you roam along the boardwalk searching for the original Gregory & Paul's Diner or Ruby's Bar & Grill amidst gift stores selling Coney T-shirts, sandals, and sunglasses, you'd better keep clear of the costumed characters posing for tips—something you may have thought only happened in Times Square. It is all part of the transformations that have swept the neighborhood since the area was rezoned in 2009. Many turn-of-the-century buildings, including the Henderson's Music Hall, the Bank of Coney Island, and the Shore Hotel, have been torn down in expectation of new development. Most of the grungy arcade game parlors along Surf

Avenue have been boarded up, while a new fancy amusement park called
Luna Park has substituted the old gritty amusements. There are talks of new
fancy residential developments here too. In 2011, the city approved a luxury
mixed-use 428,000-square-foot project called Ocean Dreams, which will
include glass and steel towers ranging from 14 to 22 stories, 415 market-rate
condos with views of the ocean, and almost 25,0000 square feet of commercial space. Stanley "Stan" Fox began working in his family's arcade at 12
years of age. Now 63, he told me what he thinks of the changes:

> They are turning Coney Island into a theme park, which it never was. It was a
> collection of large and small-sized amusements; a lot of mom-and-pops, some big
> parks like Steeplechase and Wonder Wheel, surrounded by lil' shops.... There's
> still a few mom-and-pops, but most of the games here, many closed down. There's
> still some life, but I think in a few years they might disappear, unfortunately.

A Brief History of Decline at Coney Island

Facing the Atlantic Ocean on the southern tip of the Brooklyn shore, the
peninsula of Coney Island developed over the 19th and early 20th centuries
from a gracious seaside resort of Victorian hotels and private beaches to
a popular midway of vaudeville theaters, bathhouses, arcades, dance halls,
and thrill rides, which attracted New Yorkers, immigrants, and visitors alike.
At the turn of the century, Coney Island had become a popular display
of magnificent architectures, electric arcade games, and never-before-seen
technological innovations. This is why it has been described as the utopian
laboratory of modern mass culture[3] and as the place best representing the
zeitgeist of New York City in the industrial age:[4] in the late 19th and early
20th centuries, electric lights, bizarre machineries, roller coasters, and even
baby incubators were all pioneered in Coney Island.

The first glorious amusement parks at Coney Island were strongly
indebted to the City Beautiful Movement and particularly to Burnham's
"White City," a model for an idealized, harmonious urban environment
unknown to most American city dwellers of the time. Dreamland and
Luna Park featured monumental buildings and slender towers, all generously decorated and orderly articulated among green spaces, wide canals
and picturesque lagoons (Figure 5.1). The pioneering steel structures that
characterized Coney Island in the 1940s—the vertiginous Parachute Jump,
the Wonder Wheel, and the many roller coasters—embodied the 1939–1940

Figure 5.1 Coney Island, in Luna Park (between ca. 1910 and ca. 1915).

World's Fair's quest for a revolutionary technological utopia (Figure 5.2). But Coney Island was also renamed "The Nickel Empire" and "The People's Playground" because it provided accessible recreation for the working classes of New York[5] and of the entire world. In 1925, an Italian immigrant named Giuseppe Cautela wrote: "When you bathe at Coney Island, you bathe in the American Jordan. It is holy water. Nowhere else in the United States will you see so many races mingle in a common purpose for a common good."[6] According to author Michael Immerso, "Coney Island was more than an incubator of amusement parks. A playground for the masses, it became the resort of last resort for an entire generation of Americans that lived through the Great Depression and staked a claim to a portion of its beach and boardwalk."[7]

A prototype for the artificial, light-fed, congested consumer landscape that would forge Manhattan in the following years, Coney Island was the creature of visionary ambitions as much as the product of unscrupulous entrepreneurship. Yet the very ruthless development that had given birth to Coney Island's glory at the turn of the century was to become its worst foe after World War II, when the peninsula became the fiery battlefield

Figure 5.2 Loop the Loop, Coney Island, New York, 1903.

of conflicting redevelopment utopias, social unrest, political ambitions, and greedy speculations. Throughout all these years, both city planning and private development have waged a ferocious war against Coney Island, a war that is still unfolding today.

Coney Island's history of decline begins in 1938, when Robert Moses assumed control of the area as city park commissioner; in 1941, he widened the boardwalk inland, erasing dozens of arcade amusements and vernacular architectures, including the municipal bathhouse and the ruins of the legendary Dreamland Park, which had opened in 1904 and had been destroyed by fire seven years later.[8] By making extensive use of eminent domain, Moses also razed several blocks of amusements at the site of Dreamland's fairground to clear land for new venues: the New York Aquarium (1957) and the Abe Stark ice skating rink, "a dark brown prison covered in barbed wires."[9] Both were surrounded by vastly unused parking lots, as was common practice in the era of modernist urban planning.

Later in 1953, while running the city's Slum Clearance Committee, Moses again had huge swaths of land rezoned to make room for high-rise housing projects: the Coney Island Houses, completed in 1956, destroyed more lots of amusements and hundreds of private houses.[10] After the urban renewal plans took place and old middle-class houses were replaced with towering public housing projects, local crime rates soared, giving rise to episodes of gang violence and racial conflicts that culminated in the 1960s and 1970s. In these dark years, fewer people ventured into Coney Island, forcing amusement owners to abandon their properties, while repeated episodes of arson obliterated much of the remaining structures in the amusement area. Coney's heyday had come to an end.

In 1964, Coney's last remaining large amusement park, Steeplechase,[11] which had opened in 1897 and had thrived since then, was shut down. The property was sold to Fred Trump, millionaire real estate developer with large development ventures in Brooklyn and Queens, and father of future US president Donald Trump. Fred had ambitious visions for Miami-style luxury condominiums on the ocean waterfront and spent years struggling with the city to get the area rezoned to residential uses. But Trump's plans were opposed by the Lindsay administration, which instead claimed it intended to clear the land and redevelop it as a public park. Realizing that there was a chance the city might landmark the dilapidated Steeplechase Pavilion (which dated back to 1907) and crush his development visions, Trump rushed to have it demolished: in the summer of 1966, he organized a "funeral party for the amusement industry," where young women in bikinis handed out stones which Trump invited the press to throw through the stained-glass walls of the pavilion; weeks later, he had it bulldozed.[12] But Fred Trump's dreams of luxury condos on the beach never approached reality, nor did the city's plans.

In the early 1970s, Norman Kaufman, an amusement operator who had leased the property from Trump, created a makeshift amusement park on the site and publicly disclosed plans to eventually resurrect the historic Steeplechase. In 1969, however, the city purchased the lot from Trump, and proceeded to sue Kaufman with lengthy legal battles in order to terminate the lease.[13] In 1981, the small park was eventually evicted, and the lot remained vacant for two more decades.

In the late 1970s, the Koch administration came up with yet another plan to revitalize Coney Island—this time by bringing in gambling and casinos, as had been done in Atlantic City, New Jersey. The plan created a frenzy of land speculation in which property was bought up in stock, while the few remaining rides were quickly removed to prepare land for future development. However, the state legislature never legalized gambling, and the land ended up with even more vacant lots.

In the mid-1980s, Harlem businessman Horace Bullard, founder of the Kansas Fried Chicken chain, spent a fortune buying up land at Coney Island, and revealed visionary plans for a vintage theme park inspired by the original Steeplechase; this time, the plan was approved by the city in 1986. But in the midst of the late 80s' economic crisis, the park failed to materialize. The deal was finally broken when Mayor Giuliani took office in 1994 and decided to build a baseball stadium on its site. Dropping the idea of a large theme park, Bullard announced his intentions to restore the once-glorious Thunderbolt roller coaster, which had been prominently featured in Woody Allen's 1977 romantic comedy *Annie Hall*, as the centerpiece of a scaled-down amusement park. But in an unpredictable turn of events, in November 2000, claiming that the roller coaster was in immediate danger of collapse, Giuliani ordered an early-morning raid and had it bulldozed. The Thunderbolt now gone, a new stadium was built on the property, a move that crushed Bullard's dreams but worked out pretty well for Fred Wilpon, real estate developer and majority owner of the New York Mets.[14]

The demolition of the Thunderbolt, which had been seen by historic preservationists and Coney enthusiasts as a sort of monument to survival, was the climax of a decades-long struggle of city planning against the livelihood of Coney Island's amusement industry. In fact, the history of development at Coney Island for over 70 years has been the history of its progressive obliteration: unimaginative city planning, private greed, and political opportunism have reduced the "People's Playground" to a wasteland, culminating with a devastating wave of demolitions during the first Bloomberg term—and with new, unexpected twists and turns in the latest years.

Coney Island Before the Rezoning

For decades, Coney Island's notorious reputation as a violent urban jungle was reinforced by alarming press and TV reports telling frightening stories of gang attacks and street shootings. Especially during the bleak days of the 1970s, movies like *The Warriors*, which tells the story of a Coney Island street gang engaged in an epic turf battle for survival, presented the American public with images of Coney Island as an urban inferno, popularizing the image of an "urban dystopia, a marginal space inhabited by the underbelly of the city where urban problems are endemic and untreatable"[15] (Figure 5.3).

Figure 5.3 Stills from the movie *The Warriors* (1979).

Still today, Coney Island is to some people nothing but an infamous, impoverished, and crime-ridden ghetto where the food is bad and the people are trashy. For other New Yorkers, however, Coney Island will always hold a special role as a beloved, one-of-a-kind retreat from the stress of city life. Despite the loss of many of its open-air rides over the last decades, Coney Island has somehow managed to survive ebbs and flows, thanks to attractions that continue to draw visitors and locals: its beach and boardwalk, the legendary Cyclone roller coaster, the Wonder Wheel, the open-frame steel relic of the Parachute Jump, the historic Nathan's Famous hot dogs, and a few remaining old-fashioned penny arcade houses. Signs of Coney's past funky days are still alive in today's burlesque and freak shows, the flamboyant "Mermaid Parade," and the music festivals on the beach. Like the haven and playground of the immigrants and working-class New Yorkers in past decades, Coney's boardwalk is still today a beloved place for people of all colors, ages, and incomes.

Over the last years, Coney Island has been home to people from about 50 countries, with nearly half the population consisting of recent immigrants.[16] As of the 2000 census, there were 51,574 people living in Coney Island: 59.6% were white, 32.4% were black or African American, 17.9% were Hispanic, and 4.5% were Asian. Coney Island is a predominantly low-income neighborhood, with a median household income of $21,654 as of 2009, as opposed to an average $76,800 for New York in the same year.[17] The large predominance of a low-income population in the neighborhood is due in large part to the several public housing complexes in the area, including nine New York City Housing Authority projects, containing approximately 4,093 housing units and 9,385 residents. In addition, a large proportion of residents in Coney Island are Section 8 voucher recipients or employ other forms of subsidies to rent or finance their homes.[18]

As of the 2000 census, 32.9% of all households were below poverty level, with a 12.9% unemployment rate, against an estimated 5.4% for the whole New York City metropolitan area. Census data also shows that the number of impoverished black families moving into the area grew 10 times between 1970 and 1990.[19]

Coney Island today attracts a predominantly native tourism from Brooklyn and the larger New York metropolitan area. If it's true that the district's tourism activity is in part "driven by nostalgia and by the few remaining vestiges of its storied past,"[20] Coney Island serves still as the public beach and amusement area for thousands of native New Yorkers who just can't afford to go elsewhere (Figures 5.4 and 5.5). A mix of white, Hispanic, and African American low- and middle-income families can linger along the boardwalk, bathe in the ocean, or join the free street parades and music shows for the price of a subway ride and a hot dog.

Until 2008, when the last original amusement park (Astroland) was demolished, the amusement area was managed by a small number of business owners with long-time connections to the neighborhood. In 2008, 75% of the area's 4,030 businesses had fewer than 5 employees, and almost 90% had fewer than 10.[21] It was the clustering of many independent operators

Figure 5.4 Sunbathing at the Coney Island beach in 2014.

Figure 5.5 Food stand along Surf Avenue, 2010.

that has given the place its unique character: unlike Six Flags, there were no gates at Coney Island, and no general admission tickets.

The social and ethnic diversity of its population and the anarchic palimpsest of its derelict urban fabric, coupled with the relative lack of privatized and controlled spaces, have always allowed for a very peculiar form of tourism at Coney Island, one where visitors could roam freely among

rides and attractions without the constraints of corporate rules.[22] And the
Coney Island boardwalk, with the diversity of its funky historic businesses,
has always represented a safe retreat from the homogeneity of the chain-
controlled and commodified city.

Rezoning Coney Island

Amid turbulent ups and downs, the "People's Playground" has somehow managed to survive over 70 years of relentless attacks by city
planning and private development. However, the summer of 2009
marked a turning point for Coney Island, one that was destined to
revolutionize its future development for good. On July 29, 2009, the
New York City Council approved a rezoning plan that city officials
claimed would "bring this beloved icon back to life, renewing Coney
Island's legacy for generations to come."[23] But the plan was controversial: it envisioned the radical demapping of over 61 acres formerly
zoned for outdoor amusements and their reduction to about 27 acres.
Of these, 15 would be occupied by a combination of high-rise hotels
and indoor shopping and entertainment. Only 12 acres would actually
be outdoor amusements of the kind recognizable as traditional seaside
entertainment.[24]

The preparatory process for the rezoning had started already in
September 2003, when Mayor Bloomberg, the city council, and the
Brooklyn borough president formed the Coney Island Development
Corporation (CIDC) to produce a development blueprint for the area.
The CIDC was created as a subsidiary department of the New York City
Economic Development Corporation (NYCEDC), the nonprofit local
development corporation that is owned and financed by the city and fully
controlled by the mayor.

The city's primary intention was to revitalize Coney Island as a potential
site for the 2012 Olympics. However, when the bid for the Olympics was
lost to London in July 2005, the CIDC came up with a rezoning scheme
that envisioned the conversion of large areas to residential uses to lure high-
end residential development into the neighborhood. This draft was later
integrated into a comprehensive plan developed by the Department of City
Planning (DCP), named the Coney Island Comprehensive Rezoning Plan.

According to a statement by city planning commissioner Amanda Burden in 2009, the plan

> will preserve amusements in their historic location in perpetuity as Mayor Bloomberg promised. In addition to creating a year-round 27-acre amusement and entertainment district, the plan will also make possible the much needed and long awaited revitalization of the surrounding neighborhood. The plan will reestablish the area as South Brooklyn's economic engine, bringing new jobs, retail services and affordable housing to the Coney Island community.[25]

The renderings released in 2009 depicted a landscape dense with spectacular rides and attractions—with just a hint, far away in the horizon, of a cluster of super-tall condominium and hotel towers. Yet, aside from such triumphal representations, the plan dictated a substantial inflation of the residential destination of the area—a use that many see as incompatible with the livelihood of a large amusement district[26]—and a radical reduction of its outdoor amusements.

The rezoning covers 19 blocks bounded by the New York Aquarium to the east, West 24th Street to the west, Mermaid Avenue to the north, and the Riegelmann Boardwalk to the south. It prescribes the remapping of 9.3 acres zoned for parkland at KeySpan Park, which is to be replaced by two parks along the Riegelmann Boardwalk: a 9.39-acre park for the amusement area, and a 1.41-acre neighborhood park. In the immediate surroundings of the amusement area, the plan foresees hotel towers, indoor amusements, retail, and restaurants. To the north and west of the amusement area, the plan fosters the redevelopment of underutilized land by rezoning it to a mix of residential, service, and retail uses, with the goal of creating 4,500 new units of housing and about 500,000 square feet of new retail. Around 25 high-rise buildings will be scattered throughout the area—to serve them, car parking will be accommodated in multilevel garages that will have to be "wrapped" by active uses (shops, restaurants) on the street frontages to avoid a dull streetscape (Figures 5.6 and 5.7). In an attempt to emulate the carnival feeling of old Coney Island, the Department of City Planning has also insisted on enforcing cosmetic prescriptions to keep street life "vibrant" and to recreate a sense of the "picturesque." The plan promised to strengthen Coney Island's "unique character" and adopt specific requirements and restrictions aimed at fostering an active street life: "To promote a vibrant active district … , new developments … would be required to have amusements occupying half of the total street frontage, and the ground floor level of hotels would be required to have active uses such as restaurants, retail and entertainment venues."[27]

Figure 5.6 Rendering: a rezoned beach, boardwalk, and amusement area at Coney Island.

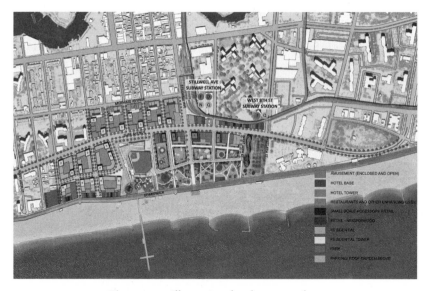

Figure 5.7 Illustrative development plan.

A new special zoning district was created, called the "Special Coney Island District," stretching 17 blocks between the New York Aquarium, the Riegelmann Boardwalk, Mermaid Avenue, and West 22nd Street. The special district is regulated by specific prescriptions on density, bulk, and parking and is composed of three subdistricts, each with its own special zoning regulations:

- Coney East (what today remains of the amusement area) will be rezoned to expand its range of uses, including hotels, enclosed entertainments, retail and restaurants. Hotel towers, whose height will range from 150 to 270 feet, will be allowed on Surf Avenue, in front of the main subway station.

- Coney West (now filled with vacant lots) will be rezoned for residential uses with retail and entertainment uses on the ground floor along Surf Avenue, and amusements and retail along the boardwalk. Residential towers will be allowed along Surf Avenue, with the highest towers at the corners of Surf Avenue and the intersecting streets.

- Coney North/Mermaid Avenue will be rezoned for residential towers with ground-floor retail along Surf Avenue and Mermaid Avenue.

The rezoning has introduced a combination of new residential and commercial uses to Coney Island, including new retail and amenities that will benefit a district whose retail supply is currently very poor.[28]

But despite the city's promises of thousands of new jobs and housing units for Coney Island residents, many locals feared they had more to lose than to gain from the proposed plan. According to the city:

> The preliminary assessment could not rule out the possibility that the proposed actions would: (1) add a substantial new population with different socioeconomic characteristics compared to the size and character of the existing population, (2) displace uses that have a "blighting" effect on property values in the area; or (3) introduce a substantial amount of a more costly type of housing compared to existing housing.[29]

The plan allows for the development of around 1,750 housing units in Coney North and roughly 2,700 residential units west of KeySpan Park. Of these, 607 new units would be set as "affordable" housing through the city's inclusionary zoning program. But the inclusionary zoning bonus, granted to developers who opt to keep aside 20% of their units as "affordable," has so far proven of little use at Coney Island. Similar programs adopted under the Bloomberg administration in other parts of the city haven't been utilized by developers in sufficient numbers to create a significant number of affordable units.

Although the environmental statement anticipated an indirect residential displacement of 1,497 residents due to soaring rental prices, no forms of mitigation were deemed necessary, as "a population loss of this magnitude would not substantially alter the demographic composition of the study area."[30] But a 2009 study by the Edward J. Bloustein School of Planning and Public Policy revealed, on a low estimate, a loss of at least 3,000 existing units of affordable housing due to expiring rental subsidies and particularly because a large majority (85%) of Section 8 units in the area are currently under contracts that are set to expire over the next few years, and are likely not to be renewed because of upward pressure in the local housing market. The study concludes that "the creation of 607 units—the number of new affordable units in Coney Island anticipated through the city's inclusionary housing program—will not even begin to mitigate the damage this potential rezoning will have on Coney Island's residents."[31] Moreover, the increased allowable density as a result of the rezoning is encouraging investors to develop the many "soft sites" (underdeveloped parcels with low-rise buildings, especially concentrated north of Surf Avenue) to their full capacity, thus demolishing the older structures, including what remains of Coney Island's surviving historic buildings, as occurred in the fall of 2010.

The plan also entirely redefines the role of the amusement industry at Coney Island. While Coney Island has always been primarily an open-air seasonal destination, the plan proposes to transform it into a year-round destination with indoor entertainment. Coney Island has always had multiple independent operators, yet city officials seemed to favor a new management carried out by a single major operator. The indoor amusements that the plan foresees may end up feeling more like Disney's highly controlled consumption outlets in the new Times Square than the grungy arcade houses of old Coney. The presence of pricey hotels and residential towers will also take its toll in the surrounding public space, where forms of control, noise ordinances, and other regulations will likely be enforced to protect the comfort of new residents. The proposed high-rise hotels could forever transform a skyline currently defined by historic landmarks like the Wonder Wheel and the Parachute Jump. According to a *Huffington Post* journalist, a cut-down amusement area, overshadowed by soaring high rises, "will be too small to accommodate new, iconic rides and would not leave much space for future generations of visionaries to carry forward Coney Island's traditions of inventiveness and artistry."[32]

But despite dozens of heated public hearings and the clear "no" of local activists, Coney Island enthusiasts, and historic preservationists, the plan was hastily approved without significant modifications from its original layout on July 29, 2009.

The Limbo of Coney Island

Shortly before the first rezoning drafts were released in September 2005, Joseph J. Sitt, a real estate tycoon with strong political connections in the neighborhood,[33] and CEO of development firm Thor Equities, purchased the 168,000-square-foot Washington Bath House lot west of the current amusement area for $13 million. Owning property that was now potentially earmarked for rezoning to residential uses, Sitt flipped it the same year to Taconic Investment Partners for $90 million—for a thick $77 million profit.[34] Between 2003 and 2006, Thor Equities proceeded to purchase almost every piece of property (about 10 acres) inside the traditional amusement area: in the winter of 2007 and then again in 2008, the developer evicted dozens of small businesses and ride operators, and swiftly purchased the largest remaining amusement park at Coney Island, Astroland. The park, which had opened in 1962, closed at the end of 2008: a few weeks later, rides were dismantled and sold (Figure 5.8).[35]

Thor Equities' real plans for Coney have always been unclear, especially since they have changed so much from year to year. In 2005, when the economy was booming, Thor released dazzling renderings of a resort area sporting

Figure 5.8 Ticket booths standing in a desolate wasteland, Coney Island, 2008.

luxury high-rise condo towers with the promise to bring a Vegas-style development to South Brooklyn.[36] Four years later, in the midst of the 2009 recession, Thor presented new designs that included what seemed to be a small gated amusement park, featuring high-rise hotels and large retail stores. Thor Equities' requests to the city to boost the maximum retail size limit in the rezoning plan from 2,500 to 10,000 square feet led many critics to assume that the developer intended to turn the area into a megamall on the ocean. In reality, many questioned Thor Equities' intentions of actually building anything at Coney Island—a bias that came from his reputation of acquiring property, requiring zoning changes, and then flipping the land to other developers for a profit. This is exactly what Thor had done during the first Bloomberg administration with the Albee Square Mall site in downtown Brooklyn, which he purchased for $25 million in 2001 and resold post-rezoning in 2004 to Arcadia Realty Trust and MacFarlane Partners for five times the amount.[37]

In November 2008, the city started negotiations to reacquire some of the land from Joe Sitt to go on with its plans. They offered the developer $110 million for the parcels required for the plans of a nine-acre outdoor amusement district. Sitt declined and reportedly demanded double the amount.[38] After lengthy negotiations, in November 2009, the city finally negotiated to purchase the land from Thor Equities for an astounding $95.6 million deal. According to the *New York Times*, "while Mr. Sitt got much less than the $140 million he had wanted for 10.5 of the 12.5 acres he owned, the $95.6 million for 6.9 acres came to more than $300 a square foot,"[39] an amount comparable to that of certain Manhattan areas. After the land was finally purchased in December 2009, the city issued a request for proposals for an interim amusement operator (on a 10-year lease) to run a temporary park on the now city-owned property: the bid was won by Zamperla Group, which also operates Victorian Gardens in Central Park and has cooperated with amusement parks around the globe, including Disney, Universal Studios, and Six Flags. The NYCEDC offered the company far more favorable leasing conditions than any other locally owned business in Coney Island had ever enjoyed. A 10-year lease was signed for a $100,000 annual rent plus a reported 10% of the gross profit in the first year of operation: "To put this number in perspective, consider that Boardwalk businesses like Ruby's and Cha Cha's have been paying $100,000 annual rent in recent years,"[40] notes the *Amusing the Zillion* blog.

In the summer of 2010, four giant pinwheels and crescent moons reminiscent of the long-gone Luna Park were put into place by the front gate of a brand-new amusement park, whose 19 rides, although state of the art, have a nostalgic allure to them (Figure 5.9). The cheerful opening of "Luna Park" on Memorial Day 2010 was such an overwhelming success that Central Amusement International (CAI, of which Zamperla is majority

Figure 5.9 Rides at Luna Park by Zamperla, 2014.

shareholder) promptly scheduled to open another $12 million expansion in the adjacent lots before the summer of 2011.[41]

But good times were not to last: just a few weeks after the opening of the new park, Thor Equities started to demolish most of the remaining historical buildings in Coney Island's amusement zone: the Henderson's Music Hall (built in the late 1880s, it had been renovated in 2004 and was the last surviving example of the music halls that thrived at Coney Island at the turn of the century), the Bank of Coney Island (a 1923 neoclassical revival building that testified to Coney's past prosperity), and the Shore Hotel (built in 1903 and Coney Island's last operational hotel) were all razed to the ground in a matter of weeks.[42]

Thor Equities' wave of demolitions started a few months after the New York State Office of Parks, Recreation, and Historic Preservation had issued a determination that Coney Island's amusement district met the criteria for inclusion on the State and National Register of Historic Places, naming each of these endangered structures as the district's "key buildings."[43] However, the city's Landmarks Preservation Commission denied them landmark designation and refused the creation of a historic district at Coney Island. The idea of a "Coney Island Historic District"—a two-block-long corridor along Surf Avenue that would preserve some of these historic structures—was proposed by preservation and advocacy groups including the Municipal Arts Society, the New York Landmarks Conservancy, the Historic Districts Council, Coney Island USA, and Save Coney Island. The designation of the area as a historic district would have provided tax incentives to rehabilitate these historic buildings. But the Landmarks Preservation Commission, whose chair is directly appointed by the mayor, played a long waiting game at Coney Island and didn't calendar any of the buildings until 2010,[44] long after all properties of Thor Equities had been reduced to rubble. Aside from the iconic Cyclone Roller Coaster,[45] the Wonder Wheel,[46] and the Parachute Jump,[47] only one historical building outside of the amusement area has survived the wrecking ball: the Shore Theater, a neo-Renaissance theater built in the 1920s and boarded up since the late 1970s, which was given landmark status in December 2010.

Thor Equities' rush to demolition was part of a strategy that has become routine in today's New York: to head off the lengthy landmarking process and take full advantage of the potential that comes with rezoning (in this case, the plan allows for 30-story high-rise hotels), small-scale historical buildings are easily sacrificed to pave the way for more profitable development. In the Bloomberg years, thousands of historical buildings were demolished each year—usually right before or right after rezoning plans were getting final approval. During the 2002–2006 building boom, the number of demolition permits rose from 3,386 in 2002 to a record 6,480 in 2006.[48]

In a TV interview on NY1,[49] Thor Equities CEO Joe Sitt declared: "Every one of these buildings is just horrible, rundown relics with nothing exciting about them."[50] In reality, most of these buildings had great potential and were open for business before Thor Equities' acquisition led to the eviction of tenants and businesses in 2008 and 2009. After demolition, the developer promptly released vague renderings of one-story retail boxes, reminiscent of a suburban strip mall, which would replace the old buildings. The *New York Observer* claimed that Thor's renderings were "almost designed to inspire distaste," with "a Burger King-like joint on the corner, next to a taco restaurant with signage highly suggestive of Taco Bell."[51]

"This is a tale of two Coney Islands," claimed advocacy group Save Coney Island:

> Luna Park is laying the groundwork for an exciting summer, while a block away Thor is planning to lay waste to Coney Island's heritage, threatening to ruin all at once the area's past, present, and future. The Bloomberg administration needs to decide: Will this summer be remembered as the beginning of Coney Island's rebirth? Or will be remembered as the summer that the City allowed an opportunistic developer to demolish Coney Island's history?[52]

But as Thor Equities' demolitions in Coney Island continued, worse was yet to come: on the day after the 2010 season ended, almost all remaining boardwalk businesses, some of which were in place for over 40 years, received immediate eviction notices, this time from the executives of CAI/Zamperla, who ran the newly built Luna Park: "They didn't have the vision that we have for the Boardwalk.... It's a business decision," said Zamperla's CEO.[53] Local businesses like the bizarre Shoot the Freak and legendary food joints and bars like Ruby's, Cha Cha's, Paul's Daughter, Grill House, Gyro Corner, Beer Island, and Pio Pio Riko all had two weeks to vacate the premises they had occupied for decades. Some of them united in a lengthy legal battle to have their leases renewed for at least one more year. In 2012, only two of them, Paul's Daughter (which had opened at Coney as Gregory & Paul's Diner in 1962) and Ruby's Bar, were offered eight-year leases with the stipulation that they invest hundreds of thousands of dollars in the rehabilitation of their stores.[54]

Death by Rezoning?

The word "preservation" seems ironic in a neighborhood that has experienced so much demolition.[55]

In 2009, a *Huffington Post* reporter wrote that, with the adoption of the Coney Island rezoning plan, Mayor Bloomberg was finally "on the cusp of completing the work of Moses and Trump."[56] As a matter of fact, it was the very city-initiated planning process for Coney Island that sparked the frenzy of land speculation that has ravaged the amusement district and most of its historical landmarks over the last few years. Once it appeared that the zoning status quo would change, Thor Equities cleared land to pave the way for higher returns. Between 2007 and 2010, most of the remaining historical buildings at Coney Island were obliterated, while the old amusement district was reduced to a fraction of its former size. However, while Thor Equities has been largely responsible for the blighting of present-day Coney Island, it is the city's plan that poses the greatest danger to the amusement district's future: "Coney Island's amusement district has survived the pressures of the New York City real estate market thanks to its special amusement-only zoning. Land that is rezoned to allow for other uses, however, will be lost to amusements forever," a reporter claims.[57] As of today, the outdoor amusements at Coney Island occupy around 3 acres. Before the plan's approval, over 61 acres were still zoned for outdoor amusements, while the legendary Coney Island of the past had over 100 acres of parkland, including rides, arcades, bathhouses, hotels, houses, and retail. The approved rezoning plan shrinks the amusement area *in perpetuum*. Only the opening of Zamperla's new Luna Park has managed to counterbalance some of the losses accumulated in such a short time.

Slogans Versus Reality

The plan was presented as the city's response to Coney Island's chronic decline. By accommodating new housing, retail, and entertainment, and by bringing in new jobs, the plan promised to "ensure that future generations can enjoy an open, affordable, urban 21st century Coney Island that does justice to its illustrious history and enduring appeal."[58] However, the plan has failed to address the demands of local residents and businesses, and to recognize Coney Island's key potential as a large-scale, diversified amusement district that honors its past glories. While opening up the doors to new injections of capital may generate new jobs for locals in the hotel, retail and food service industry, the ripple effects of such a massive upzoning in an overwhelmingly impoverished community are also representing a serious threat to the livelihood of local residents and businesses.

Participation

> The plan ... is the product of over 300 public meetings with numerous stakeholders, ranging from elected officials, residents, property and business owners, to Coney Island enthusiasts from New York City and beyond.[59]

The plan has been presented as the result of an intensive public outreach process. In reality, many residents, grassroots organizations, and advocacy groups claim that their voices and proposals have fallen on deaf ears. Activist groups Save Coney Island[60] and Coney Island USA, the Municipal Art Society, and even the *New York Times* on many occasions urged the city to expand the amusement area and to remove four high-rise towers from the heart of the amusement district; Coney Island's Community Board 13 also recommended the relocation of the hotel towers, while the New York Landmarks Conservancy and the Historic Districts Council pushed for the preservation of some of Coney's historical buildings. All of their requests remained unanswered: despite dozens of public hearings, none of the several civic coalitions opposing the rezoning or asking for amendments has been able to substantially affect the plan.

Housing

> The plan will reestablish the area as South Brooklyn's economic engine, bringing new jobs, retail services and affordable housing to the Coney Island community.[61]

To create affordable housing, the plan provides incentives to developers who decide to set off 20% of the developed units as "affordable." Of the thousand housing units proposed, 607 units would be designated as affordable to households making up to 80% of the area median income (AMI; in New York City, the AMI for a family of four in 2009 was $70,900). However, the median household income in this part of Coney Island, at $22,315 in 2009,[62] is nowhere near these numbers: as a result, the rezoning isn't likely to produce much housing that is actually affordable to Coney Island locals. Moreover, since the inclusionary zoning tool applied in this rezoning plan is voluntary, it is questionable how many of these "affordable" units will ever be built.

According to the city, by the time of the rezoning, about one-quarter of the housing stock in the rezoned area was subsidized housing, with 42% of the rental units being subsidized and 34% having some form of rent regulation.[63] The presence of so many affordable units served to justify the plan's focus on high-end, market-rate residential development. But subsidized units do not exist in perpetuity, and as rental contracts expire, upward pressures on the market incentivize landlords to opt out of subsidy programs and to convert their units into market-rate housing, as we have already seen happening in Harlem and elsewhere across the city. As a case in point, in the summer of 2007, two years before the rezoning was adopted, all Mitchell-Lama[64] units in the Trump Village mega housing complex east of Coney's amusement area were converted to pricey market-rate apartments. The same year, several other Mitchell-Lama buildings in the area were converted to market-rate housing, including Ocean Towers, a 360-unit development that was sold for $5.9 million to Cammeby's International in 2007 and has been recently resold to Proto Property Services and Community Development Trust for $35.6 million, seven times the price.[65] In an effort to halt the loss of affordable units, in November 2009, city officials announced a $21 million deal to renovate the Luna Park housing complex (one of the state's biggest Mitchell-Lama developments, which houses around 6,000 people in almost 1,600 apartments) under an agreement that will keep the apartments in the Mitchell-Lama program for 20 more years.[66]

Meanwhile, on September 8, 2011, the city council approved a luxury 415-unit, mixed-use project on two vacant parcels on the western end of Riegelmann Boardwalk, nine blocks west of the Coney Island Special District. The 428,000-square-foot project, known as Ocean Dreams, would include three residential towers with 415 market-rate condos, ranging from 14 to 22 stories; 418 parking spaces; and up to 24,750 square feet of commercial space. The same year, private beachfront condominiums were under construction on the Coney Island boardwalk at West 32nd Street, with sales prices ranging from $510,000 for a one-bedroom to $1.55 million for a penthouse.[67]

One housing development with an affordable housing component that has been completed in the rezoned area is called Coney Island Commons. The housing complex was presented by the city in early 2013 as a response to the displacement caused by Hurricane Sandy, which hit the shore of Coney Island on October 29, 2012. The city announced that residents displaced from their homes because of the storm could have access to affordable housing units in the new mixed-use development via a lottery organized by the Department of Housing Preservation and Development (HPD). Storm victims were given a 25% preference in the lottery. Completed at the end of 2013, it consists of two residential buildings plus a 40,000-square-foot YMCA, and has a total of 195 units—39 of which are reserved for the displaced. The remaining 156 apartments will be affordable to households earning up to 60% of AMI—equal to an income of $49,800 per year for a family of four.

In early 2015, rumors were out that the tallest building south of downtown Brooklyn would rise in place of a low-rise strip mall on Neptune Avenue, north of the amusement area. The $450 million, 40-story tower would include 544 market-rate apartments and three levels of retail space.[68] The architectural renderings showed a Whole Foods, a Gap, a Ralph Lauren, and a Duane Reade in the ground-floor mall.[69]

Small Local Businesses

> Through the development of year-round uses and job opportunities for the residents, [the plan seeks to] facilitate the economic revitalization of the peninsula.[70]

On paper, the Coney Island rezoning is meant to "enhance and protect existing uses and previously existing uses."[71] But the plan doesn't include any serious strategy aimed at preserving locally owned retail and at avoiding the forced relocation of local businesses. Despite anticipating the displacement of a few dozen small retailers, the city deemed mitigations unnecessary, claiming that "the proposed actions would re-introduce similar businesses with similar products and services, catering to both a residential and visitor consumer population."[72]

Many businesses along the Surf and Mermaid Avenue corridors will be directly displaced by the rezoning. As these small businesses get evicted, most of the new tenants will likely be large companies that can afford higher rents. This is already happening along Surf Avenue, where chains are gradually replacing the old arcades and food joints. Other small local stores in the area will be threatened with indirect displacement, as many are located in single-story buildings that claim only a fraction of maximum allowable density allowed under the rezoning—an incentive for investors and landlords to demolish them to build denser and taller structures. Most of these businesses are small local stores, including car workshops and bodegas catering to the existing community near the amusement district.

The Role of the Amusement Park

The plan seeks to … facilitate the development of a vibrant year round, 27-acre urban amusement and entertainment district … laying the groundwork for the development of a 12-acre urban amusement park preserving and expanding amusement uses in their historic boardwalk location in perpetuity.[73]

In early 2007, the Municipal Art Society (MAS), a New York–based urban think tank, launched the initiative Imagine Coney, which included a public call for ideas and workshops with international experts and amusement industry leaders, to craft a more sustainable vision for development at Coney Island and to emphasize the potential of Coney's amusement industry as a crucial engine for growth in the area. In a testimony for the City Planning Commission in May 2009, the MAS highlighted several key points for development at Coney Island, which included an expansion of the outdoor amusement area to 27 acres by retaining the existing zoning code (amusement only) to allow for future growth—an indispensable step to make Coney Island able to compete with other world-class amusement parks; safeguarding Coney Island's architectural heritage through the aggressive preservation of historical buildings; and introducing regulations to keep large-scale, generic retail out of the amusement district.[74] The MAS's recommendations were in support of a different, more imaginative approach to redevelopment, one that focused on the amusement area as an economic engine for the area and as a provider of quality jobs. But the city vigorously dismissed the call for a larger amusement area. In 2008, city planning chief Amanda Burden warned the public against raising any further objections: "It is imperative that the rezoning process and timeline not be jeopardized by any reconsideration of our proposed rezoning boundaries or urban design parameters…. It is imperative that this rezoning proceeds expeditiously, otherwise the Coney Island amusement area that we know and love will cease to exist."[75]

The MAS's testimony emphasizes the underlying contradictions of a plan that claims to capitalize on the legendary "brand" of Coney Island while at the same time radically scaling down its prime vocation as a world-class amusement park. In 2015, the de Blasio administration announced new plans to take six privately owned lots by condemnation to complete its 2009 plans for a "Wonder Wheel Way," a pedestrian promenade that will connect the three remaining historical landmarks of Coney Island: the Cyclone Roller Coaster, the Wonder Wheel, and the Parachute Jump. More rides and attractions along this stretch will fall victim to this development plan, including the horror-themed Ghost Hole ride at 12th Street and Bowery, and the old-fashioned High Striker. According to Save Coney Island spokesman Juan Rivero: "There are numerous places around the globe that have built glorious parks that pay tribute to Coney Island. Here, where we have the original, the city has been all too happy to shrink it out of existence."[76] The theme park industry has one of its most legendary progenitors at Coney Island: still today, hundreds of parks around the world are inspired by the former magnificence of Coney. Luna Park, in Melbourne, Australia, features a giant entrance gate inspired by the iconic face of George C. Tylou, who founded Steeplechase Park in 1897. Coney Island Park in the Cincinnati area features a range of classic rides that pay tribute to the legend of Coney Island. Full-size replicas of Coney's Wonder Wheel stand in Disney's California Adventure Park and in Yokahama Park in Japan.

Fortunately, the constant additions of new rides at Zamperla's Luna Park have managed to keep the park vibrant and crowded over the last seasons. In the summer of 2010, thanks to the opening of the new park, the number of visitors to Coney Island tripled to 12.8 million compared to rezoning-year 2009.[77] Although small if compared with the 27 acres that the MAS had called for, Luna Park has become the main catalyst for visitors and locals in a renewed Coney Island. With its entrance reminiscent of the original 1903 Luna Park, it has a general admission ticket in the form of credits (Luna cards) or unlimited ride wristbands. Over the last years, the park has been adding new attractions, from a ride inspired by Leonardo da Vinci's flying machines in 2013 to a fancy revisitation of the iconic Thunderbolt in 2014. For the 2011 season, the park expanded with a new addition called Scream Zone, which hosts the first new roller coasters built in New York since the opening of the Cyclone in 1927.

How Coney Island Survived the Storm but Found Itself Remade in Plastic

On October 29, 2012, Hurricane Sandy carved a path of devastation along Brooklyn's southern shoreline, ravaging the Coney Island waterfront and destroying innumerable businesses and houses on the peninsula. All businesses along the boardwalk and on Stillwell and Mermaid Avenues were flooded and severely damaged. A few days after the mayhem, it seemed like Coney Island had gone back to its darkest days: gangs were seen looting liquor stores, pharmacies, and even private homes in what seemed like an eerie postapocalyptic landscape of fallen street signs, mud, and sewer waters.

While the largest amusement operators managed to swiftly repair the damages to their rides, most poor residents and small business owners did-n't recover so quickly:[78] too many didn't possess flood insurance as it was too expensive or impossible for them to get. Over a quarter of the approx-imately 50,000 residents in the neighborhood suffered severe damage to their houses and properties, according to FEMA. The feds spent $44 mil-lion for temporary homes for evacuated residents, or for repair jobs on the properties that could be repaired,[79] while the city managed to funnel $72 million in federal aid to small businesses—a drop in the water consid-ering that over 18,000 businesses that employed at least 200,000 workers were hit by the storm.[80]

A few months after Sandy, in the summer of 2013, it seemed like life was back to normal in the amusement area and along the beach and the board-walk, which were again bustling with visitors. But things weren't as rosy just a few blocks away, in the poor residential areas north of the waterfront, where a real recovery was still to be seen. Many small businesses unable to get assistance or loans from the city had shut their doors for good after the storm; many others were struggling to stay open.

If there is a lesson to be learned after Katrina's destruction of New Orleans in 2005, it is that natural disasters can pave the way for develop-ment of a kind that would have been unthinkable before the tragedy. In 2013, the Bloomberg administration and the NYCEDC managed to funnel about $90 million in federal money for recovery to be used in five storm-impacted city areas, including Coney Island. But these funds are not for small businesses of the kind that populated the streets of Coney Island, and most mom-and-pops battered by the storm won't stand to benefit: the funds are dedicated to large "transformational projects" of the kind that only top developers can bring.[81] Yet another example of Naomi Klein's "disaster cap-italism" in action: in the years following Sandy, struggling small businesses have been shutting down or leaving in droves, clearing the ground for an invasion of Manhattan-like corporate retail in Coney Island (Figures 5.10 and 5.11). Shortly after Sandy, new franchises started popping up at every corner, including a new Applebee's and an IT'Sugar candy store in Thor Equities' retail building along Surf Avenue, adding to the already-present Popeye's and Dunkin' Donuts in the Stillwell Avenue Terminal. In 2014 and 2015, new food franchises opened along Surf Avenue, including Florida-based burger chain Checkers, a Subway Cafe, and New York–based pizzeria chain Grimaldi's, turning Surf Avenue into a real "Mecca for franchises."[82]

Figure 5.10 IT'Sugar candy store along Surf Avenue, 2014.

Figure 5.11 Nets Shop by Adidas, Stillwell Avenue, 2014.

More chains moved into the neighborhood in 2015, including New York City's first Wahlburgers, and rumors have it that Pizza Hut and LA-born frozen yogurt franchise Red Mango will soon have their spots on Coney Island's "franchise restaurant row."[83]

Meanwhile, another change came in 2015 to threaten the character of Coney Island: in several nearby areas of the Brooklyn shoreline, including Brighton Beach, the Parks Department started replacing sections of the wooden Boardwalk with synthetic walkways made of recycled plastic lumber and a 10-foot-wide concrete lane for emergency vehicles in the middle. The $10 million pilot project, which was launched by the Bloomberg administration in 2009,[84] was presented after Sandy as an ecological alternative for a more resilient boardwalk. The plans are to soon extend the works to Coney's famous 2.5-mile-long Riegelmann Boardwalk. But this decision isn't sitting all too well with Coney Islanders.[85] The tropical hardwood zigzagging boardwalk not only has been a symbol of Coney Island for over 80 years, but also has shown its resiliency by withstanding the destructive force of Sandy much better than those sections remade in recycled plastic and concrete along other waterfront areas. Residents expressed their frustration at community meetings, and local councilman Mark Treyger tried to convince the Landmarks Commission to give the Riegelmann Boardwalk landmark status. But their input was received with indifference.[86]

De Blasio failed to respond to the concerns of local councilpersons and the community, and the new administration sees no problem in going ahead with Bloomberg's plan, to the great disappointment of those who had believed the new mayor was the anti-Bloomberg. By the end of 2015, several sections of the boardwalk on the Brooklyn southern shore had already been remade in recycled plastic and concrete.

Ironically, piles of the same wood that New York City wanted removed were sent 4,000 miles away to create a walkway inside the $60 million USA Pavilion at the 2015 Milan Expo.[87] Other stacks of wood from the famous boardwalk were sold or given away by contractors to be used as upscale wall coverings in a West Village restaurant, as floors in the Barnes Foundation's new museum in Philadelphia, and even as high-end design lounge chairs: an ironic turn of events that seems to epitomize the ability of branding to create value out of nothing, and to turn even public losses into private profit. This is something I will dig deeper into in the next chapter.

6

The Power Branders
of New York City

Always remember: a brand is the most valuable piece of real estate in the
world; a corner of someone's mind.[1]

When the city announced in 2014 that pop celebrity and recent
Manhattan transplant Taylor Swift would become global ambassador for the "Welcome to New York" city branding campaign, New Yorkers
did not seem impressed. The choice of a 24-year-old Nashville-bred singer,
who had just moved to the city and into her $20 million Tribeca apartment,
and whose "Welcome to New York" song had been labeled as a "gentrification anthem," generated a firestorm of media controversy, with headlines
like "Taylor Swift's Unwelcome P.R. Campaign" and "New York City Has
Rejected Taylor Swift."[2] The choice of Swift over more tenured New York
celebrities, say, Robert de Niro or even Jennifer Lopez, however, was an
accurate indication of how marketers and branding consultants have chosen
to represent the "new New York"[3] to the world: hygienic and safe for a new
population of millennials whose food of choice is a latte Frappuccino rather
than a pizza or a bagel.[4]

Some people say that a great product needs no advertising, while others
say that a good brand will sell almost any product. In an era in which our
cities have become just another product to be sold in the global marketplace,
city producers will work hard to give them the finest advertising they can.
And hip branding campaigns can provide cities with that certain competitive edge that will attract new city consumers—businesses, professionals, and
tourists. But the realm of city marketing has expanded way beyond glossy
leaflets and brochures of times past. Today, city magazines, consumer guides,

lifestyle magazines, movies, and even city-based TV shows all play a major role in training us to be consumers of a city that has become, in all effects, a commodity. In the late 1990s and early 2000s, the TV sensation *Sex and the City* managed, more than any institutional marketing campaign, to popularize a fashionable "New York way of life" for an international mass audience, making New York a city of aspiration for millions of women (and even men) around the world. Almost everything represented in the show, from the trendy restaurants to the groovy bars, from the fashion catwalks to the upscale apartments, conformed to the charming vision of a hyper-consumerist urban lifestyle (Figure 6.1). In the show, Manhattan had become "a sophisticated wonderland, replete with nightclubs and cocktails, spacious terraces and skyline views, elegant shopping streets and sidewalks filled with stylish women"[5]—a tantalizing, cleaned-up version of reality. In sum: a brand.

The spectacular success of this and other recently produced urban-based TV shows, with the corollary of desires, dreams, and emulative behaviors around a liberal, trendy, and fashionable urban lifestyle they have helped generate reveals the huge appetite of an ever-growing population of consumers for glittering representations of urban life, and their seductive power. After all, today's world has a cultural obsession with the city, fueled by a whole new marketing emphasis on trends and lifestyle choices that are exquisitely urban. The urban myth advertised by the media, and the conspicuous consumption of experiences and goods it suggests, have become the new handbooks for both urban and suburban individuals. For many of us, the choice to "consume" one city instead of another (and with the city, the urban experiences and the "urban

Figure 6.1 A movie still from the series *Sex and the City*, Season 1, Episode 4.

way of life" it offers) has become an indicator of lifestyle or status, or even an essential step in the process of individual construction of the self.

But isn't this consumerist approach turning us into passive spectators of a show that has been staged for us by image-making experts and media-savvy individuals? Haven't we all become consumers of the city?

Representations of the City

Earlier in the book, I described the "symbolic space" of the city as that dimension in which the countless representations of the city in the arts and literature, the media, institutional slogans, and the popular imagination crystallize over time. It's a clash of dissonant representations, which includes our subjective perceptions of the city and those representations produced by alternative culture, but also official narratives codified in the slogans of elected officials and the popular imagery of the city we see on TV and in the newspapers.

Urban scholars Hubbard and Hall said that the entrepreneurial city is "an imaginary city, constituted by a plethora of images and representations."[6] They are referring to the symbolic space of the city, a space in which our direct, individual perception and experience of the urban realm is constantly permeated, challenged, and reframed by more established representations and discourses propagated through press reports, official statements, and the visual media.[7] The way we see the city is constantly reshaped by a number of different powerful actors—including the media and cultural producers, but also city government and the real estate and development industries—each producing specific representations of what the city is, has been, or ought to be.

Clearly, different representations reflect each group's specific visions and their own social and economic agendas. Inasmuch as different representations of the city reflect the interests of specific groups, it is important to understand *who* are the actors in charge of producing dominant representations, *why* they produce them, and for *whom*.

Power and Representations of Space

Marx argued that the capitalist relations of production are the foundation of society, while legal, political, and cultural forms are "superstructures" that serve to reproduce its economic structure—capitalism: in this framework, popular media are "means of production" owned and managed by the elites, and their aim is to disseminate a specific hegemonic culture that reflect the elites' values and interests, while defusing or even invalidating alternative or conflicting standpoints.[8] This is a claim that still stands true today, if we look at the role mainstream media often play in educating viewers along certain ideological orientations that are promoted as beneficial to everyone, even when they aren't.

With the concept of cultural "hegemony,"[9] Gramsci described how the ruling classes of post-1870 industrial Western Europe established and maintained their control over the masses by establishing a position of moral and intellectual leadership. According to Gramsci, it was the imposition of a hegemonic culture—a dominant ideology that reflected bourgeois ethics and interests—that ensured the dominance of the capitalist elite and justified the social, political, and economic status quo. According to Lefebvre, capitalist societies are the arenas of a constant struggle, in which the institutional cultural space of state power tends to establish its hegemony by gradually incorporating the affective, personal space of our everyday lives under its control.[10]

In other words, the dominant culture of capitalism has a tendency to devour and co-opt all forms of alternative culture and make them part of its inner workings. This is something we have seen occurring over and over again in modern times, for instance, each time rebellious elements of youth counterculture (from street art to hip hop music and other subcultures) have been appropriated and exploited for the profit of corporate apparel giants like Nike or Adidas.[11]

Mass culture is hence a bloody battlefield where the struggle between capital's desire for hegemony and individuals' response to these hegemonic messages is played out.[12]

Power and Branding

Over the last four decades, the application of marketing and branding principles to the toolkit of urban governance has become one of the hallmarks of the shift to urban entrepreneurialism. City branding consists of the formulation and communication of a unified "image" of the city, one that delivers a very filtered impression of a much more complex reality: usually, city branding campaigns call attention to "business friendly," "green," "vibrant," "multicultural," "high-tech" urban destinations that may appeal to the favored class of city consumers. Their role is to emphasize specific positive qualities of the city while downplaying its negative attributes—crime, poverty, or social inequalities have notably no room in these glittering representations. As a result, all forms of urban promotion and marketing presuppose a process of manipulation of the city's image, or "city re-imaging,"[13] which simplifies the city's complexity and marginalizes pesky realities or other possible perspectives. It is an image of urban living that reflects the demands of the regime of consumption and capital accumulation and gives precise instructions about the way people should make use of space.[14] A rather eerie example is provided by the billboards and banners at construction sites: sanitized renderings of spectacular architectures completed with digitalized images of young executives sitting on park benches while using their laptops, of athletic joggers in branded jumpsuits, or of dressed-up women window-shopping in front of apparel stores. These images not only tell us, "These are the desired people we want in this new development," but also tell us, "This is how people should behave in here."

This process of manipulation is inextricably connected to the question of power: according to British cultural theorist Stuart Hall, the role of power in the process of production of representations is "to stop the flow of possible multiple meanings, to narrow the range and diversity of possible meanings."[15] A similar perspective is shared by Lefebvre. In his view, the production of hegemonic "representations of space" results in what he calls "dominant space"—a uniform, unimaginative space that disciplines human interactions and flattens diversity, as its only function is to serve the interests of capital.[16]

In the process of producing and consuming representations of the city, both city producers and city consumers are mutually linked: while city marketing campaigns and branding strategies produce representations of urban lifestyles as appealing as possible to affluent consumers, the latter's demand for specific spaces and experiences, strongly influenced by the media, leads to the production of a city that is more and more tailor-suited to their demands and desires.

The Corporate Branding of Cities

Although forms of urban boosterism have been quite common practice in Western cities since at least the 19th century,[17] a consistent application of marketing and branding principles to the sphere of public management emerged only in the early 1970s, as city producers turned to aggressive growth-oriented agendas to promote localities in a regime of increasingly fierce interurban competition for investment, visitors, and consumers.[18] In this phase characterized by the emergence of new "entrepreneurial," growth- and competition-oriented urban governments, marketing and branding strategies began to be deliberately integrated into broader policies of urban restructuring to provide cities a competitive edge in the global marketplace, and to attract inward investment from companies, visitors, and prospective residents.

Sociologist Miriam Greenberg draws a parallel between city branding and corporate branding, whose origins she traces back to the times of economic crisis in the late 1960s and early 1970s: in these years, global companies started employing branding strategies as part of more generalized internal restructuring processes, which usually entailed cuts on manufacturing expenses by outsourcing production to developing countries where labor was cheap, and an emphasis on aggressive advertising and marketing strategies directed to the mass consumers inland. Similar restructuring processes were adopted by municipal governments across the US in the midst of the urban crisis of the 1970s, when potentially unpopular, neoliberal pro-market reforms that were conducted backstage were combined with new promotional strategies which borrowed heavily from the advertising culture of the corporate world.[19]

Today, in an entrepreneurial era in which cities are run like businesses, the notions of "corporate branding" and "corporate identity" are routinely translated to the sphere of public management.[20] Corporate branding presupposes a regime of fierce competition in a global marketplace in which companies need to differentiate their products from those of their competitors[21] and is strongly related to the emergence of the so-called experience economy[22] in which, branding specialists say, what is sold is not a product but a memorable experience or, as Naomi Klein puts it, "a way of life, an attitude, a set of values, a look, an idea."[23]

Translated to the realm of urban policy, the manufacturing, staging, and communication of a city brand is believed to bestow a place with a memorable identity, which will provide that certain *je ne sais quoi* in the struggle for capital investment and tax-paying businesses and residents. The corporate branding of cities thus consists of the manufacturing of a single, consistent representation of the city as a one-of-a-kind destination, and of its consistent communication at every level of interaction with city consumers (residents, prospective citizens, visitors, investors, and businesses) through all forms of marketing channels. In so doing, branding sets the strategic base upon which different marketing programs can be launched.[24]

Essential to the translation of corporate branding principles to city branding are the concepts of "company brand" and particularly "corporate identity"[25]—the crucial interface of communication with consumers that "articulates the corporate ethos, aims and values and presents a sense of individuality that can help to differentiate the organization within its competitive environment."[26] In the corporate world, a brand is successful when it embodies intangible attributes to which consumers can easily relate, because, as the branding logic goes, "consumers relate to a product with their brain, but to a brand with their heart."[27] A similar logic is applied to the branding of cities in the "destination branding" industry. The branded city "is given an ontological status as a 'personality' with a specific identity and set of values."[28] This "personality" orientates the emotions and needs of a target market of city consumers in a mobile, globalized society in which choosing a destination over another becomes an indicator of lifestyle or even social status.

The city brand is then condensed into a collection of images that are mass-reproduced in different forms of media including tourism and business magazines, travel and real estate sections of newspapers, in-flight magazines of major airlines, travel brochures, and urban lifestyle magazines, or broadcasted on TV ads or online on city homepages. In some cases, this brand is summarized in catchy slogans aimed at conveying the city's "personality" in a concise, memorable way. But today, most promotional brochures and video ads present an increasingly generic selection of urban imagery—fashionable star-architectures, gleaming office buildings, vibrant ethnic neighborhoods, bike lanes and the ever-present jogging promenades—while slogans such as "Always Turned On" for Atlantic City, "Cleveland Rocks!" for Cleveland, "Keep Austin Weird" for Austin, and "So Very Virginia" for Charlottesville suggest how branding campaigns consist of rather lofty values and concepts that don't necessarily have much to do with any specific experience the city has to offer.

In fact, the very idea of a straightforward city "identity" is a rather abstract construction that whitewashes the complexity of a rich and multifaceted organism and the multiplicity and diversity of its residents. This unifying narrative for the city is nothing but a hegemonic representation[29] that has less to do with the city to which it is applied than with the private interests of city producers that are in charge of manufacturing it. After all, contrary to a company's board of directors, how can cities reach a shared consensus on issues such as "identity," "mission," and "values"? This is the dilemma with city branding: although branding initiatives are shaped behind closed doors at the board meetings of elite interest groups, they are then championed to residents as a collective citizen endeavor.[30]

Over the last four decades, city producers have been at the front line of unprecedented branding and marketing efforts in major cities around the globe. To attract businesses and tourists, the city is presented as a playground for consumption, leisure, and entertainment. In this vision, issues of social inequality, poverty, or conflict need no mention. Routinely, "amenities that are considered attractive to Florida's creative class and, more generally, to tourists—are most prominent, while images that refer to work, schools, and public safety—factors that are important to many residents—are largely absent."[31] In so doing, city branding is based on a misrepresentation of the city and its citizens[32] as it strives to turn almost every possible exploitable aspect of city life—from its historical landmarks to its ethnic neighbor-hoods, from its underground art scene to its nightlife—into a commodity for sale.

But there's more. Cities willing to join the global branding competition often end up caught in a zero-sum game in which public resources are diverted from local needs toward image-enhancing ventures whose benefits are often questionable.[33] They routinely invest public funds in the promotion of flagship architectures, sport arenas, art museums, and entertainment complexes or strive to attract large international events such as the expos or the Olympics, and sometimes they may even do so at great risk for the city budget, as happened with Rio de Janeiro's overspending for the 2016 Olympics. This is why branding strategies, although often labeled as apolitical practices of city management, have instead thick political ramifications. Branding is not limited to the advertising and promotion of localities; instead, it articulates into a broader set of practices of production of the urban space.[34]

In a detailed history of branding endeavors in New York City from the fiscal crisis through the de Blasio years, I will illustrate how branding practices have triggered processes of sweeping reorganization of the symbolic, physical, and socioeconomic space of the city. I will tell the story of how the apocalyptic urban jungle of the 1970s has gradually dissolved to make room for a new New York, a pricey wonderland for the new hordes of global consumers.

A History of branding in New York from the Fiscal Crisis to the Early 2000s

> That gleaming filmic metropolis, born with the rise of the talkies in the early 1930's, had been displaced in the late 1960's by what was, in many ways, its exact opposite: the cinematic vision of the city as a gritty urban battleground.... Films as varied as "Taxi Driver," "Death Wish," "Little Murders," and "Escape From New York" inflated a city struggling with immense social and economic problems into a spectacularly dysfunctional urban environment, separated by an almost unbridgeable gulf from the rest of the country. But in one of the swiftest and most stunning transformations in the history of cities, New York emerged in the mid-1990's from its decades of troubles to become the safest big city in the country—a burgeoning, prosperous and essentially orderly (indeed, some might say too orderly) metropolis.[35]

The 1970s are regarded by many as the time when New York City hit rock bottom. Economic stagnation battered the city particularly hard during the administration of Abraham Beame, as trading on the stock exchange dropped precipitously, while the city's welfare spending continued unabated. The city's tax base was further eroded by the relentless "white flight" of middle- and upper-class families to the suburbs, while the inner city remained stuck in a spiral of poverty and unemployment; the city's poorest neighborhoods were ravaged by the heroin epidemic and by the spread of violent crime associated with drug abuse, while innumerable buildings in the poorest areas of Harlem, the Bronx, and Brooklyn had been left abandoned or boarded up (Figure 6.2). Meanwhile, the city's subway system was wrecked by vandalism and continuous breakdowns, the once-glorious Times Square had become a haven for prostitutes and shady sex shops, and Central Park by night was notorious in the nation as the dreadful site of muggings, murders, and rapes. Labor strikes, racial tensions, and soaring crime rates led to a widespread belief that New York City's collapse was imminent, and that its decline was irreversible. Horror stories about New York City culminated with the city blackout in the summer of 1977, which initiated a spiral of devastation and looting in low-income areas in Manhattan, Brooklyn, and the South Bronx. By the

Figure 6.2 Macombs Road, Bronx/ *World Telegram & Sun* photo by Phil Stanziola, 1964.

end of the 1970s, not only many large corporations and tourists but also nearly a million people, mostly middle-class residents, had abandoned the city since the 1950s—a population loss that would not be recouped until the 1990s.

As a consequence, the 1970s represented one of the bleakest periods for the "image" of New York City, which was perceived worldwide as an unmanageable, apocalyptic mayhem.[36] Shocking representations of a crime-ridden, anarchic metropolis were constantly propagated in movies, novels, and frightening TV and press reports. These images of a decaying, pathological urban nightmare terrorized middle-class Americans and amplified conservative political discourses about the causes of the "urban crisis,"[37] consolidating citizen support for the tough policies of welfare reform and war on drugs of the era to come.

According to Greenberg, it was in this decade that a sentiment emerged among New York's city producers that the horrific public perceptions associated with the city were contributing to the exacerbation of the broader social and economic crisis,[38] as they were holding back prospective businesses and tourists. Only the manufacturing of a brand-new, cleaned-up city image would bring New York back to its feet.

It was in this decade that powerful groups representing New York's business elite, the real estate industry, and the financial sector became increasingly involved in the making of urban policy, while local authorities assumed the role of enablers of the private initiative—a task they zealously carried out by endorsing growth-oriented and business-prone policies and by financing private ventures as engines of development.[39]

Image Cleansing

As already mentioned in chapters 2 and 4, by mid-1975 New York City was on the verge of insolvency. As a response to this emergency, a "crisis regime"[40] was put in place, which brought about a sweeping reorientation of policy priorities away from the provision of public services and toward a regime of municipal assistance to privately led development and growth initiatives. Until 1974, federal subsidies and huge borrowings had allowed the city to function and to sustain its strong welfare system, which provided among the best public health, housing, and education in the country. However, once the city's financial management was put under the control of supra-governmental emergency institutions like the Municipal Assistance Corporation and the Emergency Financial Control Board, a sweeping process of restructuring was initiated, which dictated austerity measures and drastic cuts on city services amidst an unprecedented wave of subsidies to the business community. Along with the wave of tax breaks, subsidies, development grants and zoning changes to stimulate development of high-end office and residential space in Manhattan, funds were channeled into a sweeping operation of image restructuring that would forever transform the public perception of the gritty, anarchic metropolis into that of a cleaned-up, business-friendly city.

In 1976, the Department of City Planning released a report titled *Economic Recovery: New York City's Program for 1977–1981*. Based on the assumption that New York's grim image had to be turned upside down to appeal to the international business community, the report dictated a revamping of the Office of Economic Development (today's New York City Economic Development Corporation [NYCEDC]) and called for a comprehensive marketing program funded by the city, the state, and private companies to "convey New York's advantages as a place to do business and to stress the City's positive attitude toward business."[41] The concerted application of branding strategies borrowed from the corporate industry was a crucial step in the transition to an "entrepreneurial" system of urban governance.[42]

Soon, a powerful marketing machine was set in motion, which brought together the crème de la crème of New York's city producers: elected officials, real estate players, and a bundle of business-led associations such as the New York City Partnership[43] (NYCP), the Convention and Visitors' Bureau[44] (CVB), and the Association for a Better New York[45] (ABNY). In 1971, they launched the first attempt at a citywide promotional campaign called "The Big Apple," which was popularized through TV news and magazine ads. Fully funded by New York's elite of realtors and hoteliers, "The Big Apple" campaign proved successfully that New York could again be a magnet for visitors. But the onset of the fiscal crisis in 1975 and the terrible events of 1977 (the "summer of Sam" murders and the citywide blackout) demonstrated that the real city was still shouting its anger, and no upbeat marketing campaigns could keep the mainstream media away from depicting New York as an unmanageable urban jungle.[46]

In 1977, at the height of the city's fiscal crisis, the New York State Department of Commerce (DOC) under Commissioner William Doyle (a former marketing manager at Chase Manhattan Bank and member of the ABNY) decided to commit the largest amount of its annual budget to hire a professional marketing firm. Its role was to craft effective image communication campaigns depicting the city's advantages and strengths to visitors and business managers. With the passage of the Omnibus Tourism Bill in June 1977, the DOC committed $4.3 million to finance the state's first sweeping branding campaign. The iconic, pop-style "I ♥ NY" logo was the product of advertising agency Wells Rich and Greene and *New York Magazine* artistic director Milton Glaser, and became immediately the most commonly recognized symbol of New York City.[47] Besides placing the logo on TV ads, posters, and the now-legendary white T-shirts, the "I ♥ NY" campaign also included other promotional measures, from tourist package deals like Broadway show tours or family-friendly TV and radio ads featuring the "I Love New York" theme song, to outdoor events at major city landmarks. The campaign proved incredibly successful, and revenues in the tourist industry skyrocketed.[48]

Gradually, in the late 1970s, "the mainstream media began to cover New York City's apparent recovery, and to do so as dramatically as they had the city's recent demise."[49] To press reporters and media producers, New York City appeared to be finally on the rebound. In 1973, after long delays, the Twin Towers of the World Trade Center were finally completed: although the whole operation turned out to be a huge drag on the city's finances,[50] it had an immense symbolic significance, as the brand-new towers, still largely vacant, were promptly marketed as the symbols of the revitalization of downtown Manhattan and the icons of a reborn city (Figure 6.3). Their sparkling silhouettes appeared so often in marketing brochures and tourist guides that visitors came to identify them with the city itself: the 1981 cover of *Time* magazine portraying an exultant Edward Koch with the Twin Towers in the background symbolized to American readers the resurgence of New York City.[51]

Figure 6.3 World Trade Center Towers and the New York City skyline.

Behind the Image: The Socioeconomic
Restructuring of New York City

According to Miriam Greenberg, the "I ♥ NY" campaign was "the publicly visible, populist face of a more controversial process of pro-business economic restructuring,"[52] which became the hallmark of the mayoral administration of Edward Koch (1977–1989), and which entailed cuts across the board on social services, public housing, schools, hospitals, sanitation, and public infrastructure, coupled with generous subsidies to private ventures and to privately led programs of office and market-rate housing construction.

The result was an increasingly polarized city: while the Wall Street boom fueled an unprecedented wave of speculation in office building construction, the percentage of New Yorkers living under the federal poverty line rose consistently along with homelessness rates.[53] Crime and decay, although gradually fading from the glossy pages of lifestyle magazines and marketing brochures, were still a big part of New Yorkers' daily experience, and became particularly severe in the last two of Ed Koch's three terms as mayor. The administration's response was a hard line on "quality of life" issues. By the mid-1980s, the term "quality of life"[54] had turned from a government agenda to reduce inequality (as part of Lyndon Johnson's 1964 war on poverty program) to a slogan to justify increased police enforcement against petty crime: instead of attempting to eradicate the causes of poverty, the focus was shifted toward what some pundits have called the "criminalization of poverty"—a philosophy that the mayoral administration of Rudolph Giuliani would fully endorse in the 1990s.

In 1989, David Dinkins became the city's first-ever black mayor. The tourist industry had been hit hard by the stock market crash and the recession of 1989–1992, and the city government was left with a very tight budget for tourism and business promotion. In 1992, Dinkins organized a European road show to promote the city to foreign investors, but the tour was deemed a publicity failure.[55] Dinkins's half-hearted campaign to reframe the "quality of life" focus to benefit disadvantaged New Yorkers and minority groups[56] was short-lived: in late 1993, he was defeated by Giuliani in his bid for reelection. Giuliani immediately resurrected Koch's "quality of life" policing campaign and used it as a tool to promote a cleaned-up city that would reattract visitors and businesses: the campaign, based on a "zero tolerance" approach on minor crimes such as begging, panhandling, or graffiti writing, translated into an aggressive crackdown on poor and homeless people.[57] According to author and activist Randy Shaw, "Giuliani's platform defined 'quality of life' as protecting the middle-class and business community from the homeless and poor people that the War on Poverty's 'quality of life' terminology was designed to assist."[58] During Giuliani's first term, the New York City Police Department headed by Commissioner William Bratton adopted aggressive policing strategies based on James Q. Wilson's "broken windows" approach. This was based on the harsh repression of minor offenses, on the theory that maintaining an orderly urban environment acts as a deterrent for petty crime and antisocial behavior, preventing escalation into more serious crimes. And indeed, crime declined precipitously under Giuliani's tenure, with violent crimes dropping 56% and robberies going down 67% in eight years.[59] The extent to which his administration deserves all the credit, however, is disputed, as crime had started declining before Giuliani's election, reflecting a national trend already in progress since the Dinkins years.[60] But what escalated dramatically instead were the many outrageous cases of police brutality and civil rights abuse, mostly directed toward young men of color.[61]

Under Giuliani, "zero tolerance" was an integral part of a citywide campaign to maintain order in an era of unprecedented social inequalities, many of which were the product of the very reforms that the mayor's administration had enforced:[62] Giuliani's welfare-to-work[63] initiative and the dismantling of social services for the neediest New Yorkers were the trailblazers for the major neoliberal shifts in federal policy that would come in the Clinton years. While conservative media celebrated Giuliani for "turning the city around," progressive pundits dismissed his "quality of life" campaign as an operation to protect the welfare of wealthy New Yorkers and the safety of tourists in the midst of an increasingly unequal and polarized city.[64]

By the late 1990s, the image of New York City had become that of a shiny, business-friendly global city. But New York's renaissance as a place to visit and to do business may have been less the result of the mayor's "quality of life" campaigns and more the consequence of major shifts in the administration's economic priorities. The hotel occupancy tax was reduced, while an unprecedented platform of corporate tax breaks and incentives was enacted to attract or retain major corporations, hotels, and financial institutions in the city. Investors took advantage of public/private financing to embark on new residential and office development ventures in downtown Manhattan, including Battery Park City, the World Financial Center, and the refurbishment of South Street Seaport. Meanwhile, Times Square, which throughout the 1960s and 1970s had become an infamous symbol of the city's decline, was turned around to symbolize yet another success of the Giuliani administration. In 1990, New York State had taken possession of six of the nine historic theaters on 42nd Street, some of which were renovated for Broadway shows, some demolished, and some converted into multiplex movie theaters or megastores. In 1992, the Times Square Alliance started a program of "clean-up" for the area by increasing security, evicting porn theaters and sex shops, and attracting tourist- and family-friendly attractions like Planet Hollywood and other global franchises. The renewed Times Square attracted a number of large financial, publishing, and media firms, whose headquarters were also "branded" thanks to zoning ordinances requiring building owners to display huge illuminated LED billboards—the Times Square of today. Under Giuliani, more attempts at revamping the New York brand were set in motion: the obsolete Convention and Visitors Bureau was revamped, its operation and budget expanded, and its name changed to NYC & Company to become the city's official tourism marketing organization. The new body, composed of 13,000 members including hotels, restaurants, attractions, and convention centers, was geared especially toward attracting tourists to the new sparkling downtown in Lower Manhattan, symbolized by the towers of the World Trade Center. By 2000, the city had managed to attract 37.4 million yearly visitors, up from 28.5 million in 1995. According to data released by NYC & Company, by the year 2000, business travel increased to 11.7 million travelers, while the city also gained ground as a family-friendly travel destination, with an overall 45% increase in family travel (up to 10.5 million) since 1996. Visitor spending in New York City rose to $17 billion, accounting for a total economic impact calculated at $24.9 billion.[65] In the summer of 2001, Giuliani announced the results of these extraordinary efforts:

> Tourism continues to be one of the engines powering New York City's economy. Last year's record number of visitors is a testament to New York City's broad appeal to people from all over the world. In addition to our historic reductions in crime, we have made significant improvements in quality of life, and great advances in both economic vitality and cultural achievement. There is great energy in New York City now—and tourists come here to be a part of it.[66]

If Koch had been no man to eschew public exposure, having appeared in more than 70 movies and TV shows as himself, Giuliani was an even bolder marketer of himself. During his time in office, through his tightly controlled

press office and his commissioners, Giuliani managed to consistently satu-
rate the media, advertising the results of his "quality of life" campaigns and
celebrating the successes of his administration.[67] He succeeded in selling the
narrative that a city as unmanageable as New York could be indeed "turned
around": if Giuliani had turned New York City into a profitable, tourist- and
business-friendly brand, there was hope for all cities in distress. In so doing,
Giuliani became probably the first of a future generation of "branded" city
mayors[68]—a practice that the Bloomberg administration would heavily bor-
row from in the following years. The branding of Giuliani swelled after the
tragedy of September 11, once again a time of crisis for New York City,
whose image was now tied to the horrors of devastation, terrorism, danger, and mourning. As mayor of a wounded city, Giuliani gained the attention of the international community and was praised for his engagement
in the rescue and recovery operations during the crisis. In the aftermath of
the terrorist attacks, the controversies surrounding his figure quickly disappeared from the media, as Giuliani became, in the words of Oprah Winfrey,
"America's Mayor,"[69] a man whose courage and prowess were celebrated
worldwide. *Time* magazine named him "Person of the Year" for 2001, while
Queen Elizabeth II made him an honorary knight of the British Empire in
2002. After 9/11, Giuliani thus came to symbolize to the world the endur-
ance and resilience of the entire city. But despite Giuliani's international
recognition, New York was again in the midst of a terrible emergency, and
had to deal not only with a devastating loss of jobs and tax revenues but also
with the flight of hundreds of companies in the aftermath of the attacks.
Before 9/11, there was a projected $545 million surplus in the city budget;
after the attack, the city had a $1.3 billion shortfall. Almost 15,000 businesses
in the area close to the World Trade Center were destroyed, damaged, or
disrupted.[70] The New York City Partnership estimated that the economic
impact of the attack would likely total $83 billion in damage to New York
City's economy. As an article in the *Wall Street Journal* announced, it was time
to "turn around" once again the public perception of the city to reinject
confidence in visitors, consumers, and businesses:

> For the city's official marketers New York isn't just a wounded city, but a chal-
> lenged brand ... [and] like all challenged brands, it needs ... an overarching
> scheme to reposition itself in the American popular consciousness.[71]

Businesses and tourists had to be persuaded once again that the city, despite
the tragedy, was a safe and profitable destination. Thus, while federal aid was

channeled into a new wave of tax breaks and incentives for the corporate sector, new marketing campaigns were launched to emphasize the "resilience" of the city in the aftermath of the tragedy.

On the one side, a massive corporate retention strategy was pursued that consisted of million-dollar tax breaks and other subsidies to companies that were threatening to leave the city after the attacks, "regardless of whether companies actually stay in the city, or ever intended to leave in the first place."[72] This strategy would continue under Giuliani's successor Michael Bloomberg, who would allow a large chunk of federal aid for reconstruction to be funneled into subsidies for corporate and banking giants.[73] On the other side, the New York City Partnership and the ABNY, in concert with city and state agencies such as NYC & Company, the NYCEDC, the Empire State Development Corporation (ESDC), and the newly created Lower Manhattan Development Corporation (LMDC),[74] and assisted by professional marketing firms, mobilized to craft a new citywide branding campaign. As recommended by marketing consultants, a campaign would be successful only if it managed to push aside the memory of the tragedy and focus on New York's ability to rebound.[75] Two campaigns were thus launched in 2001: the "New York Stronger Than Ever" campaign was targeted at patriotic tourists from the United States and international sympathizers from across the world and aimed to attract national and international events like the 2004 Republican National Convention and the 2012 Olympics. The campaign featured TV commercials and giant billboards advertising the resilient city and its generous sponsors (American Express, Mercedes Benz, and AOL Time Warner, among others). Simultaneously, a new $40 million marketing operation was launched to mark the 25th anniversary of the 1977 "I ♥ NY" campaign: it featured advertisements on the radio, on the Internet, and in newspapers and magazines, as well as an energetic TV ad that emphasized the vibrancy of the city and highlighted its "businesses, theaters, restaurants, and stadiums"; it also featured Mayor Giuliani, Governor Pataki, celebrities, and people from the streets sporting T-shirts with the "I ♥ NY" logo and proudly repeating, "I love New York." The message was that New York was back and thriving, as Pataki announced in October 2001.[76]

For the occasion, Milton Glaser had crafted pro bono a new logo—a reiteration of the "I ♥ NY" logo, but with a black stain over the heart, as a symbol of New York's wounded heart. But the ESDC, which was the copyright holder, urged Glaser to either take the black mark off of the heart or discontinue using the logo.[77] City marketing could well capitalize on the tragedy, but only up to a certain extent: vulnerability was no suitable brand to attract visitors and businesses, as alarming reports from marketing consultancy firms had convinced the city that the memory of the tragedy, although still popular among patriotic US visitors, was no good sale to wealthy business travelers and corporations considering relocation.[78]

This shift became clear by the opening of what would become New York's top tourist attraction for many years, the viewing platform at Ground Zero, when the city cleared the fences of the thousands of memorabilia, floral wreaths, US flags, and photos that honored the missing and the deceased in the terrorist attack (Figure 6.4). City officials had realized it was time to adopt a completely different strategy.

The Corporate Branding of NYC in the Time of Bloomberg

In 2001, Michael R. Bloomberg succeeded Giuliani with a staggering $73 million privately funded campaign. He inherited a city with a sinking economy, a huge budget deficit, and a bleak image tied to the horrors of 9/11. As he took office, Bloomberg addressed the city's image crisis by bringing the branding machine to a whole new level. The branding efforts led by Bloomberg throughout his three mandates have constituted probably the most literal translation of the principles of "corporate identity" and "corporate branding" into the realm of urban management. He channeled unprecedented investments from both the private and the public sector and worked on an extensive restructuring of the municipal city marketing agencies to create a hierarchically integrated marketing apparatus modeled on the structure of a business corporation.[79] Soon after taking office, the mayor clarified his intentions of manufacturing a unified city brand to be sold in the global marketplace:

> New York is in a fierce, worldwide competition; our strategy must be to hone our competitive advantages. We must offer the best product—and sell it, forcefully....We'll take advantage of our brand. New York is the best-known City on the planet....Yet, as a City, we've never taken direct, coordinated custody of our image. By changing that, we can realize additional City revenues immediately. Many companies are interested in sponsorship agreements, similar to their sponsorship of major sporting and charitable events. We'll do this in a way that protects the integrity of our services and that creates financial returns benefiting all New Yorkers.[80]

Figure 6.4 Ground Zero Memorial, public viewing platform. Adorned with flowers, letters, and patches of deceased officers, the first Ground Zero Memorial installation was removed in 2002.

In 2002, Bloomberg created two new city marketing agencies, NYC Big Events and a "Permanent Host Committee," to secure high-profile events that could provide a platform to showcase the city both nationally and internationally. In 2003, the NYCEDC organized a series of "road shows" to

market the city around the world, from London to Beijing. The host committee was successful in hosting high-profile events such as the 2003 WNBA
All-Star game, the Grammys, and the 2004 Republican National Convention.
With the pursuit of the contested bid for the 2012 Olympic Games as the
keystone for an unprecedented branding campaign,[81] Bloomberg started
marketing the city as "the world's second home" at public speeches and conventions.[82] Television ads were broadcasted with the tagline: "The Olympic
Games in New York. We've been training for this forever." Meanwhile, a
2002 report was produced by corporate consulting firm McKinsey and Co.
that would have a crucial influence on the future moves of Bloomberg's
branding machine.[83] If the city wanted to compete in the global marketplace, according to the report, it had to diversify its economy beyond Wall
Street and attract new industries, especially high-end global companies in
the fields of information, media, and technology. The report advised against
the use of traditional corporate retention strategies (a standard practice that
had reached its climax during the administration of Giuliani and continued
during the first years of Bloomberg) and suggested focusing instead on specific branding strategies targeting the industries' top executives: these had to
emphasize the city's highly skilled talent pool, its high-end residential space,
its first-class amenities, and its cultural vibrancy and quality of life—elements
that the report deemed crucial to the locational decisions of wealthy managers and professionals.[84] In January 2003, Bloomberg finally unveiled to
reporters what seemed to summarize the city's new strategy:

> The more I learn about this institution of New York City, the more I see
> the ways in which it needs to think like a private company…. If New York
> City is a business, it isn't Wal-Mart—it isn't trying to be the lowest-priced
> product in the market. It's a high-end product, maybe even a luxury product.
> New York offers tremendous value, but only for those companies able to cap-
> italize on it.[85]

Bloomberg's "luxury city" message was targeted at an elite market made
up of the wealthiest global companies—companies whose dominant concern in locational decision making was not about costs but rather about
enhancing their brand image by associating it with that of a winning global
city. Bloomberg's message to the business world was pretty clear-cut: not all
companies are invited to move here, only those that can afford to pay for
the unique advantages that New York has to offer—the upper crust of the
global corporate market.[86]

In 2002, while overseas the city was sold to the Olympic Committee and international tourists as a beacon of inclusion and cultural diversity, NYC & Company filled the city with over 1,000 banners on city streets with taglines such as "NYC—Banking Capital of the World," "NYC—Real Estate Capital of the World," and "NYC—Financial Capital of the World." The huge gap between two marketing messages as divergent as "the world's second home" and "the luxury city" epitomizes the bipolar, double-faced approach of the branding campaigns led during Bloomberg's first term, based on distinct marketing messages for each different target group. While the Olympic campaign celebrated the color and diversity of "the world's second home," and following campaigns such as "This Is New York City" presented New York as a welcoming city of openness and creativity, in VIP business meetings the city was marketed as a luxury brand to an elite of powerful companies and investors.[87]

The use of such a two-faced approach not only testifies to the ambiguity of the representational universe of marketing messages in the broadest sense but also poses the question of how could two such conflicting representational universes translate into a consistent policy agenda? The answer, as will be clarified in the following sections, is quite simple: the city would be re-engineered as a luxury enclave for the wealthy, while public campaigns would advertise it to middle-class locals and visitors as an inclusive, diverse, and open city. Marketing slogans and factual policy had split their paths, never to join again.

Bloomberg's Branding Machine in Action

> There was a day when everybody said NYC does not need to advertise, it's the Big Apple, everyone is going to come here.... Those days are long over.... We are in the days of good communications and great transportation and a media that shows people that there are other cities around the world. We are in a very competitive battle.... You have to have a coordinated strategy; you can't just say ... they're going to come to us.[88]

Bloomberg understood that the establishment of a supervising body capable of coordinating a broad array of marketing efforts was paramount for a consistent and effective branding of the city, and in 2003 he instituted a new entity called New York City Marketing (NYCM), designed to manage the city brand, articulate marketing campaigns, and craft sponsorships with private companies. Bloomberg appointed marketing executive Joseph Perello, a former advertising agency director and business consultant for the

New York Yankees, as its president and chief marketing officer (CMO). The CMO's task was to oversee all marketing efforts in cooperation with other city agencies, and to partner with corporations interested in cosponsorship agreements. NYCM's activities were also closely tied to the development agendas of three other city-affiliated quasi-governmental agencies: the NYCEDC, responsible for promoting urban development across the five boroughs; NYC & Company, the official city agency for tourism; and NYC Big Events, the marketing division the mayor had established with the task of attracting events in the aftermath of 9/11. NYCM, the NYCEDC, NYC Big Events, and NYC & Company well represented the interests of the city's most powerful city producers, including members of the real estate, financial, media, and banking elites, and their operations were strictly overseen by growth advocate and Deputy Mayor Daniel Doctoroff. NYCM, which in June 2003 was transformed into a local development corporation, became Bloomberg's and Doctoroff's centralized marketing authority. Its new status meant that the agency, although largely funded with public money, could act unrestrained by public scrutiny. Over the following years, CMO Perello assembled a team of business leaders and marketing firms to guide the agency's first marketing operations: in its early years, NYCM forged corporate partnerships, surveyed all of the city's brands, secured copyrights, contracted licensing royalties, and negotiated advertising and promotion space on the city's street furniture. As Daniel Doctoroff anticipated in 2003, almost every aspect of city life was now up for grabs for corporate sponsors:

> Similar to sports franchises and cultural institutions that use stadiums and exhibits as their canvas for corporate support, New York City can do the same. The difference here is that the entire City will be our canvas.[89]

Thanks to the centralized management of the city's trademarks, NYCM could sell the New York City brand to corporations interested in partnership deals. Several requests for proposals were issued to offer licensing rights for a range of products including apparel, souvenirs, and gadgets. The office was also charged with licensing the New York City brands and logos in films and television productions.

Starting in 2003, a number of corporate sponsorships were set in motion. The same year, the city entered into a contract with Snapple, a five-year, $166 million deal that gave the New York–born beverage company exclusive rights to sell its beverages through vending machines placed in various city agencies, police stations, and even sanitation depots, as well as in 1,200

New York City public schools. In return, Snapple guaranteed at least $8 million a year to New York City schools for five years, and about $13 million a year to the city, based on sales. Snapple would also spend $12 million a year on cross-advertising that also promoted the city.[90] Soon after, several other citywide sponsorship deals were set in motion. In December 2004, NYCM announced a $19.5 million contract with The History Channel: under the 3.5-year agreement, the network was allowed self-promotion on several city properties and street furniture; in return, the city would get $19.5 million, of which $3.5 million would be spent to restore historical sites and to create the NYC Heritage Tourism Center in Lower Manhattan, $15 million would be directed to promote the city on the channel, and another $1 million would be spent on educational programs for city schools sponsored by the network.[91] Later in 2005, a new partnership was developed with Universal Studios for the premiere of the *King Kong* movie: the deal allowed Universal free use of Military Island, one of the plazas created by the DOT at Times Square, where a 20-foot sculpture of King Kong was erected for the event. In the following years, other sponsorship agreements were developed with American Express, OpenTable, Sony Pictures, Travelocity, Time Out New York, and Spanish street furniture design firm Cemusa, among others.

In less than one year, Bloomberg's branding machine started to bear fruit. A Young & Rubicam study ranked New York City as the 13th most powerful global brand of 2,400 brands analyzed in 2004: according to the report, brand attributes for New York City were "unique," "authentic," and "dynamic."[92] By 2005, New York City tourism represented a $24 billion industry with more than $5 billion in city, state, and federal tax revenues.[93]

But it wasn't until 2006 that Bloomberg laid the groundwork for the creation of what Greenberg calls his "massive new branding apparatus,"[94] when he merged the three existing city marketing agencies and put them under his control, creating a single, vertically organized municipal marketing agency. Both NYCM and NYC Big Events were merged with the city's tourism and convention agency NYC & Company, creating a new, unified governing body. A private nonprofit corporation, NYC & Company until 2006 was a membership-based organization financed by dues collected from its members, but when the mayor took direct control of its operations, he supplemented the newly created entity with an annual budget that rose to $103 million over five years. In so doing, Bloomberg applied the business model of a corporation to a governmental body that eluded public scrutiny:[95] according to *New York Magazine* reporter Michael Idov, "on paper, Bloomberg got rid of two agencies; in reality, he created a kind of superagency free from the bureaucratic confines of City Hall."[96] Finally, top marketing professionals from the world of advertising were appointed as managers of the revamped agency: power brander George A. Fertitta, a former Madison Avenue veteran whose ad agency specialized in marketing luxury goods,[97] was appointed as its CEO and brought in his own team of advertising executives and creative professionals. NYC & Company's public funding escalated to $22.5 million yearly. But NYC & Company's direct revenues from sponsorships and deals far outweighed its public funding, with a budget estimated at $60 million in 2010.[98]

To further promote and enhance the image of New York around the world, NYC & Company also worked to create the first ever unified brand identity for the city. In 2006, the agency hired branding firm Wolff Olins to manufacture the city's first official "corporate identity" through the design of a new logo for New York City and the revamping of the official city website. Today, the new logo has been integrated across city and government services, from taxi cabs to municipal services, from travel brochures to TV ads, providing a ubiquitous, consistent, and instantly recognizable symbol to both residents and visitors, while the renewed website was expanded with new interactive features, so that it could compete with the most established online guides.[99] The revenues from advertising on the website (which became www. nycgo.com in 2009) amounted to $2 million in 2009 and reached $3 million by 2011.[100]

In his 2006 State of the City address, Bloomberg boldly announced that he would bring a staggering 50 million tourists to New York City by 2015, up from the 32.5 million he inherited in 2002 and from an estimated 43 million in 2006.[101] Bloomberg's ambitious goal would be fulfilled four years ahead of schedule, in 2011.

In 2007, the marketing division of NYC & Company unveiled its first global branding campaign: the $30 million "This Is New York City" campaign, designed by global advertising agency Bartle Bogle Hegarty, boasted dreamy images of a colorful urban paradise, and included television, print, online, and outdoor ads. The campaign's centerpiece was a TV ad that combined film and animation and featured iconic images from the five boroughs, including the Statue of Liberty, Times Square, the Empire State Building, the Wonder Wheel in Coney Island, the Lenox Lounge in Harlem, the Brooklyn Bridge, the Unisphere in Queens, and the Staten Island Ferry. The family-friendly commercial showed a psychedelic New York City, almost remindful of the Beatles' classic 1968 animated feature film *Yellow Submarine*. The ad aired on television in Spain, Ireland, France, and the United Kingdom, and on domestic networks through the partnership with The History Channel and other cable partners (Figure 6.5). The outdoor and print advertisements highlighted different segments of the New York City experience—from shopping and fashion to entertainment and food—and were placed on bus shelters in Brazil, Portugal, Italy, and Spain, and domestically in cities such as Boston, Philadelphia, Miami, and San Antonio, through the city's street furniture contract with advertising company Cemusa, which managed 3,000 bus shelters, 7,000 street poles, and 1,000 telephone kiosks in the city.[102]

"This Is New York City" presented New York as a magical wonderland of experiences unmatchable by any other destination in the world, a place of "unparalleled diversity, excitement, culture, shopping and entertainment."[103] But most important, the campaign constituted the first attempt to promote all of the five New York City boroughs as tourist destinations, each with its own distinct flavor.

Figure 6.5 Stills from the "This Is New York City" TV ad, 2007, designed by Bartle Bogle Hegarty.

The idea of a campaign to officially promote all of the five boroughs as tourist destinations, something that would have been unimaginable just a decade earlier, had become a sure bet by 2007, when an unprecedented boom in the housing market had profoundly transformed the face of once-deprived neighborhoods in Brooklyn, Queens, and Harlem. By 2007, all of the outer boroughs had seen a sustained drop in crime rates, all of them had witnessed soaring housing values due to their proximity to the booming housing market in Manhattan, all of them had been penetrated by big corporate retailers and banks, and many sported their own hip artistic scene and vibrant nightlife: in sum, by the late 2000s, most of the outer boroughs fulfilled the necessary prerequisites to be marketed as tourist-friendly destinations, and some had even started their own local branding campaigns. As a case in point, in 2007, Brooklyn was experiencing an unprecedented wave of luxury hotel construction spurred by the city's rezoning plans for Williamsburg and downtown Brooklyn; this boom prompted the Brooklyn Tourism and Visitors Center to create its own interactive tourism website (visitbrooklyn.org) and Borough President Markowitz to brand Brooklyn as "the perfect destination for business, conference and leisure travelers from around the globe,"[104] while lifestyle magazines labeled it as "America's coolest restaurant neighborhood."[105]

Similar transformations were occurring in other boroughs as well: while luxury waterfront developments were transforming Queens' once-industrialized Long Island City into a hip residential destination, large parts of the Bronx and Staten Island were being rezoned for luxury residential units and hotels. By the early 2010s, the hotel industry experienced for the first time a staggering expansion in the outer boroughs: in the 2008–2011 period, 42% of new hotel developments built in New York City were located out of Manhattan, with the majority in Queens (22%) and Brooklyn (15%).[106] In 2007, despite the global financial crisis, the city managed to attract a record 46 million visitors, 1.5 million more than in 2006:[107] the combination of Bloomberg's bold marketing campaigns and a weak dollar had contributed to make New York one of the few large cities in the United States that had seen a constant increase in tourism since 9/11.

Yet Bloomberg and Fertitta were confident that more could be done. As internal reports were showing that one of the most common negative perceptions about the city was that it was prohibitively expensive, outdoor ads were placed across European cities declaring that, with the weakness of the dollar, New York had become a relative bargain for European visitors.[108] Meanwhile, according to the heads of NYC & Company, other common negative perceptions about the city, such as its crime and the rudeness of New Yorkers, had to be overcome with a new marketing overdose of urbanity and glamour:

> Mr. Fertitta said he would rather foreigners picture "Sex and the City" than "Law & Order." ... To change people's negative views of New York's grime, crime and prices, he said, the city can piggyback on the invaluable boost it gets from pop-culture cynosures like Carrie Bradshaw.... "To some people, New York City is 'Sex and the City' and the best shoes in the world," Mr. Fertitta said. "They want to see where Carrie Bradshaw sat on the stoop."[109]

Consequently, in 2007, a smaller campaign was crafted with the goal of highlighting New Yorkers' friendliness toward visitors—or at least to reverse a common perception of New Yorkers as jaded and unfriendly: the campaign "Just Ask the Locals" consisted of posters of New York celebrities giving local shopping and dining tips that were disseminated in bus shelters across the city. New York celebrities like Robert de Niro, Julianne Moore, Jimmy Fallon, and Puff Daddy contributed to the campaign pro bono. In early 2008, hotel occupancy rates kept growing, to above 80%, compared to about 60% across the rest of the country, prompting Bloomberg to announce he was confident that the city would reach his goal of attracting 50 million annual visitors by 2012.

Changing Economy, Changing Strategies

> Wrong would be to have a luxury campaign at this time. Right would be to have a family friendly, offer-driven program.[110]

At the end of 2007, the economy was changing for the worse, and the unfolding of a global recession challenged the mayor and the heads of NYC & Company to re-examine their marketing strategies. The programs adopted since 2008 thus focused on a dual strategy: on one hand, because the United States was suffering the consequences of the subprime mortgage crisis and a devastating recession, the image of New York as a prohibitively expensive enclave for the super-wealthy had to be replaced with that of a more approachable and affordable destination, and domestic campaigns had to be made more appealing to average middle-class American families, rather than wealthy business executives; on the other hand, the NYC brand had to be sold more aggressively than ever before overseas, where money was still flowing. As the number of domestic visitors plunged, the city started investing massively in promotion across the Atlantic: NYC

& Company opened a slate of international offices in 17 countries worldwide, including Moscow, Shanghai, Seoul, Tokyo, and Mumbai, and started
launching separate marketing campaigns in each country:

> While the efforts all share the upscale New York brand identity, they are tai-
> lored in unique ways. Asian ads focus on our main icons to entice first-time
> visitors. European markets get bombarded with messages meant to encourage
> repeat visits and a "live like a local" experience. In Italy and Germany, NYC &
> Company has been selling the notion of the city's "energy" and "vibrancy," as
> opposed to any specific sites. It's less Broadway and more Bedford Avenue—a
> place where you go to be cool.[111]

Meanwhile, to a domestic tourist market impoverished by the recession, the
chic imagery of a "Sex and the City"–inspired urbanity was no longer considered an easy sale: the brand of New York City had to be purged of any
remaining "luxury" pedigree to be made appealing to a more disenchanted
and less wealthy US consumer market.

As reports were showing that family trips to favored destinations like
Disney World were dropping, NYC & Company experts responded by
strenuously promoting the city as a family-friendly destination with a series
of low-budget packages for family trips to the city called "New York: The
Real Deal," and later "Get More NYC," which offered deals and savings on
dining, hotels, and shopping and featured characters from Sesame Street as
"NYC family ambassadors."[112]

In line with the core idea of developing different niche marketing messages directed at different consumer targets, these family-friendly campaigns
were conducted side by side with the first global marketing efforts aimed at
bringing visitors from the LGBT community to the city. To highlight the gay-
friendliness of New York, the "Rainbow Pilgrimage" campaign was launched
in 2009, marking the 40th anniversary of the gay rights movement started by
the Stonewall Riots in 1969. Later in 2011, after New York State passed the
same-sex marriage law, NYC & Company jumped in with the "NYC I Do"
marketing campaign, opening the city to the juicy market of wedding and
honeymoon destinations for gay couples, and reaping a staggering $259 mil-
lion from same-sex marriages in the first year of the law allowing the practice,
with at least 8,200 gay-marriage licenses issued in 2011.[113]

The new efforts were again successful, as 2009, despite the global
economic slump, marked New York City as the most popular US destination for the first time in over two decades, with over 45.6 million

visitors, ahead of traditional top destinations like Orlando or Las Vegas.[114] Despite a slight reduction in public funding since the recession (city contributions had dropped to $17 million compared to $22.5 in 2006) and a total budget of $37 million (down from $44 million in 2006), NYC & Company was able to maintain record revenues thanks to sponsorships, advertising, and licensing agreements, and through the popular nycgo.com website, which in 2009 alone generated $2 million worth of advertising.

In 2010, to encourage more Americans and foreigners to keep coming to the city, NYC & Company unveiled another iteration of the "This Is New York City" campaign, which emphasized the energy, excitement, and diversity of the city: a colorful, frantic TV ad featured MTV-like images of a dynamic, edgy, young city of music, funky nightlife, concerts, fashion shows, sports events, and crowded streets. The ad was targeted especially at young tourists, and it was one of the most explicit in promoting all five boroughs as tourist destinations—"five cities in one," as the ad put it:

> This is five cities in one: the Bronx, Brooklyn, Manhattan, Queens, and Staten Island, home to every color, culture, fashion and flavor you can think of. This is knishes, kebabs, pizza, pâté, satay and all the best the rest of the world has to offer. This is where the ball drops and curtains rise. This is Broadway, Off Broadway, Off Off Broadway, beyond Broadway. This is people watching, celebrity sightings, and sample sale prices on the cutting edge of style. This is raw, sophisticated, beautiful, avant-garde. This is energy so exhilarating you can feel it in your soul. This is all of the above, all at the same time. This is New York City.[115]

The outdoor campaign ran across the United States, as well as in international markets in Australia, Brazil, Canada, and Europe, and included promotional packages from leading corporate partners such as American Airlines, American Express, AT&T, Travelocity, and the Nickelodeon cable channel, which in return promoted travel to the city. The online campaign featured the addition of a micro-site at nycgo.com/getmorenyc with personalized travel itineraries (Family, Gay, One Day, Two Day, and Shopping) and the possibility for visitors to engage with social media features via Twitter and Facebook. In 2010, tourism to New York City reached record numbers, with 48.7 million visitors and $31 billion in visitor spending.

Meanwhile, many Manhattan neighborhoods that had been traditionally more reluctant to embrace tourism—like Harlem and Lower Manhattan—saw a massive influx of new hotel openings, including the Aloft Harlem, Mondrian

SoHo, James New York, Sheraton Tribeca New York Hotel, W New York Downtown, and Doubletree New York City in the Financial District.

"Five Cities in One"

Visitors to New York City should know that in every borough of our great city, there are neighborhoods with great restaurants, shops and cultural institutions....We've focused on bringing more tourists to neighborhoods outside of Manhattan, and it's paid off with more hotels being built and tourism-related economic activity happening in those boroughs.[116]

Increasing tourism opportunities in Lower Manhattan, a neighborhood that had been for long disconnected from major tourist routes, was a top priority in anticipation of the 10th anniversary of 9/11. For the opening of the World Trade Center Memorial in September 2011, the city launched the campaign "Get More NYC: Lower Manhattan," designed to showcase to global visitors the recovery of Lower Manhattan and to promote hotels, dining, and shopping venues in a heavily transformed neighborhood. The campaign, which featured outdoor media ads throughout the city's five boroughs, on taxicab monitors, and on social media, included special travel itineraries, coupons, and special offers at Lower Manhattan shops, restaurants, hotels, galleries, and museums. These promotional efforts were, as usual, coupled with a range of fiscal strategies to stimulate commercial development in the district. The NYCEDC's creation of a Lower Manhattan Business Expansion Program granted property tax abatements to medium-sized and small businesses with plans to locate to or expand their operations downtown through the Lower Manhattan Relocation and Employment Assistance Program and the Lower Manhattan Sales and Use Tax Exemption. Such efforts capitalized on a decade-long revitalization program that had started in 2002 with the Job Creation and Worker Assistance Act, which eliminated the commercial rent taxation on all leases at the World Trade Center site and included special sales and use tax exemptions to assist in the recovery from the impact of 9/11. Marketing efforts and tax incentives to businesses were also coupled with massive investments in new cultural events for the opening of the 9/11 Memorial, including the Sol LeWitt outdoor exhibition at City Hall Park and the 10th anniversary of the River to River Festival, Lower Manhattan's largest free summer arts festival. Meanwhile, the private property market downtown had prepared for the opening of the 9/11 Memorial with a remarkable growth in the hotel industry: by 2011, almost 800 new hotel rooms had been created, adding to a total 5,000 hotel rooms in the downtown area,[117] and joining the growing number of upscale restaurants and fashion boutiques. New hotels included the World Center Hotel, which overlooks the September 11 Memorial and the Freedom Tower with a "View of the World Terrace Club" located on the 20th floor; the 42-story-high Andaz Wall Street; the 58-story-high W New York Downtown; and Hilton's Doubletree Financial District—all featuring luxury amenities for business visitors like private meeting rooms, working spaces, private clubs, and spas.

Uptown, the "Destination Harlem" campaign was launched in 2012 for the opening of the Aloft Harlem Hotel near Columbia University, the first new hotel to open in the neighborhood since 1967. But more swaths of the city were yet to be absorbed under the marketing umbrella of NYC & Company. Countless other initiatives were launched in the following years to capitalize on each neighborhood's potential as a tourist destination. The "Neighborhood x Neighborhood" initiative was launched in 2013 to bring more visitors to neighborhoods far beyond traditional tourist routes, including Bushwick, Coney Island, and Washington Heights.[118]

As a result of the combination of such rampant marketing efforts, in 2011 the city managed to attract a record 50.5 million visitors, way ahead of Bloomberg's own predictions. The success prompted the mayor to announce the even more ambitious goal to draw 55 million visitors to the city by 2015[119]—a goal that would be achieved one year in advance under the new administration of Bill de Blasio. As NYC & Company's original five-year contract with the city expired in the summer of 2011, city hall swiftly reinvested in it $66 million over five years.[120] In December 2012, Mayor Bloomberg announced that, despite the disruption caused by Hurricane Sandy, New York had again broken records with 52 million visitors, a new all-time high.[121] In 2013, the city drew a new record 54.3 million visitors—a whopping 54% increase since Bloomberg had taken office 12 years before.

Incentives

Contrary to Bloomberg's "luxury city" manifesto (according to which a successful city like New York doesn't need to use any discounts to lure high-profile businesses) and his early promises to end the practice of "bribing companies" to stay in the city, his administration did not fully discontinue Giuliani's tradition of granting generous tax breaks and other subsidy packages to large businesses.

Initially, Bloomberg had made headlines for killing an unprecedented subsidy package that Giuliani had agreed on with the New York Stock Exchange (NYSE) in 1998, which included a staggering $1.4 billion in enticements to retain the NYSE in Manhattan after its officials had started quite unrealistic rumors of moving to New Jersey.[122] Soon after 9/11, however, taxpayers' money was again funneled into a large program of incentives to large businesses, for example, in the form of community development grants administered by the LMDC to retain businesses in Lower Manhattan after the World Trade Center attacks. The largest part of these funds went to financial and banking giants, including Bank of America and Metlife, among others. Public money was also allocated to large "sport entertainment corporations" to finance new baseball stadiums for the Yankees ($1.2 billion) and the Mets ($600 million), and further subsidies were provided for the recently completed arena for the Nets (Barclays Center) at the Atlantic Yards development site in Brooklyn. Bloomberg's and Doctoroff's vision of a new football stadium for the Jets on Manhattan's Far West Side did not become a reality, but hundreds of millions of dollars in city subsidies have been chaneled to finance the transformation of the rezoned area into a brand-new mixed-use extension of Midtown.[123]

Meanwhile, major incentives were given specifically to the hospitality business, in line with the goal to make the city a top tourist destination. In the early 2000s, major donations were assigned by the ESDC and the LMDC to luxury hotel chains in Lower Manhattan, including the Ritz Carlton ($325,000) and Tribeca Grand Hotel ($150,000) in 2002 and the Millennium Hilton ($300,000) and Embassy Suites Hotel ($267,000) in 2003.[124] In 2010, a staggering $15 million in Federal Recovery Zone bonds was allocated to finance the revamping of an industrial building into a 73-room boutique luxury Wythe Hotel in Williamsburg, Brooklyn, in an effort to advance the transformation of the neighborhood into a viable alternative to Manhattan for upscale tourism.[125]

Continuity: Enter de Blasio

Taylor Swift [as New York Ambassador] is perfect: Doesn't the Statue of Liberty say, "Give me your bland, your wealthy, your gentrifying elites yearning to live in a condo in a giant, open-air mall?"[126]

By the time Bill de Blasio succeeded Bloomberg as mayor, tourism had become New York's fastest-growing economic sector and one of the city's top industries, sustaining an estimated 350,000 jobs and generating nearly $39 billion in direct spending across all five boroughs.[127] De Blasio also inherited Bloomberg's ultra-efficient branding machine, which had been set in motion since NYC & Company had taken charge of branding in 2006.

After eight consecutive record-breaking years, by 2014 the economy of tourism in New York City was so rosy that de Blasio could proudly announce that New York City wouldn't even consider running for the 2024 Olympics bid, because, quite simply, it didn't need to: "Our tourism industry couldn't be stronger. Our international reputation couldn't be better, our brand couldn't be more well respected all over the world," he said. "And so we thought, in a classic New York phrase, 'If it ain't broke, don't fix it.'"[128] De Blasio insisted instead on the necessity of bringing more visitors to the outer boroughs, by channeling more efforts for the promotion of Staten Island, Brooklyn, the Bronx, and Queens as spectacular tourist destinations in their own right:

> So we know and love the fact that millions and millions of people go to the Empire State Building or the Statue of Liberty. But we want them also to go out into neighborhoods all over the five boroughs, experience the most wonderful cuisine from all over the world, experience folklore and culture from all over the world, experience wonders like Coney Island that are irreplaceable.... If you talk about this five borough phenomenon, some of the statistics are amazing. Since 2008, 48 percent of hotel development in the city of New York has occurred outside of Manhattan. That is an amazing vote of confidence in the city and in the outer boroughs.[129]

In 2015, NYC & Company announced that pop singer Taylor Swift would be the city's global welcome ambassador for its "Welcome to New York" campaign (Figure 6.6): "We could not identify a more fitting representative of the 'new New York City' to tell our story to a new generation of travellers, especially millennials," said power brander and new CEO of NYC & Company Fred Dixon at a press conference of the US Travel Association's annual trade convention. Sure enough, this sanitized, young, and rather hipsterish brand of "new New York" sells well: another record was set in 2014, with 56.4 million visitors and an all-time-high $61.3 billion in overall economic impact,[130] prompting the mayor to announce that the city was on the "Road to 10 Million More Visitors" by 2021.[131] If six consecutive years of relentless increases in tourist numbers—and the record 60 million tourists who visited the city in 2016[132]—are any indication, 67 million tourists in 2021 is an easy bet.

Figure 6.6 Stills from the "Welcome to New York" video featuring Taylor Swift's "Welcome to New York" hit from her "1989" album.

Branding the City to a Pulp

NYC & Company's efforts to capitalize on almost any exploitable aspect of city life to market New York to its citizens and to the outside world have been unprecedented in terms of management, performance, and success. By expanding the scope of branding initiatives across all five neighborhoods; by incorporating elements of underground and off-culture into the compass of the tourist market, and locking them into partnerships with private companies (the absorption of underground or even once-illegal events such as *rooftop films*[133] into its official programs is a case in point); by granting large corporations temporary use of public space for promotional events like movie premieres; and even by assigning official sponsorship of traditional festivities to big media conglomerates (such as "Syfy's 31 Days of Halloween" in 2011[134]), branding strategies under the direction of NYC & Company have hastened a process of commodification of the urban experience that is unprecedented in its pervasiveness, and that is likely to become a prototype for the branding of big cities worldwide in the coming years. In the New York City of today, branding has become a structuring element of everyday life, and the presence of NYC & Company is to be felt just about everywhere: the NYC logo is displayed on all city vehicles, brochures, and online platforms; the company controls all advertising on street furniture, taxicab monitors, street poles, city facades, online platforms, and TV channels; it centrally manages hundreds of city events (including Broadway week, Off-Broadway week, restaurant week, comedy week); and it routinely allows the use of central public spaces to private entertainment companies to promote their products. In New York, so it seems, all facets of city life are now branded, from its historical landmarks to its ethnic neighborhoods, from its underground art scene to its sleazy nightlife. There's no escape from branding's intrusive gaze.

But the branding process goes beyond strategies to attract tourism and moves into the realm of governance. Starting with the Bloomberg administration, the marketing models of promotional culture have permeated the very idea of public management and political communication. In the branded city, citizens and visitors alike are becoming a valued customer base, whose feedback is needed to fine-tune the product's efficiency: the establishment in March 2003 of a 311 "customer service line," which allows New Yorkers to report common nuisances (from noise complaints to pest reports), has been a major success: it gives city officials a clear idea of what is going on in the minds of their constituents while making residents feel in touch with a transparent and friendly administration.

NYC & Company also acts as a public relations department that supervises almost every interaction between New York and the rest of the world, and between the mayor and his constituents.[135] In so doing, NYC & Company has contributed to forging new social and power relations, and this is one of the most remarkable and enduring legacies of the Bloomberg administration, one that survives even during the years of de Blasio. As *Bloomberg Business* journalist Tom Lowry wrote in 2007 about the former mayor, "Bloomberg sees New York City as a corporation, its citizens as customers, its sanitation workers, police officers, clerks, and deputy commissioners as talent. He is the chief executive."[136] Under this model of governance, the city is equaled to a product or service that can be sold to the citizen-customers, while Bloomberg has become, as Miriam Greenberg argues, the most notable of a "new generation of CEO politicians."[137] Just as much as the CEO is the face of a company to its employees and customers, the CEO-mayor represents the values and missions of the city brand. All of the mayor's bold initiatives, from PlaNYC 2030's "For a Greener, Greater New York," through the New Housing Marketplace ("Creating Housing for the Next Generation"), have been heavily branded with catchy slogans and public presentations to galvanize New Yorkers and arouse public interest and support. Bloomberg's constant TV appearances, his weekly radio shows on CBS New York, and his numerous public talks have given him a global stature that has allowed him to move way beyond the realm of New York City politics after leaving office.

And things certainly haven't changed under de Blasio, another branded mayor who chose to brand himself as the anti-Bloomberg in 2013. His "progressive" brand and approachable character attracted those New Yorkers who resented the cold, technocratic, self-referential, data-driven Bloomberg way. Although some say the new mayor hasn't been as savvy in administering his brand as Bloomberg was, de Blasio has managed to sell rezoning and development plans that are just as intimidating and monumental as his predecessor's, yet insisting these projects are somehow inspired by "progressive" goals of community building and housing affordability. When faced with low approval ratings in 2015, de Blasio repeatedly blamed the perceived failures of his administration on nothing else than communication mishaps. "I need to communicate better," he kept on declaring when discussing his midterm accomplishments[138]—a sign that the new mayor knows all too well the importance of packaging over substance in politics, as we will see in the next chapter.

7

A Different Brand of Mayor

De Blasio won ... because better than anyone else, he articulated the sense
of loss that many New Yorkers are feeling these days. He acknowledged
the residents of the city who are always looking over their shoulders, waiting for the next rent hike, the next demolition, the next conversion of a
local store to a national chain. He spoke to the folks who are barely hang-
ing on as the city gets bigger and stronger and richer around them.[1]

Since taking the reins, de Blasio has proven to be far from the radical
leftist that many feared. Rather, he has arguably been a solid real estate
advocate.[2]

It was de Blasio's third day as mayor of New York City. On January 3,
2014, New York was hit by the second snowstorm of the winter, which
left five inches of snow and shut down all the major highways and airports.
On NY1, images began circulating of the newly elected mayor shoveling
the sidewalk of his house in Park Slope in front of the cameras. The photo
op emphasized the image of an approachable, feet-on-the-ground kind of
mayor. Pointing to Bloomberg's absence from the city during a similar bliz-
zard in 2010, during which the former mayor was visiting his vacation home
in Bermuda, reporters emphasized the striking difference between the way
the new mayor and his predecessor presented themselves to the public: de
Blasio appeared amicable and warm-hearted, whereas Bloomberg had been
seen as distant and inaccessible.[3]

Bill de Blasio was elected mayor of New York City in November 2013,
25 years after the election of the last Democrat in office (David Dinkins in
1989), and on the heels of two decades of sweeping urban transformations
under the administrations of Rudolph Giuliani and Michael Bloomberg. In
his service as public advocate between 2010 and 2013, de Blasio had made
headlines for launching the "NYC's Worst Landlords Watchlist" to publicly

track the city's most negligent landlords and pressure them to make repairs in their properties, and had successfully opposed the New York City Housing Authority's (NYCHA's) decision to cut around 2,600 Section 8 vouchers issued to low-income New Yorkers in 2010. Conscious of the growing dissatisfaction of struggling middle-class New Yorkers with their former mayor, de Blasio's campaign was based on an aggressive anti-Bloomberg rhetoric. If Bloomberg had reassured the real estate elites and the financial industries by promising (and leading) an era of unprecedented growth and record-high profits, de Blasio chose to speak straight to the souls of underprivileged and middle-class New Yorkers who had been left behind by Bloomberg's "luxury city" agenda. Throughout his campaign, he made headlines with his "tale of two cities" message, which placed the issue of inequality at the center of a new, progressive political agenda for New York City:

> This is a place that in too many ways has become a tale of two cities, a place where City Hall has too often catered to the interests of the elite rather than the needs of everyday New Yorkers.[4]

De Blasio promised to tackle inequality in one of the most unequal cities on the planet, and to take bold actions that would finally benefit ordinary citizens struggling to make ends meet or to survive in their rapidly changing neighborhoods. He vowed to put an end to New York's housing crisis by creating or preserving 200,000 affordable units, which he promised would be feasible by making inclusionary zoning a mandatory program rather than a voluntary incentive. He committed to revising New York City's convoluted property tax system, which today allows for grotesque disparities because of its reliance on property assessments that have little or nothing to do with actual market values. He also vowed to address the strain of the working poor by broadening living-wage legislation and by expanding laws mandating companies to offer paid sick days to their employees. He pledged to secure universal prekindergarten and after-school programs with a tax increase on the wealthiest New Yorkers, and to put an end to the NYPD's practice of "stop and frisk," which had been contested in the Bloomberg years for its racial profiling of young men of color.

Especially in matters of urban development, de Blasio's mayoral campaign promises sounded like a fierce rebuttal of Bloomberg's three terms in office. As he said in a 2013 interview:

> Towering, glitzy buildings marketed to the global elite is not the type of development New Yorkers are looking for. I look forward to working with the real

estate community to spur the development, in all five boroughs, of real afford-able housing, mixed-income neighborhoods, sustainable and vibrant density, and new spaces for small and new businesses to grow and thrive.[5]

The media started playing on the "radicalism" of de Blasio by empha-sizing selected episodes of his past, like a 10-day trip to Nicaragua in the late 1980s to volunteer for the Sandinistas during the Nicaraguan revolu-tion. Conservative pundits depicted him as a dangerous socialist who would make a U-turn not only from the "luxury city" agenda of his billionaire predecessor but also from the capitalist consensus on a free-market approach to city building. The New York Post referred to him as "Che de Blasio," while Republican opponent Joe Lhota foreshadowed New York's return to the bleak days of decay of the 1970s if de Blasio won the election. On the other hand, liberal media emphasized his progressive appeal by focusing on his multicultural family (particularly his wife, a black woman who once identi-fied as a lesbian, and his 15-year-old biracial son).

"America Shifts Left" was the headline of a Washington Post article on victory day, in which de Blasio was referred to as an "ebullient progres-sive,"[6] while the New York Times celebrated the revolutionary shift that de Blasio's election would bring about, predicting that his mayoralty would bear a much broader significance for the history of the nation, way beyond the limits of local politics.[7] A parade of VIP liberal New Yorkers, including Hollywood star Susan Sarandon and Sex and the City actress Sarah Jessica Parker, gave de Blasio their public endorsement. The buzz around the new mayor was reminiscent of the halo the media created around the figure of Barack Obama during the 2008 presidential elections, shifting the focus from the fact that many of de Blasio's campaign donors were, as usual, repre-sentatives of New York City's big real estate and financial industries—again, New York's city producers.[8] Opponent Christine Quinn, whose campaign elaborated the "Tale of Two de Blasios" slogan, emphasized this contradic-tion and accused him of double-talk and flip-flopping on key issues.[9]

The media also seemed to play down the fact that de Blasio had a more mainstream curriculum than it seemed, and that he certainly was no stranger to the corridors of power. De Blasio had volunteered for David Dinkins's mayoral campaign in 1989, and had served in the US Department of Housing and Urban Development (HUD) as a regional director for New York and New Jersey. Before becoming New York City's public advo-cate in 2010, he had served as a city council member from 2001 to 2009. De Blasio had also worked as Hillary Clinton's campaign manager during her

2000 Senate race, and once in office he endorsed, although belatedly, her unsuccessful candidacy for the 2016 presidential race, calling her "the candidate who I believe can fundamentally address income inequality effectively, the candidate who has the right vision, the right experience and the ability to get the job done."[10]

De Blasio made headlines with his promises to end public giveaways to luxury housing developers. Yet his record was certainly not that of a staunch antidevelopment activist. In city council, de Blasio had been a strong supporter of Bloomberg's Atlantic Yards mega-plan in downtown Brooklyn, which he strenuously defended by pointing to the jobs, services, and affordable housing it would bring to the local community.[11] With the promise of creating opportunities for affordable housing, he also supported projects for the development of two luxury towers with spectacular waterfront views inside Brooklyn Bridge Park.[12] According to *Politico* commentator Dana Rubinstein, "de Blasio's record as a councilman demonstrated a willingness to work with developers to spur economic development and tackle the city's affordable housing crisis, using an approach to land use that at times bore a strong resemblance to Bloomberg's own."[13]

In fact, lost among the media buzz around de Blasio's "radicalism" was the fact that his solutions to New York City's inequality and housing crisis didn't differ much from those of his predecessor. In a speech he gave at NYU's Wagner School of Public Service in July 2012, he emphasized his pro-growth stance, touting aggressive real estate development as the only way to solve the city's affordable housing crisis:

> First and foremost, when given the choice to grow or to sit idle, we need to grow and we have to be aggressive about it.... The things I value as a progressive—good jobs and affordable housing—cannot happen if projects stall or never materialize. If we aren't doing everything possible as a City government to spur on development, even if valid compromises are included, we risk nothing getting built at all, and that is the worst possible outcome.[14]

The equation more development = more affordable units had been a mantra of the Bloomberg administration for over a decade, yet its meager results in terms of actual affordable housing production had by then become obvious to many low- and middle-income New Yorkers. But de Blasio's tying of upzoning for more density with a mandatory inclusionary zoning program seemed like a practical—although not radical—strategy to create a larger number of affordable units while maximizing profits for developers and increasing tax returns for the city. A mandatory inclusionary zoning program would also help developers overcome the opposition of the many antidevelopment activist groups across the city. In sum, far from the "radical" tones of his campaign rhetoric, de Blasio's stance on development was that of a pro-development liberal, or a "development pragmatist."[15]

De Blasio in Office

We're going to take an entirely different approach is the simple answer.... We are looking at the notion of what city planning is with fresh eyes.... This is about using the planning process to achieve a bigger set of strategic goals. That includes the creation of affordable housing, that includes facilitating job development, that includes trying to address inequality.[16]

In his inaugural address on January 1, 2014, de Blasio reiterated his campaign pledge to finally address New York City's economic and social inequalities. But when the list of mayoral appointees emerged in early 2014, people started wondering whether the new administration would really stick to its promise of making a clean break from past administrations. Their credentials in the world of big business and finance unsettled ordinary citizens, while they reassured the New York elites that the radical stances of pre-election de Blasio would loosen up once in office.

De Blasio had run for mayor aggressively contesting the NYPD's notorious "stop and frisk" policy. He notably released a TV ad in which his biracial teenage son promised that his father would finally put an end to racial profiling in the streets of New York. But in what came as a surprise for most, de Blasio reappointed Giuliani's former commissioner William Bratton as head of the NYPD—the man under whom the NYPD had incorporated the controversial policy in the first place, as a centerpiece of Giuliani's "law and order" platform.

Just like Bloomberg did before him, de Blasio hired a former Goldman Sachs executive, Alicia Glen, to be his deputy mayor for housing and economic development. For 12 years, Glen had headed Goldman Sachs' Urban Investment Group, a division that has massively invested in low-income communities across the United States. As reported by *Gothamist* in 2013:

Glen's Urban Investment Group played a large part in the Bloomberg administration's development agenda over the past decade, helping fund much of the uneven development that has priced out many New Yorkers from neighborhoods across the city. If you're into what Franklin Avenue has become in Crown Heights, then Glen's the person for you.[17]

As deputy mayor, Glen now controls the activity of 26 city agencies and has a final say on all rezoning and land use plans. Most important, she has been tasked with implementing de Blasio's housing plan—the cornerstone of the mayor's electoral promises—coordinating the preservation of 120,000 and the creation of 80,000 units of affordable housing over the next decade.

Another of de Blasio's eyebrow-raising choices was to retain Bloomberg's appointee and another former Goldman Sachs executive Kyle Kimball as the president of the New York City Economic Development Corporation (NYCEDC). When asked about this choice and how this seemed like a repudiation of his campaign promises, de Blasio simply responded: "I think I've tried to articulate repeatedly the theory under which we're working here.... I've set forth an exceedingly clear, aggressive, progressive agenda. It's there: black and white. It's the exact same one I put forward in the primary and the general election– it ain't changing."[18]

De Blasio appointed Carl Weisbrod, a well-respected urban development insider, as chair of the City Planning Commission and director of the Department of City Planning (DCP). Under Koch, Weisbrod had served as the executive director of the DCP and was appointed president of the 42nd Street Redevelopment Project, heading up the first efforts to revitalize the seedy Times Square by cleaning up the area and striking a major deal with Disney to take over the New Amsterdam Theater. In the early 1990s, under Dinkins, he became founding president of the NYCEDC. His long resume also includes working as the founding president of the Alliance for Downtown New York, the nation's largest business improvement district, which channeled funds in the revitalization of Lower Manhattan, particularly after 9/11. More recently, he was partner of the real estate consulting firm HR&A Advisors,[19] which oversaw the rezoning of the Hudson Square area in Manhattan, and president of Trinity Real Estate, the real estate division of Trinity Church that owns large real estate holdings in the neighborhood and has been a major applicant for the Hudson Square rezoning.[20] He is responsible for steering the city's rezoning initiatives in new disadvantaged areas of the city, like East New York, and for implementing the new mandatory inclusionary zoning policy.

In another unexpected move, in 2014 de Blasio appointed Scott Walsh, vice president of development for Forest City Ratner, the realtor that pushed for the massive Atlantic Yards rezoning project

and a long-time de Blasio fundraiser,[21] to join the Rent Guidelines
Board—the panel responsible for establishing annual rent adjustments
for the over one million apartments that are under the city's rent stabilization program. The choice dismayed housing activists. Although
New Yorkers were surprised when in June 2015 the board voted, for
the first time in its 46-year history, for a rent freeze on rent-regulated
apartments with one-year leases, fulfilling one of de Blasio's electoral
promises, the only opposing votes came from de Blasio appointees,
including Scott Walsh.[22] De Blasio also appointed campaign donor
Jonathan Greenspun, managing director of Mercury Public Affairs, a
lobbying firm serving clients including leaders in the real estate industry, as chair of the New York City Commission on Human Rights,
which is entrusted with ensuring fairness in the provision of housing,
employment, and credit.[23]

These appointments to the top positions of the city-planning machine
baffled those middle-class New Yorkers who believed in a radical cut with
past policies. In opposition to the anti-Bloomberg rhetoric of his campaign,
they suggested a choice of continuity, announcing that more of the same
was on the way.

Further disappointment came in 2016, when the federal government
began to investigate allegations that de Blasio's nonprofit, "The Campaign
for One New York," had received millions in contributions from powerful interest groups, including unions, lobbyists, and developers.[24] Many
of these contributions came from real estate firms engaged in some of
the largest residential development projects across the city,[25] like Two
Trees Management, whose $1.5 billion redevelopment plan for the old
Domino Sugar refinery on the Brooklyn waterfront was approved by the
city in 2014.[26] Aides to the mayor were subpoenaed by state and federal
prosecutors, who conducted several investigations into the mayor's fundraising operations. In March 2017, the prosecutors announced they would
not file charges against the mayor or his aides, despite Manhattan District
Attorney Cyrus Vance commenting that some of the team's fundraising
practices appeared "contrary to the intent and spirit of the law."[27] As a
public advocate, de Blasio had vocally criticized corporate donations to
politicians. The multiple investigations into his fundraising practices have
infuriated many of those who had supported the new mayor on the basis
of his moral values.

De Blasio's Housing Plan: Doubling Down on Bloomberg's Plan

After over a decade of outrageous luxury development under Bloomberg, by 2013 the scarcity of affordable housing in New York had become the buzzword in all local media—and fixing it became the promise of all mayoral candidates. But the real estate frenzy in which New York City had been engulfed since the years of Bloomberg, and that was the result of an almost 40-year-long neoliberal shift in urban development policy, is far from being over.

By the end of the Bloomberg years, about a third of the city's residents were spending at least half of their income in rent, and fixing the affordable housing crisis became a centerpiece of de Blasio's campaign. Four months into his term, he unveiled his "Housing New York: A Five-Borough, Ten-Year Plan," pledging it would provide for affordable housing to all struggling New Yorkers, even those at the bottom of the social ladder, by building 80,000 new units and preserving 120,000 affordable units in 10 years. The $41.1 billion plan would increase protections for low-income tenants and would require landlords to include below-market units in all developments that would benefit from zoning changes across the city. In his introduction to the plan, de Blasio stated:

> Our affordable housing policies must reach every New Yorker in need, which is why this plan thinks big about the changes we need to make—in government and in the private sector—to make this a city where everyone rises together, and everyone has a safe and decent home. If you're in a community where affordability is disappearing, we want to protect it. If your family lives in a rent-regulated apartment, this plan is focused on helping you keep it. If you're a senior trying to remain in the neighborhood you helped to build, we are fighting to help you stay. If you are a building owner or developer intent on building or preserving affordable apartments, we will support you. This is a five-borough, ten-year plan. It will marshal people and resources from every corner of this city behind a singular purpose: to make this city again a place where our most vulnerable, our working people, and our middle class can all thrive.[28]

De Blasio's agenda highlighted several strategies, some of which would indeed set it apart from Bloomberg's housing approach. Among these were the introduction of a mandatory inclusionary zoning program, an emphasis on affordability for low-income households, the introduction of new mixed-income housing programs to supersede the previous "80/ 20" agreement, an increase of the Department of Housing Preservation and Development's annual capital funding, attention to prevent abuses of vacancy and luxury decontrol provisions, and the expansion of low-cost permanent supportive housing for the homeless by reallocating a portion of the existing funding for homeless shelters.

Some major aspects of the plan, however, bear a striking resemblance to Bloomberg's housing plan. Rezoning across the board, just like under Bloomberg, is at the core of de Blasio's housing agenda. The city aims to identify new locations near mass transit that may be suitable for development of mixed-income high-rise units that would also include affordable housing. Just like under Bloomberg, new buildable sites could be created by decking over rail facilities and other large infrastructures, by strengthening coastal infrastructure to facilitate waterfront developments, and by offering incentives for environmental remediation on Brownfield sites. Just like with Bloomberg, the emphasis is on dense development, which will be facilitated by removing rules preventing the construction of micro housing units for single-person households, by allowing developers to build higher also in contextual zoning districts, and by easing restrictions on the transferability of development rights. There is also a proposal to allow private developers to build mixed-income housing on land owned by the NYCHA to generate revenue that may help cut the NYCHA's budget deficit—a plan that had been advanced by the Bloomberg administration and that de Blasio had once strongly criticized, so much so that the *New York Post* jumped in with the headline "De Blasio Recycles Bloomberg Housing Plan He Once Bashed."[29]

De Blasio's housing plan, designed under the supervision of Deputy Mayor Alicia Glen, is to be financed in large part (73%, or $30 billion) from the private sector, together with other city, state, and federal funds. According to the city, the plan will create 194,000 construction jobs and nearly 7,100 permanent jobs. The massive scale of the plan, which dwarfs in size even Koch's housing plan of the 1970s and 1980s; the promise of major upzonings that will loosen height restrictions and favor development in new strategic areas across the city; and the continued reliance on incentives and subsidies to private developers, have been welcomed by the real estate and construction community, which has lined up in support of de Blasio.[30] According to a *Business Insider* reporter, the coupling of more development with affordable housing provisions "looks designed to create a win-win: more density, more development, more affordable housing as part of that development, more developer profits, and more real estate taxes collected by the city."[31] But is it so? According to Tom Angotti, once again there is little guarantee that the "affordable housing" produced will be affordable to those who need it the most, because the very definition of affordability remains unchanged in a city where "low income" is defined as 50% to 80% of the area median income (AMI), or up to $67,000 a year for a family of four.[32] The risk is that, as usual, only the development industry might end up as the winner.

Two massive zoning changes were essential to make de Blasio's housing vision a reality. One, called mandatory inclusionary housing (MIH), would require developers to include affordable units in all rezoned areas. The other, called zoning for quality and affordability (ZQA), would entail yet another massive series of amendments to the 1961 zoning resolution to allow for taller buildings, eliminate strict parking requirements for affordable housing located near subway lines, and change shape regulations for new constructions in certain areas to better accommodate state-of-the-art ground-floor retail.

In 2015, more details of the ZQA and MIH plans were unveiled. The administration identified several areas across the five boroughs to be rezoned for higher density. These included East Harlem and Washington Heights in Manhattan, East New York in Brooklyn, Flushing and Long Island City in Queens, the Jerome Avenue corridor in the Bronx, and the Bay Street corridor in Staten Island. For each neighborhood or area, the city would choose one of three different options, or a combination of different options, through which developers may respond to the affordable housing mandate:[33] either 25% of units affordable to be reserved to households earning 60% of AMI (around $46,620 for a family of three, so that a two-bedroom apartment would cost about $1,150 a month); 30% of units to be set aside for households earning around 80% of AMI ($62,150 for a family of three, and $1,550 rent for a two-bedroom apartment); or, in cases where the developers got no government subsidy, 30% of units affordable to be reserved for households earning 120% of AMI ($93,240 for a family of three, with a two-bedroom apartment renting for about $2,330) in so-called emerging (call them gentrifying) markets. The latter option would not be available in Manhattan south of 96th Street on the east side and south of 110th Street on the west side.

What is clear by looking at these figures is that most of the units envisioned under de Blasio's plan once again won't be in the reach of the majority of New Yorkers who need them the most,[34] in a city where half of renters make less than 60% of the AMI, and where almost one million citizens make less than 50% of AMI (or about $39,000 for a family of three). Most important, these levels of "affordability" are nowhere near the average incomes of the vast majority of residents currently living in the poorest areas slated for rezoning. For instance, as of 2013, the median household income in East Harlem, one of the first areas earmarked for rezoning, was $28,800, or 37% of AMI. In the Jerome Avenue area of the South Bronx, it was just $25,000, less than one-third of AMI. In Inwood, in the area east of 10th Avenue that's currently slated for rezoning, the neighborhood's median income was only $21,000.[35]

It is undeniable that, in cities like New York, middle- and upper-middle-class apartments are easier to build, not only because they are more profitable for developers, but also because wealthy buyers can take advantage of generous tax deductions, while federal subsidies are extremely tight for low-income households.[36] And mayors have little power to change what gets decided in Washington. But what about the much-trumpeted housing for the most vulnerable New Yorkers? The plan calls for about 16,000 units for families making less than $25,000, yet about one-fourth of the city's population is in this income bracket. According to a *Gothamist* reporter:

> That's…far less than the 60,000 homeless people, the estimated 250,000 rent-stabilized apartments lost in the last 20 years, the 270,000 people on the waiting list for public housing, and the 425,000 low-income apartments the Housing First Plan estimated that the city needed in 2014.[37]

To make matters worse, if there's anything we learned during the Bloomberg years, it is that rezoning has almost invariably resulted in escalating property prices, which in turn has contributed to intensify waves of gentrification and displacement of existing residents and businesses. Lately, the rezoned area of the South Bronx (recently rebranded "the Piano District") has seen residential sale prices more than double in only two years between 2012 and 2014. De Blasio's announcement in 2015 that he would establish a fund to provide free legal aid and support to protect tenants facing eviction doesn't change the reality that the city's very rezoning policies will presumably be the number-one factor encouraging landlords to evict low-income tenants. In 2016, the administration pledged $76 million in legal assistance for tenants facing eviction, but this will assist only New Yorkers living in rent-regulated apartments.[38]

The truth is that gentrification is *built into* de Blasio's housing plan. The plan will produce far more units than any effort led since the times of Ed Koch. Most of these units will be built in very disadvantaged neighborhoods, but their standard of affordability will likely attract middle-income transplants escaping from the rising costs in more expensive neighborhoods, while they will still be out of the reach of locals.

There Is No Alternative

> I'm still hearing the same arguments as in the previous administration.... Where are all the low-income residents in downtown Brooklyn? They're in North Carolina, South Carolina. I get letters from them saying they couldn't afford to stay.[39]

De Blasio's plan has been presented with the bottom line that there is no alternative to harnessing the force of high-end private development if the city aims to build more housing for the poor, especially in a regime of disappearing federal subsidies, in which programs for low-income families such as Section 8 are accepting no new applicants.[40] At a city council zoning subcommittee meeting in February 2016, Deputy Mayor Alicia Glen insisted that, if levels of affordability are set too low, developers just won't build, and "we can't just sit by and do nothing as market pressures change the city," while HPD Commissioner Been told the council: "Don't make the perfect the enemy of the good."[41]

Yet we have seen it all before. De Blasio's plan seems to rely on the same strategies that made big real estate so fond of Bloomberg: incentivizing the production of more units by loosening zoning regulations in strategic areas across the city, and granting generous giveaways to luxury developers with the condition that they include a percentage of affordable units in the upscale developments that continue to pop up in gentrifying neighborhoods across the city. But "the majority of new housing, invariably built for the luxury market, is still bound to drive up housing prices and rents and displace more affordable units than it creates."[42] The monolithic consensus among city producers that more development will wash away the housing crisis remains unchallenged. Yet this was already done under Bloomberg, with miserable results: luxury development was the number-one factor of displacement for middle- and low-income New Yorkers during the Bloomberg years.

New Yorkers and the Plan: Thanks, but No Thanks

> The hostility simmering in East New York and beyond, coming from many of the very people who voted Mr. de Blasio into office on a platform of reducing inequality, is not just a challenge to the mayor's efforts to add thousands of units for lower-income residents. It has also raised legitimate questions, housing activists say, about whether the city can build without further gentrifying large areas.[43]

> The accelerated development of market-rate housing has had a disastrous ripple effect as other landlords are incentivized to push tenants out to take advantage of rising rents. Williamsburg, Brooklyn and West Chelsea have seen the largest production of affordable housing in recent years. They are also two of the most rapidly gentrifying and unaffordable neighborhoods in NYC.[44]

The plan was okayed by the real estate industry and endorsed by its most powerful lobby, the Real Estate Board of New York, whose president Steven Spinola called it "a realistic road map for solutions."[45] Praise also came from Bill Rudin,[46] CEO of Rudin Management, who has led the conversion of St. Vincent's Hospital in the West Village into a super-luxury 10-building condo complex called Greenwich Lane. Prices at Greenwich Lane will average $8.8 million per condo unit, with the penthouse set to hit the market for $45 million.[47] In 2013, de Blasio had vocally protested against that development, leading a "Hospitals Not Condos" rally along with top personalities like singer Harry Belafonte and *Sex and the City* star Cynthia Nixon.[48]

But when the public review process for the MIH plan was started in September 2015, New Yorkers didn't welcome it just as cheerfully. The experience of 10 years of Bloomberg had made them wary of city producers coming in with promises of bringing "affordable housing" by maximizing development. By November 2015, four of the five borough presidents and most of the city's 59 community boards had voted against the plan, including almost all community boards in poor neighborhoods like Queens and the Bronx. Queens borough president Melinda Katz said of the MIH plan: "There are concerns that the proposed new mandatory inclusionary [plan] may replace existing affordable housing with housing deemed affordable that is not within reach to the current residents."[49] Her dismay was echoed by Bronx borough president Ruben Diaz, who asked: "Will neighborhood residents even be able to live in these apartments?"[50] As for the ZQA, preservationists also made the argument that raising height caps up to 30%, as the plan allows, would further compromise the character of neighborhoods, particularly in those districts where it took years of effort from community activists to obtain some restrictions to prevent out-of-scale development.

But the opposition of community boards and borough presidents didn't prevent the plans from moving ahead. "Those advisory votes are meaningful, but they're not the final word," de Blasio said in November 2015. "When it comes to anything that might be new development, the community [board is] often negatively disposed. That's not a news flash. We know that. What we're talking about is a different approach to development."[51]

On February 4, 2016, the City Planning Commission approved both plans with minor tweaks, sending them to city council to hold public hearings. Before the final decision in city council in March 2016, resistance to the plans escalated. On February 9, protesters attended a council hearing, chanting, "De Blasio's plan ain't affordable for me," and had to be escorted out.[52] Other rallies in the following weeks were held outside city hall, with banners that read "Affordable for whom?" Concerns about the plans were also raised by some council members, as well as city comptroller Scott Stringer and public advocate Letitia James. City representatives assured the public that, while they recognized that MIH alone wouldn't be able to produce enough units for the many low-income New Yorkers in need of housing, the city would use more tools to produce affordable housing for those in deep poverty.[53] But the expiration in January 2016 of the state's 421-a tax exemption program, which was used to incentivize developers in exchange for affordable housing, may put de Blasio's affordable housing vision in jeopardy. As of this writing, the renewal of the program has been derailed after months of negotiations because of the inability of the real estate lobbies to reach an agreement with labor unions demanding union labor and wages included in the program.

As the city council vote neared, Real Affordability for All, a coalition of 65 tenant organizations, unions, and other housing advocacy groups, organized a rally with around 1,000 protesters in front of city hall, demanding modifications to the MIH plan and insisting that at least 30% of new housing be affordable to those making 30% of AMI. On March 22, 2016, in a frantic session during which some shouting protesters had to be escorted out, city council approved both plans, with a 40-to-6 vote, with one abstention, to pass the ZQA plan, and a 42-to-5 vote to approve a revised MIH plan.[54] The revised version of the MIH introduced the requirement for an additional 5% of affordable units if the affordable housing component is built off-site (at another location). It also added a new affordability option that allows developers a choice of creating 20% of units in their developments for households making 40% of AMI, or about $31,000 for a family of three, in rezoned neighborhoods. According to the Association for Neighborhood and Housing Development, this tweak could help close to half a million families that would have been left out in the initial proposal.[55] But there is no guarantee that this will be the case, as it will be the council members' duty to select the most appropriate from among the four affordability options on a case-by-case basis, and ultimately it will be left to the developers to decide the mix of affordability brackets they will choose to include in their developments.

Rezoning More of New York City: From East New York ...

"We see what's going on around in the city," said Joyce Scott-Brayboy, 58, a local community board member and retired city worker. "No to that in East New York. No. No."[56]

East New York. A vast impoverished area in the predominantly black section of Eastern Brooklyn, which Manhattanites know mostly from shooting reports on local TV and for its notorious reputation as Brooklyn's murder capital. It is an area ravaged by years of "blockbusting"[57] and ensuing foreclosures in the 1970s, which have made it today a relatively unpopulated neighborhood scattered with vast vacant lots. Yet it sits not far from neighborhoods like Bedford-Stuyvesant and Bushwick, which had similar reputations until not long ago but in a matter of a few years have changed beyond recognition because of the influx of young hipsters, middle-class professionals, galleries, and cafes. Despite its poverty and the general shortage of services, this is an area where the presence of many public housing complexes provides for a large number of affordable housing units, in a city where urban development has made almost any parcel of urban land prohibitively expensive.

In recent years, the neighborhood has seen the first influx of new hordes of Brooklyn expats who are unable to pay skyrocketing rents in other parts of the borough. This is the last frontier of urban renewal—and the testing ground of de Blasio's massive housing plan. But according to the *New York Times*, "nowhere is the distrust of his strategy deeper than in Brooklyn, Mr. de Blasio's home borough, where it can seem as if it is only a matter of time before development transforms even the poorest neighborhoods beyond recognition, straining the subways, packing schools and pushing longtime residents out."[58] The rezoning plan envisioned by the city will apply to a massive area of eastern Brooklyn (around 190 blocks) comprising a portion of the area of Ocean Hill west of Broadway Junction and the main portion of East New York and Cypress Hills to the east, bounded by Fulton Street to the north, Pitkin Avenue to the south, Sheffield Avenue to the west, and Lincoln Avenue to the east. The plan promises to provide for nearly 6,300 new housing units by 2030, bringing the area back to its original 1960s population of around 66,000 residents. The densest developments will be allowed along the main arteries like Atlantic Avenue, where the rezoning allows for 12- to 14-story residential buildings with retail on the ground floor. Less tall buildings (8 to 10 stories) will be allowed on Pitkin Avenue. Liberty Avenue and Fulton Street will be lined with 6- to 8-story buildings. Through the implementation of MIH, a percentage of new housing will be set aside as permanently affordable. The rezoning will also result in almost a million square feet of commercial space, a new 1,000-seat school, upgrades in transportation infrastructure, and streetscape improvements. To avoid raising the costs of construction (which ultimately translates into higher prices), the plan will waive parking requirements for affordable and senior developments within a mile of the subway. The plan also promises to implement measures to preserve existing government-assisted units whose affordability programs are about to expire and to invest $36 million in legal services to residents who may be facing landlord harassment, to limit the wave of evictions that the rezoning will likely produce.

When the city started the public review process for the East New York rezoning, locals were outraged. Things got worse when a report by Comptroller Scott Stringer was released on December 2015, stating that most of the newly built affordable housing units would be unaffordable to the majority of locals, and that nearly 50,000 low-income residents in 22,000 unprotected housing units would risk displacement if the plan went through. According to the report, the affordability price ranges envisioned in the plan would allow only 1,724 (and possibly even less, or about 948) out of 6,312 new apartments to be in the reach of local residents through the city's affordable housing lotteries.[59] Fortunately, the modifications to the MIH made in 2016 may allow for an extra option for families making about $31,000, more in line with the median income of East New York. It remains to be seen if developers will choose to go for this very low-income bracket option.

At public hearings in early 2016, the plan encountered harsh resistance. Pointing to the price range of the newly planned "affordable" housing, local activists and long-time residents showed little trust that de Blasio's plan was meant to improve the neighborhood *for them*: it was wealthier newcomers that the plan was aiming to attract.[60] Communities for Change and Real Affordability for All, among other groups, demanded more resources to preserve the existing affordable housing units, an increased supply of very low- and low-income units to house locals, and increased investments in programs to prevent commercial displacement of local small businesses.

... to East Harlem

> When we watch TV we see de Blasio promote this plan as an affordable housing plan.... But this is pure propaganda. We did the math and we realized after reading the report on housing and his ten-year plan that this is not truly an affordable housing plan. It favors the creation of luxury housing that we don't consider affordable.[61]

A similar opposition has targeted de Blasio's implementation of the MIH plan in East Harlem, where the area between Madison/Lexington Avenue between 115th and 132nd Streets has been slated for rezoning. At community meetings and public rallies, residents have vocally opposed the plan, arguing that it will disrupt the lives of the many low-income tenants and small business owners in the neighborhood, and that it will wipe out the social and cultural fabric of "El Barrio" as they know it.[62] Locals have complained about the affordability ranges included in the plan, claiming they don't reflect the actual income of the people living in the area. For many low-income residents in East Harlem, being eligible to get these affordable units will be impossible. Most are already struggling with two or three low-wage jobs just to make ends meet in a local housing market that, although prohibitive, is more affordable than most of the housing the plan envisions. They are scared they will lose their homes. Residents also complained about de Blasio's NYCHA's "Next-Gen" program—a plan first envisioned by the Bloomberg administration which allows developers to build up to 50% market-rate housing on playgrounds, lawns, community facilities, and parking lots belonging to NYCHA complexes. In the summer of 2015, local residents united in the Movement for Justice in El Barrio organized several "Consultas del Barrio," a series of community meetings and workshops, the results of which have been summarized in a 10-point community plan to preserve rent-stabilized housing in the neighborhood. The plan was delivered to the members of the community board and the community invited the administration to discuss it, but to no avail.[63]

East New York and East Harlem are only the trailblazers for more rezoning efforts to come through the pipeline across the five boroughs, like Jerome Avenue west of the Grand Concourse in the Bronx, West Flushing along Flushing Creek in Queens, Long Island City, and Bay Street in Staten Island.

But despite the gigantic scale of de Blasio's housing efforts and their relatively stronger focus (compared to Bloomberg's plan) on the demands of working-class New Yorkers, very few housing units will be available for struggling citizens[64]—particularly those African Americans and Latinos who represented the largest constituency of the new mayor in the 2013 elections.

In 2015, the city released reports stating that over 40,000 units had been produced in the two years since 2014. But of all these, only about 15% went to households making less than $39,000, and just 5% were for people making less than $23,000. The large majority of units were reserved for much wealthier households.[65] According to *City Limits* reporter Gregory Jost, "the core components [of the plan] benefit higher income bands, new arrivals, and industries like finance and real estate … and leaves the majority of those most threatened with displacement with no hope of even qualifying to play the lottery, let alone win it."[66]

Yet again, rezoning is employed by city producers not as a tool to provide housing to struggling New Yorkers, but as a bridgehead for capital to penetrate into new underexploited urban frontiers.

What About Small Businesses?

There are some small businesses that are probably going to just fail because they're not very good businesses.[67]

What good are money-management courses and networking events if you can't stay in business because of the exorbitant rent increases?[68]

For almost a decade, a mysterious blogger under the pen name of Jeremiah Moss has chronicled the loss of innumerable mom-and-pop businesses that have shut their doors across the city because of skyrocketing rents in his *Vanishing New York* blog. James and Karla Murray have instead chosen photography to document New York City's storefronts before they disappear, devoting a photographic testament to the most iconic establishments across the five boroughs: bodegas, hairdressers, stationeries, kosher joints, tobacconists, and laundromats. Of all the stores they photographed in their 2011 book, only about a third are still standing today: most have closed up shop or given way to corporate chains. Over a decade of citywide rezonings, land speculations, and corporate bidding wars for available commercial space has produced a Darwinian habitat where corporate retail proliferates, and where mom-and-pops have become an endangered species. Today, the ubiquitous presence of vacant storefronts all across the city is one of the most disturbing effects of the rampage against small business: warehoused storefronts can be kept vacant for years, until landlords find the next large enough retail chain to move in.

It is a well-known fact that the Bloomberg years were a living hell for New York's small businesses: during Bloomberg's tenure, there were 83,211 commercial eviction warrants issued, and 168,000 stores closed without a court fight. This equals about 800 to 1,000 stores closing *per month*, each year, for over a decade.[69] When running for public advocate in 2009, de Blasio made protecting struggling small businesses a centerpiece of his campaign. He was also among the champions of a Small Business Jobs Survival Act (SBJSA) proposal that has been the subject of discussion for decades in New York, without ever seeing the light of day. The bill would give commercial tenants the right to demand 10-year leases with the right to renewal, and would give low-earning tenants the opportunity to bring lease renewals to arbitration if they think the new terms are unacceptable.[70] But the bill was denied a vote at city council for over 30 years, opposed as it was by city hall and the real estate elites interested in maximizing profits from commercial properties in a booming city. In 2009, Speaker Quinn denied a vote on the bill, which at that time had 32 sponsoring council members.[71]

In his campaign for mayor and once in office, however, de Blasio declined to discuss the SBJSA any further, and his battle changed focus abruptly. While real estate speculation, exorbitant commercial rents, and a lack of tenant protections fully disappeared from his political talks, he started pointing to the "dramatic increase in inspections and nuisance fines on small businesses." His solution to the problem was hence based on "improving the regulatory climate in the city" to alleviate "the incredible burden on small businesses from the rapid rise in fines."[72] "In my 30 years advocating for small business," says Sung Soo Kim, historical small business advocate and cofounder of the New York City Small Business Congress and the Coalition to Save New York City Small Businesses, "no elected official has exhibited as dramatic a change in small business policy as our Mayor Bill de Blasio. He has gone the gamut, changing his assessment of the crisis from 'rent gouging and extortion' to 'fines and lack of access to loans,' a complete flip-flop from the last election."[73]

Proposals for the introduction of forms of commercial rent control or fairer lease negotiation opportunities, the most powerful strategy to help local businesses in rapidly gentrifying neighborhoods, have been routinely dismissed by de Blasio officials. When confronted with the concerns of small business owners, Deputy Mayor Alicia Glen quite smugly declared that such solutions would not help solve "the problem that people think the problem is."[74] The SBJSA currently has 27 sponsoring members, which is the needed majority at city council. Yet, no vote on this legislation has been called so far by city council. Council Speaker Melissa Mark-Viverito had sponsored the bill when she was a council member during the administration of Bloomberg, only to suddenly withdraw her support in 2014 as council speaker (the most powerful position in city government after the mayor) during the self-proclaimed "progressive" administration of Bill de Blasio.[75]

As a result, no radical change is about to come for small businesses under the new mayor. The same policies of the Bloomberg years are still in place and are producing similar results: in 2014, there was an average of 488 eviction warrants issued to small businesses per month, compared with 485 such warrants in 2012 and 499 in 2013 under Bloomberg. And in 2015, there were 542 court evictions per month.[76] If anything has changed under de Blasio, it has changed for the worse. And de Blasio's rezoning plans will do their part to impact also those small mom-and-pop businesses that managed to make it through a decade of hell under Bloomberg, as well as prospective small businesses that may be looking for a chance in New York's frantic market: zoning regulations to improve ground-floor retail space are very likely to be paralleled by exorbitant rent increases, and this in the last decade has almost invariably meant that big chains have replaced small local stores unable to renew their leases. The influx of new residents will also penalize those many small businesses and family and neighborhood stores that are unable to cater to a new population of consumers.

The administration has launched two programs to support small retailers under threat: NYC Business Solution, a service offered by the Department of Small Business Services to support businesses with legal advice and assistance, and Small Business First. The latter was unveiled in 2014 with the aim to "improve the regulatory climate in New York City and help businesses avoid penalties and fines."[77] But only two years later, in 2016, the *Daily News* and ProPublica published a frightening report showing the dark side of the "regulatory climate" for small business owners in New York City. The report investigated the NYPD's alleged systematic practices of entrapment and extortion against small and immigrant business owners of bodegas, laundromats, and liquor stores in poor and minority neighborhoods like East Harlem, Inwood, Washington Heights, and Flushing.[78] In about 18 months since 2013, the report found 646 cases filed by the NYPD against business owners for alleged violations, and found that 90% of such actions were against small businesses located in minority or immigrant neighborhoods.[79]

"How Are You Enjoying the de Blasio Revolution?"

De Blasio must be credited for some significant achievements he obtained during his tenure. By the second half of his term, New York City's economy had registered a steady increase in employment (248,000 new jobs were created in his first two years in office) and in wages, especially in the outer boroughs.[80] And tourism keeps on setting new records year after year. De Blasio has also managed to adopt measures to alleviate the plight of some working-class New Yorkers. He won a battle to secure free full-day universal prekindergarten care after only eight months in office, without the tax on the wealthy (those with incomes above $500,000) that he had called his "number one proposal" during the mayoral campaign.[81] He is campaigning for a $15 minimum wage for city employees by the end of 2018, and has also managed to expand paid sick leave, a landmark law that has brought worker benefits to 3.4 million private- and nonprofit-sector working New Yorkers, opening the way for other cities, including Philadelphia and Oakland, and the states of California and Massachusetts to enact similar legislation.

Although misdemeanor arrests increased slightly at the beginning of his tenure, he was responsible for strongly reducing the NYPD's stop-and-frisk policy, which had skyrocketed during the Bloomberg years. By the end of 2015, the number of stop-and-frisk encounters dropped to around 23,000, from a record 685,000 in 2011 during Bloomberg's tenure.[82]

De Blasio, who has made combating inequality a centerpiece of his administration's rhetoric, has championed himself as a crusading progressive also on the national stage. In 2014, he began embarking on a road show of public talks and appearances across the United States, to illuminate other city governments about his solutions to fix what he called "the crisis of our time." But when it comes to affordable housing—one of the centerpieces of his progressive agenda for New York City—many struggling New Yorkers haven't seen much of a change. Over a decade of rezoning across the board during the Bloomberg years has taught residents in low-income neighborhoods that whenever the city comes out with a rezoning plan, regardless of vague promises of affordable housing, prices will go up, and if they are tenants or small business owners, their permanence in the community will be at risk. They have understood that, if a rezoning plan is adopted, it will accelerate the gentrification of their neighborhood and trigger developments that will transform its social and cultural fabric beyond recognition. Regardless of the quotas reserved for "affordable" units, they are conscious that the majority of new housing will invariably be aimed at wealthier residents. They have seen it all before, and they have come to distrust the words of elected officials, even of those who run for mayor as the "anti-Bloomberg." Notably, the biggest opposition to de Blasio's agenda was to be found in Brooklyn, the mayor's home borough, and it has been strong particularly among many of those Latin and African American voters who cheered his election into office in 2013.

"How Are You Enjoying the De Blasio Revolution?" was the title of a December 2015 cover story for *New York Magazine*, which pointed to the mayor's very poor approval ratings only two years into his term.[83] In May 2015, a poll released by Quinnipiac University showed that only 44% of voters approved of de Blasio's job performance after one and a half years in office.[84] Five months later, this number declined to 38% according to a Marist College poll. Notably, support for the mayor dropped 9 points among African American voters and 12 points among Latinos.[85] The same month, three out of five New Yorkers disapproved of de Blasio's handling of the city's homelessness and affordable housing crisis, despite both issues having been at the core of his political agenda, according to a survey conducted by Siena College and the *New York Times*.[86] A recent Quinnipiac University poll showed that 50% of New Yorkers would not approve of his re-election in 2017.[87]

These numbers are significant, considering the polls were conducted in moments of general economic prosperity for the city. The numbers suggest that de Blasio may have disappointed both sides of the city: middle-class voters have seen a mayor who in talks and public appearances seemed too focused on the plight of the poor, while at the same time, poor New Yorkers haven't seen the change they were expecting under the new mayor. But there is another issue capable of disconcerting both the rich and the poor, and that few would have expected to get worse under the new administration: the rising number of homeless people on the streets of New York.

The Other Side of New York

"We cannot let children like Dasani down,"[88] said de Blasio at a public speech a few weeks after his 2013 election. Dasani was a then-11-year-old homeless girl whose touching story, reported in a widely read *New York Times* series,[89] testified to the horrible conditions of the 22,000 children living in the grim homeless shelters of New York City—a sad legacy of the Bloomberg administration, and living proof of the failure of its affordable housing policies. It was a shameful legacy that de Blasio vowed to amend.

The number of homeless people hit all-time-high levels during the latter years of Bloomberg. Despite promises to cut homelessness by two-thirds by the end of his time in office, the number of people living in the streets or in homeless shelters increased year after year during his tenure, reaching a record of over 50,000 people living in homeless shelters by the end of 2013. Meanwhile, because of skyrocketing rental prices, in little more than a decade under Bloomberg, the number of official evictions in New York City rose from 21,945 in 2005 to 26,857 in 2014 (and this number doesn't take into account the probably larger number of informal evictions). Between 2002 and 2010, the number of families entering homeless shelters after an eviction quadrupled.[90] Bloomberg eliminated permanent housing assistance programs for homeless families, particularly after 2005, when he ended the practice of giving priority access to NYCHA public housing units and federal Section 8 vouchers to homeless families.[91] He replaced these programs with the so-called Homeless Stability Plus, and later with the Advantage program, which offered two years of rental assistance to a selected number of working families living in shelters. Homeless advocates criticized both programs as ineffective, and state funding for these programs was cut in 2011 by Governor Cuomo.

De Blasio had not been deaf to the problem. He had invested in programs for homeless prevention and had restored the policy of the NYCHA to reserve a small number of apartments for families leaving the shelters. In 2014, he launched Living in Communities, or LINC, a voucher program designed to move shelter families into stable housing. The vouchers provide short-term rental assistance to those leaving the shelter system. Initially the program encountered several obstacles, particularly due to budget disputes with Albany, since the state rejected the city's proposal to set the rent levels at the federal "Fair Market Rent" limits, which would have made the program competitive with federal Section 8 vouchers. As a result, in many cases landlords were refusing to accept the vouchers.[92] Later in 2015, the administration devoted additional funds to raise the rent levels in the LINC program, making landlords less reluctant to accept the vouchers.[93] In 2014, the city also set aside around 750 of the 5,500 NYCHA vacant apartments available every year for the homeless, and this number was doubled one year later.[94]

But the tragic reality of homelessness, which had intensified in the times of Koch, and escalated further under the tenures of Dinkins, Giuliani, and Bloomberg, seems to have only gotten worse under de Blasio's watch. And merciless tabloids have been quick to point it out with headlines such as "De Blasio Proves He's Clueless About the Homeless Crisis."[95] But there is truth to these stories. By November 2015, a federal report indicated that New York was officially the United States' homeless capital, with a staggering 75,323 homeless people, including 58,000 sleeping in city shelters, even as the number of homeless people nationwide was sinking.[96] By the end of 2016, the number of homeless individuals in the city shelter system had risen to an all-time record of over 60,000.[97]

When faced with this growing political emergency, de Blasio for too long dismissed the phenomenon as the creation of tabloids and political opposers, and blamed the emergency on the failures of the Bloomberg administration, the lack of adequate communication with the press, and the resistance of New York State Governor Cuomo, who had refused to support several proposals to address the situation.[98] Only at the end of 2015, as his ratings were dropping and homelessness had become an emergency covered almost daily by all major city magazines, did he decide to take action. He unveiled a $2.6 billion plan aimed at moving people out of the shelter system by creating 15,000 supportive housing units for the homeless, including veterans, the mentally ill, and disabled people, over a 15-year period.[99] He removed Commissioner of the Department of Homeless Services Gilbert Taylor and announced plans to overhaul the department along with the other agency dealing with combating homelessness, the Human Resources Administration.[100] He also announced a new homelessness outreach program called HOME-STAT, which employs specially trained staff of the NYPD's homeless outreach unit along with social workers, to provide a daily count of homeless people living in the city streets and allow outreach teams to respond to calls from residents reporting the presence of homeless people on the street.[101] Meanwhile, NYPD Commissioner Bratton announced that the department would try to pass legislation that makes it illegal for homeless people to panhandle within 10 feet of any ATM, among other measures. But homeless advocates claim that HOME-STAT may simply revive the Giuliani method of criminalizing the homeless on the street, leading to more arrests rather than offering any alternative shelter. A member of advocacy group Picture the Homeless commented: "The Mayor and the police commissioner are trying to show people they're doing something, to get the public off the back, but there's nothing to it ... except more surveillance and more police targeting homeless African-Americans and Hispanics....We need housing. It's really simple."[102]

Afterword

Engineering the City for the Elite

There's never been a clearer sign that 21st-century New York is nothing but an amusement park for the world's wealthy and their children. It has ceased to be a real place for the rest of us.[1]

Zuccotti Park, Financial District, December 6, 2011. On the heels of an unprecedented wave of bank foreclosures that has devastated the nation, Occupy Wall Street (OWS) activists and housing rights advocates across the country launch an International Day of Action. By joining forces with the hundreds of community-based organizations that have burgeoned after the bursting of the subprime mortgage crisis, the Occupy Our Homes chapters of OWS move to direct action by reclaiming vacant foreclosed homes for homeless families, disrupting auctions of bank-owned houses, and blocking eviction procedures from New York City to Minneapolis, from Portland to San Francisco.[2] In Harlem, the Occupy Harlem movement stages a rally at 125th Street, condemning the privatization of Harlem's public housing and the eviction of low-income tenants, and advocating the boycott of predatory lending banks and financial corporations.

Fast forward to 2012, in Chelsea. Light poles near the Highline are patched with flyers saying: "Attention High Line tourists. West Chelsea is not Times Square.... Please consider how you would feel if 3 million people a year from around the world trampled your street, your neighborhood, and your local park." This innocent flyer sparks a storm of media controversy, with some claiming it is more than the bitter rant of some elitist snob: it expresses perfectly the frustration of New Yorkers with the transformation of their city into a massive tourist trap.[3] American art critic Jerry Saltz jumps into the controversy, claiming: "For me, the High Line is the harbinger of a bad pathogen now transforming public space into fussy, extra-busy, over-designed, high-maintenance mannered playgrounds, curated experiences, and crowd-pleasing spectacles."[4]

Full speed ahead to 2016, at 335 East 27th Street. New York City's long-awaited first micro-apartment units are unveiled with great fanfare. More than 60,000 people have applied to live in 14 super-small affordable dwellings with retractable beds that pull down from the wall, which the city presented as a "new model for development of affordable housing."[5] Only 14 of the 55 tiny units in the building, whose sizes range from 265 to 360 square feet, have "affordable" rents ranging from $914 to $1,873 a month, while the market-rate units range between $2,670 and $3,220.[6] Since the average price per square foot in the building, called Carmel Place, is over $100 against an average $55 in the rest of the neighborhood, one has to question whether this new breed of luxury micro-units represents a sensible solution to New York City's affordable housing dilemma.[7]

Now let me tell you another tale of two New Yorks, circa 2017. There's a gilded-age city of gleaming glass towers where Wall Street managers, Hollywood celebrities, exiled Russian oligarchs, and Middle East billionaires live their glamorous lives or stash their offshore cash. And then there's a city where even the professional middle class is one rent hike away from eviction. It's a city of creatives, freelancers, students, artists, teachers, nurses, clerks and firefighters struggling with exorbitant rents; of storeowners living under the constant threat that their businesses will shut down; and of thousands of families coming in and out of the shelter system.

And these two New Yorks, where the rich devour more and more of the urban space, while ordinary citizens are stuck, are growing further apart.

A brand-new global class of city consumers has been born, and they're ousting the rest of us—the working classes, the middle classes, and even the upper middle classes—from the city we love. The sheer scale of their consuming power is entirely changing the rules of the urban development game, which today seems focused exclusively on producing a city that is more custom-tailored to their ostentatious consumption demands. In the process, ordinary New Yorkers are pushed further out of this gilded city of unaffordable rents, or left to observe their neighborhoods while they gradually morph into exclusive enclaves for the super-wealthy.

Meanwhile, the power of city producers has never been greater. Those who count in real estate, banking, and finance have managed to ensure that their interests are safeguarded at city hall, in Albany, and in Washington. They have ensured that, regardless of who sits at different levels of government, the fundamental rules of the game (opening up more avenues for profit and being subsidized in the process) will remain untouched. Their ambitious agenda, based on a relentless use of rezoning and branding, is driving an era of unprecedented urban transformations and prompting the physical, social, and symbolic re-engineering of districts and communities across the board, from Flushing to East Brooklyn, from Staten Island to the South Bronx. No corner is off-limits to capital: the whole of the city is up for grabs, and new spectacular tides of creative destruction are on the horizon.

City producers and city consumers are transforming the city into a repackaged wonderland of lavish real estate, dotted by pockets of poverty where a new urban underclass lives its daily struggles. New York, like no other city, encapsulates the contradictions and inequalities that surround the process of neoliberal urbanization: it only takes a subway ride from Billionaire's Row to Spanish Harlem to get a visual reminder of the way the rich and poor live in the city. Even though a trend toward a concentration of wealth among the city's top earners goes back at least four decades, it has widened precipitously over the last 15 years. By the end of Bloomberg's tenure, the top 1% of earners in New York City brought in 40% of the city's total income.[8] And things have only worsened under de Blasio's watch.[9] Today, New York has among the highest levels of income inequality in the United States, concurring globally with the likes of Rio de Janeiro and Sao Paulo. And the most unequal of all US counties is unsurprisingly Manhattan.[10] Here, the average apartment in 2015 was priced at a whopping $1.95 million.[11] In this island of wealth and inequality, median rentals have increased consecutively for years, and today, at above $4,000 a month, they are among the highest on the globe. And things aren't much better in Brooklyn and Queens, where rents are at around $3,000 a month.[12] Prepare to see more of the same happening soon in the South Bronx, where residents in Mott Haven have recently learned that their neighborhood is currently being marketed as "the Piano District" to hip newcomers, courtesy of developers Somerset Partners and Chetrit Group.[13]

It's the System, Stupid!

Developers can relax—Mayor Bill de Blasio won't turn New York City into a communistic realm where no one can build a candy store without including "affordable" apartments.... There are enough fully entitled, publicly approved mega-projects underway to keep the tower cranes busy for four more years—no matter what policies City Hall adopts—and to advance the Bloomberg-era vision far into the future.[14]

New York's harsh social inequalities have come a long way, and de Blasio won't be able to change the rules of a game that was established way before he moved his first steps into the world of politics. They are the result of a political turn that, grown out of the "neoliberal euphoria"[15] of the laissez-faire economics of the early 1970s, has morphed into a system of crony capitalism, where an ever larger government is there to give blessings to well-connected special interest groups. It is a system that through corporate welfare, financial deregulation, and the public financing of private losses, has made sure that inequality was built into it, at the federal as much as at the local level.

This system, which certainly hasn't changed after the 2007/2008 financial crisis (and the ensuing government-sponsored trillion-dollar bank bailout), has traditionally translated into a chronic shrinking of federal spending on housing, services, and infrastructures, at the same time when government was handing out special tax privileges and public funding to big private ventures. In cities, it is a system in which the enormous sway of city producers (the local elite) and city consumers has changed the rules of the game entirely. Those cities that won at the game, like New York or San Francisco, keep attracting top industries and global consumers, and have gradually morphed into citadels where the most outrageous wealth at the top clashes with unimaginable poverty at the bottom. Those that didn't make it are sinking in a downward spiral of poverty, disinvestment, and population loss: these are cities like Youngstown, Ohio, where almost 40% of residents live below the poverty line, or Flint, Michigan, where even tap water can kill you.

The CEOs of the Urban Regime

Mayors these days are often celebrated on the global stage as innovative game-changers, and there's been a growing media emphasis on how they can inspire change and policy shifts to higher levels of government. But a mayor can only do so much to address the demons of poverty and inequality.

De Blasio campaigned on the promise of undoing the Bloomberg legacy. Once in office, his promises of a clean break with past policies were thwarted by the interests of developers and big business, the power of higher levels of government (the governor and the state senate), the total withdrawal of funding for housing by the federal government, and an implicit acceptance of the golden rules of the urban development game. A game that is based on the physical, social, and symbolic re-engineering of low-income communities across the board, to encourage high-end residential and commercial investment and the influx of new, more affluent city consumers.

Despite the enormous hope surrounding the new mayor's policy platform, he has continued an approach to housing development that was used to devastating effect under Bloomberg, with just some trimming around the edges. As a result, in the first four years of his tenure we have seen more of the same: more rezonings serving as a bridgehead for upscale development in working-class neighborhoods, more ultra-luxury glass towers piercing the city skyline, more record sales of multimillion *pied-à-terre* to foreign investors, and more small businesses, many of them long-lived cultural touchstones, wiped out by massive rent hikes and skyrocketing property values. What de Blasio has strived to do to a larger extent compared to Bloomberg is to harness the forces of the market to extract more benefits for the larger community, such as a slightly increased quota of "affordable" housing units in new developments, although, as we have seen, very few of them will be in the reach of those who need them the most. And de Blasio, who has spent a lot of time raising his national profile as champion of progressive economic policies across the United States, recently had to admit that he expects no interest from higher levels of government in helping cities cope with issues of inequality:[16] unsurprisingly, throughout the 2016 presidential race, the issue of housing as a fundamental key to address urban poverty was nowhere to be heard in the talks of political candidates from both sides of the political spectrum.

It must be hard for an administration that vowed to address economic injustice to live up to such big expectations in the world's capital of inequality, or to invoke preservation in the world's capital of creative destruction, a city where thousands of buildings are demolished each year, and over 56,000 new building permits were issued in 2015 alone, the highest recorded figure since the 1960s.[17]

When it comes to urban development and housing, very few New Yorkers have seen much of a radical change since the new mayor was elected into office. What housing activists and local residents have witnessed, instead, was an about-face on many stances that were of the utmost importance to them.

The truth is, the mayor of New York is only the chief executive officer of an urban regime that was in place long before his administration, and that will continue to reign over the city beyond his tenure. CEO-mayors may come and go, but the regime is here to stay. And city producers will do all they can to keep the city building machine alive, regardless of who sits in office.

What we are witnessing, in New York City and other levels of government elsewhere around the world, is an always deeper chasm separating the control rooms of decision making and the people affected by them. And there's a growing mistrust against the inner workings and the very meaning of representative democracy, in a world where figurehead leaders are elected on a program, only to flip-flop on their electoral promises once in office and once acquainted with the corridors of power. And nothing better explains the deep disconnect between the established norms of representative democracy and the voting public than two major events that shook the world in 2016: the unanticipated UK vote for Brexit and the results of the 2016 US presidential election.

Out of the blue, against all odds, the people have shouted their discontent and their mistrust for the promises and rhetoric of established leaders. In the case of the election of Donald J. Trump, in a paradoxical turn of events, the most well known of city producers in his home city of New York, yet an outcast in Washington, has been chosen by the working classes in the Rust Belt and across rural America as the vanguard against the undue power of elite wealthy cities over the rest of the country, and as an antidote to an establishment that was promising to uphold the trajectory that brought them to their dire straits. Like them or not, these phenomena articulate a clear and sudden rise in popular dissent against elite rule, and they may teach policymakers a crucial lesson: working and middle-class citizens have had enough of established practices of power that have proven time and again their utter distance from the people's daily needs and desires.

It is said that Einstein defined madness as doing the same thing over and over again and expecting different results. Many are feeling that they have been engaging in this demonstration of madness long enough. The elite city is a policy choice, not some inevitable God-given mandate.[18] And even at the local level, there are things that can be done to arrest this mess. When did people tell their government bureaucracies to drain city budgets to subsidize big corporations and banking giants? Or to give out massive tax breaks to developers and buyers of luxury units, when affordable housing is shrinking at a record pace? Since when has producing offshore deposit boxes in the sky for the 1%, while being publicly subsidized for doing so,[19] become the new normal? There must be something better than this. As people wake up and challenge the established consensus around city building, there will be a chance for us to see another kind of creative destruction. And hopefully, it will be the creative destruction of established norms, slogans, and political practices that have made this system so disconnected from the needs of the citizens of New York, as well as the citizens of the world.

Acknowledgments

I would like to thank a number of people who have helped me in the long and rocky journey that was the writing of this book. This project has gone through a number of evolutionary stages, starting as academic research and then morphing into a more trade-oriented book that will hopefully be accessible to everyone. I was very fortunate to have Roz Foster as my literary agent: since the day we started working together, she has shown boundless dedication and enthusiasm for this project. She is a real professional in the publishing industry and I can't thank her enough for her patience, intellect, and insight. I am incredibly grateful to Lise Vogel for her love and emotional support during my crazy New York years. Her loyalty has given me strength also in the many times when difficulties and insecurities threatened to overwhelm me. She is an inspiring woman, a brilliant thinker, and the best of friends: I couldn't imagine my time in New York without her. I would also like to thank Michael Zimmer, my first introduction to New York City, a visionary man and a quintessential New Yorker, who died in 2008 but whose memory lives in my heart.

I would like to thank David McBride, my editor at Oxford University Press, for his feedback and insights, and editorial assistant Kathleen Weaver for her competence and efficiency. I also warmly thank project manager Emma Clements for her tireless dedication, and marketing and publicity managers Erin Meehan and Jonathan Kroberger for their guidance. I am very grateful to Peter Marcuse, who guided me during my first years in New York City at Columbia University. I am also strongly indebted to my friend Tom Angotti, whose research on rezoning and community planning in New York City has been a fundamental resource for this book, and who has provided me with his friendly assistance and encouragement for years. I can't thank him enough for taking the time to read drafts of this book and offering his feedback. I also would like to thank a thousand times Loretta Lees for her constant encouragement and support. My gratitude goes also to those other scholars whose lectures and seminars in New York City and Berlin have nurtured my love and passion for urban research: particularly

Neil Brenner, Margit Mayer, Rosemary Wakeman, David Harvey, Tom Slater and the late Neil Smith, whose warmth and enthusiasm will be sorely missed. Special thanks go also to Harald Bodenschatz for his guidance and friendship, and to Elisabeth Asche for offering sage advice during my time at the Center for Metropolitan Studies in Berlin. I thank Robert Beauregard and Enrico Gualini for their insights.

I also would like to thank the students at the doctoral colloquia of Professor Marcuse at Columbia University, and particularly Kostantin Kontokosta, Ingrid Olivo, Cuz Potter, and Justin Steil, for their constructive criticism and suggestions. I am especially indebted to my colleagues at the Center for Metropolitan Studies in Berlin: I thank Anne Vogelpohl, Sabine Horlitz, Noa Ha, Sasha Disko, Kristina Graaf, Manuel Lutz, Cordelia Polinna, and Stefan Höhne for their feedback and for our beautiful conversations.

I owe a strong debt of gratitude to all those who took the time to share their knowledge of the neighborhood stories I have chronicled in the book and allowed me to be a part of their community. I warmly thank Erica Razook, Craig Schley, Nellie Hester Bailey, and Michael Henry Adams for helping me get to know a piece of the real Harlem and the daily life, dreams, and struggles of its residents. I thank Tricia Vita for her painstaking dedication and knowledge of Coney Island, and the many people I met at the People's Playground. I thank all the members of Save Coney Island, and particularly Juan Rivero, Amanda Deutch, and Diane Carlin, for their amazing energy and inspiration. Without their support, this work wouldn't have been possible. I also would like to thank all those New Yorkers who let me interview them and shared their life stories. I would like to thank Alex Garvin for his help, and Yvette Clairjeane from the counsel's office of the Department of City Planning for her patient assistance. I thank Jerry Krase, Stanley Fox, Keith and Adriana de Cesare, Bettina Damiani, Patricia Mchugh and Philip Tonda Heide.

I am indebted to my dear friends Giovanni Ometto, who helped me carry out some of my street interviews, and the lovely Valentina Belli, who has designed the concept for the iconic cover of this book. I thank my wonderful family for their support and for always having been by my side in difficult times. My achievements were made possible by their dedication and constant encouragement through the years. Lastly, I would like to thank a thousand times New York City, its streets, and its people, for always making me feel at home.

List of Figures

Notes

FOREWORD

1. O'Connell, "15 Reasons."
2. Leon, "Skyscraper Boom."
3. Trejos, "Berlin."
4. Ozimek, "Richard Florida."
5. Nezik, "Tourism Troubles."
6. White, "London."
7. Clack, "Would You Live in Cupboard?"
8. Blackwell, "Urban Renaissance."
9. Richter, "San Francisco."
10. Misener, "9 Private Islands."
11. Earth Porm, "7 Castles."
12. Graff, "What $350,000 Buys."
13. Carroll, "Never Be Able to Buy."
14. Smith, "Conversation."

INTRODUCTION

1. Solomont, "220 CPS."
2. Navarro, "Long Lines."

CHAPTER I

1. Kelley, "Disappearing Acts," 64.
2. REBNY, website.
3. *New York Times*, "Harlem Is Booming."
4. Hackman, "When Harlem Becomes White."
5. Makalani, "Sociological Analysis of Renaissance," 12.
6. *New York Times*, "Landlord Brings in Negroes."
7. William Blumstein, then head of the store, finally gave in to pressures from local residents and promised to hire 35 African Americans for clerical and sales positions. In 1938, Reverend Adam Clayton Powell Jr. led the Greater New York Coordinating Committee for Employment and secured agreements

with Woolworth's, Kress, A. S. Beck, and other major businesses to cease their discriminating hiring policies.

8. Schoener, *Harlem on My Mind*, 132–134.
9. Schoener, *Harlem on My Mind*, 237–238.
10. Sterne, "Harlem's Dreams."
11. Felber, "Apollo Theater."
12. According to calculations by Schaffer and Smith, "Gentrification of Harlem," 358, based on census data.
13. "The western corridor of Central Harlem is experiencing the beginning of gentrification. Above-average increases in income and rent levels as well as in the number of high-income families were matched by a rapid increase in sales activity" (Schaffer and Smith, "Gentrification of Harlem," 357).
14. Novy, "Marginalized Neighborhoods," 172.
15. Hicks, "Street Vendors."
16. NYPD, "2001 Crime Statistics."
17. Furman Center, "Trends."
18. Waldman, "Harlem, Hero's Welcome."
19. The UMEZ began operations in 1995 and made its first round of grants and loans in 1996. In 2000, the UMEZ's operations were extended through December 2009. Legislation enacted in 2009 extended again the UMEZ's program through December 2011.
20. Maurrasse, *Listening to Harlem*, 38.
21. Maurrasse, *Listening to Harlem*; Hyra, *New Urban Renewal*.
22. Quoted in Hyra, *New Urban Renewal*, 75.
23. Dunlap, "Changing Look of Harlem."
24. Zukin, *Naked City*, 87.
25. Novy, "Marginalized Neighborhoods," 167.
26. Maurrasse, *Listening to Harlem*, 97.
27. Novy, "Marginalized Neighborhoods," 202.
28. Starting in 2007, the BID also started cooperating with the Department of City Planning and issued reports and recommendations for the rezoning of 125th Street as a cultural and shopping hub.
29. Cardwell, "Casting Call (Smile!)."
30. Sadly, the Lenox Lounge closed the same year, in December 2012, because of the escalating rental price.
31. Kaufman, "Must-see Harlem."
32. *Uptown Magazine*, "Toast to Luxury."
33. *Uptown Magazine*, "Toast to Luxury."
34. From the website of BET: "'Harlem Heights' will provide a window into the fascinating world of New York's young, Black and fabulous crowd. Set against the backdrop of the increasingly gentrified neighborhood of Harlem, the series features a diverse cast of eight young adults from different backgrounds who

share common goals—making the post-college leap into adulthood and finding love and success in the big city on their own terms."

35. Burden, "Statement at City Planning Commission."

36. City of New York, DCP, "125th Street Original Proposal."

37. City of New York, DCP, "125th Street Press Release," 2007.

38. Feltz, "Redlining."

39. City of New York, DCP, "125th Street Corridor Rezoning."

40. Feltz, "Redlining."

41. See Buettner, "Faltering Harlem Housing Deal."

42. Hyra, *New Urban Renewal*, 137.

43. Williams, "Council Approves Rezoning."

44. Durkin, "Council Approves Rezoning."

45. Vornado Realty Trust, developer of the demised "Harlem Park" office tower at
    125th Street and Park Avenue, and Kimco Realty, which has purchased a two-
    story building at 125th Street and Frederick Douglass and evicted its long-time
    tenants to replace the building with a new retail complex, are both linked
    to donations for hundreds of thousands of dollars to Representative Charles
    B. Rangel's fundraising operation since the 2004 election cycle, according to
    Hernandez, "Real Estate Developers."

46. Williams, "Council Approves Rezoning."

47. Rudish and Lombardi, "Council OKs Rezoning Plan."

48. Barron, quoted in Chung, "Council Passes Rezoning."

49. Topousis, "Rezoning OK'd."

50. Dickens, quoted in Durkin, "Council Approves Rezoning."

51. Gale, personal interview, 2014.

52. Tucker, "Zoned Out."

53. Henry, "Community Fights Gentrification."

54. Bailey, quoted in Chaban, "Harlem's Future?"

55. Rhodes-Pitts, quoted in Warner, "Rezoning Harlem's Main Street."

56. Craig Schley, quoted in Tucker, "Zoned Out."

57. Gale, personal interview, 2014.

58. CUF, "Attack of the Chains?"

59. A commentator on *Jeremiah's Vanishing New York Blog*, April 9, 2008.

60. Heilpern, "Princess of the City."

61. Williams, "City's Sweeping Rezoning Plan."

62. City of New York, DCP, "125th Street Rezoning Plan."

63. City of New York, DCP, "Final Environmental Impact Statement," 1.0–17.

64. The theater, whose facade and lobby will be restored, is set to become the
    centerpiece of a massive redevelopment project which will include a 26-story
    Renaissance Hotel by Marriot, 200 residential rental units, half of which will
    be below-market rate, retail and cultural space. See City Realty, "Victoria
    Theater Site."

65. Henry Adams, quoted in Irwin, "Landmarking the Black Capital."
66. Angotti, *New York for Sale.*
67. Barnes, "Harlem on the Rise."
68. A commentator on *Curbed New York,* April 30, 2008.
69. Halstead Property, website.
70. Douglas Elliman Real Estate, website.
71. Freeman, *There Goes the 'Hood,* 53.
72. Hyra, *New Urban Renewal,* 4.
73. Freeman, *There Goes the 'Hood,* 92.
74. Beveridge, "Affluent, White Harlem?"
75. Fanelli, "Census Trends."
76. Zhang, "West Harlem, Identity Crisis."
77. Spike Lee, quoted in Coscarelli, "Spike Lee's Rant."
78. Williams, "Evolving Harlem."
79. In his book, Freeman documents both the positive and negative sides to the mixing of the new gentry with indigenous residents. Among the positive sides are the dropping crime rates, cleaner streets, and better services, including supermarkets, chain stores, food delivery services, ATM machines, and taxis—in sum, services that are common in most Manhattan neighborhoods but were for too long lacking in Harlem. The other side of the coin, however, is that other kinds of businesses and services, including social services aimed at the poor, are likely to disappear in the gentrifying neighborhood. See Freeman, *There Goes the 'Hood,* 154.

    In his book *Listening to Harlem,* David J. Maurrasse interviewed Harlem locals to find what their perception of the changing neighborhood was. When asked about what they liked most of the changes in the neighborhood, 22% indicated the availability of new businesses, while another 20% pointed to the rehabilitation and construction of new housing. When asked about what they liked least, however, an overwhelming majority (62%) indicated the escalating costs of living in the neighborhood as the worst aspect of change. When asked whether they knew anyone who had been forced to move because of rising rents, over 58% of respondents answered yes. See Maurrasse, *Listening to Harlem,* 77–86.
80. Freeman, *There Goes the 'Hood,* 105.
81. Gale, personal interview, 2014.
82. Henry Adams, quoted in Feltz, "Redlining."
83. *CBS New York,* "Police Focus."
84. Freeman, *There Goes the 'Hood,* 105.
85. Williams, "Old Sound in Harlem."
86. Mays, "Brownstone Residents."
87. Mays, "Brownstone Residents."
88. Corcoran, "1Q-2001 Manhattan Report."
89. Corcoran, "1Q-2007 Manhattan Report."

90. Fusfeld, "Closing Prices."
91. Budin, "Neil Patrick Harris."
92. Warerkar, "Record-Setting Townhouse."
93. Carlos, personal interview, 2014.
94. A Harlem real estate broker, personal interview, 2014.
95. Bailey, "Harlem."
96. Trotta, "Black New York."
97. If an apartment is rent regulated, increases each year can't exceed a fixed amount set annually by the Rent Guidelines Board; however, when an apartment is vacated, rents can climb much faster. When the rental price rises above $2,500 (under the 2011 Rent Act), the unit exits from the rent regulation system and is valued at market rate.
98. Jones, "Subsidized Housing."
99. Associated Press, "New Laws."
100. Stulberg, "City to Landlords."
101. Morgenson, "Rent Tactics."
102. Associated Press, "New Laws."
103. Jones, "Subsidized Housing."
104. Del Signore, "Tenants Sue Owner."
105. Lowery, "Harlem Growth Plans." Also see, Solis, "Lenox Terrace Landlord."
106. Solis, "Lenox Terrace Residents."
107. Chiaramonte, "Tenants Flee."
108. Suh, "East Harlem Tenants."
109. Kapp, "Tenants Evacuated."
110. U.S. Census Bureau, 2010.
111. A policy of housing discrimination and segregation "formally began in 1935 when the Federal Home Loan Bank Board helped create 'residential security maps' to indicate the level of risk for real estate investments in 239 cities. The maps defined most black neighborhoods as ineligible for loans, including Harlem" (Feltz, "Redlining").
112. Mays, "East Harlem Leaders."
113. Budin, "Harlem's Tallest Buildings."
114. Solis, "City Moving Forward."
115. A commentator on *Curbed New York*, May 1, 2008.
116. REBNY, "REBNY Retail Report Fall 2005."
117. NRA, "Obamacare."
118. Ryley, "Retail Vacancies by Neighborhood."
119. Ryley, "Harlem Losing Soul."
120. Mazor, "Razing Rage in Harlem."
121. Pruitt, "Developers Back Off."
122. Bagli, "Blighted Area?"
123. Bagli, "Blighted Area?"
124. Moss, "Boro Hotel."

125. Moss, "Lenox Lounge Stripped."
126. CUF, "Attack of the Chains?"; CUF, "Chain Reaction"; Irwin, "Landmarking the Black Capital."
127. REBNY, "REBNY Retail Report Fall 2011."
128. CUF, "State of the Chains, 2012."
129. Melton, "Mark-Viverito."
130. Clarke, "Extell Makes Deal."
131. Schaffer and Smith, "Gentrification of Harlem," 352.
132. Regina Smith, quoted in Feiden, "Big Retailers Moved Uptown."

CHAPTER 2

1. Moss, "125th Street."
2. Lefebvre, *Production of Space*, 347.
3. See Harvey, *Urbanization of Capital*; and Harvey, *Urban Experience*.
4. Harvey's writings have identified urbanism as the spatial manifestation of the process of accumulation of surplus capital. He explains that the capitalist system is inherently unstable and requires constant accumulation to ensure its survival, which results in regular crises of overaccumulation that must be dealt with through numerous "spatial fixes." Harvey's argument is based on the idea that space can function as an alternative "fix," or a "safety valve" for capital accumulation. He distinguishes three different circuits of capital accumulation: the primary circuit is centered on the production and consumption of commodities; the secondary circuit revolves around the production of the built environment; and the tertiary circuit consists of investments in social services and technological innovation. Investment in the production of the built environment can provide a profitable "secondary circuit" of surplus capital absorption, which can be used when overaccumulation problems arise in the primary circuit of commodity production—that is, whenever profitable reinvestment in the primary circuit of capital is made difficult (e.g., because of lack of demand or high labor wages) and when such barriers cannot be easily overcome (e.g., by disciplining labor, outsourcing production, or opening new export markets). See Harvey, *Urbanization of Capital*; Harvey, *Urban Experience*; Harvey, "Globalization."
5. Loomis, "Consuming the City."
6. Brenner, Marcuse, and Mayer, "Cities for People."
7. This section draws on Harvey, *Urban Experience*; and Lefebvre, *Production of Space*.
8. Jacobs, *Death and Life*, 4.
9. Harvey, *Urban Experience*, 44.
10. Van Riper, "Ford to City."
11. See Fainstein, *City Builders*; Weber, "Extracting Value."
12. See Harvey, "Managerialism to Entrepreneurialism."

13. Weber, "Extracting Value."

14. Moody, *Welfare State to Real Estate*, 76.

15. Fainstein, *City Builders*, 48–49.

16. Moody, *Welfare State to Real Estate*, 78.

17. The 421-a property tax exemption was established to stimulate residential con-
    struction in New York City in times of crisis. It exempted landlords from pay-
    ing increases in property taxes resulting from their construction. For instance,
    if a vacant lot was initially valued at $5 million but its value rose to $30 million
    after construction, the $25 million increase in value wouldn't be taxed during
    the exemption period.

18. The J-51 tax abatement was first introduced in the 1950s to encourage capital
    improvements and repairs, by reducing the taxable assessed value in properties
    repaired or renovated by their landlords. Through the years, the program was
    expanded to benefit the conversions of industrial buildings to residential uses,
    or the conversion of rental buildings to co-ops or condos.

19. Soffer, *Ed Koch*.

20. See Sanders, *Celluloid Skyline*; Greenberg, *Branding New York*; Macek, *Urban
    Nightmares*.

21. Schwartz, "New York City and Subsidized Housing."

22. Moody, *Welfare State to Real Estate*, 150.

23. Moody, *Welfare State to Real Estate*, 150.

24. Schwarz, "Gentrification and Its Discontents."

25. In Marxist economic theory, the term is never explicitly used. The con-
    cept, however, is described in *The Communist Manifesto* and expanded in the
    Grundrisse and volume IV of *Das Kapital*, and refers to the interrelated pro-
    cesses of accumulation and destruction of wealth occurring in capitalism.

26. Schumpeter, *Capitalism*, 83.

27. Lefebvre, *Production of Space*, 360.

28. Weber, "Extracting Value."

29. Brenner, Marcuse, and Mayer, "Cities for People," 178.

30. Weber, "Extracting Value."

31. Weber, "Extracting Value," 520–521.

32. Lefebvre, *Production of Space*.

33. This notwithstanding, the three dimensions of space are intensely contested
    in capitalist societies. The *social space* of the city, administered by regulations
    and policies aimed at enhancing the market value of urban land, is constantly
    contested by social movements and citizen groups who strive to challenge the
    dictates of capital profitability and prioritize the value of neighborhoods as
    spaces for community building and everyday-life social practices. The *physical
    space* of the city, dominated by planning arrangements required to ensure the
    smooth extraction of value from urban land, is challenged by the multiform
    practices of collective mobilization that strive to reappropriate it, reinvent it,
    or self-manage it (through occupations, forms of community-based planning,

establishment of land trusts, etc.). The *symbolic space* of the city, monopolized
by dominant institutional representations aimed at enhancing the city's competitiveness in the global market, is constantly scrutinized and challenged in
the arts, literature, and the media, and in the personal perceptions of city users,
leading to the production of alternative narratives and counterrepresentations
of what the city is, or ought to be.

34. NYU, "NYU Space Planning."

35. Molotch, "Growth Machine," 309.

36. The growth machine thesis has been the object of discussion and critique
    in urban geography. Some critics have pointed to its almost exclusive focus
    on human agency, which de-emphasizes the influence that broader structural
    social relations play in guiding growth policies. According to some commenta-
    tors, a flaw of the growth machine thesis lies in its notion of locally tied elites
    concerned almost exclusively with property development, which on one hand
    excludes other potential political concerns, and on the other does not take into
    account the influence of extra-local, super-national, and transnational forces.
    See Rodgers, "Urban Geography."

37. Harvey, *Urban Experience*, 47–48.

38. See Logan and Molotch, *Urban Fortunes*. See also Molotch, "Growth Machine."

39. Logan and Molotch, *Urban Fortunes*, 51.

40. Gutekunst-Roth, "Note: New York."

41. Gutekunst-Roth, "Note: New York."

42. Newfield and du Brul, *Permanent Government*.

43. Harvey, *History of Neoliberalism*, 45.

44. See Stone, "Summing Up"; and Stone, *Regime Politics*.

45. See Stone, "Summing Up"; and Stone, *Regime Politics*.

46. My account of city producers is based on some of the main pivots of urban
    regime theory (the coalition between governments and nongovernmental
    organizations; the relative stability of urban regimes, which operate across dif-
    ferent administrations). It takes into account the multiscalar nature of urban
    governance, where decisions affecting local development are often made at
    extra-local levels, including the national, the super-national, and the transna-
    tional level. It also takes into account the contribution of heterogeneous forces,
    such as grassroots organizations and advocacy groups that strive to have a say in
    the decision-making process affecting the city.

47. In the scheme that follows, I summarize some of the ways in which city pro-
    ducers contribute to reshaping the physical, social, and symbolic space of
    the city:

    **City producers and the production of the physical space—Urban
    development:** Local governments manufacture flexible planning blueprints
    to encourage privately led real estate development in strategic areas of the city
    or accommodate development proposals launched by individual developers
    through ad hoc land use plans. As urban land is re-engineered to maximize its

market value, underperforming property markets are obliterated or rehabilitated to pave the way for new capital investments.

City producers and the production of the social space—Urban policy: The corporate and real estate industries lobby governments to enforce measures aimed at facilitating real estate growth and business expansion. This can be accomplished through advantageous fiscal policies by which public budgets are used to absorb the risks of private investment, but also through investments in technology innovations, or even through structural changes in labor and welfare policy aimed at enhancing the productivity of companies.

City producers and the production of the symbolic space—City branding and city marketing: Local coalitions of interests, including elected officials, strive to manufacture attractive images of the city through city marketing and branding initiatives. The manufacturing of dominant representations of a consumerist urbanity through branding and marketing campaigns is aimed at stimulating consumer demand for the commodified city from high-value industries, investors, visitors, and newcomers.

48. Lefebvre, *Production of Space*, 337.
49. In Marxist political economy, commodification occurs when something is assigned a value in the marketplace that goes beyond its sheer use value, making it into a marketable commodity.
50. See Lefebvre, *Production of Space*; Harvey, *Urban Experience*.
51. Marx and Engels, *German Ideology*, 131.
52. See Harvey, "Managerialism to Entrepreneurialism."
53. Lefebvre calls it "abstract space" (Lefebvre, *Production of Space*, 49–50).
54. Florida, *Who's Your City?*, 7.
55. See Lloyd and Clark, "City as Entertainment; Florida, *Cities and Creative Class*; Glaeser and Saiz, "Rise of Skilled City."
56. Lloyd and Clark, "City as Entertainment," 362.
57. Let's see in more detail how:

City consumers and the production of physical space—Physical upgrading: New geographies of consumption emerge in gentrifying neighborhoods, in districts that are catalysts for tourism, and areas that are undergoing large-scale redevelopment plans. In these areas, city consumers' demand for residential space, retail, services, and amenities is met by public policy and private efforts directed at a physical upgrade of the built environment: the old housing stock can be demolished or rehabilitated according to new consumer tastes and preferences; new urban apartments are built for a more affluent population; new office buildings are created to meet the demands of in-moving companies and their employees; parks, squares, and streetscapes are sanitized and refurbished; bike lanes materialize everywhere; large-scale chain retail and hipster specialty shops settle in; and "obsolete" local businesses that don't cater to the refined tastes of the new consumers are forced to shut their doors or relocate. Elsewhere, waterfront industrial areas are refurbished and turned into residential communities, high-tech hubs, or office districts, while stunning flag-ship architectures mushroom all over the city.

City consumers and the production of social space—Social trans-formations: Entrepreneurial urban policy mobilizes resources to attract dif-ferent groups of city consumers, by implementing "creative" development agendas favoring the arts and cultural events, subsidizing specific businesses through tax incentives, enforcing forms of control to keep the inner city safe, and stimulating the gentrification of inner-city working-class districts. In areas where new city consumers settle, the old neighborhood life gradually dis-solves: long-time social networks are threatened as households who can't afford to live in the upgraded district are displaced by wealthier residents; small local businesses, intimidated by the competition of larger and more powerful retail-ers or by escalating rental prices, are forced to relocate or shut down. The old community's socioeconomic and cultural capital erodes, while a new com-munity emerges, with new habits, new lifestyles, new consumption patterns, new rules, and even a new political voice.

City consumers and the production of symbolic space—Rebranding: In districts undergoing development, even nefarious reputa-tions of times past can be gradually substituted by new, glittering brands of urban living. Real estate developers, city officials, and even the local media strive to craft new narratives of "urbanity," "diversity," and "sustainability," to which the new in-movers can easily relate as customers. Gradually, the con-sumption of the city becomes a crucial aspect of the daily practices of most city users, including its residents, to which the city is presented as a landscape of consumption.

58. There are two main interpretations that link the urban development proc-ess to the practices of production and consumption of space. Demand-side (or consumption-side) explanations stress the importance of the living pref-erences of new affluent urbanites as the crucial engine of urban transforma-tions: according to this view, city consumers are the major drivers of an urban restructuring process that revolves around their consumption patterns. In other words: what consumers want determines how the city is built. On the other hand, supply-side explanations emphasize the dependency of consumption patterns upon the dictates of capital accumulation. In other words, our envi-ronment is built in such a way that it affects the way we consume.

59. With regard to the production of gentrified space for affluent city consumers, urban scholar Kevin Fox Gotham argues that the need for such space is "cre-ated and marketed, and depends on alternatives offered by property capitalists who are primarily interested in producing the built environment from which they can extract the highest profit." See Fox Gotham, "Redevelopment for Whom?." See also Firat, "Social Construction of Consumption Patterns."

60. See Harvey, "Right to the City."

61. Smith, "New Globalism."

62. See Lees, Slater, and Wyly, *Gentrification*. See also Lees, Shin, and Morales, *Planetary Gentrification*.
63. Smith, "New Globalism."

CHAPTER 3

1. Goodman, "New York Allowed Gentrification."
2. REBNY, "Invisible Engine."
3. Mahoney, "REBNY Members."
4. The program had been established as a 10-year tax abatement for new construction in 1971, at a time when the city was desperate for property investments. It wasn't until 2006, however, that the program was used to subsidize luxury developments in exchange for including a percentage of affordable units, on- or off-site. Until 2016, most newly constructed housing developments in New York City were eligible for a 10- to 25-year exemption from property taxes under this program. See King, "Calls for Public Discussion."
5. See King, "Calls for Public Discussion."
6. Mitsubishi's ownership was short-lived, and the building was purchased by a group led by Goldman Sachs and Jerry I. Speyer in 1996.
7. Fung, "Foreigners Purchase City Condos."
8. AFIRE, "Annual Foreign Investment Survey."
9. Sorkin, "Hotel Buying Spree."
10. Angotti, *New York for Sale*.
11. Story, Fehr, and Watkins, "$100 Million Club."
12. Fiscal Policy Institute, Good Jobs New York, and National Employment Law Project, "Overview of Job Quality."
13. Gross, "Subsidies in the City."
14. On August 1, 2002, the deal was pronounced dead by NYSE Chairman Richard Grasso.
15. CUF, "State of the Chains, 2016."
16. CUF, "Attack of the Chains?"
17. SBE Council, "Small Business Tax Index 2015."
18. Pratt Center for Community Development, "Saving Independent Retail."
19. The public advocate is one of the three city offices elected by voters. He or she serves as a mediator between New Yorkers and the local government and advises the mayor on all relations with the electorate. The public advocate responds to complaints about city services, investigates disputes, and provides oversight over city agencies. Bill de Blasio served as public advocate between 2010 and 2013, before his election as mayor of New York. The city comptroller, elected directly by city voters, is the city's chief financial officer. He or she is responsible for advising the mayor and city council on financial matters, overseeing the city's budget, and auditing the performance and finances of city agencies. The five borough presidents are elected by direct popular vote

but have only limited power and a minimal discretionary budget. Borough presidents are responsible for appointing community boards but have an advisory role on issues relating to their borough, including land use decisions and financial needs.

20. These include the New York City Economic Development Corporation (NYCEDC), the Department of Transportation (DOT), the Department of Buildings (DOB), the Department of City Planning (DCP), the Department of Housing Preservation and Development (HPD), and dozens of other agencies related to economic development and land use, including the Department of Finance, the Department of Small Business Services, and the mayor's office of Operations and Long-term Planning and Sustainability (OLPTS).

21. Clarke, "Goldman Sachs."

22. Of the remaining six members, five are appointed by each of the five borough presidents, and one by the public advocate.

23. The 51 members of city council (1 member for each of the 51 districts) are elected by New Yorkers. Bills passed by a simple majority are sent to the mayor, who may sign them into law. If the mayor vetoes a bill, the council has 30 days to override the veto by a two-thirds majority vote.

24. See Peyser, "Melissa Mark-Viverito."

25. *The Real Deal*, "Affordable Lender CPC."

26. Putzier, "De Blasio's Donors."

27. Angotti, "Real Power."

28. Velsey, "Twilight of an Era."

29. Pogrebin, "Preservation and Development."

30. Pogrebin, "Preservation and Development."

31. See Lloyd and Clark, "City as Entertainment"; Florida, *Rise of Creative Class*; Florida, *Cities and Creative Class*; Florida, *Who's Your City?*; Glaeser and Saiz, "Rise of Skilled City."

32. See Florida, *Rise of Creative Class*; Florida, *Cities and Creative Class*; Florida, *Who's Your City?*.

33. Florida, *Rise of Creative Class*.

34. According to Florida (*Who's Your City?*, 84), a 2002 survey released by strategic planning consultancy firm Next Generation Consulting found that "three-quarters of recent college graduates first choose where to live, *then* look for a job in that market."

35. The term "perpetual travelers" or "permanent tourists" is used to describe a population of temporary urban residents who live in such a way that they can't be considered legal residents of any of the countries in which they spend time. By lacking a legal permanent residence status, they are able to avoid the legal obligations that come with residency, such as income and property taxes, social security contributions, and so on.

36. The term was coined by Norma McCaig, president of Global Nomads International. In 1984, she used the term to define "anyone of any nationality

who has lived outside their parents' country of origin (or their 'passport country') before adulthood because of a parent's occupation." The group may include children of employees in the diplomatic or military sector, international businesses, missionary organizations, and intergovernmental or voluntary agencies. As a social group, they share the experience of having been uprooted from their hometown and of having experienced the cultures and languages of different countries.

37. Florida, *Who's Your City?*, 79.
38. Florida, *Rise of Creative Class*.
39. See Peck, "Creative Class." See also Malanga, "Curse of Creative Class," and Kotkin and Siegel, "Too Much Froth."
40. Peck, "Creative Class," 747.
41. Peck, "Creative Class," 760.
42. Currid, "Global Creative Hub."
43. City of New York, DCP, "Employment Patterns in New York City."
44. Klinenberg, "Solo Nation."
45. Lloyd and Clark, "City as Entertainment."
46. Smith, "New Globalism."
47. Kim, "Hedonic and Utilitarian Shopping Motivations."
48. Alpha shoppers are the most enthusiastic shoppers, with high levels of motivation in all aspects of shopping and consuming. Usually, alpha shoppers have a relatively low degree of education, and most are middle- to low-income individuals. Hedonistic motivations play a large role in their consumption behavior. Beta shoppers are individuals that have strong shopping motivations, but not as high as alpha shoppers. They associate both hedonistic and utilitarian shopping motivations (Kim, "Hedonic and Utilitarian Shopping Motivations").
49. Kim, "Hedonic and Utilitarian Shopping Motivations," 76.
50. *Trendwatching*, "Citysumers."
51. Zukin, "Urban Lifestyles."
52. Porter, Blaxil, Hervé, and Mixer, "Inner Cities."
53. *The Suburbanization of New York: Is the World's Greatest City Becoming Just Another Town?* is the title of a book edited by Jerilou and Kingsley Hammett, published in 2007.
54. See Judd and Fainstein, *Tourist City*; Fainstein, "Tourism."
55. Michael Bloomberg, quoted in Powell, "Despair?"
56. Urry, *Tourist Gaze*.
57. Moss, "Disney World."
58. Moss, "Disney World."
59. See Judd and Fainstein, *Tourist City*.
60. Sassen and Roost, "The City."
61. Kotkin, "Where Inequality Is Worst."
62. CWF, "Empire State of Inequality."
63. Stilwell and Lu, "10 Most Unequal Big Cities."
64. FPI, "Grow Together?," 15.

65. Moody, *Welfare State to Real Estate*, 200.

66. Gross, "Don't Hate Them."

67. Parrot, "Incomes Gap Widens."

68. Parrot, "Incomes Gap Widens."

69. FPI, "Grow Together?," 16.

70. Katz, "Gentrification Hangover."

71. Kroll, "Billionaire's Daughter."

72. Rice, "Stash Pad."

73. Korn, "NYC's Luxury Housing Market."

74. Plitt, "$110K/Month Pad."

75. Rosenberg, "Buyer Outed."

76. Marino, "2015, Shattering Records."

77. McKee, "Tax Breaks for Billionaires."

78. Satow, "Want a Green Card?"

79. Rice, "Stash Pad."

80. Rice, "Stash Pad."

81. Solomon, "Hermès Birkin Bag."

82. Davidson, "World's Most Expensive Basketball Sneaker."

83. Olmsted, "$1,000 Ice Cream Sundae?"

84. *New York Daily News*, "Serendipity 3."

85. McGeehan, "Manhattan Area Codes."

86. Bloomberg, quoted in Yakas, "Old Man Bloomberg."

CHAPTER 4

1. Caro, *Power Broker*.

2. See Harvey, *Limits to Capital*; Harvey, *Urban Experience*; Harvey, "Globalization."

3. The program, which ended in 1974 with over 2,000 urban renewal projects across the country, caused great controversy for its disregard for the livelihood of low-income and especially minority communities across the nation.

4. Caro, *Power Broker*.

5. Each use was mapped with the letters "R" (for residential), "C" (for commercial), or "M" (for manufacturing), followed by a number, 1 through 10, whereby a higher number meant a higher building density.

6. By the 1970s, however, as larger lots became scarcer, many buildings were built through special permits from the City Planning Commission that allowed them to rise straight up from the street line, with no setbacks or pedestrian plazas.

7. In 1965, the Landmarks Preservation Commission was established as a result of these events with the mission to protect historical landmarks in New York City.

8. In 1951, 12 so-called community planning councils had been introduced in Manhattan by Borough President Robert F. Wagner, with advisory powers on local planning and budgetary matters. The model was soon adopted by other

borough presidents across the city. In 1968, the city was divided into 62 community districts and each board was given the responsibility for advising the City Planning Commission on matters relating to the development of their communities.

9. Today, the key participants in the ULURP process are the Department of City Planning, the City Planning Commission, the borough presidents, the borough boards, city council, and the mayor. But only the commission and city council have a binding say. Any decision made by city council is considered final unless the mayor vetoes a council action within five days of the vote.

10. City of New York, CPC, "Rules for Processing Plans," 1.

11. Angotti, *New York for Sale*.

12. Jahr, "All Together Now."

13. Murphy, "Whose Dreams Will Decide?"

14. Murphy, "Whose Dreams Will Decide?"

15. Marcus, "City Zoning," 720.

16. Marcus, "City Zoning," 726.

17. Fainstein, *City Builders*.

18. Moody, *Welfare State to Real Estate*; Fainstein, *City Builders*.

19. Notably, with the elimination of the Board of Estimate, whose functions in land use and budget decisions were reassigned to the city council and the mayor.

20. Pristin, "Council Approves Zoning Plan."

21. City of New York, DCP, "Unified Bulk Program."

22. Stern, "Gotham's Developers."

23. Although the city's campaign finance laws pose strict restrictions on the amount of contributions that candidates can receive, it prescribes no limitations if a candidate chooses to use his or her own money to finance a campaign.

24. Nagourney, "2011 Elections."

25. As a result of a 1993 referendum, a two-term limit was imposed on the mayor, city council members and citywide elected officials. A council proposal to extend term limits was turned down by voters in 1996.

26. Chen and Barbaro, "Bloomberg Wins 3rd Term."

27. Chen, "Bloomberg Biggest Giver."

28. Purnick quotes head of the Community Service Society David Jones, claiming: "I think the personal funding has clearly kept the not-for-profit community very pro-Bloomberg. It chills dissent. You are going to watch what you say" (Purnick, *Mike Bloomberg*, 197).

29. Chen, "Bloomberg Biggest Giver."

30. *Noticing New York*, "Bloomberg's Increasing Wealth."

31. *Forbes*, "World's Billionaires 2007"; *Forbes*, "World's Billionaires 2009."

32. *Forbes*, "World's Billionaires."

33. Moody, *Welfare State to Real Estate*, 166.

34. In the words of NYU Professor Mitchell Moss, quoted in McGrath, "The Untouchable."

35. Greenberg, *Branding New York*.
36. Porter, Ketels, Habiby, and Zipper, "New York City."
37. Bloomberg, "State of the City."
38. Steinberg, "Planning the Neoliberal City."
39. Michael Bloomberg, quoted in Brash, *Bloomberg's New York*, 85.
40. Title of a report by Moss, "New York City Won Olympics."
41. Brash, *Bloomberg's New York*, 50–53.
42. Jay Kriegel, quoted in Brash, *Bloomberg's New York*, 51.
43. Brash, *Bloomberg's New York*, 248–253.
44. Fainstein, "Urban Renewal."
45. Angotti, *New York for Sale*, 210.
46. Angotti, *New York for Sale*, 208.
47. An anonymous analyst, quoted in Kolben, "Ratner Arena, Olympics."
48. Angotti, *New York for Sale*, 216.
49. Angotti, *New York for Sale*.
50. Confessore, "Another Step."
51. Brown, "Atlantic Yards Eminent Domain Battle."
52. Doctoroff, quoted in Porter, Ketels, Habiby, and Zipper, "New York City," 10.
53. See Cardwell, "Once at Cotillions," and Satow, "Remake New York."
54. McGrath, "The Untouchable."
55. Burden, quoted in Satow, "Remake New York."
56. Burden, quoted in Satow, "Remake New York."
57. Watanabe, "Contextual Zoning."
58. Watanabe, "Contextual Zoning"; Nicas, "Bloomberg Machine."
59. Angotti, *New York for Sale*, 2008.
60. Nicas, "Bloomberg Machine," 2.
61. Bloomberg, quoted in Lueck, "Bloomberg Draws Blueprint."
62. Cardwell and Bagli, "25-Year Outline."
63. Finn, "PlaNYC Initiative."
64. ICLEI Local Governments for Sustainability USA and the Mayor's Office for Long-Term Planning and Sustainability, "Process Behind PlaNYC," 6–8.
65. Finn, "PlaNYC Initiative"; Paul, "PlaNYC."
66. Paul, "PlaNYC."
67. Krueger and Agyeman, "Sustainability Schizophrenia."
68. See APA, Diversity Committee of the New York Metro Chapter, "Written Response to PlaNYC 2030," and Marcuse, "PlaNYC Is Not a Plan."
69. Finn, "PlaNYC Initiative," 15.
70. See City of New York, IBO, "Fewer New Apartments Likely," and New York City Comptroller, "Rents Through the Roof!"
71. Arden, "Bloomberg Housing Plan."
72. CUF, "Reviving the City."
73. City of New York, OLTPS, "PlaNYC, Greener, Greater," 12.
74. City of New York, DCP, "Celebrating DCP Rezonings."

75. City of New York, IBO, "Fewer New Apartments Likely"; New York City Comptroller, "Rents Through the Roof!"; Furman Center for Real Estate and Urban Policy, "Key Findings."
76. Paul, "Affordable Housing."
77. See Paul, "Affordable Housing"; and Angotti, "Building and Zoning."
78. Hartman, "Right to Stay Put"; Hartman, "Case for Right to Housing"; Fullilove, *Root Shock*; Newman and Wyly, "Right to Stay Put"; Turffrey, "Human Cost."
79. Hartman, "Right to Stay Put"; Hartman, "Case for Right to Housing"; Turffrey, "Human Cost"; Fullilove, *Root Shock*.
80. Angotti, "Building and Zoning."
81. City of New York, OLTPS, "PlaNYC, Greener, Greater," 12.
82. City of New York, OLTPS, "PlaNYC Progress Report 2010," 11.
83. City of New York, OLTPS, "PlaNYC Update 2011," 21.
84. City of New York, IBO, "Fewer New Apartments Likely," 11.
85. New York City Comptroller, "Rents Through the Roof!"
86. New York City Comptroller, "Rents Through the Roof!"
87. Coalition for the Homeless, "State of the Homeless 2013."
88. City of New York, IBO, "Fewer New Apartments Likely."
89. Flegenheimer, "Flooded Tunnels."
90. Kaplan, "Cuomo, Aid Appeal."
91. Bloomberg quoted in Chaban, "Hurricane, Bloomberg Bullish."
92. Turetsky, "Seas Rise, Storms Surge."
93. Rayman, "Flood Zone."
94. See Rayman, "Flood Zone."
95. Daly and Townsend, *Valuing the Earth*, 267.
96. UNEP, "Towards a Green Economy," 16.
97. Owens, "Land, Limits, Sustainability." Quoted in Finn, "PlaNYC Initiative."
98. Burden, quoted in Treskon, "Constructing an Oppositional Community," 297.
99. City of New York, DCP, "Greetings from the Chair."
100. Burden, "Interview."
101. NYCHDC, "Income Eligibility."
102. Thirteen Metrofocus, "New Yorkers Out in the Cold?"
103. Burden, "Interview."
104. Angotti, "Zoning Without Planning?"
105. See Angotti, "Zoning Without Planning?"; Bloustein, "Gentrification and Rezoning."
106. Burden, "Interview."
107. Angotti, "Zoning Instead of Planning."
108. Angotti, "Zoning Without Planning?"
109. See Marcus, "City Zoning," 717; Nicas, "Bloomberg Machine," 29.
110. Smith, "Theory of Gentrification"; Smith, "Gentrification and Rent Gap."
111. Weber, "Extracting Value."

112. Smith, "New Globalism," 446.

113. Gross, "Reshaping the City."

114. Busà, "Unsustainable Cost," 194–195.

115. Newman and Wyly, "Right to Stay Put," 38–42; Busà, "History of Decline and Revival"; Busà, "125th Street Rezoning."

116. Burden, quoted in Satow, "Remake New York."

117. Slater, Curran, and Lees, "Gentrification Research," 1144.

118. Slater, Curran, and Lees, "Gentrification Research," 1145.

119. Hartman, "Right to Stay Put"; Smith, *New Urban Frontier.*

120. See CUF, "Reviving the City"; and ICP, "Cost of Good Intentions."

121. Newman and Wyly, "Right to Stay Put."

122. A commentator on *Curbed New York,* 2009.

123. A commentator on *Curbed New York,* 2009.

124. Bloustein, "Gentrification and Rezoning," 7.

125. Bloustein, "Gentrification and Rezoning," 4.

126. Bram and Anderson, "Declining Manufacturing Employment."

127. Wolf-Powers, "Up-Zoning Mixed Use Neighborhoods."

128. Fung, "Push to Restart Manufacturing."

129. FPI, "State of Working New York."

130. City of New York, DCP, "Employment Patterns in New York City."

131. Curran and Hanson, "Getting Globalized."

132. Curran, "Frying Pan to Oven," 1427.

133. Curran, "Frying Pan to Oven."

134. A commentator on *Curbed New York,* 2009.

135. A commentator on *Curbed New York,* 2009.

136. Lefkowitz, "The Holdouts."

137. Busà, "City Producers, City Consumers."

138. GOLES, "No Go for Local Business."

139. Bloustein, "Gentrification and Rezoning," 15.

140. Pratt Center for Community Development, "Downtown Brooklyn's Detour."

141. FUREE, "Out of Business," 14.

142. Angotti, *New York for Sale,* 208.

143. City of New York, "No. 7 Subway Extension," 5–3.

144. See Lefkowitz, "The Holdouts."

145. Baird-Remba, "City Releases Plan To Rezone."

146. CUF, "Chain Reaction."

147. Hammett, and Hammett, *Suburbanization of New York.*

148. Lefkowitz, "The Holdouts."

CHAPTER 5

1. A commentator on *Curbed New York,* 2009.

2. A commentator on *Curbed New York,* 2009.

3. Kasson, *Amusing the Million,* 8.

4. Koolhaas, *Delirious New York*, 29.

5. The addition of subway service in 1920 allowed visitors from throughout the city to reach Coney Island for a five-cent ticket. It was said that over one million visitors a day visited Coney Island. Many of these were poor immigrants, who at the time made up about 40% of the city's population.

6. Cautela, "Coney," 238.

7. Immerso, "Coney Island Cornerstones."

8. Denson, *Coney Island*.

9. Matassa, "Whaddya Want?," 56.

10. Denson, *Coney Island*.

11. The first Steeplechase Park was opened in 1897 by George C. Tilyou, a visionary salesman and entrepreneur. Right after the park was destroyed by fire in 1907, a second Steeplechase Park was opened in time for the 1908 summer season. Tilyou's second Steeplechase Park was rebuilt with steel, glass, and concrete.

12. Denson, *Coney Island*, 138.

13. Denson, *Coney Island*, 205–210.

14. "In 2000, when plans for a Brooklyn ballpark were being finalized, Jeff Wilpon—a top New York Mets executive and the man whose minor-league team would play in the new park—mentioned to Mr. Giuliani that the Thunderbolt was an eyesore that looked dangerous. Say no more. Whether by coincidence or design, the Thunderbolt was now squarely in City Hall's sights." The case ended in court. In September 2003, "a federal jury in Manhattan ruled that the city had no justification for tearing down the Thunderbolt, and in doing so had trespassed on Mr. Bullard's property. It also determined that one city official, who was integral in the decision to demolish, had acted with 'deliberate indifference'" (Barry, "About New York").

15. Matassa, "Whaddya Want?," 3.

16. New York State Comptroller, "Economic Snapshot."

17. SocioWiki, "Presence of the Past."

18. Section 8 is a Federal housing assistance program for low-income individuals or families. Under the voucher program, tenants pay only a portion of the rent, while the rest is guaranteed by the federal government. City of New York, DCP, "FEIS for Coney Island Rezoning Proposal," 3–20.

19. SocioWiki, "Presence of the Past."

20. Rivero, "Coney Island," 17.

21. New York State Comptroller, "Economic Snapshot," 1.

22. Matassa, "Whaddya Want?"

23. Burden, "Statement of Commissioner."

24. Save Coney Island, "FAQs."

25. Burden, "Statement of Commissioner."

26. In February 2007, City Planning Commissioner Amanda Burden herself told an audience at a breakfast sponsored by local business magazine *Crain's Business*: "Amusements are incompatible with immediate adjacent residential use" (Calder, "Cyclone").

27. City of New York, DCP, "Coney Island Comprehensive Rezoning Plan."

28. The "Reasonable Worst Case Development Scenario" projects that the plan would increase total residential use in 2019 by 2,407,941 square feet (383.8%), commercial use by 403,980 square feet (152.7%), and amusement use by 251,411 square feet (264.9%). An additional 4,019 parking spaces and 411,300 square feet of hotel use would also be introduced in the neighborhood. See Coney Island, "FEIS," 3–14.

29. Coney Island, "FEIS," 3–8.

30. Coney Island, "FEIS," 3–36.

31. Bloustein, "Rezoning New York City."

32. Treiman, "Bloomberg Killing Coney Island."

33. Local City Councilman Domenic Recchia has been a close childhood friend of developer Joe Sitt. See Bagli, "Beyond Sideshows."

34. Fung, "Coney Island Keeper."

35. A few rides are still in storage. One of the stars from the gate was donated to the Smithsonian Air Space Museum. The Rocket was donated to the city.

36. Sargen, "Makeover of Coney Island."

37. Fung, "Coney Island Keeper."

38. Miller, "Whose Coney Island?."

39. Bagli, "Seeking Revival."

40. Amusing the Zillion, "Under Construction."

41. *The Real Deal*, "Major Revenue for City."

42. Amusing the Zillion, "R.I.P. Coney Island's Shore Hotel."

43. While it can't protect the buildings within the district from demolition, an inclusion on the Registers of Historic Places could make grants and tax credits available for redevelopment projects that rehabilitate and reuse historic properties in the amusement area. The determination of eligibility released on August 12, 2010, states that the amusement district is "nationally significant . . . as the birthplace of the modern American amusement industry." It also claims that the area's surviving historic buildings are "valuable cultural assets worthy of recognition and consideration in preservation planning" (New York State Office of Parks, Recreation and Historic Preservation, "Coney Island's Historic District," 2).

44. Almost ironically, on December 14, 2010, after all properties of Thor Equities had been razed to rubble to make them ripe for development, the Landmarks Preservation Commission belatedly approved the designation for the Shore Theater, a neo-Renaissance theater built in 1924 and boarded up since the late 1970s, giving it landmark status.

45. The Cyclone roller coaster, opened in 1927, was declared a New York City Landmark in 1988 and a National Historic Landmark in 1991.

46. Coney Island's Wonder Wheel, opened in 1920, was named an official New York City Landmark in 1989.

47. The Parachute Jump was built for the 1939 New York World's Fair in Flushing Meadows and brought to Coney in 1941 as part of the Steeplechase Park. It was completely restored in 2002–2003.
48. Pincus, "Demolition Permits."
49. Broadcasted on September 27, 2010.
50. Yet, the buildings had great potential, as a set of architectural renderings commissioned by the Save Coney Island advocacy groups in June 2010 showed: "These renderings show that the historic buildings of Coney Island still have life in them and still have a future," said Simeon Bankoff, executive director of the Historic Districts Council. "It's now up to the City to say whether that's better than acres of rubble" (Save Coney Island, "Potential of Endangered Buildings."
51. Brown, "New Coney Island?"
52. Save Coney Island, "History in Danger."
53. Amusing the Zillion, "Out with the Old."
54. Amusing the Zillion, "50 Years on Coney Island Boardwalk."
55. Matassa, "Whaddya Want?," 79.
56. Treiman, "Bloomberg Killing Coney Island."
57. According to Treiman, "Bloomberg Killing Coney Island."
58. Burden, "Statement of Commissioner."
59. Burden, "Statement of Commissioner."
60. In 2009, Save Coney Island filed an eventually unsuccessful lawsuit against the city right after the rezoning passed. The lawsuit was filed on the basis that the city had failed to perform an adequate environmental review of the proposed plan—for example, the city had failed to adequately study a meaningful alternative to the proposed rezoning or to properly consider the impacts that the presence of high-rise hotels and residential towers would have on the pedestrian experience at Coney Island.
61. Burden, "Statement of Commissioner."
62. City Data, "Coney Island Neighborhood."
63. City of New York, DCP, "DEIS for Coney Island Rezoning Proposal."
64. The State of New York's Mitchell-Lama subsidy program was signed into law in 1955. It focused on the development of affordable housing, both rental and cooperatively owned, for low- and middle-income residents.
65. Kusisto, "Complex Upgrade."
66. Jones, "Coney Island Housing Complex."
67. Amusing the Zillion, "1st Private Beachfront Condos."
68. Smith, "40-Story Tower."
69. Rosenberg, "Future Tallest Tower."
70. Burden, "Statement of Commissioner."
71. City of New York, DCP, "DEIS for Coney Island Rezoning Proposal," 3–14.
72. City of New York, DCP, "DEIS for Coney Island Rezoning Proposal," 3–17.
73. Burden, "Statement of Commissioner."
74. Municipal Art Society, "Comments on Draft Scope."

75. Burden, quoted in Brown, "Municipal Art Society."
76. Rivero, quoted in Save Coney Island, "Rezoning Vote."
77. New York State Comptroller, "Economic Snapshot."
78. Weichselbaum, "Hurricane Sandy."
79. Weichselbaum, "Hurricane Sandy."
80. Bidon, "How Sandy Changed the Game."
81. Bidon, "How Sandy Changed the Game."
82. Back in 2012, the popular blog Amusing the Zillion asked, "Will Coney Island's Surf Ave Become a Mecca for Franchises?"
83. Amusing the Zillion, "Coney Island 2016."
84. The plan was approved by the city despite the resistance of local Community Board 13, whose majority (21 to 7) voted against it.
85. Rosenberg, "Concrete Likely for Boardwalk."
86. Rosenberg, "Concrete Likely for Boardwalk."
87. Amusing the Zillion, "Boardwalk Bunco."

CHAPTER 6

1. Hegarty, *Advertising*.
2. See North, "Taylor Swift Unwelcome." Also see Barnes, "Rejected Taylor Swift," and Shepherd, "Taylor Swift's New Song."
3. In the words of Fred Dixon, president and CEO of NYC & Company, at the IPW Press Conference, June 2015, https://www.youtube.com/watch?v=t2Y7Go_xhsg.
4. Stuart, "Taylor Swift Tourism Campaign."
5. Sanders, "Mythic Movie Dream."
6. Hubbard and Hall, "Entrepreneurial City," 7.
7. Gunn, *Vacationscape*.
8. Marx and Engels, *German Ideology*.
9. Gramsci, *Prison Notebooks*.
10. Kipfer, "Urbanized Gramsci," 205. Also, scholar Tony Bennet alerted us that "the bourgeoisie can become a hegemonic, leading class only to the degree that bourgeoisie culture ideology is able to accommodate, to find some space for, opposing class cultures and values. A bourgeoisie hegemony is secured not via the obliteration of working class culture, but via its articulation to bourgeoisie culture and ideology. . . ." See Bennet, "Popular Culture and Return to Gramsci."
11. Klein, *No Logo*.
12. Procter, *Stuart Hall*, 1.
13. Smith defines it as "the deliberate (re)presentation and (re)configuration of a city's image to accrue economic, cultural and political capital" (Smith, "Conceptualizing City Image Change, 399.")
14. Lefebvre, *Production of Space*, 50–53.

15. Hall, *Cultural Representations*; Hall, "Representations and Media."

16. Lefebvre, *Production of Space*, 50–53, 370.

17. Ward, *Selling Places*.

18. See Harvey, "Managerialism to Entrepreneurialism"; Hubbard and Hall, "Entrepreneurial City"; Greenberg, *Branding New York*.

19. Greenberg, *Branding New York*; Greenberg, "Branding, Crisis, Utopia," 118.

20. Kavaratzis, "City Branding"; Kavaratzis and Ashworth, "Place Marketing."

21. Kotler, *Marketing Management*.

22. Pine and Gilmore, *Experience Economy*.

23. Klein, *No Logo*, 23.

24. Kavaratzis, "City Branding," 63–65.

25. Kavaratzis, "City Branding."

26. Van Riel and Balmer, "Corporate Identity," 355.

27. Arnold, *Handbook of Brand Management*, 12.

28. Stigel and Frimann, "City Branding," 248.

29. Or "representation of space," as Lefebvre puts it. See Lefebvre, *Production of Space*, 370.

30. Greenberg, *Branding New York*.

31. Grodach, "Urban Branding," 193.

32. Zukin, *Cultures of Cities*.

33. Grodach, "Urban Branding," 183.

34. Brash, *Bloomberg's New York*, 103.

35. Sanders, "Mythic Movie Dream."

36. Sanders, *Celluloid Skyline*; Sanders, "Mythic Movie Dream"; Greenberg, *Branding New York*; Greenberg, "Branding New York"; Macek, *Urban Nightmares*.

37. Macek, *Urban Nightmares*.

38. Greenberg, "Limits of Branding," 393.

39. Moody, *Welfare State to Real Estate*; Greenberg, *Branding New York*.

40. Bailey, *Crisis Regime*.

41. City of New York, DCP, "Economic Recovery," 34.

42. Greenberg, "Limits of Branding."

43. The New York City Partnership was founded by David Rockefeller in 1979. Affiliated with the New York City Chamber of Commerce and Industry, it was a business advocacy group committed to lobby the government, labor, and the nonprofit sector for legislation favorable to economic growth and business development.

44. The Convention and Visitors Bureau was created in 1934 to attract travel and conventions to the city. It changed its name to NYC & Company in 1999, under the administration of Rudolph Giuliani.

45. The Association for a Better New York (ABNY) is active in lobbying local government to promote the city's position as a corporate business capital.

46. Greenberg, *Branding New York*, 163.

47. The logo has continued to sell for decades, and became especially prominent following the 9/11 attacks on the city, when visitors to the city purchased and wore the shirts bearing the "I Love New York" logo as a sign of their support.

48. Greenberg, "Limits of Branding," 402.

49. Greenberg, *Branding New York*.

50. "The towers were finally completed . . . for a price of $900 million, five years behind schedule and $500 million over budget, creating a public finance fiasco that dragged New York deeper into debt. . . . Thus, many have argued that the multi-million dollar public debt incurred in building and maintaining this new symbol of Downtown's financial might have contributed heavily to the city's spiraling fiscal crisis of the mid-1970s" (Greenberg, "Limits of Branding," 392).

51. Greenberg, "Limits of Branding," 402.

52. Greenberg, "Branding, Crisis, Utopia," 119.

53. Moody, *Welfare State to Real Estate*.

54. Particularly during the Nixon years, the term was redefined toward issues that had little to do with social inclusion and more with middle-class well-being. See Vitale, *City of Disorder*. Under the mayoral administration of Ed Koch, "an agenda originally targeted at uplifting the nation's poor became a buzzword for addressing the daily problems of transit, crime, and pollution affecting the urban middle-class" (Shaw, "Politics of Homelessness").

55. Stohr, "I Sell New York."

56. Shaw, "Politics of Homelessness."

57. Smith, "New Globalism"; Shaw, "Politics of Homelessness."

58. Shaw, "Politics of Homelessness."

59. Allison, "How Much Credit Does Giuliani Deserve."

60. Levitt, "Understanding Why Crime Fell."

61. Among these, the torture of Abner Louima, horribly assaulted and sexually abused by police officers, or the shootings of unarmed, innocent suspects like Amadou Diallo or Patrick Dorismond, a father of two who was shot by an undercover police officer on March 16, 2000. See McArdle and Erzen, *Zero Tolerance*.

62. Moody, *Welfare State to Real Estate*, 132–133.

63. Giuliani began aggressively reforming the municipal welfare system soon after taking office, and his policies were already well under way before 1996, when Bill Clinton signed the Personal Responsibility and Work Opportunity Act and ended "welfare as we know it."

64. See Mazelis, "Spotlight on NYC Police Brutality."

65. NYC & Company, "37.4 Million People Visited NYC."

66. Giuliani, quoted in NYC & Company, "37.4 Million People Visited NYC."

67. Cole, "Against the Giuliani Legacy."

68. Greenberg, *Branding New York*.

69. Oprah Winfrey called Rudolph Giuliani "America's Mayor" at a 9/11 memorial service held at Yankee Stadium on September 23, 2001.

70. Hochberg, "Small Business."
71. Shalit, "Brand New."
72. Greenberg, *Branding New York*, 258.
73. Fox Gotham and Greenberg, "From 9/11 to 8/29."
74. The LMDC was created after 9/11 by Giuliani and then-governor George Pataki to channel nearly $10 billion in federal funds for the reconstruction of Lower Manhattan.
75. Greenberg, *Branding New York*.
76. Pataki, quoted in *CNN*, "$40 Million Advertising Campaign."
77. See Greenberg, "Limits of Branding," 412.
78. Greenberg, "Branding, Crisis, Utopia," 126–127.
79. Greenberg, *Branding New York*.
80. Bloomberg, "State of the City."
81. Brash, *Bloomberg's New York*.
82. Bloomberg, "Speech at Republican National Convention."
83. Some of the report's major conclusions are reported in Brash, *Bloomberg's New York*.
84. Brash, *Bloomberg's New York*.
85. Bloomberg, quoted in Cardwell, "Worth the Cost."
86. Greenberg, "Branding, Crisis, Utopia," 131.
87. Greenberg, "Branding, Crisis, Utopia," 122–123.
88. Bloomberg, quoted in Rangan, Elberse, and Bell, *Marketing New York*.
89. Doctoroff, quoted in City of New York, "Bloomberg appoints Perello."
90. Herszenhorn, "What Will It Be?"
91. Rangan, Elberse, and Bell, *Marketing New York*.
92. Rangan, Elberse, and Bell, *Marketing New York*.
93. Rangan, Elberse, and Bell, *Marketing New York*.
94. Greenberg, "Branding, Crisis, Utopia," 123.
95. Greenberg, "Branding, Crisis, Utopia"; Brash, *Bloomberg's New York*.
96. Idov, "Another Fifty Million People."
97. Prior to his appointment, George A. Fertitta was the chairman and founder of Margeotes Fertitta Powell, a New York City–based advertising agency whose clients include major corporate giants such as the Coca Cola Company, Disney, Campbell Soup Company, McGraw-Hill, Bacardi, Godiva Chocolatier, SunCom Wireless, Radisson, and Seven Seas Cruises, among others.
98. Greenberg, "Branding, Crisis, Utopia," 126.
99. Greenberg, "Branding, Crisis, Utopia," 125.
100. Idov, "Another Fifty Million People."
101. City of New York, "Bloomberg and Tisch Announce City's Plan."
102. Under the agreement, Cemusa would design, install, and maintain 3,300 new bus stop shelters, 330 new newsstands, and 20 public toilets and pay the city $1 billion over 20 years for the rights to sell advertising on these structures (Rangan, Elberse, and Bell, *Marketing New York*). The city received a share of the ad revenues as well as 22.5% of the ad space for its own agencies and for corporate

partners, and secured $18 million worth of free ad space a year in international Cemusa markets, including Spain. As a result, Spanish travel to New York City promptly increased by 25% (Idov, "Another Fifty Million People.").

103. Michael Bloomberg, quoted in City of New York, "Bloomberg Launches 'This Is New York City.'"

104. Heilman, "Gotham Glory."

105. Heilman, "Gotham Glory."

106. NYC & Company, "New York City Hotel Industry."

107. Lee, "Foreign Tourists."

108. McGeehan, "Remaking the City's Image."

109. McGeehan, "Remaking the City's Image."

110. NYC & Company official, quoted in Greenberg, "Branding, Crisis, Utopia," 129.

111. Idov, "Another Fifty Million People."

112. Such family-friendly campaigns have been repeated ever since: in 2011 the city declared a "Smurfs Week" to promote the feature film by Sony Entertainment and Columbia Pictures, and made the Smurfs 2011's "NYC family ambassadors." Other NYC family ambassador characters were the Muppets in 2012, Where's Waldo? in 2013, Curious George in 2014, Dora the Explorer in 2015, and the Teenage Mutant Ninja Turtles in 2016.

113. Goldman, "Gay Marriage."

114. Fickenscher, "NYC Tourism."

115. NYC & Company, 2010 TV ad, "See More Be More."

116. Michael Bloomberg, quoted in NYC & Company, "Bloomberg and NYC & Company Announce Campaign."

117. City of New York, "Bloomberg and Officials Announce Campaign."

118. NYC & Company, "Bloomberg and NYC & Company Announce Campaign."

119. NYCEDC, "New York City Breaks Tourism Record."

120. Idov, "Another Fifty Million People."

121. NYCEDC, "Mayor Bloomberg Announces New York City Breaks Tourism Record."

122. On August 1, 2002, almost four years after the first version of this deal was announced, it was pronounced dead by NYSE Chairman Richard Grasso. Yet, according to reports by Good Jobs New York, taxpayers were still paying for approximately $100 million in expenses associated with the plan in 2012. See Good Jobs New York, "Spotlight."

123. Goldensohn, "Hudson Yards Debt."

124. Figures by Good Jobs New York, "Spotlight."

125. Fung, "Bklyn Developer Wins."

126. Clint Irwin from the Bronx, comment in Marcus, "Taylor Swift Explaining New York Vocabulary."

127. NYC & Company, "Annual Summary 2013."

128. De Blasio, quoted in City of New York, "Transcript."
129. De Blasio, quoted in City of New York, "Transcript."
130. City of New York, "Road to 10 Million More Visitors."
131. City of New York, "Road to 10 Million More Visitors."
132. Sugar, "More tourists visited NYC in 2016."
133. Rooftop films started in 1997 as a series of illegal summer screenings of movies on the roof of a tenement building in the East Village, but by 2011 had become a legitimate, nonprofit organization with a massive program including 47 events over the course of the summer.
134. With the launch of "Syfy's 31 Days of Halloween," sponsored by the American science fiction cable channel, "ownership of the Halloween experience was delivered to Syfy by blanketing the City through traditional media, press coverage, experiential events and more." See NYC & Company, "Annual Summary 2011."
135. Greenberg, "Branding, Crisis, Utopia," 132.
136. Lowry, "CEO Mayor."
137. Greenberg, "Branding, Crisis, Utopia," 117.
138. Grynbaum, "De Blasio Still Trying."

CHAPTER 7

1. Goodyear, "De Blasio Feels Your Pain."
2. Putzier, "Love-hate Relationship."
3. Pareene, "De Blasio's Impossible Task."
4. Walker, "De Blasio Tells 'A Tale of Two Cities.'"
5. Samtani, "Mayoral Candidates Get Candid."
6. Dionne Jr., "America Shifts Left."
7. The *New York Times* noted, "The elevation of an assertive, tax-the-rich liberal to the nation's most prominent municipal office has fanned hopes that hot-button causes like universal prekindergarten and low-wage worker benefits … could be aided by the imprimatur of being proved workable in New York." See Grynbaum, "De Blasio Draws Liberal Eyes."
8. See New York City Campaign Finance Board, Election Cycle 2013, http://www.nyccfb.info/searchabledb/SimpleSearchResult.aspx?cand_id=326&cand_name=de+Blasio,+Bill&election_cycle=2013. See also Taylor, "De Blasio Attracts Donors."
9. Fermino, "Christine Quinn Unleashes Attack."
10. Grynbaum, "De Blasio Endorses Hillary Clinton."
11. Pazmino, "State of Atlantic Yards."
12. Goldenberg, "De Blasio Position Assailed."
13. Rubinstein, "De Blasio, Development Pragmatist."
14. The full text is available here: http://genius.com/Bill-de-blasio-fostering-economic-growth-in-new-york-city-annotated.

15. Rubinstein, "De Blasio, Development Pragmatist."
16. De Blasio, quoted in Rubinstein, "For Planning."
17. Rivlin-Nadler, 2013.
18. De Blasio, quoted in Barkan, "De Blasio Says No Contradiction."
19. Janison, "NYC Planning Chair."
20. See HR&A Advisors, "Council Approves Rezoning."
21. Bredderman, "De Blasio Appoints Exec."
22. Velsey, "Rent Freeze!"
23. Fermino, "De Blasio Names Chair."
24. Daly, "Tell New York the Truth."
25. Putzier, "De Blasio's Donors."
26. Putzier, "De Blasio's Donors."
27. Neumeister and Long, "No charges to be filed."
28. City of New York, "Housing New York."
29. Gartland, "De Blasio Recycles Housing Plan."
30. Velsey and Colvin, "De Blasio Unveils Housing Plan."
31. Barro, "De Blasio Left Wing?"
32. Angotti, "Two Housing Plans."
33. Farkas and Newman, "Rezoning Plan."
34. Wishnia, "De Blasio's Controversial Plan."
35. Farkas and Newman, "Rezoning Plan."
36. Hertz, "Make Housing Assistance Easy."
37. Wishnia, "De Blasio's Controversial Plan."
38. Wishnia, "What Does 'Affordable Housing' Mean?"
39. Letitia James, quoted in Wishnia, "What Does 'Affordable Housing' Mean?"
40. Wishnia, "What Does 'Affordable Housing' Mean?"
41. Quoted in Wishnia, "What Does 'Affordable Housing' Mean?"
42. Angotti, "Two Housing Plans."
43. Yee and Navarro, "Some See Risk."
44. East Harlem Preservation, "Dumbing-Down East Harlem."
45. Goldman, "$41 Billion Plan."
46. Samtani, "Execs Laud de Blasio's Plan."
47. Samtani, "Rudin's St. Vincent's Condos."
48. Anderson, "'Hospitals Not Condos' Rally."
49. Gartland, "De Blasio's Plan."
50. Quoted in Wishnia, "De Blasio's Controversial Plan."
51. Fermino and Durkin, "Manhattan Board Votes."
52. Navarro, "Council Hearing."
53. Calmes, "Mayor's Zoning Proposals."
54. Savitch-Lew, "Ayes and Nays."
55. Association for Neighborhood and Housing Development, "ANHD Helps Win Deeper MIH Affordability."
56. Yee and Navarro, "Some See Risk."

57. Blockbusting is an illegal and discriminatory scheme through which unscrupulous brokers use scare tactics to convince residents to sell their homes at a deflated price, by making them believe that tenants from minority groups may soon move into the area, and that this will lead to a decline in the value of their properties. Once the properties are vacated, brokers can buy them up at reduced prices, only to resell them later at an inflated price.

58. Yee and Navarro, "Some See Risk."

59. New York City Comptroller, Scott M. Stringer, "Mandatory Inclusionary Housing."

60. Bredderman, "De Blasio Commissioners."

61. Josefina Salazar, quoted in King, "East Harlem Tenants Group."

62. Roberts, "East Harlem Residents Protest."

63. Roberts, "East Harlem Residents Protest."

64. According to a 2016 Housing and Vacancy Survey report compiled by the Citizens Budget Commission, the number of severely rent-burdened households in the very low-income and extremely low-income brackets amounted to 379,000 in 2014. For these residents, the plan reserves only 40,000 units. Almost three times this number (116,000 units) will be instead set aside for households making between $41,951 and $67,121, while around 22,000 apartments will be earmarked for households making between $100,681 and $138,435 (which in New York is considered to be "middle income"). See Cheney, "De Blasio Housing Plan."

65. Wishnia, "What Does 'Affordable Housing' Mean?"

66. Jost, "Housing Plan Misses Big Question."

67. Alicia Glen, quoted in Rubinstein, "Official Dismisses Idea."

68. Take Back NYC, "De Blasio Continues Anti-Small Business Policy."

69. Woolums, "Mayor and Speaker Are M.I.A."

70. Woolums, "Mayor and Speaker Are M.I.A."

71. Woolums, "Mayor and Speaker Are M.I.A."

72. Bill de Blasio for Mayor, "One New York, Rising Together."

73. Quoted in Woolums, "Mayor and Speaker Are M.I.A."

74. Alicia Glen, at the Municipal Arts Society Summit 2015. On that occasion, "MAS Director Carol Colleta, revealed to DM Glen that 100 percent of the people polled in the audience supported commercial rent control for NYC, to which she quipped 'anybody in the audience who actually [has] done any real estate finance? It is a very complicated issue, like most issues, and I'm not sure that necessarily adopting commercial rent control would lead to solve the problem that people think the problem is.' DM Glen's answer implies that her background in real estate finance at Goldman Sachs gave her knowledge about the regulation of commercial leases and rents that the audience would not have. The reality is, what would someone who worked at Goldman Sachs before joining the de Blasio administration, know about owning a small business?" (Take Back NYC, "De Blasio Continues Anti-Small Business Policy.")

75. Rivlin-Nadler, "Law That Would Help."

76. Take Back NYC, "1994–2015 NYC Court."

77. City of New York, "De Blasio Administration Announces 'Small Business First' Initiative."

78. Riley, "NYPD Running Stings."

79. Riley, "NYPD Running Stings."

80. McGeehan, "De Blasio's New York."

81. The tax on the wealthy was killed in Albany by Cuomo, although the governor still provided full funding for de Blasio's universal prekindergarten plan.

82. New York Civil Liberties Union, "Stop-and-Frisk Data."

83. Rice, "De Blasio Revolution."

84. Barkan, "De Blasio's Approval Ratings."

85. Marist Poll, "11/3."

86. Calder, "NYers Think de Blasio Clueless."

87. Dawsey, "Poll."

88. De Blasio, quoted in Katz, "On Homelessness."

89. Elliott, "Invisible Child."

90. Coalition for the Homeless, "State of the Homeless 2015."

91. Coalition for the Homeless, "State of the Homeless 2015."

92. Goldensohn, "LINC Homeless Rent Vouchers."

93. Coalition for the Homeless, "State of the Homeless 2015."

94. Savitch-Lew, "Advocates Like, and Critique."

95. Goodwin, "De Blasio Proves He's Clueless."

96. Stewart, "New York's Rise in Homelessness."

97. Gartland, "NYC Homeless Population."

98. Rice, "De Blasio Revolution."

99. Stewart, "De Blasio Unveils Plan."

100. Fermino, "Head of Homeless Services."

101. Katz, "HOME-STAT."

102. Katz, "HOME-STAT."

AFTERWORD

1. Ferro, "New Steampunk Condo Development."

2. Christie, "Occupy Protesters."

3. Dailey, "Chelsea to High Line Tourists."

4. Saltz, "Problem of Public Art."

5. Greenspan, "Micro-Apartments."

6. Huen, "Inside Luxury Micro-Apartment Building."

7. Greenspan, "Micro-Apartments."

8. Bellafante, "Mayor Puts Wall Street First."

9. Raymond, "Report."

10. Misra, "Towering Income Inequality."

11. Frank, "Manhattan Real Estate Prices."
12. Alberts, "Rents Rise."
13. Cheney-Rice, "Meet the Artists."
14. Cuozzo, "NYC Development Surge."
15. Joseph Stiglitz, quoted in Martin, "Nobel-Prize Winning Economist Stiglitz."
16. Rubinstein, "Expect No Help."
17. Cohen, "Developers Rushed."
18. Leon, "Skyscraper Boom."
19. Massive private developments like the Bank of America Tower or the Goldman Sachs headquarters have taken advantage of millions in Liberty Bonds, in subsidy packages from the city and the state, or in special lease arrangements. See Good Jobs New York Database, http://www.goodjobsny.org/economic-development/major-corporate-giveaways. But developers of luxury residential buildings are also benefiting from tax breaks or exemptions. For instance, Extell benefited from generous tax abatements through the 421-a tax exemption program for the ultra-luxury One57 condominium building, whose penthouse was sold in 2015 for a staggering $100.5 million. See Solomont, "One57."

Bibliography

BOOKS

Arnold, David. 1992. *The Handbook of Brand Management*. London: Economist Books.

Angotti, Tom. 2008. *New York for Sale: Community Planning Confronts Global Real Estate*. Cambridge, MA: MIT Press.

Bailey, Robert W. 1984. *The Crisis Regime: The MAC, the EFCB, and the Political Impact of the New York City Financial Crisis*. New York: Suny Press.

Brash, Julian. 2011. *Bloomberg's New York: Class and Governance in the Luxury City*. Athens: University of Georgia Press.

Caro, Robert A. 1974. *The Power Broker: Robert Moses and the Fall of New York*. New York: Knopf Doubleday Publishing.

Daly, Herman E., and Kenneth N. Townsend. 1993. *Valuing the Earth: Economics, Ecology, Ethics*. Cambridge, MA: MIT Press.

Denson, Charles. 2004. *Coney Island: Lost and Found*. Berkeley, CA: Ten Speed Press.

Fainstein, Susan. 1994. *The City Builders: Property, Politics and Planning in London and New York*. Cambridge, MA: Blackwell.

Florida, Richard. 2002. *The Rise of the Creative Class: And How It's Transforming Work, Leisure and Everyday Life*. New York: Basic Books.

———. 2005. *Cities and the Creative Class*. New York: Routledge.

———. 2008. *Who's Your City?: How the Creative Economy Is Making Where to Live the Most Important Decision of Your Life*. New York: Basic Books.

Freeman, Lance. 2006. *There Goes the 'Hood. Views of Gentrification from the Ground Up*. Philadelphia: Temple University Press.

Fullilove, Mindy Thompson. 2004. *Root Shock: How Tearing up City Neighborhoods Hurts America, and What We Can Do About It*. New York: One World/Ballantine.

Gramsci, Antonio. 1971. *Selections from the Prison Notebooks of Antonio Gramsci*, edited and translated by Quintin Hoare and Geoffrey Nowell-Smith. New York: International Publishers.

Greenberg, Miriam. 2008. *Branding New York: How a City in Crisis Was Sold to the World*. London and New York: Routledge.

Gunn, Clare A. 1972. *Vacationscape: Designing Tourist Regions*. Austin: University of Texas at Austin, Bureau of Business Research.

Hegarty, John. 2011. *Hegarty on Advertising*. London and New York: Thames and Hudson.

Hall, Stuart. 1997. *Cultural Representations and Signifying Practices*. London: Sage in Association with the Open University.

Hammett, Jerilou, and Kingsley Hammett. 2007. *The Suburbanization of New York: Is the World's Greatest City Becoming Just Another Town?* New York: Princeton Architectural Press.

Harvey, David. 1982: *The Limits to Capital*. Oxford: Blackwell.

———. 1985. *The Urbanization of Capital: Studies in the History and Theory of Capitalist Urbanization*. Baltimore: Johns Hopkins University Press.

———. 1989. *The Urban Experience*. Baltimore: Johns Hopkins University Press.

———. 2007. *A Brief History of Neoliberalism*. Oxford: Oxford University Press.

Hyra, Derek S. 2008. *The New Urban Renewal: The Economic Transformation of Harlem and Bronzeville*. Chicago: The University of Chicago Press.

Jacobs, Jane. 1992 [1961]. *The Death and Life of Great American Cities*. New York: Vintage.

Judd, Dennis R., and Susan S. Fainstein. 1999. *The Tourist City*. New Haven, CT: Yale University Press.

Kasson, F. John. 1978. *Amusing the Million: Coney Island at the Turn of the Century*. New York: Hill and Wang.

Klein, Naomi. 2002. *No Logo: Taking Aim at the Brand Bullies*. New York: Picador.

Koolhaas, Rem. 2001 [1978]. *Delirious New York: A Retroactive Manifesto for Manhattan*. New York: Monacelli Press.

Kotler, Philip. 2000. *Marketing Management: The Millennium Edition*. London: Prentice Hall.

Lees, Loretta, Tom Slater, and Elvin K. Wyly. 2008. *Gentrification*. New York: Routledge.

Lees, Loretta, Hyun Bang Shin, and Ernesto Lopez Morales. 2016. *Planetary Gentrification*. Cambridge, UK: Polity Press.

Lefebvre, Henri. 1991 [1974]. *The Production of Space*. Oxford: Blackwell.

Logan, John R., and Harvey Molotch. 1987. *Urban Fortunes: The Political Economy of Place*. Berkeley: University of California Press.

Macek, Steve. 2006. *Urban Nightmares: The Media, the Right, and the Moral Panic over the City*. Minneapolis: University of Minnesota Press.

Marx, Karl, and Friedrich Engels. 2004 [1932]. *The German Ideology: Part One*, edited by J. C. Arthur. New York: International Publishers.

Maurrasse, David J. 2006. *Listening to Harlem: Gentrification, Community, and Business*. New York and London: Routledge.

McArdle, Andrea, and Tanya Erzen. 2001. *Zero Tolerance: Quality of Life and the New Police Brutality in New York City*. New York: New York University Press.

Moody, Kim. 2007. *From Welfare State to Real Estate: Regime Change in New York City, 1974 to the Present*. New York: New Press.

Newfield, Jack, and Paul du Brul. 1981. *The Permanent Government: Who Really Rules New York?* New York: Pilgrim Press.

Pine, Joseph B., and James H. Gilmore. 1999. *The Experience Economy: Work Is Theatre & Every Business a Stage*. Boston: Harvard Business School.

Procter, James. 2004. *Stuart Hall*. London and New York: Routledge.

Purnick, Joyce. 2010. *Mike Bloomberg: Money, Power, Politics*. New York: Public Affairs.

Rangan, V. Kasturi, Anita Elberse, and Marie Bell. 2008. *Marketing New York City*. Boston, MA: Harvard Business School.

Sanders, James. 2001. *Celluloid Skyline: New York and the Movies*. New York: A. A. Knopf.

Schoener, Allon. 2007. *Harlem on My Mind*. New York: New Press.

Schumpeter, Joseph Alois. 1994 [1942]. *Capitalism, Socialism and Democracy*. London: Routledge.

Smith, Neil. 1996. *New Urban Frontier: Gentrification and the Revanchist City*. London: Routledge.

Soffer, Jonathan. 2010. *Ed Koch and the Rebuilding of New York City*. New York: Columbia University Press.

Stone, Clarence N. 1989. *Regime Politics: Governing Atlanta, 1946–1988*. Lawrence: University Press of Kansas.

Urry, John. 1990. *The Tourist Gaze: Leisure and Travel in Contemporary Societies*. London: Sage.

Vitale, Alex. 2008. *City of Disorder: How the Quality of Life Campaign Transformed New York Politics*. New York: New York University Press.

Ward, Stephen Victor. 1998. *Selling Places: The Marketing and Promotion of Towns and Cities 1850–2000*. London: Routledge.

Zukin, Sharon. 1995. *The Cultures of Cities*. Malden, MA and Oxford, UK: Blackwell.

_____. 2010. *The Naked City: The Death and Life of Authentic Urban Places*. New York: Oxford University Press.

BOOK CHAPTERS, ARTICLES, PAPERS, LECTURES, REPORTS

Alberts, Hana R. 2015, May 14. "Rents Rise Across New York City, But Brooklyn's Set a Record." *Curbed New York*. http://ny.curbed.com/2015/5/14/9961270/rents-rise-across-new-york-city-but-brooklyns-set-a-record.

Allison, Wes. 2007, September 1. "How Much Credit Does Giuliani Deserve for Fighting Crime?" *Politifact*. http://www.politifact.com/truth-o-meter/article/2007/sep/01/how-much-credit-giuliani-due-fighting-crime/.

Amusing the Zillion. 2010, November 1. "Out with the Old in Coney Island: Only 2 of 11 Boardwalk Businesses Invited Back." http://amusingthezillion.com/2010/11/01/out-with-the-old-in-coney-island-only-2-of-11-boardwalk-businesses-invited-back/.

_____. 2010, December 2. "Under Construction: Luna Park Coney Island's $1.4M Sodexo-Run Restaurant & More." http://amusingthezillion.com/2010/12/02/under-construction-luna-park-coney-islands-1-4m-sodexo-run-restaurant-more/.

———. 2010, December 13. "R.I.P. Coney Island's Shore Hotel, Henderson Next on Hit List." https://amusingthezillion.com/2010/12/13/r-i-p-coney-islands-shore-hotel-henderson-next-on-hit-list/.

———. 2011, December 20. "Coney Island's 1st Private Beachfront Condos on Boardwalk." https://amusingthezillion.com/2011/12/20/update-coney-islands-1st-private-beachfront-condos-on-boardwalk/.

———. 2012, July 17. "50 Years on Coney Island Boardwalk for Paul & His Daughter." http://amusingthezillion.com/2012/07/17/50-years-on-coney-island-boardwalk-for-paul-his-daughter/.

———. 2012, December 19. "Will Coney Island's Surf Ave Become a Mecca for Franchises?" http://amusingthezillion.com/2012/12/19/will-coney-islands-surf-ave-become-a-mecca-for-franchises/.

———. 2015, May 4. "Boardwalk Bunco: Milan Expo's USA Pavilion Has Boardwalk from Coney Island, Brooklyn to Get Plastic & Concrete." http://amusingthezillion.com/2015/05/04/boardwalk-bunco-milan-expos-usa-pavilion-has-boardwalk-from-coney-island-brooklyn-to-get-plastic-concrete/.

———. 2016, January 11. "Coney Island 2016: Pizza Hut Express Signs Lease on Coney Island's Surf Ave." http://amusingthezillion.com/2016/01/11/coney-island-2016-pizza-hut-express-signs-lease-on-coney-islands-surf-ave/.

Anderson, Lincoln. 2013, August 22. "De Blasio to Lead 'Hospitals Not Condos' Rally at Former St. Vincent's Site, with Belafonte, Sarandon, Cynthia Nixon, Others." *The Villager*. http://thevillager.com/2013/08/22/de-blasio-to-lead-hospitals-not-condos-rally-at-former-st-vincents-site-with-belafonte-sarandon-cynthia-nixon-others/.

Angotti, Tom. 2005, May 17. "Zoning Instead of Planning in Williamsburg and Greenpoint." *Gotham Gazette*. http://www.gothamgazette.com/index.php/development/2767-zoning-instead-of-planning-in-williamsburg-and-greenpoint.

———. 2009, May 26. "Zoning Without Planning?" *Gotham Gazette*. http://www.gothamgazette.com/article/fea/20090526/202/2928.

———. 2010, October 24. "The Real Power in City Planning." *Gotham Gazette*. http://www.gothamgazette.com/index.php/development/616-the-real-power-in-city-planning.

———. 2011, July 18. "Mayor Still Looks to Building and Zoning to Ease Housing Crunch." *Gotham Gazette*. http://www.gothamgazette.com/index.php/development/787-mayor-still-looks-to-building-and-zoning-to-ease-housing-crunch.

———. 2014, June 12. "A Tale of Two Housing Plans," *The Indypendent,* issue 197. https://indypendent.org/2014/06/12/tale-two-housing-plans.

APA, Diversity Committee of the New York Metro Chapter. 2007, March 30. "NY Metro's Written Response to PlaNYC 2030." http://www.nyplanning.org/docs/PlaNYC_2030_response_DiversityCommittee.pdf.

Arden, Patrick. 2011, September 15. "Bloomberg Housing Plan Hits Milestones, Obstacles." *City Limits*. http://citylimits.org/2011/09/15/bloomberg-housing-plan-hits-milestones-obstacles/.

Associated Press. 2015, September 3. "New Laws Prevent Landlords from Pressuring Tenants Out." *Crain's New York Business.* http://www.crainsnewyork.com/article/20150903/REAL_ESTATE/150909956/new-laws-prevent-landlords-from-pressuring-tenants-out.

Association for Neighborhood and Housing Development. 2016, March 18. "ANHD Helps Win Deeper MIH Affordability." http://anhd.org/anhd-helps-win-deeper-mih-affordability/.

Association of Foreign Investors in Real Estate. 2015/2016. "Annual Foreign Investment Survey." http://www.afire.org/content.asp?contentid=155.

Bagli, Charles V. 2009, April 10. "Beyond Sideshows, the City and a Developer Face Off Over Coney Island's Future." *New York Times.* http://www.nytimes.com/2009/04/11/nyregion/11coney.html?_r=1.

———. 2009, November 11. "Seeking Revival, City to Buy Land in Coney Island." *New York Times.* http://www.nytimes.com/2009/11/12/nyregion/12coney.html.

———. 2011, February 4. "Blighted Area? These Business Owners Beg to Differ." *New York Times.* http://www.nytimes.com/2011/02/05/nyregion/05metjournal.html.

Bailey, Nellie Hester. 2008, June 16. "Harlem: Resisting Displacements." *Black Star News.* http://www.blackstarnews.com/ny-watch/others/harlem-resisting-displacements.html.

Baird-Remba, Rebecca. 2016, August 31. "City Releases Plan To Rezone Jerome Avenue In The Bronx." *New York Yimby.* http://newyorkyimby.com/2016/08/city-releases-plan-to-rezone-jerome-avenue-in-the-bronx.html.

Barkan, Ross. 2013, December 21. "De Blasio Says No Contradiction in Keeping Bloomberg Development Commissioner." *Observer.* http://observer.com/2013/12/de-blasio-says-no-contradiction-in-keeping-bloomberg-development-commissioner/.

———. 2015, May 12. "Bill de Blasio's Approval Ratings Are the Lowest They Have Ever Been." *Observer.* http://observer.com/2015/05/bill-de-blasios-approval-ratings-are-the-lowest-they-have-ever-been/.

Barnes, Jonathan. 2007, July. "Harlem on the Rise. A Look at a Multi-Layered Community." *The Cooperator.* http://cooperator.com/articles/1475/1/Harlem-on-the-Rise/Page1.html.

Barnes, Tom. 2014, November 18. "New York City Has Rejected Taylor Swift." *MIC.* https://mic.com/articles/104538/new-york-city-has-rejected-taylor-swift#.fBzVzuMKL.

Barro, Josh. 2013, September 18. "Is Bill De Blasio Really That Left Wing?" *Business Insider.* http://www.businessinsider.com/is-bill-de-blasio-really-that-left-wing-2013-9?IR=T.

Barry, Dan. 2003, October 4. "About New York; Giuliani Razed Roller Coaster, and the Law." *New York Times.* http://www.nytimes.com/2003/10/04/nyregion/about-new-york-giuliani-razed-roller-coaster-and-the-law.html?scp=1&sq=giuliani%20thunderbolt%20bullard&st=cse.

Bellafante, Ginia. 2013, August 16. "A Mayor Who Puts Wall Street First." *New York Times*. http://www.nytimes.com/2013/08/18/nyregion/a-mayor-who-puts-wall-street-first.html?pagewanted=all&mtrref=undefined.

Bennet, Tony. 1986. "Popular Culture and the Return to Gramsci." In *Popular Culture and Social Relations*, edited by Tony Bennet, Colin Mercer, and Janet Woollacott, 11–19. Milton Keynes: Open University Press.

Beveridge, Andrew. 2008, August. "An Affluent, White Harlem?" *Gotham Gazette*. http://www.gothamgazette.com/index.php/demographics/4062-an-affluent-white-harlem.

Bidon, Timothy. 2013, August 17. "How Sandy Has Changed the Game in Coney Island." *The Indypendent*. https://indypendent.org/2013/08/17/HOW-SANDY-HAS-CHANGED-GAME-CONEY-ISLAND.

Bill de Blasio for Mayor. 2013. "One New York, Rising Together." http://www.archivoelectoral.org/archivo/doc/One%20New%20York%20Rising%20TogetherBillDeBlasioDemocraticPrimariasDemocratasAlcaldeNYEEUU2013.pdf.

Blackwell, Angela Glover. 2015, May 4. "Urban Renaissance or Cities of the One Percent?" *Huffington Post*. http://www.huffingtonpost.com/angela-glover-blackwell/urban-renaissance-or-cities_b_6793896.html.

Bloomberg, Michael. 2003, January 23. "State of the City. News from the Blue Room."

Bloomberg, Michael. 2004, August 30. "Speech at the Republican National Convention in New York City." *Washington Post*. http://www.washingtonpost.com/wp-dyn/articles/A46503-2004Aug30.html.

Bloustein. 2007, Spring. "Gentrification and Rezoning Williamsburg-Greenpoint." School of Planning and Public Policy, Rutgers University. http://rwv.rutgers.edu/wp-content/uploads/2013/08/Rezoning-in-Williamsburg-2007.pdf.

———. 2009, Spring. "Rezoning New York City—Lower East Side and Coney Island." School of Planning and Public Policy, Rutgers University, Development Studio. http://rwv.rutgers.edu/wp-content/uploads/2013/08/Rezoning_Presentation_June20_09.pdf.

Bram, Jason, and Michael Anderson. 2001. "Declining Manufacturing Employment in the New York–New Jersey Region: 1969–99." Federal Reserve Bank of New York. *Current Issues in Economics and Finance* 7, no. 1: 1–6. http://www.newyorkfed.org/research/current_issues/ci7-1.pdf.

Bredderman, Will. 2015, March 12. "De Blasio Appoints Forest City Ratner Exec to Rent Guidelines Board." *Observer*. http://observer.com/2015/03/de-blasio-appoints-forest-city-ratner-exec-to-rent-guidelines-board/.

———. 2016, January 6. "De Blasio Commissioners Face Off With Protesters Over Brooklyn Rezoning Plan." *Observer*. http://observer.com/2016/01/de-blasio-commissioners-face-off-with-protesters-over-brooklyn-rezoning-plan/.

Brenner, Neil, Peter Marcuse, and Margit Mayer. 2009. "Cities for People, Not for Profit." *City* 13, nos. 2–3: 176–184.

Brown, Eliot. 2008, August 4. "Landowners Bring Atlantic Yards Eminent Domain Battle to State Court." *Observer*. http://observer.com/2008/08/landowners-bring-atlantic-yards-eminent-domain-battle-to-state-court-updated/.

———. 2010, April 28. "The New Coney Island? Sitt Sees Fast Food in Place of Current Buildings." *New York Observer*. http://observer.com/2010/04/the-new-coney-island-sitt-sees-fast-food-in-place-of-current-buildings/.

———. 2008, October 27. "Burden to Municipal Art Society: Don't Mess with City's Coney Plans." *New York Observer*. http://observer.com/2008/10/burden-to-municipal-art-society-dont-mess-with-citys-coney-plans/.

Budin, Jeremiah. 2013, September 5. "Neil Patrick Harris Bought Record-Setting Harlem Townhouse." *Curbed New York*. http://ny.curbed.com/archives/2013/09/05/neil_patrick_harris_bought_recordsetting_harlem_townhouse.php.

———. 2014, January 10. "Harlem's Tallest Buildings Will Look Like a Sci-Fi Castle." *Curbed New York*. http://ny.curbed.com/archives/2014/01/10/harlems_tallest_buildings_will_look_like_a_scifi_castle.php.

Buettner, Russ. 2010, August 11. "Faltering Harlem Housing Deal Won City Cash." *New York Times*. http://www.nytimes.com/2010/08/12/nyregion/12harlem.html.

Burden, Amanda. 2006, October 9. "Interview." *Planetizen*. http://www.planetizen.com/node/21476.

———. 2008, March 10. "Statement at the City Planning Commission on the 125th Street Rezoning."

———. 2009, July 30. "Statement of Commissioner Amanda Burden on the Adoption of the Coney Island Revitalization Plan."

Busà, Alessandro. 2012. "A History of Decline and Revival, of Heroes and Villains at the People's Playground." In *The World in Brooklyn: Gentrification, Immigration, and Ethnic Politics in a Global City*, edited by Judith de Sena and Timothy Shortell, 147–185. Lanham, MD: Lexington Books.

———. 2013. "The Unsustainable Cost of Sustainability: PlaNYC and the Future of New York City." *Critical Planning* 20: 193–216.

———. 2014. "After the 125th Street Rezoning: The Gentrification of Harlem's Main Street in the Bloomberg Years." *Urbanities* 4, no. 2: 51–68.

———. 2014. "City Producers, City Consumers: The Rezoning and Branding of New York City Under the Administration of Michael R. Bloomberg (2002–2013)." Doctor of Urban Planning Thesis, Department of Urban Planning, Technical University of Berlin.

Calder, Rich. 2007, March 26. "Cyclone Swirls Around Coney Island Builder." *New York Post*. http://www.nypost.com/p/news/regional/item_uRMWWxL-9ZL6xI dBiXNUC2L.

———. 2015, November 18. "Most NYers Think de Blasio Is Clueless on Homeless Crisis." *New York Post*. http://nypost.com/2015/11/18/most-nyers-think-de-blasio-is-clueless-on-homeless-crisis/.

Calmes, Maggie. 2016, February 4. "Planning Commission Sends Mayor's Zoning Proposals to City Council." *Gotham Gazette.* http://www.gothamgazette.com/index.php/government/6143-planning-commission-sends-mayors-zoning-proposals-to-city-council.

Cardwell, Diane. 2003, January 8. "Mayor Says New York Is Worth the Cost." *New York Times.* http://www.nytimes.com/2003/01/08/nyregion/mayor-says-new-york-is-worth-the-cost.html.

———. 2007, January 15. "Once at Cotillions, Now Reshaping the Cityscape." *New York Times.* http://www.nytimes.com/2007/01/15/nyregion/15amanda.html?pagewanted=all.

———. 2010, June 23. "Casting Call (Smile!) for a New Hotel in Harlem." *New York Times.* http://query.nytimes.com/gst/fullpage.html?res=9C01E4D81738F937A15755C0A9669D8B63.

Cardwell, Diane, and Charles Bagli. 2007, April 20. "Mayor to Unveil 25-Year Outline for Greener City." *New York Times.*

Carroll, Rebecca. 2015, December 29. "I'll Never Be Able to Buy a Home. The Super Wealthy Broke the System." *The Guardian.* http://www.theguardian.com/commentisfree/2015/dec/29/home-ownership-super-wealthy-broke-the-system.

Cautela, Giuseppe. 1925, November. "Coney." *The American Mercury,* 280–285.

CBS New York. 2015, September 22. "Police to Focus on 125th Street in Harlem in Effort to Deal with Homelessness." *CBS New York.* http://newyork.cbslocal.com/2015/09/22/homeless-harlem-125th-street/.

Center for an Urban Future. 2008, July. "Attack of the Chains? A Borough-by-borough Analysis of New York City's Largest Retailers." *New York by the Numbers* 1, no. 1. http://www.nycfuture.org/images_pdfs/pdfs/Attackofthechains.pdf.

———. 2009, February. "Reviving the City of Aspiration: A Study of the Challenges Facing New York City's Middle Class." http://www.nycfuture.org/images_pdfs/pdfs/CityOfAspiration.pdf.

———. 2010, December. "A Chain Reaction: This Year's Borough-by-Borough Analysis of New York City's Largest Retailers." *New York by the Numbers* 3, no. 1. http://nycfuture.org/pdf/A_Chain_Reaction.pdf.

———. 2012, December. "State of the Chains, 2012." https://nycfuture.org/pdf/State-of-the-Chains-2012.pdf.

———. 2016, December. "State of the Chains, 2016." https://nycfuture.org/research/state-of-the-chains-2016.

Center for Working Families. 2011, April. "Empire State of Inequality: New York's Growing Wealth Divide." http://www.cwfny.org/wordpress/wp-content/uploads/2011/04/Empire-State-of-Inequaltiy.pdf.

Chaban, Matt. 2008, February 20. "Harlem's Future? Despite Some Support, Many Fear Worst from Rezoning." *Architect's Newspaper.* http://archpaper.com/news/articles.asp?id=1192.

————. 2012, November 29. "Even in a Hurricane, Mayor Bloomberg Bullish on Waterfront Development." *Observer.* http://observer.com/2012/10/even-in-a-hurricane-mayor-bloomberg-bullish-on-waterfront-development/.

Chen, David W. 2009, January 26. "At \$235 Million, Bloomberg Was Biggest Giver in U.S." *New York Times.* http://www.nytimes.com/2009/01/27/nyregion/27bloomberg.html?ref=nyregion.

Chen, David W., and Michael Barbaro. 2009, November 3. "Bloomberg Wins 3rd Term as Mayor in Unexpectedly Close Race." *New York Times.* http://www.nytimes.com/2009/11/04/nyregion/04mayor.html?pagewanted=all.

Cheney, Brandan. 2016, July 27. "De Blasio Housing Plan Shapes Up as Historic-scale Trade-off." *Politico New York.* http://www.politico.com/states/new-york/city-hall/story/2016/07/de-blasios-housing-plan-wont-fix-affordable-housing-crisis-102249.

Cheney-Rice, Zak. 2015, November 19. "Meet the Artists of 'Piano District,' the NYC Neighborhood Invented by White Developers." *Mic.* https://mic.com/articles/128862/meet-the-artists-of-piano-district-the-nyc-neighborhood-invented-by-white-developers#.RQAai9FRz.

Chiaramonte, Perry. 2007, September 12. "Tenants Flee Wobbly Building in Harlem." *New York Post.* http://www.nypost.com/p/news/regional/item_Kr09P88ReNsJuSERz2pRfM.

Christie, Les. 2011, December 6. "Occupy Protesters Take Over Foreclosed Homes." *CNN Money International.* http://money.cnn.com/2011/12/06/real_estate/occupy_movement_spreads/index.htm.

Chung, Jen. 2008, May 1. "City Council Passes 125th Street Rezoning." *Gothamist.* http://gothamist.com/2008/05/01/harlem_rezoning_1.php.

City Data. n.d. "Coney Island Neighborhood in Brooklyn, New York (NY), 11224 Detailed Profile." Accessed April 12, 2011. http://www.city-data.com/neighborhood/Coney-Island-Brooklyn-NY.html.

City of New York. 2003, April 2. "Mayor Michael R. Bloomberg Appoints Joseph M. Perello as Chief Marketing Officer for New York City. Marketing Officer Will Leverage City's Image and Assets to Generate New Revenue Streams for New York." Press release.

————. 2004. "No. 7 Subway Extension—Hudson Yards Rezoning and Development Program FGEIS." http://www1.nyc.gov/assets/planning/download/pdf/plans/hudson-yards/hy_chap5_t_fgeis_final.pdf.

————. 2006, June 8. "Mayor Bloomberg and NYC & Company Chairman Tisch Announce City's Plan to Create Single Marketing and Tourism Organization." Press release. http://www.nyc.gov/portal/site/nycgov/menuitem.c0935b9a57bb4ef3daf2f1c701c789a0/index.jsp?pageID=mayor_press_release&catID=1194&doc_name=http%3A%2F%2Fwww.nyc.gov%2Fhtml%2Fom%2Fhtml%2F2006a%2Fpr190-06.html&cc=unused1978&rc=1194&ndi=1.

———. 2007, October 10. "Mayor Bloomberg Launches 'This Is New York City'—First-Ever Multimedia Global Communications Campaign to Promote NYC." Press release.

———. 2011, May 19. "Mayor Bloomberg and Officials Announce Campaign to Promote All of Lower Manhattan to Visitors from Around the World." Press release. http://www.nyc.gov/portal/site/nycgov/menuitem.c0935b9a57bb4ef3daf2f-1c701c789a0/index.jsp?pageID=mayor_press_release&catID=1194&doc_name=http%3A%2F%2Fwww.nyc.gov%2Fhtml%2Fom%2Fhtml%2F2011a%2Fpr168-11.html&cc=unused1978&rc=1194&ndi=1.

———. 2014, June 2. "Transcript: Mayor de Blasio Delivers the Luncheon Address at the 2014 NYU International Hospitality Industry Investment Conference." http://www1.nyc.gov/office-of-the-mayor/news/263-14/transcript-mayor-de-blasio-delivers-luncheon-address-the-2014-nyu-international-hospitality.

———. 2014, July 25. "De Blasio Administration Announces 'Small Business First' Initiative to Reduce the Regulatory Burden on Small Businesses Across the Five Boroughs." http://www1.nyc.gov/office-of-the-mayor/news/372-14/de-blasio-administration-small-business-first-initiative-reduce-regulatory.

———. 2015. "Housing New York. A Five-Borough, Ten-Year Plan." http://www.nyc.gov/html/housing/assets/downloads/pdf/housing_plan.pdf.

———. 2015, March 18. "Mayor de Blasio and NYC & Company Announce 'Road to 10 Million More Visitors.'" http://www1.nyc.gov/office-of-the-mayor/news/180-15/mayor-de-blasio-nyc-company-road-10-million-more-visitors-.

City of New York, City Planning Commission. 1991, July. "Rules for the Processing of Plans Pursuant to Charter Section 197-a." https://www1.nyc.gov/assets/planning/download/pdf/about/publications/rules_197a.pdf.

City of New York, Department of City Planning. 1976. "Economic Recovery: New York City's Program for 1977–1981."

———. 1999. "Unified Bulk Program." http://tenant.net/land/zoning/unifiedbulk/unifprgm.pdf.

———. 2007, September 28. "125th Street Corridor Rezoning: Draft Environmental Impact Statement (DEIS)."

———. 2007, October 1. "125th Street Original Proposal."

———. 2007. "125th Street Press Release."

———. 2008. "125th Street Rezoning Plan."

———. 2008, February 29. "Final Environmental Impact Statement for 125th Street Corridor Rezoning and Related Actions." https://www1.nyc.gov/assets/planning/download/pdf/applicants/env-review/125th/0100_feis.pdf.

———. 2009. Coney Island Comprehensive Rezoning Plan.

———. 2009, January 16. "Draft Environmental Impact Statement (DEIS) for the Coney Island Rezoning Proposal."

———. 2009, June 5. "Final Environmental Impact Statement (FEIS) for the Coney Island Rezoning Proposal." http://www.nyc.gov/html/oec/downloads/pdf/dme_projects/08DME007K/FEIS/08DME007K_FEIS_03_Socioeconomic_Conditions.pdf.

———. 2013. "Celebrating DCP Rezonings."

———. 2013. "Greetings from the Chair, Amanda M. Burden."

———. 2016, July. "Employment Patterns in New York City." http://www1.nyc. gov/assets/planning/download/pdf/data-maps/nyc-economy/employment-patterns-nyc.pdf.

City of New York, Independent Budget Office. 2012, June. "Recession, Funding Shifts, and Changing Goals Mean Fewer New Apartments Likely to Be Built." Fiscal Brief. http://www.ibo.nyc.ny.us/iboreports/nhmp2012.pdf.

City of New York, Operations and Long-Term Planning and Sustainability. 2007. "PlaNYC, A Greener, Greater New York." http://www.nyc.gov/html/planyc2030/html/home/home.shtml.

———. 2010. "PlaNYC Progress Report 2010."

———. 2011. "PlaNYC Update 2011."

City Realty. 2016, August 23. "Work Begins at the Victoria Theater Site, See How It Will Transform Harlem's Skyline." City Realty. https://www.cityrealty.com/nyc/market-insight/features/the-new-skyline/work-begins-victoria-theater-site-see-how-will-transform-harlems-skyline/5446.

Clack, David. 2014, January 10. "Would You Live in a Cupboard for £40 per Week?" Now. Here. This. http://now-here-this.timeout.com/2014/01/10/would-you-live-in-a-cupboard-for-40-per-week/.

Clarke, Katherine. 2016, February 16. "Goldman Sachs' Essex Crossing Bet to Top $500M." The Real Deal. http://therealdeal.com/2016/02/16/goldman-sachs-essex-crossing-bet-to-top-500m/.

———. 2014, April 16. "Extell Makes Deal for Harlem Pathmark Official." The Real Deal. http://therealdeal.com/2014/04/16/extell-makes-deal-for-harlem-pathmark-official/.

CNN. 2001, October 2. "New York City Is Launching a $40 Million Advertising Campaign to Encourage Tourists and Business Travelers to Visit in the Wake of the Terrorist Attacks, New York Gov. George Pataki Announced Tuesday." CNN. http://edition.cnn.com/2001/TRAVEL/NEWS/10/02/nyc.tourism/.

Coalition for the Homeless. 2013, March 5. "State of the Homeless 2013. 50,000: The Bloomberg Legacy of Record Homelessness." http://coalhome.3cdn.net/5029926c66cd17b044_osm6btn4k.pdf.

———. 2015. "State of the Homeless 2015." http://www.coalitionforthehomeless.org/state-homeless-2015/.

Cohen, Michelle. 2016, January 29. "Developers Rushed to Get Nearly 8,000 Permits Ahead of 421-a Tax Break Expiration." 6sqft. https://www.6sqft.com/developers-rushed-to-get-nearly-8000-permits-ahead-of-421-a-tax-break-expiration/.

Cole, Williams. 2001, May 1. "Against the Giuliani Legacy." The Brooklyn Rail. http://brooklynrail.org/2006/05/local/against-the-giuliani-legacy.

Coney Island. 2009. "Final Environmental Impact Statement (FEIS)." http://www.nyc.gov/html/oec/downloads/pdf/dme_projects/08DME007K/FEIS/08DME007K_FEIS_03_Socioeconomic_Conditions.pdf.

Confessore, Nicholas. 2005, December 16. "Another Step for Downtown Brooklyn Project." *New York Times*. http://www.nytimes.com/2005/12/16/nyregion/another-step-for-downtown-brooklyn-project.html?mtrref=ny.curbed.com&gwh=4964C4A8813178C7712C3A8D944DF027&gwt=pay&_r=0.

Corcoran. 2001. "1Q-2001 Manhattan Report." Corcoran Group Real Estate.

Corcoran. 2007. "1Q-2007 Manhattan Report." Corcoran Group Real Estate.

Coscarelli, Joe. 2014, February 25. "Spike Lee's Amazing Rant Against Gentrification: 'We Been Here!'" *New York Magazine*. http://nymag.com/daily/intelligencer/2014/02/spike-lee-amazing-rant-against-gentrification.html.

Cuozzo, Steve. 2014, January 15. "NYC Development Surge to Continue Under de Blasio." *New York Post*. http://nypost.com/2014/01/15/nyc-development-surge-to-continue-under-de-blasio/.

Curran, Winifred. 2007. "From the Frying Pan to the Oven: Gentrification and the Experience of Industrial Displacement in Williamsburg, Brooklyn." *Urban Studies* 44, no. 8: 1427–1440.

Curran, Winifred, and Susan Hanson. 2005. "Getting Globalized: Urban Policy and Industrial Displacement in Williamsburg, Brooklyn." *Urban Geography* 26, no. 6: 461–482.

Currid, Elizabeth. 2006. "New York as a Global Creative Hub: A Competitive Analysis of Four Theories on World Cities." *Economic Development Quarterly* 20: 330–350.

Dailey, Jessica. 2012, May 24. "Chelsea to High Line Tourists: We Pretty Much Hate You." *Curbed New York*. http://ny.curbed.com/2012/5/24/10368018/chelsea-to-high-line-tourists-we-pretty-much-hate-you.

Daly, Michael. 2016, April 29. "It's Time for 'Honest' Bill de Blasio to Tell New York the Truth." *The Daily Beast*. http://www.thedailybeast.com/articles/2016/04/29/it-s-time-for-honest-bill-de-blasio-to-tell-new-york-the-truth.html.

Davidson, Alastair. 2016, March 18. "Photo: World's Most Expensive Basketball Sneaker Going on Sale for $4 Million." *Give Me Sport*. http://www.givemesport.com/733244-photo-worlds-most-expensive-basketball-sneaker-going-on-sale-for-4-million.

Dawsey, Josh. 2016, August 1. "Poll: Most New Yorkers Say Bill de Blasio Doesn't Deserve Re-election." *Wall Street Journal*. http://www.wsj.com/articles/poll-bill-de-blasio-doesnt-deserve-re-election-in-2017-1470078172.

Del Signore, John. 2008, October 16. "Tenants Sue Owner of Big Harlem Building over Displacement Tactics." *Gothamist*. http://gothamist.com/2008/10/16/tenant_lawsuit.php.

Dionne Jr., E. J. 2013, November 6. "America Shifts Left." *Washington Post*. https://www.washingtonpost.com/opinions/ej-dionne-jr-america-shifts-left/2013/11/06/2119e06e-470e-11e3-b6f8-3782ff6cb769_story.html.

Dunlap, David W. 2002, February 10. "The Changing Look of the New Harlem." *New York Times*. http://www.nytimes.com/2002/02/10/realestate/the-changing-look-of-the-new-harlem.html?pagewanted=all&src=pm.

Durkin, Erin. 2008, May 1. "City Council Approves 125th Street Rezoning." *Columbia Spectator*. http://www.columbiaspectator.com/2008/05/01/city-council-approves-125th-street-rezoning.

Earth Porm. n.d. "7 Castles That Are Cheaper Than an Apartment in San Francisco." *Earth Porm*. http://www.earthporm.com/apartment-in-san-francisco/.

East Harlem Preservation. 2015, December 11. "Dumbing-Down East Harlem: A Forked-Tongue Approach to Rezoning." http://eastharlempreservation.org/rezoning-and-dumbing-down-east-harlem/.

Elliott, Andrea. 2013, December 9. "Invisible Child. Girl in the Shadows: Dasani's Homeless Life." *New York Times*. http://www.nytimes.com/projects/2013/invisible-child/.

Fainstein, Susan. 2005. "The Return of Urban Renewal: Dan Doctoroff's Great Plans for New York City." *Harvard Design Magazine* 22 (Spring/Summer): 1–5.

———. 2007. "Tourism and the Commodification of Urban Culture." *The Urban Reinventors Paper Series*. http://www.urbanreinventors.net/2/fainstein/fainstein-urbanreinventors.pdf.

Families United for Racial and Economic Equality (FUREE). 2008, July. "Out of Business: The Crisis of Small Businesses in Rezoned Downtown Brooklyn." FUREE and the Community Development Project of the Urban Justice Center. https://cdp.urbanjustice.org/sites/default/files/oob_31jul08.pdf.

Fanelli, James. 2010, December 26. "Census Trends: Young, White Harlem Newcomers Aren't Always Welcomed." *NY Daily News*. http://www.nydailynews.com/new-york/census-trends-young-white-harlem-newcomers-aren-welcomed-article-1.475634.

Farkas, Ava, and Sara Newman. 2015, November 19. "Rezoning Plan Will Cause More Displacement in New York." *People's World*. http://peoplesworld.org/rezoning-plan-will-cause-more-displacement-in-new-york/.

Feiden, Douglas. 2012, December 6. "Big Retailers Moved Uptown in Greatest Numbers in 2012; Survey Shows 11.2% Rise in Corporate Chains in Harlem, Washington Heights and Inwood." *New York Daily News*. http://www.nydailynews.com/chain-reaction-leads-uptown-article-1.1227884.

Felber, Garrett. 1995. "Apollo Theater." In *The Encyclopedia of New York City*, edited by Kenneth T. Jackson. New Haven: Yale University Press.

Feltz, Renee. 2008, February 22. "Redlining: Why So Few Harlemites Own Property." *The Indypendent*. https://indypendent.org/2008/02/22/redlining-why-so-few-harlemites-own-property.

Fermino, Jennifer. 2013, August 21. "Mayoral Hopeful Christine Quinn Unleashes Attack on Opponent Bill de Blasio, Paints Him as Flip-Flopper." *New York Daily News*. http://www.nydailynews.com/news/election/christine-quinn-slams-bill-de-blasio-flip-flopper-article-1.1432375.

———. 2014, November 21. "Bill de Blasio Names Chair for City's Commission on Human Rights, Eight New Commissioners." *Daily News*.

http://www.nydailynews.com/blogs/dailypolitics/de-blasio-names-chair-city-commission-human-rights-blog-entry-1.2019782.

————. 2015, December 16. "De Blasio Removing Head of Homeless Services, Restructuring NYC's Approach to Homelessness." *New York Daily News.* http://www.nydailynews.com/new-york/de-blasio-removing-head-homeless-services-article-1.2466761.

Fermino, Jennifer, and Erin Durkin. 2015, November 30. "Manhattan Board Votes Down Zoning Changes Needed for de Blasio's Housing Plan." *Daily News.* http://www.nydailynews.com/news/politics/manhattan-board-votes-de-blasio-zoning-article-1.2450610.

Ferro, Shane. 2014, December 3. "This New Steampunk Condo Development Is Proof That New York Is Over." *Business Insider.* http://uk.businessinsider.com/steampunk-condo-development-proves-that-new-york-is-over-2014-12?r=US&IR=T.

Fickenscher, Lisa. 2010, January 4. "NYC Tourism Fell Less Than Forecast in 2009." *Crain's New York Business.* http://www.crainsnewyork.com/article/20100104/FREE/100109987.

Finn, Donovan. 2008, July. "New York City's PlaNYC Initiative: Does Greener Really Mean Greater?" Paper presented at the joint ACSP/AESOP conference, Chicago, IL. http://www.hunter.cuny.edu/ccpd/repository/files/planyc2030-does-greener-really-mean-greater.pdf.

Firat, A. Fuat. 1987. "The Social Construction of Consumption Patterns: Understanding Macro Consumption Phenomena." In *Philosophical and Radical Thought in Marketing,* edited by A. Fuat Firat, Nikhilesh Dholakia, and Richard P. Bagozzi, 251–267. Lexington, MA: Lexington Books.

Fiscal Policy Institute. 2010, December 13. "Grow Together or Pull Further Apart? Income Concentration Trends in New York." http://www.fiscalpolicy.org/FPI_GrowTogetherOrPullFurtherApart_20101213.pdf.

————. 2012, September 2. "The State of Working New York 2012: Disappointingly Weak Recovery." http://fiscalpolicy.org/wp-content/uploads/2012/09/fpi-SWNY-2012-data-show-a-disappointingly-weak-recovery.pdf.

Fiscal Policy Institute, Good Jobs New York, and National Employment Law Project. 2011. "An Overview of Job Quality and Discretionary Economic Development Subsidies in New York City." http://www.fiscalpolicy.org/FPI_GJNY_NELP_SubsidizedEmployersCreateLowWageJobs.pdf.

Flegenheimer, Matt. 2012, October 30. "Flooded Tunnels May Keep City's Subway Network Closed for Several Days." *New York Times.* http://www.nytimes.com/2012/10/31/nyregion/subways-may-be-shut-for-several-days-after-hurricane-sandy.html.

Forbes. n.d. "The World's Billionaires." *Forbes.* Accessed May 4, 2016. http://www.forbes.com/profile/michael-bloomberg/.

————. 2007, March 8. "The World's Billionaires 2007." *Forbes.* http://www.forbes.com/lists/2007/10/07billionaires_Michael-Bloomberg_C610.html.

————. 2009, March 11. "The World's Billionaires 2009." *Forbes*. http://www.forbes. com/lists/2009/10/billionaires-2009-richest-people_Michael-Bloomberg_ C610.html.

Fox Gotham, Kevin. 2001. "Redevelopment for Whom and for What Purpose?" *Critical Perspectives on Urban Redevelopment* 6: 431–454.

Fox Gotham, Kevin, and Miriam Greenberg. 2008. "From 9/11 to 8/29: Post-Disaster Recovery and Rebuilding in New York and New Orleans." *Social Forces* 87, no. 2: 1039–1062.

Frank, Robert. 2016, January 5. "Manhattan Real Estate Prices Shatter Records." *CNBC*. http://www.cnbc.com/2016/01/04/manhattan-real-estate-prices-shatter-records.html.

Fung, Amanda. 2009, June 28. "Coney Island Keeper—Thor Equities' Joe Sitt Gives City a Ride for Its Money." *Crain's New York Business*. http://www.crainsnewyork.com/article/20090628/SMALLBIZ/306289868/coney-island-keeper.

————. 2010, December 21. "Bklyn Developer Wins Stimulus Cash for Hotel." *Crain's New York Business*. http://www.crainsnewyork.com/article/20101221/REAL_ESTATE/101229976/bklyn-developer-wins-stimulus-cash-for-hotel.

————. 2011, June 19. "New York City Pushes to Restart Manufacturing—Initiatives Focus on Creating Industrial Space, Access to Capital." *Crain's New York Business*. http://www.crainsnewyork.com/article/20110619/SMALLBIZ/306199973.

————. 2011, October 7. "Foreigners Purchase One-third of City Condos." *Crain's New York Business*. http://www.crainsnewyork.com/article/20111007/REAL_ESTATE/111009913/1009?template=smartphone.

Furman Center. 2008. "Trends in New York City Housing Price Appreciation." Furman Center for Real Estate and Urban Policy, State of New York City's Housing and Neighborhoods 2008. http://furmancenter.org/files/Trends_in_NYC_Housing_Price_Appreciation.pdf.

Furman Center for Real Estate and Urban Policy. 2009, June. "Key Findings on the Affordability of Rental Housing from New York City's Housing and Vacancy Survey 2008." http://furmancenter.org/files/Key_Findings_HVS_2008.pdf.

Fusfeld, Adam. 2011, June 15. "Closing Prices at 2280 FDB Are Tops in Harlem." *The Real Deal New York City Real Estate News*. http://therealdeal.com/blog/2011/06/15/closing-prices-at-2280-frederick-douglas-boulevard-marketed-by-halstead-property-development-marketing-and-developed-by-phoenix-realty-group-are-tops-in-harlem/.

Gartland, Michael. 2015, May 19. "De Blasio Recycles Bloomberg Housing Plan He Once Bashed." *New York Post*. http://nypost.com/2015/05/19/de-blasio-recycles-bloomberg-housing-plan-he-once-bashed/.

————. 2015, November 17. "De Blasio's Affordable-Housing Plan Doesn't Have Many Backers." *New York Post*. http://nypost.com/2015/11/17/de-blasios-affordable-housing-plan-doesnt-have-many-backers/.

———. 2016, October 20. "NYC Homeless Population Reaches Historically Tragic Number." *New York Post*. http://nypost.com/2016/10/20/nyc-homeless-population-reaches-historically-tragic-number/.

Glaeser, Edward L., and Albert Saiz. 2004. "The Rise of the Skilled City." *Brookings-Wharton Papers on Urban Affairs*.

Goldenberg, Sally. 2015, July 31. "De Blasio Position Assailed at Brooklyn Bridge Park Hearing." *Politico New York*. http://www.capitalnewyork.com/article/city-hall/2015/07/8573131/de-blasio-position-assailed-brooklyn-bridge-park-hearing.

Goldensohn, Rosa. 2015, July 22. "Hudson Yards Debt Will Cost City Another $368M Through 2019, Data Shows." *DNAinfo*. https://www.dnainfo.com/new-york/20150722/hells-kitchen-clinton/hudson-yards-debt-will-cost-city-another-368m-through-2019-study-finds.

———. 2015, November 9. "80 Percent of LINC Homeless Rent Vouchers Aren't Being Used, City Says." *DNAinfo*. https://www.dnainfo.com/new-york/20151109/fort-greene/80-percent-of-homeless-rent-vouchers-arent-being-used-city-says.

Goldman, Henry. 2012, July 24. "Gay Marriage Produced $259 Million for New York City Economy." *Bloomberg News*. http://www.bloomberg.com/news/2012-07-24/gay-marriage-produced-259-million-for-new-york-city-economy-1-.html.

———. 2014, May 5. "De Blasio Unveils $41 Billion Plan for Affordable Housing." *Bloomberg*. http://www.bloomberg.com/news/articles/2014-05-05/de-blasio-unveils-41-billion-plan-for-affordable-housing.

Good Old Lower East Side. 2008, December. "No Go for Local Business: The Decline of the Lower East Side's Small Business Identity." Good Old Lower East Side and the Community Development Project of the Urban Justice Center. https://cdp.urbanjustice.org/sites/default/files/Small_Business_report_FINAL.pdf.

Good Jobs New York. 2013. "Spotlight on Economic Development." http://www.goodjobsny.org/economic-development/new-york-stock-exchange.

Goodman, J. David. 2016, March 30. "How New York Allowed Gentrification for $16 Million." *New York Times*. http://www.nytimes.com/2016/03/31/nyregion/nursing-homes-sale-to-condo-developer-raises-questions-for-city.html.

Goodwin, Michael. 2015, September 30. "De Blasio Proves He's Clueless About the Homeless Crisis." *New York Post*. http://nypost.com/2015/09/30/de-blasio-proves-hes-clueless-about-the-homeless-crisis/.

Goodyear, Sarah. 2013, September 11. "Bill de Blasio Feels Your Pain." *Citylab*. http://www.citylab.com/politics/2013/09/bill-de-blasio-feels-your-pain/6861/.

Graff, Amy. 2015, September 21. "This Is What $350,000 Buys You in San Francisco's Crazy Housing Market." *SFGate*. http://blog.sfgate.com/ontheblock/2015/09/21/this-is-what-350000-buys-you-in-san-franciscos-crazy-housing-market/.

Greenberg, Miriam. 2003. "The Limits of Branding: The World Trade Center, Fiscal Crisis and the Marketing of Recovery." *International Journal of Urban and Regional Research* 27, no. 2: 386–416.

———. 2008, May. "Branding New York." *The Brooklyn Rail.* http://brooklynrail. org/2008/05/express/branding-new-york.

———. 2010. "Branding, Crisis, and Utopia: Representing New York in the Age of Bloomberg." In *Blowing up the Brand: Critical Perspectives on Promotional Paradigms,* edited by Melissa Aronczyc and Devon Powers, 115–143. New York and Oxford: Peter Lang.

Greenspan, Elizabeth. 2016, March 2. "Are Micro-Apartments a Good Solution to the Affordable-Housing Crisis?" *New Yorker.* http://www.newyorker.com/ business/currency/are-micro-apartments-a-good-solution-to-the-affordable-housing-crisis.

Grodach, Martin. 2009. "Urban Branding: An Analysis of City Homepage Imagery." *Journal of Architectural and Planning Research* 26, no. 3: 181–197.

Gross, Courtney. 2008, August 25. "Reshaping the City: Who's Being Heard, and Why?" *Gotham Gazette.* http://old.gothamgazette.com/article/iotw/20080825/ 200/2619.

———. 2010, April 13. "Subsidies in the City." *Gotham Gazette.* http://www.gothamgazette.com/index.php/economy/496-subsidies-in-the-city-part-i; http://www. gothamgazette.com/index.php/about/495-subsidies-in-the-city-part-ii.

Gross, Daniel. 2005, April 18. "Don't Hate Them Because They're Rich—The Trickle-Down Effect of Ridiculous, Ostentatious Wealth." *New York Magazine.* http://nymag.com/nymetro/news/culture/features/11721/.

Grynbaum, Michael M. 2013, December 31. "De Blasio Draws All Liberal Eyes to New York City." *New York Times.* http://www.nytimes.com/2014/01/01/nyre-gion/de-blasio-draws-all-liberal-eyes-to-new-york-city.html.

———. 2015, October 30. "Bill de Blasio Endorses Hillary Clinton, to Little Fanfare from Campaign." *New York Times.* http://www.nytimes.com/2015/10/31/nyre-gion/bill-de-blasio-finally-endorses-hillary-clinton.html.

———. 2015, December 28. "Mayor de Blasio Still Trying, Fitfully, to Promote Himself." *New York Times.* http://www.nytimes.com/2015/12/29/nyregion/ mayor-de-blasio-still-trying-fitfully-to-blow-his-own-horn-better.html.

Gutekunst-Roth, Gayle. 1977. "Note: New York—A City in Crisis: Fiscal Emergency Legislation and the Constitutional Attacks." *Fordham Urban Law Journal* 6, no. 1: 65–100.

Hackman, Rose. 2015, May 13. "What Will Happen When Harlem Becomes White?" *The Guardian.* http://www.theguardian.com/us-news/2015/may/13/ harlem-gentrification-new-york-race-black-white.

Hall, Stuart. 1997. "Representations and the Media." Lecture at University of Westminster in London. Transcript available online at http://www.mediaed.org/ assets/products/409/transcript_409.pdf.

Hartman, Chester. 1984. "The Right to Stay Put." In *Land Reform, American Style*, edited by Charles C. Geisler and Frank J. Popper, 302–318. Totowa, NJ: Rowman and Allanheld.

———. 1998. "The Case for a Right to Housing." *Housing Policy Debate* 9, no. 2: 223–246.

Harvey, David. 1989. "From Managerialism to Entrepreneurialism: The Transformation in Urban Governance in Late Capitalism." *Geografiska Annaler, Series B, Human Geography* 71, no. 1: 3–17.

———. 2001. "Globalization and the 'Spatial Fix.'" *Geographische Revue* 2: 23–30.

———. 2008. "The Right to the City." *New Left Review* 53 (September–October). https://newleftreview.org/II/53/david-harvey-the-right-to-the-city.

Heilman, Jeff. 2007, December. "Gotham Glory." *Meetings Focus*. http://www.meetingsfocus.com/Magazines/ArticleDetails/tabid/136/RegionID/235/ArticleID/9607/Default.aspx#top.

Heilpern, John. 2010, May. "Princess of the City." *Vanity Fair*. http://www.vanityfair.com/culture/2010/05/otl-burden-201005.

Henry, Imani. 2005, December 4. "Community Fights Gentrification in Harlem." *Worker's World*. http://www.workers.org/2005/us/harlem-1208/.

Hernandez, Raymond. 2008, July 27. "Real Estate Developers Are Major Rangel Donors." *New York Times*. http://www.nytimes.com/2008/07/27/nyregion/27rangel.html?pagewanted=all.

Herszenhorn, David M. 2003, September 10. "What Will It Be, New York City? For $166 Million, Make It Snapple." *New York Times*. http://www.nytimes.com/2003/09/10/nyregion/what-will-it-be-new-york-city-for-166-million-make-it-snapple.html?pagewanted=all&src=pm.

Hertz, Daniel. 2016, January 21. "Why Not Make Housing Assistance to the Low-Income as Easy as Assistance to the High-Income?" *City Commentary*. http://cityobservatory.org/low-income-housing-tax/.

Hicks, Jonathan P. 1994, October 18. "Police Move Street Vendors in Harlem." *New York Times*.

Hochberg, Fred P. 2001, October 17. "Small Business, Badly Damaged." *New York Times*. http://www.nytimes.com/2001/10/17/opinion/small-business-badly-damaged.html.

HR&A Advisors. 2013, April 5. "New York City Council Approves Rezoning of Hudson Square Neighborhood." http://www.hraadvisors.com/news/new-york-city-council-approves-rezoning-of-hudson-square-neighborhood/.

Hubbard, Phil, and Tim Hall. 1998. "The Entrepreneurial City and the New Urban Politics." In *The Entrepreneurial City: Geographies of Politics, Regime and Representation*, edited by Phil Hubbard and Tim Hall, 1–25. Chichester, UK: John Wiley & Sons.

Huen, Eustacia. 2016, August 30. "Inside New York City's First Luxury Micro-Apartment Building, Where Units Start at 265 Square Feet." *Forbes*. http://www.forbes.com/sites/eustaciahuen/2016/08/30/

inside-new-york-citys-first-luxury-micro-apartment-building-where-units-start-at-265-square-feet/#4e9dc179398b.

ICLEI Local Governments for Sustainability USA and the Mayor's Office for Long-Term Planning and Sustainability. 2010, April. "The Process Behind PlaNYC: How the City of New York Developed Its Comprehensive Long-Term Sustainability Plan." http://s-media.nyc.gov/agencies/planyc2030/pdf/iclei_planyc_case_study_201004.pdf.

Idov, Michael. 2011, November 27. "And Another Fifty Million People Just Got Off of the Plane." *New York Magazine.* http://nymag.com/news/features/tourism/tourist-increase-2011-12/.

Immerso, Michael. 2010, July 14. "Coney Island Cornerstones on Surf Avenue Face Demolition." *Huffington Post.* http://www.huffingtonpost.com/michael-immerso/coney-island-cornerstones_b_646400.html.

Institute for Children and Poverty. 2006, March. "The Cost of Good Intentions: Gentrification and Homelessness in Upper Manhattan." http://www.urbancenter.utoronto.ca/pdfs/curp/Gentrification_HLN_Manhatt.pdf.

Irwin, Demetria. 2008, March 20. "Landmarking the Black Cultural Capital of the World." *Amsterdam News.*

Jahr, Nicholas. 2009, January 5. "All Together Now: Toward a Better Land Use Process." *City Limits.* http://citylimits.org/2009/01/05/all-together-now-toward-a-better-land-use-process/.

Janison, Dan. 2014, February 7. "NYC Planning Chair: Major-League Connections in Real Estate-Gov't Nexus." *Newsday.* http://www.newsday.com/long-island/politics/spin-cycle/nyc-planning-chair-majr-league-connections-in-real-estate-gov-t-nexus-1.6981431.

Jones, David R. 2006, March 30. "Subsidized Housing." *Gotham Gazette.* http://www.gothamgazette.com/index.php/development/3199-subsidized-housing.

———. 2009, November 2. "Coney Island Housing Complex Gets $21M to Stay Affordable." *The Real Deal.* http://therealdeal.com/blog/2009/11/02/coney-island-housing-complex-mitchell-lama-gets-21m-to-stay-affordable/.

Jost, Gregory. 2016, January 19. "Housing Plan Misses the Big Question of How We Got into this Mess in the First Place." *City Limits.* http://citylimits.org/2016/01/19/cityviewshousing-plan-misses-the-big-question-of-how-we-got-into-this-mess-in-the-first-place/.

Kaplan, Thomas. 2012, November 26. "Cuomo, in Aid Appeal, Cites Broad Reach of Storm." *New York Times.* http://www.nytimes.com/2012/11/27/nyregion/governor-cuomo-says-hurricane-sandy-was-worse-than-katrina.html.

Kapp, Trevor. 2012, March 9. "Tenants Evacuated from Unstable Harlem Building." *DNAinfo.* http://www.dnainfo.com/new-york/20120309/harlem/tenants-evacuated-from-unstable-harlem-building?r=rm=1.

Katz, Alyssa. 2009, December 18. "Gentrification Hangover—Can a New Era of Affordable Housing Be Created from the Wreckage of Failed Luxury Real Estate?" *American Prospect.* http://prospect.org/article/gentrification-hangover-0.

————. 2015, December 20. "On Homelessness, De Blasio Made His Bed." *New York Daily News*. http://www.nydailynews.com/opinion/homelessness-de-blasio-made-bed-article-1.2470935.

Katz, Miranda. 2015, December 18. "HOME-STAT: De Blasio's New Homelessness Plan Worries Some Advocates." *Gothamist*. http://gothamist.com/2015/12/18/de_blasio_home_stat.php.

Kaufman, David. n.d. "Must-See Harlem: 12 Great Things to See and Do." NYCgo.com. Accessed September 14, 2013. http://www.nycgo.com/slideshows/must-see-harlem.

Kavaratzis, Mihalis. 2004. "From City Marketing to City Branding: Towards a Theoretical Framework for Developing City Brands." *Place Branding* 1, no. 1: 58–73.

Kavaratzis, Mihalis, and Gregory Ashworth. 2008. "Place Marketing: How Did We Get Here and Where Are We Going?" *Journal of Place Management and Development* 1, no. 2: 150–165.

Kelley, Robin D. G. 2007. "Disappearing Acts: Harlem in Transition." In *The Suburbanization of New York: Is the World's Greatest City Becoming Just Another Town?*, edited by Jerilou Hammett, and Kingsley Hammett, 63–74. New York: Princeton Architectural Press.

Kim, Hye-Shin. 2006. "Using Hedonic and Utilitarian Shopping Motivations to Profile Inner City Consumers." *Journal of Shopping Center Research* 13, no. 1: 57–79.

King, David. 2015, November 6. "East Harlem Tenants Group Rejects De Blasio Housing Plan, Offers Its Own." *Gotham Gazette*. http://www.gothamgazette.com/index.php/government/5972-east-harlem-tenants-group-rejects-de-blasio-housing-plan-offer-its-own.

King, David Howard. 2016, February 3. "Calls for Public Discussion of New Affordable Housing Incentive Program." *Gotham Gazette*. http://www.gothamgazette.com/index.php/government/6138-calls-for-public-discussion-of-new-affordable-housing-incentive-program.

Kipfer, Stefan. 2008. "How Lefebvre Urbanized Gramsci: Hegemony, Everyday Life, and Difference." In *Space, Difference, Everyday Life: Reading Henri Lefebvre*, edited by Kanishka Goonewardena, Stefan Kipfer, Richard Milgrom, and Christian Schmid, 193–211. New York: Routledge.

Klinenberg, Eric. 2012, January 25. "Solo Nation: American Consumers Stay Single." *Fortune*. http://fortune.com/2012/01/25/solo-nation-american-consumers-stay-single/.

Kolben, Deborah. 2004, August 7. "Mayor Ties Ratner Arena to Olympics." *Brooklyn Paper*. http://www.brooklynpaper.com/stories/27/31/27_31nets1.html.

Korn, Morgan. 2012, March 22. "NYC's Luxury Housing Market Booms, While American Dream Fades for Most." *Yahoo Finance*. http://finance.yahoo.com/blogs/daily-ticker/nyc-luxury-housing-market-booms-while-american-dream-170316774.html.

Kotkin, Joel. 2014, March 20. "Where Inequality Is Worst in the United States." *Forbes.* http://www.forbes.com/sites/joelkotkin/2014/03/20/where-inequality-is-worst-in-the-united-states/#5c9d972a56ce.

Kotkin, Joel, and F. Siegel. 2004, January. "Too Much Froth: The Latte Quotient Is a Bad Strategy for Building Middle Class Cities." *Blueprint Magazine.*

Kroll, Luisa. 2011, December 19. "Billionaire's Daughter Pays Record Sum for NYC Pad. *Forbes.* http://www.forbes.com/sites/luisakroll/2011/12/19/billionaires-daughter-pays-record-sum-for-nyc-pad/#512599815936.

Krueger, Rob J., and Julian Agyeman. 2005. "Sustainability Schizophrenia Or 'Actually Existing Sustainabilities?' Toward a Broader Understanding of the Politics and Promise of Local Sustainability in the US." *Geoforum* 36, no. 4: 410–417.

Kusisto, Laura. 2013, May 28. "Complex Upgrade on Coney Island Work on Former Affordable-Housing Development Set After Sale." *Wall Street Journal.* http://online.wsj.com/article/SB10001424127887323855804578511281925509280.html.

Lee, Jennifer. 2008, July 30. "Foreign Tourists Adore New York City." *New York Times.* http://cityroom.blogs.nytimes.com/2008/07/30/foreign-tourists-adore-new-york-city/.

Lefkowitz, Melanie. 2010, October 26. "The Holdouts—If It Doesn't Start Doing Something Soon, I'm Going to Be Out of Business After 26 Years." *City Limits.* http://www.citylimits.org/news/articles/4222/the-holdouts#.US4qljA3uSo.

Leon, Joshua K. 2014, November 25. "On New York's Skyscraper Boom and the Failure of Trickle-Down Urbanism." *Metropolis.* http://www.metropolismag.com/Point-of-View/November-2014/New-Yorks-Skyscraper-Boom-and-the-Failure-of-Trickle-Down-Urbanism/.

Levitt, Steven D. 2004. "Understanding Why Crime Fell in the 1990s: Four Factors That Explain the Decline and Six That Do Not." *Journal of Economic Perspectives* 18, no. 1: 163–190. http://pricetheory.uchicago.edu/levitt/Papers/LevittUnderstandingWhyCrime2004.pdf.

Lloyd, Richard, and Terry Nicholas Clark. 2001. "The City as Entertainment Machine." In *Critical Perspectives on Urban Redevelopment*, edited by Kevin Fox Gotham, 357–378. Amsterdam: JAI.

Loomis, Alan. 2002, October 30. "Consuming the City." *Delirious LA.* http://deliriousla.com/2002/10/30/consuming-the-city/.

Lowery, Wesley. 2011, July 11. "Harlem Growth Plans Face Hurdles." *Wall Street Journal.* http://online.wsj.com/article/SB10001424052702303763404576420061628796064.html.

Lowry, Tom. 2007, June 15. "The CEO Mayor. How New York's Mike Bloomberg Is Creating a New Model for Public Service That Places Pragmatism Before Politics." *Businessweek.*

Lueck, Thomas J. 2007, April 23. "Bloomberg Draws a Blueprint for a Greener City." *New York Times*. http://www.nytimes.com/2007/04/23/nyregion/23mayor. html?pagewanted=all&_r=o.

Mahoney, Bill. 2015, April 15. "REBNY Members Gave a Tenth of All N.Y. Campaign Money." *Politico New York*. http://www.capitalnewyork.com/article/ albany/2015/04/8566024/rebny-members-gave-tenth-all-ny-campaign-money.

Makalani, Jabulani Kamau. 1976. "Toward a Sociological Analysis of the Renaissance: Why Harlem?" *Black World/Negro Digest*. February: 4–13.

Malanga, Steven. 2004, Winter. "The Curse of the Creative Class." *City Journal*. http://www.city-journal.org/html/curse-creative-class-12491.html.

Marcus, Norman. 1991. "New York City Zoning – 1961–1991: Turning Back the Clock – But With an Up-To-The-Minute Social Agenda." *Fordham Urban Law Journal* 19, no. 3: 706–726.

Marcus, Stephanie. 2014, October 28. "Taylor Swift Explaining New York Vocabulary Is Beyond Cringeworthy." *Huffington Post*. http://www.huffington-post.com/2014/10/27/taylor-swift-new-york-vocabulary_n_6056096.html.

Marcuse, Peter. 2007. "PlaNYC Is Not a Plan and It Is Not for NYC." http://www. hunter.cuny.edu/ccpd/repository/files/planyc-is-not-a-plan-and-it-is-not-for-nyc.pdf.

Marino, Vivian. 2015, December 24. "In 2015, Shattering Records in New York City Real Estate." *New York Times*. http://www.nytimes.com/2015/12/27/realestate/ in-2015-shattering-records-in-new-york-city-real-estate.html?mtrref=undefine d&gwh=804502232911806CC736D5B3C850F69A&gwt=pay.

Marist Poll. 2015, November 3. "11/3: Drop in de Blasio's Approval Rating ... Support Among Base Erodes." Marist Poll. http://maristpoll.marist.edu/113-drop-in-de-blasios-approval-rating-support-among-base-erodes/.

Martin, Will. 2016, August 19. "Nobel-Prize Winning Economist Stiglitz Tells Us Why 'Neoliberalism Is Dead.'" *Business Insider UK*. http://uk.businessinsider. com/joseph-stiglitz-says-neoliberalism-is-dead-2016-8.

Matassa, Elizabeth H. 2006. "Whaddya Want? It's Coney Island! Tourism, Play and Memory in the Illegible City." Master of Arts Thesis, Department of Geography and Anthropology, Louisiana State University.

Mays, Jeff. 2010, September 2. "Brownstone Residents Oppose Construction of Affordable Housing on 123rd Street." *DNAinfo*. https://www.dnainfo.com/ new-york/20100902/harlem/brownstone-residents-oppose-construction-of-affordable-housing-on-123rd-street.

———. 2014, January 9. "East Harlem Leaders Want More Affordable Housing at 125th St. Development." *DNAinfo*. http://www.dnainfo.com/ new-york/20140109/east-harlem/east-harlem-leaders-want-more-affordable-housing-at-125th-st-development.

Mazelis, Fred. 1999, April 6. "Spotlight on NYC Police Brutality Throws Mayor Giuliani in Crisis." *World Socialist*. http://www.wsws.org/articles/1999/apr1999/ dial-a06.shtml.

Mazor, John. 2007, October 29. "Razing Rage in Harlem." *New York Post.* http://www.nypost.com/p/news/regional/item_YYJmtFjPh5fjxyXTI08CxI.

McGeehan, Patrick. 2007, February 27. "Remaking the City's Image, with 50 Million Tourists in Mind." *New York Times.* http://www.nytimes.com/2007/02/27/nyregion/27tourism.html?pagewanted=all.

———. 2015, March 24. "Manhattan Area Codes Multiply, but the Original, 212, Is Still Coveted." *New York Times.* http://www.nytimes.com/2015/03/25/nyregion/as-manhattan-area-codes-multiply-some-still-covet-a-212.html?_r=0&mtrref=undefined&assetType=nyt_now.

———. 2016, March 7. "De Blasio's New York Feels Effects of Recovery to Relief of Business Leaders." *New York Times.* http://www.nytimes.com/2016/03/08/nyregion/new-york-is-thriving-under-mayor-de-blasio-much-to-business-leaders-relief.html?mtrref=undefined.

McGrath, Ben. 2009, August 24. "The Untouchable. Can a Good Mayor Amass Too Much Power?" *New Yorker.* http://www.newyorker.com/reporting/2009/08/24/090824fa_fact_mcgrath.

McKee, Michael. 2013, June. "Tax Breaks for Billionaires." *Metropolitan Council on Housing.* http://metcouncilonhousing.org/news_and_issues/tenant_newspaper/2013/june/tax_breaks_for_billionaires_how_the_campaign_finance_system_faile_0.

Melton, Monica. 2015, November 18. "Mark-Viverito Decries Closing of East Harlem Supermarket." *Politico New York.* http://www.capitalnewyork.com/article/city-hall/2015/11/8583485/mark-viverito-decries-closing-east-harlem-supermarket.

Miller, Michael. 2009, April 6. "Whose Coney Island?" *The Brooklyn Rail.* http://www.brooklynrail.org/2009/06/local/whose-coney-island.

Misener, Jessica. 2014, May 1. "9 Private Islands That Cost Less Than an Apartment In San Francisco." *BuzzFeed.* http://www.buzzfeed.com/jessicamisener/private-islands-that-are-cheaper-than-an-apartment-in-san#.vyN4P2BQpK.

Misra, Tanvi. 2015, April 21. "Manhattan's Towering Income Inequality, in 2 Charts." *CITYLAB.* http://www.citylab.com/housing/2015/04/manhattans-towering-income-inequality-in-2-charts/390945/.

Molotch, Harvey. 1976. "The City as a Growth Machine: Toward a Political Economy of Place." *The American Journal of Sociology* 82, no. 2: 309–332.

Morgenson, Gretchen. 2008, May 9. "Questions of Rent Tactics by Private Equity." *New York Times.* http://www.nytimes.com/2008/05/09/business/09rent.html?pagewanted=all&_r=0.

Moss, Mitchell L. 2011, November. "How New York City Won the Olympics." Rudin Center for Transportation Policy and Management, New York University. http://wagner.nyu.edu/files/faculty/publications/Olympics_in_NYC_2012_REPORT_110711.pdf.

Moss, Jeremiah. 2008, April 9. "Boro Hotel." *Jeremiah's Vanishing New York Blog.* http://vanishingnewyork.blogspot.it/2008/04/boro-hotel.html.

———. 2012, August 21. "Disney World on the Hudson." *New York Times.* http://www.nytimes.com/2012/08/22/opinion/in-the-shadows-of-the-high-line.html?mtrref=undefined&assetType=opinion.

———. 2013, January 2. "Lenox Lounge Stripped." *Jeremiah's Vanishing New York Blog.* http://vanishingnewyork.blogspot.it/2013/01/lenox-lounge-stripped.html.

———. 2015, November 23. "125th Street in Chains." *Jeremiah's Vanishing New York Blog.* http://vanishingnewyork.blogspot.it/2015/11/125th-street-in-chains.html.

Municipal Art Society. 2008, March 3. "Comments on Draft Scope of Analysis for Coney Island Rezoning Project EIS."

Murphy, Jarret. 2010, December 21. "Whose Dreams Will Decide? The Push for Neighborhoods to Have More Than a Voice." *City Limits.* http://www.citylimits.org/news/articles/4250/whose-dreams-will-decide.

Nagourney, Adam. 2001, November 7. "The 2011 Elections: Bloomberg Edges Green in Race for Mayor." *New York Times.* http://www.nytimes.com/2001/11/07/nyregion/2001-elections-mayor-bloomberg-edges-green-race-for-mayor-mcgreevey-easy-winner.html.

Navarro, Mireya. 2015, January 29. "Long Lines, and Odds, for New York's Subsidized Housing Lotteries." *New York Times.* http://www.nytimes.com/2015/01/30/nyregion/long-lines-and-low-odds-for-new-yorks-subsidized-housing-lotteries.html?smprod=nytcore-iphone&smid=nytcore-iphone-share&_r=0&mtrref=undefined&assetType=nyt_now.

———. 2016, February 9. "At Council Hearing on de Blasio's Housing Plan, Many Voices Rise." *New York Times.* http://www.nytimes.com/2016/02/10/nyregion/at-council-hearing-on-bill-de-blasios-housing-plan-many-voices-rise.html.

Neighborhood Retail Alliance. 2009, July 23. "Obamacare and Small Businesses." *Neighborhood Retail Alliance Blogspot.* http://momandpopnyc.blogspot.it/2009/07/obamacare-and-small-business.html.

Neumeister, Larry, and Colleen Long. 2017, March 16. "No Charges to Be Filed Against New York Mayor Bill de Blasio in Fundraising Probe." *Chicago Tribune.* http://www.chicagotribune.com/news/nationworld/ct-bill-de-blasio-fundraising-probe-20170316-story.html.

Newman, Kathe, and Elvin K. Wyly. 2006. "The Right to Stay Put, Revisited: Gentrification and Resistance to Displacement in New York City." *Urban Studies* 43, no. 1: 23–57.

New York City Comptroller. 2012, September. "Rents Through the Roof! A Statistical Analysis of Unaffordable Rents in New York City." http://comptroller.nyc.gov/wp-content/uploads/documents/Rents-through-the-Roof.pdf.

New York City Comptroller, Scott M. Stringer. 2015, December 2. "Mandatory Inclusionary Housing and the East New York Rezoning: An Analysis." http://comptroller.nyc.gov/wp-content/uploads/documents/Mandatory_Inclusionary_Housing_and_the_East_New_York_Rezoning.pdf.

New York City Economic Development Corporation. 2012, December 31. "Mayor Bloomberg Announces New York City Breaks Tourism Record Again in 2012 with 52 Million Visitors." Press release. http://www.nycedc.com/press-release/

mayor-bloomberg-announces-new-york-city-breaks-tourism-record-again-2012-52-million.

New York City Housing Development Corporation. n.d. "Income Eligibility." Accessed May 5, 2016. http://www.nychdc.com/pages/Income-Eligibility.html.

New York Civil Liberties Union. n.d. "Stop-and-Frisk Data." Accessed March 14, 2016. http://www.nyclu.org/content/stop-and-frisk-data.

New York State Comptroller. 2011, July. "An Economic Snapshot of Coney Island and Brighton Beach." http://www.osc.state.ny.us/osdc/rpt8-2012.pdf.

New York Daily News. 2012, May 29. "Serendipity 3 Claims Most Expensive Burger; New York City Restaurant Selling $295 Wagyu Beef Hamburger." *New York Daily News*. http://www.nydailynews.com/new-york/serendipity-3-claims-expensive-burger-new-york-city-restaurant-selling-295-wagyu-beef-hamburger-article-1.1085962.

New York Police Department. 2001. "2001 Crime Statistics." NYPD.

New York State Office of Parks, Recreation and Historic Preservation. 2010. "Determination of Eligibility for Coney Island's Historic District." http://www.saveconeyisland.net/wp-content/uploads/2010/08/determinationofeligibility.081210.pdf.

New York Times. 1920, January 27. "Landlord Brings in Negroes to Get High Rents." *New York Times*.

———. 2010, October 7. "Harlem Is Booming" supplement. *New York Times*.

New York University. n.d. "NYU Space Planning: The Core Plan." Accessed January 9, 2017. http://www.nyu.edu/community/nyu-in-nyc/core-plan-commitments/nyu- space-planning–the-core-plan.html.

Nezik, Ann-Kathrin. 2015, April 10. "Tourism Troubles: Berlin Cracks Down on Vacation Rentals." *Spiegel Online International*. http://www.spiegel.de/international/business/berlin-cracks-down-on-estimated-18-000-vacation-rentals-a-1026881.html.

Nicas, Alexander J. 2010, Fall. "The Bloomberg Machine Exploits New York City's Flawed Land Use Decision-making Process: Why Reform Is Necessary to Ensure Orderly Growth Across Administrations." Unpublished paper, St. John's University School of Law, Land Use Planning Course.

North, Anna. 2014, October 28. "Taylor Swift's Unwelcome P.R. Campaign." *New York Times*. http://op-talk.blogs.nytimes.com/2014/10/28/taylor-swifts-unwelcome-p-r-campaign/?mtrref=undefined&gwh=313F93CD18DCA2D80DFA5E1620F1C0BD&gwt=pay&assetType=opinion.

Noticing New York. 2011, October 16. "Bloomberg's Increasing Annual Wealth: 1996 to 2011." *Noticing New York*. http://noticingnewyork.blogspot.it/2011/10/bloombergs-increasing-annual-wealth.html.

Novy, Johannes. 2011. "Marketing Marginalized Neighborhoods: Tourism and Leisure in the 21st Century Inner City." PhD Thesis, submitted to the Graduate School for Arts and Sciences, Columbia University.

NYC & Company. 2000. "Record 37.4 Million People Visited NYC in 2000; 28% Growth Since 1996." Archives of the Mayor's Press Office. http://www.nyc.gov/html/om/html/2001b/pr264-01.html.

———. 2011. "Annual Summary 2011." http://www.nycgo.com/assets/files/pdf/2011annualsummary.pdf.

———. 2011, May 16. "New York City Hotel Industry Experiences Significant Growth in the Boroughs Beyond Manhattan." http://www.nycandcompany.org/press/new-york-city-hotel-industry-experiences-significant-growth-in-the-boroughs.

———. 2013. "Annual Summary 2013." http://www.nycgo.com/assets/files/pdf/2013annualsummary.pdf.

———. 2013, March 13. "Mayor Bloomberg and NYC & Company Announce 'Neighborhood x Neighborhood' Campaign Inviting Travelers to explore New York City." Press release. http://www1.nyc.gov/office-of-the-mayor/news/092-13/mayor-bloomberg-nyc-company-neighborhood-x-neighborhood-campaign-inviting.

O'Connell, Ryan. 2013, January 6. "15 Reasons Why People Move to New York City." *Thought Catalog.* http://thoughtcatalog.com/ryan-oconnell/2013/01/15-reasons-why-people-move-to-new-york-city/.

Olmsted, Larry. 2014, April 23. "$1,000 Ice Cream Sundae? What's in New York's Latest Four-Figure Dessert?" *Forbes.* http://www.forbes.com/sites/larryolmsted/2014/04/23/1000-ice-cream-sundae-whats-in-new-yorks-latest-four-figure-dessert/#4f9cd3115b22.

Owens, Susan. 1994. "Land, Limits and Sustainability: A Conceptual Framework and Some Dilemmas for the Planning System." *Transactions of the Institute of British Geographers, New Series* 19, no. 4: 439–456.

Ozimek, Adam. 2012, May 23. "Richard Florida Is Wrong About Creative Cities." *Forbes.* http://www.forbes.com/sites/modeledbehavior/2012/05/23/richard-florida-is-wrong-about-creative-cities/#61c4c5807e42.

Pareene, Alex. 2014, January 6. "De Blasio's Impossible Task: Fix Bloomberg's New York." *Salon.* http://www.salon.com/2014/01/06/de_blasios_impossible_task_fix_bloombergs_new_york/.

Parrot, James. 2011, January 18. "As Incomes Gap Widens, New York Grows Apart." *Gotham Gazette.* http://www.gothamgazette.com/index.php/economy/683-as-incomes-gap-widens-new-york-grows-apart.

Paul, Brian. 2011. "PlaNYC: A Model of Public Participation or Corporate Marketing?" http://www.hunter.cuny.edu/ccpd/repository/files/planyc-a-model-of-public-participation-or.pdf.

———. 2011, February 22. "Affordable Housing Policies May Spur Gentrification, Segregation." *Gotham Gazette.* http://www.gothamgazette.com/index.php/city/4282-affordable-housing-policies-may-spur-gentrification-segregation.

Pazmino, Gloria. 2014, June 27. "De Blasio Feels 'Very Good' About State of Atlantic Yards." *Politico New York.* http://www.capitalnewyork.com/article/city-hall/2014/06/8548137/de-blasio-feels-very-good-about-state-atlantic-yards.

Peck, Jamie. 2005. "Struggling With the Creative Class." *International Journal of Urban and Regional Research* 29, no. 4: 740–770.

Peyser, Andrea. 2014, January 9. "Melissa Mark-Viverito: A Millionaire Hypocrite Who Will Ruin NYC." *New York Post*. http://nypost.com/2014/01/09/melissa-mark-viverito-a-millionaire-hypocrite-who-will-ruin-nyc/.

Pincus, Adam. 2008, December 1. "Demolition Permits Plunge in November, Signal Development Slowdown." *The Real Deal*. https://therealdeal.com/2008/12/01/demolition-permits-plunge-in-november-signal-slowdown/.

Plitt, Ami. 2017, March 3. "$110K/Month Time Warner Center Pad is NYC's Most Expensive Non-hotel Rental." *Curbed New York*. http://ny.curbed.com/2017/3/3/14807806/midtown-time-warner-center-most-expensive-rental.

Pogrebin, Robin. 2008, December 1. "Preservation and Development, Engaged in a Delicate Dance." *New York Times*. http://www.nytimes.com/2008/12/02/arts/design/02landmarks.html?ref=nyregion.

Porter, Michael E., Mark Blaxil, Jérôme Hervé, and Jean Mixer. 1998, January 1. "Inner Cities Are the Next Retailing Frontier." The Boston Consulting Group, Inc. https://www.bcgperspectives.com/content/articles/consumer_products_retail_inner_cities_next_retailing_frontier/.

Porter, Michael E., Christian H. M. Ketels, Anne Habiby, and David Zipper. 2009, March. "New York City: Bloomberg's Strategy for Economic Development." Harvard Business School Case 709-427, p. 10. http://charlottechamber.com/clientuploads/ICV12/Case_Study.pdf.

Powell, Michael. 2011, May 23. "Despair? None Bloomberg Seems to See." *New York Times*. http://www.nytimes.com/2011/05/24/nyregion/bloomberg-remarks-ignore-new-yorks-class-divide.html.

Pratt Center for Community Development. 2008. "Downtown Brooklyn's Detour: The Unanticipated Impacts of Rezoning and Development on Residents and Businesses." http://prattcenter.net/sites/default/files/prattcenter-downtown_brooklyns_detour.pdf.

———. 2009, August 10. "Saving Independent Retail—Policy Measures to Keep Neighborhoods Thriving." *Issue Brief*. http://prattcenter.net/issue-brief/saving-independent-retail. Pruitt, A. D. 2010, March 17. "Developers Back Off on Grand Harlem Plans." *Wall Street Journal*. http://www.wsj.com/articles/SB10001424052748704688604575125980865724828.

Pristin, Terry. 2001, July 27. "Council Approves a Zoning Plan to Revitalize Long Island City." *New York Times*. http://www.nytimes.com/2001/07/27/nyregion/council-approves-a-zoning-plan-to-revitalize-long-island-city.html.

Putzier, Konrad. 2016, February 1. "De Blasio's Donors: Two Trees, Brookfield and Toll Brothers Are Among the Supporters Shelling Out the Most for Mayor's Non-Profit." *The Real Deal*. https://therealdeal.com/issues_articles/de-blasios-donors/.

———. 2016, February 1. "Real Estate's Love-hate Relationship with De Blasio." *The Real Deal*. https://therealdeal.com/issues_articles/real-estates-love-hate-relationship-with-de-blasio/.

Rayman, Graham. 2012, October 31. "Flood Zone, NYC Bloomberg's Push for Development in the Wrong Places." *Village Voice.* http://www.villagevoice.com/2012-10-31/news/flood-zone-nyc/full/.

Raymond, Adam K. 2016, December 13. "Report: Income Inequality Worse Under Mayor de Blasio." *New York Magazine.* http://nymag.com/daily/intelligencer/2016/12/report-income-inequality-worse-under-mayor-de-blasio.html.

The Real Deal. 2010, February 22. "Coney Island to Generate Major Revenue for the City, Bloomberg Says." *The Real Deal.* https://therealdeal.com/2010/02/22/coney-island-to-generate-major-revenue-for-the-city-bloomberg-says/.

———. 2013, March 12. "Affordable Lender CPC Gets $250M Citigroup Boost." *The Real Deal.* http://therealdeal.com/2013/03/12/nonprofit-lender-cpc-gets-250m-boost-from-citigroup/.

Real Estate Board of New York. 2005. "REBNY Retail Report Fall 2005."

———. 2011. "REBNY Retail Report Fall 2011."

———. 2014, March 5. "The Invisible Engine: The Economic Impact of New York City's Real Estate Industry." https://www.rebny.com/content/dam/rebny/Documents/PDF/News/Research/Policy%20Reports/AKRF_Real_Estate_Economic_Impact_Jobs_Taxes.pdf.

Rice, Andrew. 2014, June 29. "Stash Pad: The New York Real-Estate Market Is Now the Premier Destination for Wealthy Foreigners with Rubles, Yuan, and Dollars to Hide." *New York Magazine.* http://nymag.com/news/features/foreigners-hiding-money-new-york-real-estate-2014-6/.

———. 2015, December 28. "How Are You Enjoying the de Blasio Revolution?" *New York Magazine.* http://nymag.com/daily/intelligencer/2015/12/how-are-you-enjoying-the-de-blasio-revolution.html.

Richter, Wolf. 2015, May 20. "San Francisco's Housing Boom Has Gotten Over-the-Top Crazy." *Business Insider.* http://www.businessinsider.com/san-franciscos-housing-boom-has-gotten-over-the-top-crazy-2015-5?IR=T.

Riley, Sarah. 2016, April 22. "The NYPD Is Running Stings Against Immigrant-Owned Shops, Then Pushing for Warrantless Searches." *ProPublica* and the *New York Daily News.* https://www.propublica.org/article/nypd-nuisance-abatement-shop-stings-warrantless-searches?utm_campaign=sprout&utm_medium=social&utm_source=twitter&utm_content=1461326640.

Rivero, Juan. 2004. "Coney Island: Planning Nostalgic Space." Master of Architecture and Planning Thesis, Columbia University, New York.

Rivlin-Nadler, Max. 2013, December 23. "De Blasio Hires Goldman Sachs Exec To Make City More Affordable." http://gothamist.com/2013/12/23/bill_de_blasio_hires_goldman_sachs.php.

———. 2016, September 30. "Law That Would Help NYC from Being Strangled by Chain Stores Is Deserted by City Council." *Village Voice.* http://www.villagevoice.com/news/law-that-would-help-nyc-from-being-strangled-by-chain-stores-is-deserted-by-city-council-9169261.

Roberts, Liz. 2015, November 6. "East Harlem Residents Protest Against Mayor De Blasio's Rezoning Plan." *The Indypendent.* https://indypendent.org/2015/11/06/east-harlem-residents-protest-against-mayor-de-blasio%E2%80%99s-rezoning-plan.

Rodgers, Scott. 2009. "Urban Geography: Urban Growth Machine." In *The International Encyclopedia of Human Geography,* edited by Rob Kitchin and Nigel Thrift, 40–45. Oxford: Elsevier.

Rosenberg, Zoe. 2015, January 12. "Despite Outrage, Concrete Likely for Coney Island Boardwalk." *Curbed New York.* http://ny.curbed.com/archives/2015/01/12/despite_outrage_concrete_likely_for_coney_island_boardwalk.php.

———. 2015, May 29. "Buyer Outed for 432 Park Avenue's $95 Million Penthouse." *Curbed New York.* http://ny.curbed.com/2015/5/29/9955802/buyer-outed-for-432-park-avenues-95-million-penthouse.

———. 2015, August 10. "Coney Island's Future Tallest Tower Gets New Renderings." *Curbed New York.* http://ny.curbed.com/2015/8/10/9931962/coney-islands-future-tallest-tower-gets-new-renderings.

Rubinstein, Dana. 2013, August 30. "Bill de Blasio, Development Pragmatist." *Politico New York.* http://www.capitalnewyork.com/article/politics/2013/08/8533321/bill-de-blasio-development-pragmatist.

———. 2014, February 7. "For Planning, a Pro-Development Liberal." *Politico.* http://www.politico.com/states/new-york/city-hall/story/2014/02/for-planning-a-pro-development-liberal-010880.

———. 2015, October 22. "De Blasio Official Dismisses Commercial Rent Control Idea." *Politico New York.* http://www.politico.com/states/new-york/city-hall/story/2015/10/de-blasio-official-dismisses-commercial-rent-control-idea-027026.

———. 2016, March 29. "De Blasio: Expect No Help in Resolving Income Inequality." *Politico New York.* http://www.capitalnewyork.com/article/city-hall/2016/03/8595159/de-blasio-expect-no-help-resolving-income-inequality.

Rudish, Kate, and Frank Lombardi. 2008, May 1. "Council OKs Harlem Rezoning Plan; Cops Called to Clear Opponents." *Daily News.* http://www.nydaily-news.com/new-york/council-oks-harlem-rezoning-plan-cops-called-clear-opponents-article-1.331317.

Ryley, Sarah. 2009, March 31. "A Look at Retail Vacancies by Neighborhood." *The Real Deal New York City Real Estate News.* http://therealdeal.com/issues_articles/retail-gets-knocked-out/.

———. 2009, April 5. "Harlem Is Losing a Bit of its Soul." *New York Post.* http://nypost.com/2009/04/05/harlem-is-losing-a-bit-of-its-oul/.

Saltz, Jerry. 2015, December 17. "New York Has Solved the Problem of Public Art. But at What Cost?" *Vulture.* http://www.vulture.com/2015/12/how-new-york-solved-the-problem-of-public-art.html.

Samtani, Hiten. 2013, September 3. "Mayoral Candidates Get Candid." *The Real Deal.* http://therealdeal.com/issues_articles/mayoral-candidates-get-candid/.

———. 2013, December 17. "Rudin's St. Vincent's Condos Selling at $3,500 Per Square Foot." *The Real Deal.* http://therealdeal.com/2013/12/17/rudins-st-vincents-condos-selling-at-3500-per-square-foot/.

————. 2014, May 5. "Real Estate Execs Laud de Blasio's Affordable Housing Plan." *The Real Deal*. http://therealdeal.com/2014/05/05/what-real-estate-execs-think-about-de-blasios-just-released-affordable-housing-plan/.

Sanders, James. 2004, February 22. "Sex and the Mythic Movie Dream of New York City." *New York Times*. http://www.nytimes.com/2004/02/22/arts/television-sex-and-the-mythic-movie-dream-of-new-york-city.html?pagewanted=all&src=pm.

Sargen, Greg. 2005, September 18. "The Incredibly Bold, Audaciously Cheesy, Jaw-Droppingly Vegasified, Billion-Dollar Glam-Rock Makeover of Coney Island." *New York Magazine*. http://nymag.com/nymetro/realestate/features/14498/.

Sassen, Saskia, and Frank Roost. 1999. "The City: Strategic Site for the Global Entertainment Industry." In *The Tourist City*, edited by Dennis R. Judd and Susan S. Fainstein, 143–154. New Haven, CT: Yale University Press.

Satow, Julie. 2012, May 18. "Amanda Burden Wants to Remake New York. She Has 19 Months Left." *New York Times*. http://www.nytimes.com/2012/05/20/nyregion/amanda-burden-planning-commissioner-is-remaking-new-york-city.html?pagewanted=all.

————. 2015, May 15. "Want a Green Card? Invest in Real Estate." *New York Times*. http://www.nytimes.com/2015/05/17/realestate/want-a-green-card-invest-in-real-estate.html?mtrref=undefined&gwh=64E79F40F06988247A9A3D6917819839&gwt=pay.

Save Coney Island. n.d. "FAQs." http://www.saveconeyisland.net/?page_id=383.

————. 2009, July 29. "Save Coney Island on Rezoning Vote: A Sad Day for New York City." http://www.saveconeyisland.net/?p=621.

————. 2010, May 27. "Save Coney Island Hails New Luna Park, but Warns Coney's History Is in Danger." http://www.saveconeyisland.net/?p=1173.

————. 2010, June 1. "Renderings Show Potential of Endangered Coney Island Buildings." http://www.saveconeyisland.net/?p=1238.

Savitch-Lew, Abigail. 2016, March 23. "Ayes and Nays on Mayor's Zoning Changes Pave Way for Bigger Questions." *City Limits*. http://citylimits.org/2016/03/23/ayes-and-nays-on-mayors-zoning-changes-pave-way-for-bigger-questions/.

————. 2016, April 13. "Advocates Like, and Critique, de Blasio's Homeless Plan." *City Limits*. http://citylimits.org/2016/04/13/advocates-like-and-critique-de-blasios-homeless-plan/.

SBE Council. 2015, April. "Small Business Tax Index 2015." http://www.sbecouncil.org/wp-content/uploads/2015/04/BTI2015SBECouncil.pdf.

Schaffer, Richard, and Neil Smith. 1986. "The Gentrification of Harlem?" *Annals of the Association of American Geographers* 76, no. 3: 347–365.

Schwartz, Alex. 1999. "New York City and Subsidized Housing: Impacts and Lessons of the City's $5 Billion Capital Budget Housing Plan." *Housing Policy Debate* 10, no. 4: 839–877.

Schwarz, Benjamin. 2010, June. "Gentrification and Its Discontents." *The Atlantic*. http://www.theatlantic.com/magazine/archive/2010/06/gentrification-and-its-discontents/308092/.

Shalit, Ruth. 2001, November 9. "Brand New: How Do You Sell New York Now? Great Minds Are Working on It." *Wall Street Journal.*

Shaw, Randy. 2008, May 1. "The Politics of Homelessness and the 'Quality' of Urban Life." *Beyond Chron.* http://www.beyondchron.org/news/index.php?itemid=5624.

Shepherd, Julianne Escobedo. 2014, October. "Taylor Swift's New Song Is the Gentrification Anthem NYC Didn't Need." *Jezebel.* http://jezebel.com/taylor-swifts-new-song-is-the-gentrification-anthem-nyc-1648607040.

Slater, Tom, Winifred Curran, and Loretta Lees. 2004. "Gentrification Research: New Directions and Critical Scholarship." *Environment and Planning* 36: 1141–1150.

Smith, Andrew. 2005. "Conceptualizing City Image Change: The 'Re-Imaging' of Barcelona." *Tourism Geographies* 7, no. 4: 398–423.

Smith, Chris. 2013, September 7. "In Conversation: Michael Bloomberg." *New York Magazine.* http://nymag.com/news/politics/bloomberg/in-conversation-2013-9/.

Smith, Neil. 1979. "Toward a Theory of Gentrification: A Back to the City Movement By Capital, Not People." *Journal of the American Planning Association* 45, no. 4: 538–548.

———. 1987. "Gentrification and the Rent Gap." *Annals of the Association of American Geographers* 77, no. 3: 462–465.

———. 2002. "New Globalism, New Urbanism: Gentrification as Global Urban Strategy." *Antipode* 34, no. 3: 427–450.

Smith, Stephen. 2015, January 16. "40-Story Tower, Tallest in Coney Island, Planned for Trump Village Shopping Center, 532 Neptune Avenue." *New York Yimby.* http://newyorkyimby.com/2015/01/40-story-tower-tallest-in-coney-island-planned-for-trump-village-shopping-center-532-neptune-avenue.html.

SocioWiki. n.d. "The Presence of the Past: Turning Points in NYC." Accessed January 12, 2011. http://www.macaulay.cuny.edu/seminars/napoli08/index.php/Coney_Island_Context.

Solis, Gustavo. 2015, June 4. "Lenox Terrace Residents Fighting Against Proposed Commercial Rezoning." *DNAinfo.* https://www.dnainfo.com/new-york/20150604/central-harlem/lenox-terrace-residents-fighting-against-proposed-commercial-rezoning.

———. 2015, December 8. "Lenox Terrace Landlord Illegally Raising Stabilized Rents, Tenants Say." *DNAinfo.* https://www.dnainfo.com/new-york/20151208/central-harlem/lenox-terrace-landlord-illegally-raising-stabilized-rents-tenants-say.

———. 2015, December 11. "City Moving Forward with Massive East 125th Street Development." *DNAinfo.* http://www.dnainfo.com/new-york/20151211/east-harlem/city-moving-forward-with-massive-east-125th-street-development.

Solomon, Michael. 2015, June 1. "Hermès Birkin Bag Sells for Record $222,000 at Auction in Hong Kong." *Forbes.* http://www.forbes.com/sites/msolomon/2015/06/01/hermes-birkin-bag-sells-for-record-221000-at-auction-in-hong-kong/#14961c70722c.

Solomont, E. B. 2015, July 14. "One57's Tax Breaks Could Have Produced Nearly 370 Affordable Units: IBO." *The Real Deal.* http://therealdeal.com/2015/07/14/one57s-tax-breaks-could-have-produced-nearly-370-affordable-units-ibo/.

————. 2016, May 5. "220 CPS Officially Has a $250M Mansion in the Sky." *The Real Deal.* http://therealdeal.com/2016/05/05/220-cps-now-officially-has-a-250m-mansion-in-the-sky-photos/.

Sorkin, Andrew Ross. 2016, March 14. "Unpacking a Chinese Company's U.S. Hotel Buying Spree." *New York Times.* http://www.nytimes.com/2016/03/15/business/dealbook/unpacking-a-chinese-companys-us-hotel-buying-spree.html.

Steinberg, Dan. 2012, Winter. "Planning the Neoliberal City." *New Politics* XIII, no. 4. http://newpol.org/print/content/planning-neoliberal-city.

Stern, William J. 2000, Fall. "Why Gotham's Developers Don't Develop." *City Journal.* http://www.city-journal.org/html/why-gotham%E2%80%99s-developers-don%E2%80%99t-develop-12130.html.

Sterne, Michael. 1978, March 1. "In Last Decade, Leaders Say, Harlem's Dreams Have Died." *New York Times.* http://www.nytimes.com/1978/03/01/archives/new-jersey-pages-in-last-decade-leaders-say-harlems-dreams-have.html?_r=0.

Stewart, Nikita. 2015, November 18. "De Blasio Unveils Plan to Create 15,000 Units of Housing." *New York Times.* http://www.nytimes.com/2015/11/19/nyregion/de-blasio-unveils-plan-to-create-15000-units-of-housing.html.

————. 2015, November 19. "New York's Rise in Homelessness Went Against National Trend, U.S. Report Finds." *New York Times.* http://www.nytimes.com/2015/11/20/nyregion/new-yorks-rise-in-homelessness-went-against-national-trend-us-report-finds.html.

Stigel, Jorgen, and Soren Frimann. 2006. "City Branding—All Smoke, No Fire?" *Nordicom Review* 27, no. 2: 245–268.

Stilwell, Victoria, and Wei Lu. 2015, November 10. "The 10 Most Unequal Big Cities in America." *Bloomberg Markets.* http://www.bloomberg.com/news/articles/2015-11-10/the-10-most-unequal-big-cities-in-america.

Stohr, Kate. 2003, March 17. "I Sell New York." *Gotham Gazette.* http://www.gothamgazette.com/index.php/about/1751-i-sell-new-york.

Stone, Clarence N. 1987. "Summing Up: Urban Regimes, Development Policy, and Political Arrangements." In *The Politics of Urban Development*, edited by Clarence N. Stone and Heywood T. Sanders, 269–281. Lawrence: University Press of Kansas.

Story, Louise, Tiff Fehr, and Derek Watkins. 2012. "$100 Million Club. The *Times* identified 48 companies that have received more than $100 million in state grants since 2007. Some 5,000 other companies have received more than $1 million in recent years." *New York Times.* http://www.nytimes.com/interactive/2012/12/01/us/government-incentives.html#NY.

Stuart, Tessa. 2014, October 27. "Taylor Swift's 'Welcome to New York' Is Literally a Tourism Campaign Disguised as a Single." *Village Voice.* http://www.villagevoice.com/news/taylor-swifts-welcome-to-new-york-is-literally-a-tourism-campaign-disguised-as-a-single-6672401.

Stulberg, Ariel. 2015, September 3. "City to Landlords Offering Buyouts: Back Off!" *The Real Deal.* http://therealdeal.com/2015/09/03/city-to-landlords-offering-buyouts-back-off/.

Sugar, Rachel. 2016, December 19. "More tourists visited NYC in 2016 than ever before." *Curbed New York*. http://ny.curbed.com/2016/12/19/14005846/new-york-city-tourism-2016-record.

Suh, Seung. 2012, April 3. "East Harlem Tenants Forced Out of Two Buildings." *WABC online*. http://abclocal.go.com/wabc/story?section=news/local/new_york&id=8607269.

Take Back NYC. 2015. "1994–2015 NYC Court Warrants Issued Eviction Commercial."https://static1.squarespace.com/static/553fbb67e4b0c9bd03468d3c/t/571f89da746fb914371a6083/1461684700773/1994-2015+NYC+Court+Warrants+Issued+Eviction++Commercial.pdf.

Take Back NYC. 2015, December 1. "Mayor de Blasio Continues Bloomberg's Anti-Small Business Policy: Deputy Mayor Glen Turns Her Back on Women Entrepreneurs in Crisis." Press release. http://static1.squarespace.com/static/553fbb67e4b0c9bd03468d3c/t/565e0472e4b09a621bfbf864/1449002098494/For+Immediate+Release_TakeBackNYC_+Mayor+de+Blasio+Continues+Bloomberg%E2%80%99s+Anti-Small+Business+Policy_12.1.15.pdf.

Taylor, Kate. 2013, October 31. "De Blasio Attracts Silicon Valley Donors." *New York Times*. http://www.nytimes.com/2013/11/01/nyregion/de-blasio-attracts-silicon-valley-donors.html?mtrref=undefined&_r=0.

Thirteen Metrofocus. 2012, July 20. "Will Affordable Housing Plan Leave Middle Class New Yorkers Out in the Cold?" http://www.thirteen.org/metrofocus/2012/07/will-affordable-housing-plan-leave-middle-class-new-yorkers-out-in-the-cold/.

Topousis, Tom. 2008, April 30. "Rezoning OK'd for 125th Street." *New York Post*. http://www.nypost.com/p/news/regional/item_WwiGjbLIyja8crqq128giP.

Treiman, Daniel. 2009, July 22. "How Mayor Bloomberg Is Killing Coney Island." *Huffington Post*. http://www.huffingtonpost.com/daniel-treiman/coney-island-construction_b_242748.html.

Trejos, Nancy. 2014, June 20. "Berlin: European Capital of Cool." *USA Today*. http://www.usatoday.com/story/travel/destinations/2014/06/19/berlin-nightlife-kreuzberg-prenzlauer-berg/10857161/.

Trendwatching. 2011, February. "Citysumers: The Future Consumer Arena Is Urban." *Trendwatching*. http://trendwatching.com/trends/citysumers/.

Treskon, Mark. 2012. "Constructing an Oppositional Community: Sunset Park and the Politics of Organizing Across Difference." In *The World in Brooklyn: Gentrification, Immigration, and Ethnic Politics in a Global City*, edited by Judith de Sena and Timothy Shortell, 289–312. Lanham, MD: Lexington Books.

Trotta, Daniel. 2006, August 18. "Black New York Frets the Changing Face of Harlem." *Reuters*. http://www.redorbit.com/news/general/622349/black_new_york_frets_the_changing_face_of_harlem/.

Tucker, Maria Luisa. 2007, December 4. "Zoned Out: High-Rises on 125th Street? Harlem's Transformation Gathers Speed." *Village Voice*. http://www.villagevoice.com/news/zoned-out-6423919.

Turetsky, Doug. 2012, November 21. "Seas Rise, Storms Surge, and NYC Presses Ahead with Waterfront Development Projects." Independent Budget Office weblog. http://ibo.nyc.ny.us/cgi-park/?p=575.

Turffrey, Belinda. 2010, April. "The Human Cost—How the Lack of Affordable Housing Impacts on All Aspects of Life." http://england.shelter.org.uk/__data/assets/pdf_file/0003/268752/The_Human_Cost.pdf.

Uptown Magazine. 2013. "A Toast to Luxury, Lifestyle, and Living." *Uptown Magazine* Mediakit. Accessed February 11, 2013. http://uptownmagazine.com/images/mediakits/UPTOWN_NYC.pdf.

United Nations Environment Programme (UNEP). 2011. "Towards a Green Economy: Pathways to Sustainable Development and Poverty Eradication."

U.S. Census Bureau. 2010. "2000 and 2010 Census PL and SF1 Files and 1990 Census STF1 Population Division."

Van Riel, Cees, and John M. T. Balmer. 1997. "Corporate Identity: The Concept, Its Measurement and Management." *European Journal of Marketing* 31, no. 5/6: 340–355.

Van Riper, Frank. 1975, October 30. "Ford to City: Drop Dead." *Daily News.*

Velsey, Kim. 2013, July 16. "Twilight of an Era: Seth Pinsky Leaving EDC for RXR Realty." *New York Observer.* http://observer.com/2013/07/twilight-of-an-era-seth-pinksy-leaving-edc-for-rxr-realty/.

———. 2015, June 29. "Rent Freeze! Rent Guidelines Board Approves Historic Zero Percent Increase." *Observer.* http://observer.com/2015/06/rent-freeze-rent-guidelines-board-approves-historic-zero-percent-increase/.

Velsey, Kim, and Jill Colvin. 2014, May 5. "De Blasio Unveils 'Most Ambitious' Affordable Housing Plan in Nation." *Observer.* http://observer.com/2014/05/de-blasio-unveils-most-ambitious-affordable-housing-plan/.

Waldman, Amy. 2001, July 31. "In Harlem, a Hero's Welcome for New Neighbor Clinton." *New York Times.* http://www.nytimes.com/2001/07/31/nyregion/in-harlem-a-hero-s-welcome-for-new-neighbor-clinton.html.

Walker, Hunter. 2014, January 27. "Bill de Blasio Tells 'A Tale of Two Cities' at His Mayoral Campaign Kickoff." *The Observer.* http://observer.com/2013/01/bill-de-blasio-tells-a-tale-of-two-cities-at-his-mayoral-campaign-kickoff/.

Warerkar, Tanay. 2016, January 13. "Record-Setting Harlem Townhouse Sells for Just Under $5M." *Curbed New York.* http://ny.curbed.com/2016/1/13/10846846/record-setting-harlem-townhouse-sells-for-just-under-5m.

Warner, R. 2008, March 13. "Rezoning Harlem's Main Street." *Helium.* http://www.helium.com/items/927110-rezoning-harlems-main-street.

Watanabe, Andrew. 2010, May. "The Social and Spatial Imperatives of Contextual Zoning in New York City During the Bloomberg Administration." Unpublished Thesis, Columbia University, New York.

Weber, Rachel. 2002. "Extracting Value from the City: Neoliberalism and Urban Redevelopment." *Antipode* 34, no. 3: 519–540.

Weichselbaum, Simone. 2013, October 26. "Hurricane Sandy, One Year Later: Not All Fun and Games in Coney Island." *New York Daily News.* http://www.nydailynews.com/new-york/hurricane-sandy/hurricane-sandy-year-coney-island-article-1.1494779.

ʃ

White, Anna. 2015, October 12. "London to Become a Place 'We Work but Don't Live.'" *The Telegraph*. http://www.telegraph.co.uk/finance/property/11925580/ The-exodus-of-homebuyers-from-London-hits-epic-levels.html.

Williams, Timothy. 2008, February 21. "City's Sweeping Rezoning Plan for 125th Street Has Many in Harlem Concerned." *New York Times*. http://www.nytimes. com/2008/02/21/nyregion/21rezone.html?pagewanted=all.

———. 2008, May 1. "Council Approves Rezoning of 125th Street, Over Loud Protests of Some Spectators." *New York Times*. http://www.nytimes.com/2008/ 05/01/nyregion/01harlem.html.

———. 2008, July 6. "An Old Sound in Harlem Draws New Neighbors' Ire." *New York Times*. http://www.nytimes.com/2008/07/06/nyregion/06drummers. html?pagewanted=all.

———. 2008, September 6. "In an Evolving Harlem, Newcomers Try to Fit In." *New York Times*. http://www.nytimes.com/2008/09/07/nyregion/07newcom- ers.html?_r=2&oref=slogin.

Wishnia, Steven. 2015, December 18. "De Blasio's Controversial Zoning Plan Stretches Definition of Affordable." *Gothamist*. http://gothamist.com/2015/12/ 18/de_blasio_zoning_affordable.php.

———. 2016, February 10. "What Does 'Affordable Housing' Really Mean in De Blasio's New York? We're About to Find Out." *Gothamist*. http://gothamist. com/2016/02/10/affordable_housing_battle.php.

Wolf-Powers, Laura. 2005. "Up-Zoning New York City's Mixed Use Neighborhoods: Property-Led Economic Development and the Anatomy of a Planning Dilemma." *Journal of Planning, Education and Research* 24, no. 4: 379–393.

Woolums, Sharon. 2015, January 22. "Mayor and Speaker Are M.I.A. on Small Businesses." *The Villager*. http://thevillager.com/2015/01/22/mayor-and- speaker-are-m-i-a-on-small-businesses/.

Yakas, Ben. 2011, October 12. "Old Man Bloomberg: Occupy Wall Street Should Stop Being Mean to Rich People." *Gothamist*. http://gothamist.com/2011/10/ 12/old_man_bloomberg_leave_rich_people.php.

Yee, Vivian, and Mireya Navarro. 2015, February 3. "Some See Risk in de Blasio's Bid to Add Housing." *New York Times*. http://www.nytimes.com/2015/02/04/nyre- gion/an-obstacle-to-mayor-de-blasios-affordable-housing-plan-neighborhood- resistance.html.

Zhang, Christian. 2010, December 10. "For West Harlem, an Identity Crisis." *Columbia Daily Spectator*. http://www.columbiaspectator.com/2012/12/10/ west-harlem-identity-crisis.

Zukin, Sharon. 2003. "Urban Lifestyles." In *The Consumption Reader*, edited by David B. Clarke, Marcus A. Doel, and Kate M. L. Housinaux, 127–133. London and New York: Routledge.

Index

Note: Page references followed by an "*f*" indicate figure.